The Spirit and the Common Good

The Spirit and the Common Good

Shared Flourishing in the Image of God

Daniela C. Augustine

William B. Eerdmans Publishing Company
Grand Rapids, Michigan

Wm. B. Eerdmans Publishing Co.
4035 Park East Court SE, Grand Rapids, Michigan 49546
www.eerdmans.com

© 2019 Daniela C. Augustine
All rights reserved
Published 2019
Printed in the United States of America

25 24 23 22 21 20 19 1 2 3 4 5 6 7

ISBN 978-0-8028-4385-2

Library of Congress Cataloging-in-Publication Data

Names: Augustine, Daniela Christova, author.
Title: The spirit and the common good : shared flourishing in the image of God / Daniela C. Augustine.
Description: Grand Rapids : Eerdmans Publishing Co., 2019. | Includes bibliographical references and index.
Identifiers: LCCN 2019017685 | ISBN 9780802843852 (pbk. : alk. paper)
Subjects: LCSH: Common good–Religious aspects–Christianity. | Public theology. | Holy Spirit.
Classification: LCC BR115.P7 A94 2019 | DDC 261.8–dc23
LC record available at https://lccn.loc.gov/2019017685

Unless otherwise noted, Scripture quotations are from New Revised Standard Version Bible, copyright © 1989 National Council of the Churches of Christ in the United States of America. Used by permission. All rights reserved worldwide.

For the peacebuilders
in Eastern Slavonia

Contents

Foreword *by Miroslav Volf* ix

Acknowledgments xi

Prologue: The Story Behind the Text 1

1. From the Common Image to the Common Good 13

From Belief to the Practice of the Common Good 15

The Memory of a World Illuminated by the Divine Face 25

Creation, Incarnation, and Redemptive World-Mending 29

Making the Divine Community Visible in the Cosmos 44

Pentecost and the Church as the Icon of the Trinity on Earth 58

2. From the Iconoclasm of Violence to Love as the Life of the New Creation 61

Genesis's First Account of Fratricide in Light of the Iconoclasm of Violence 66

Scripture's Correlation between Violence and "Limited Goods" 77

The Call to Responsibility for the Other amidst a Violent World 89

Equality, Justice, and Peace 108

3. Recovering of Eucharistic Being in a Market-Shaped World 121

The World as Eucharistic Sacrament 128

Royal Priests and Stewards of the Cosmos in the Eucharistic Economics of the Spirit 135

The Eucharist as Pedagogy of Disciplining Desires and an Antidote to Consumerism 145

Holiness and Moral Economic Responsibility 155

4. From Forgiveness to the Common Good in the Spirit's World-Mending 160

The Spirit's Artistry of Unconditional Forgiveness 164

Forgiveness and the Redemption of Memory 175

The Challenge of Forgiving the Unforgivable 182

Justice and Legislated Forgiveness as a Civic Virtue 191

The Challenge of "The Ways of Peace" 196

Epilogue: Toward a Hagiography of a Community Committed to the Common Good 199

Pondering the Distinctives of Hagiographic Discourse and Saintly Lives 201

Making Love Visible in the Midst of War 212

Concluding Thoughts 227

Bibliography 229

Index of Subjects 245

Index of Scripture Citations 254

Foreword

Pentecostals have a reputation of being either otherworldly and mystical or aggressively worldly and political: they speak in tongues and dance in the Spirit, in seeming obliviousness to reason and utility, or they work and pray for the kingdom now, marked by health and fame, opulence and worldly power. For the outsiders, it is sometimes hard to imagine that there are forms of Pentecostalism with a very different face. In this book, which bears all the marks of very wide reading, Daniela C. Augustine presents Pentecostalism engaged for the common good and committed to peacebuilding, Pentecostalism open to people from diverse cultures and, in a sense, like the disciples on the Day of Pentecost, speaking diverse "ethno-cultural" languages.

Much of Augustine's work is rooted in the experiences of Pentecostal Christians in the part of Croatia called East Slavonia. The capital of East Slavonia is Osijek, the town in which I was born and where my father started his ministry; that's also where my brother-in-law, Peter Kuzmič, was both a minister and an educator and where I had my first teaching job as a young theologian. Ours was Pentecostalism open to the world, a Pentecostalism that stressed learning and social engagement no less than evangelism and healing.

Augustine celebrates this brand of Pentecostalism; the accounts of saintly lives from that region make visible "the life of God in flesh" and are the story behind her theoretical text. But she does more than just celebrate lives, and what she does is unique and important: she articulates this open version of Pentecostalism with the help of resources that come from Eastern Orthodoxy (and a good deal of French philosophy!). *The Spirit and the*

FOREWORD

Common Good is a creative and compelling contribution to the growing body of global Pentecostal theology. Its author is one of today's most learned and creative Pentecostal theologians.

Miroslav Volf
Henry B. Wright Professor of Theology, Yale University
Founder and Director of Yale Center for Faith and Culture

Acknowledgments

The present work originated in 2011–2012 field research on the peacebuilding agency of the Pentecostal community within the region of Eastern Slavonia during and after the 1990s war in the former Yugoslavia. I am very grateful for the gracious hospitality and logistical assistance of the Pentecostal churches in the region and the Evangelical Theological Seminary (ETS) in Osijek, Croatia. Special gratitude goes to Professor Peter Kuzmic, President of ETS; Rev. Damir Spoljarić, Senior Pastor of the Pentecostal Evangelical Church in Osijek; Bishops Josip Jendričko and Matej Lazar Kovačević (the past and present overseers of the Church of God in Croatia, respectively), as well as to David Kovačević for helping me organize and conduct over thirty interviews throughout the region.

During the summer of 2012, our son Josiah C. Augustine (curently a PhD student in Comparative Politics at George Washington University) served as my research assistant, helping me to sift through the vast archives documenting the war. His excellent research skills and insights in political science were invaluable not only during the early stages of the project but also in the shaping of its contextual prologue and epilogue.

Special recognition is due to my graduate assistants, Alejandra Guajardo and Michael Austin Kamenicky, for investing the time to help me with completing the book's bibliography.

I am grateful for the continual moral support and affirmation of Lee University's administration, especially by President Paul Conn; Vice President Debbie Murray; the Dean of the School of Religion, Terry L. Cross; the Associate Dean, Rickie Moore; and the Chair of the Department of Theology, Skip Jenkins. A 2012 summer research grant, as well as consequent travel grants by the university, funded the most critical segments of my field research in Eastern Slavonia.

The completion of the project, particularly in relation to its liturgico-theological sections, would have not been possible without generous grants by the Louisville Institute and the Appalachian College Association.

My deep gratitude goes to Michael Thomson, former Senior Acquisitions Editor at the Wm. B. Eerdmans Publishing Co., James Ernest, Vice President and Editor in Chief, Linda Bieze, Senior Project Editor; and all who worked alongside them in patiently guiding and facilitating the publication process of the volume.

As always, this book would have not come to fruition without the faithful support of my husband and best friend, Jonathan, who has been the first trusted reader, editor, and insightful reviewer of all my theological work.

Finally, since the completion of this work was spread over a few years, revised versions of some subsections within chapter 1 and chapter 3 have appeared in preceding publications. These include: "Image, Spirit and *Theosis*: Imaging God in an Image-Distorting World," in Beth Felker Jones and Jeff Barbeau, eds., *The Image of God in an Image Driven Age: Explorations in Christian Anthropology* (Downers Grove, IL: InterVarsity, 2016); "Creation as Perichoretic Trinitarian Conversation: Reflections on World-Making with Robert W. Jenson," in Stephen Wright and Christopher W. Green, eds., *The Promise of Robert Jenson's Theology* (Minneapolis: Fortress, 2017); "From Proclamation to Embodiment: The Sacrament of the Word for the Life of the World and Its Destiny in *Theosis*" in Lee Roy Martin, ed., *Toward a Pentecostal Theology of Preaching* (Cleveland, TN: CPT, 2015); and "Holiness and Economics: Towards Recovery of Eucharistic Being in a Market-Shaped World," in Lee Roy Martin, ed., *A Future for Holiness: Pentecostal Explorations* (Cleveland, TN: CPT, 2013). I am most grateful to the publishers and editors of these volumes for permission to use revised portions of the texts in the present book.

DANIELA C. AUGUSTINE
Lee University
Fall 2018

Prologue

The Story Behind the Text

A Contextual Glimpse

The last decade of the twentieth century shocked Europe with the most horrific violence the continent had witnessed since World War II—the so-called "Third Balkan War,"[1] sealing the political and economic disintegration of the former Yugoslavia. The war unleashed an ominous sociopolitical destabilization of the entire region, stirring volatile multiethnic and religious tensions with incalculable consequences. While the genesis of the conflict is still a subject of debate,[2] it is tempting to simplify the complex sociopolitical events triggering the war by casting them as a textbook legitimation of Thomas Hobbes's pessimistic anthropology with its notorious depiction of violence as the natural state of humanity, ceaselessly antagonized by competition, diffidence, and the pursuit of glory.[3] Most scholars agree, however, that the war's madness was fueled and sustained fundamentally by rampant nationalism, conflated with religious crusade

1. The term is commonly used to designate the series of conflicts erupting in the former Yugoslavia between 1991 and 2002. See Misha Glenny, *The Fall of Yugoslavia: The Third Balkan War* (London: Penguin, 1992). For a detailed history of the war, see R. Craig Nation, *War in the Balkans, 1991-2002: Comprehensive History of Wars Provoked by Yugoslav Collapse: Balkan Region in World Politics, Slovenia and Croatia, Bosnia-Herzegovina, Kosovo, Greece, Turkey, Cyprus* (Progressive Management, 2014).

2. See Peter Kuzmic, "Reconciliation in Eastern Europe," *Reconciliation in Difficult Places: Dealing with Our Deepest Differences, The Washington Forum: Perspectives on Our Common Future* (Monrovia, CA: World Vision, 1994), 47–55 (particularly, 50–51). In this article, Kuzmic focuses fundamentally on the war in Bosnia, disputing the assertions that it is ethnic and religious civil war. Rejecting the influence of preexistent ethno-religious motifs, the author emphasizes instead the ideological and territorial disputes surrounding the conflict.

3. Thomas Hobbes, *Leviathan (Or the Matter, Form and Power of a Commonwealth Ecclesiastical and Civil)* (New York: Simon and Schuster, 1962), 99. For more discussion on Hobbes, see the introduction to chapter 2 (as well as footnotes 1 and 2).

rhetoric, mobilizing support for the fight against one's neighbor in the name of God and country.[4]

Since the beginning of the conflict in Croatia (1991) until its end in Kosovo (1999), one restless question troubled the self-searching European conscience: What causes the incomprehensible "depth of hatred which has provoked atrocities and slaughter on such a wide scale for such a short time?"[5] Reflecting on the unimaginable proportions and brutality of violence, Misha Glenny, the BBC's celebrated correspondent for Central Europe, remarks: "Even for those like myself who have observed not merely the war itself but the dense web of political intrigue which led to it, the extent or nature of the violence is beyond any framework of moral comprehension."[6] Notably, Glenny's careful account and analysis of the war dispute its conventional categorization as an ethnic conflict and emphasize the close ethnographic kinship between the Orthodox Serbs, Catholic Croats, and Muslim Bosnians,[7] emphatically asserting that "most of those doing the killing are of the same ethnos."[8] Thus, the author concludes that religion constitutes the "crucial [cultural] factor dividing these people," who have been asked for centuries "to choose between competing empires and ideologies, which have invariably been defined by religion."[9] Yet Glenny also quickly dispels attempts to depict the conflict as "confessional"[10] in nature. Instead he looks for answers in the Balkan historico-political realities of nation-building that have forced the warring sides to wear "many different cultural uniforms throughout the centuries by which they identify one another as the enemy when conflict breaks out."[11]

4. See Glenny, *Fall of Yugoslavia*, 166–67, 170–71.

5. Glenny, *Fall of Yugoslavia*, 166.

6. Glenny, *Fall of Yugoslavia*, 166.

7. The Bosnians are ethnic Croats and Serbs who converted to Islam during the centuries of Ottoman rule in the Balkans. For a brief historical account of the Bosnian Slavs' conversion to Islam, see Theó Tschuy, *Ethnic Conflict and Religion: Challenge to the Churches* (Geneva: World Council of Churches, 1997), ch. 8.

8. Glenny, *Fall of Yugoslavia*, 168.

9. Glenny, *Fall of Yugoslavia*, 169.

10. Glenny, *Fall of Yugoslavia*, 168.

11. Glenny, *Fall of Yugoslavia*, 169. The concepts of ethnicity and nationality are often confused and treated as synonymous. For differentiation between the two through the lenses of political philosophy, see Ernest Renan, "What Is a Nation?" in *The Nationalism Reader*, ed. Omar Dahbour and Micheline R. Ishay (Atlantic Highlands, NJ: Humanities, 1995), 143–55. Renan discusses the historico-political process behind the development of nations, asserting that they are a relatively recent phenomenon. He explicates the violent origins of nations,

In light of this assertion, Glenny suggests that the distressing hatred deepening the conflict is cultivated by nationalist propaganda rehearsing historically accumulated mistrust and fear of the other.[12] The resulting narrative constructs offer the warring sides justification to deflect the terrifying awareness of the enemy's close kinship, the realization that "the primitive beasts on the other side of the barricade are their brothers."[13] For Glenny, precisely the inescapable recognition of kinship accounts for the ghastly proportions of violence in Bosnia—for the unprecedented scale of crimes against humanity—for the blood-chilling barbarism of the conflict memorialized in the legacy of concentration camps and mass graves, as well as in the endless accounts of utilizing rape as a weapon of war against the religious other.[14] The distressing call to responsibility mediated by the proximity of the other's face (as the recognizable image of one's sibling) is, according to Glenny, also the reason for the otherwise unexplainable tradition of "facial mutilation" in the region[15]—the literal effacement of the other in an iconoclastic act that conceals the evidence of family resemblance between enemies. Destroying

---

pointing out that they represent "former conquest that has been at first accepted, and then forgotten, by the masses of the [conquered] people." At the time these "annexations were made nobody thought of natural limits, the rights of nations, or wishes of provinces" (148). Therefore, Renan points out that, given the fact that nations are formed by violence and held consequently by common interests, nationhood cuts at the very root of race or ethnicity (150). He states: "The truth is that no race [ethnicity] is pure, and that to base politics on ethnographic analysis is tantamount to basing it on a chimera" (150). See also Max Weber, "Ethnic Groups," in *Theories of Ethnicity: A Classical Reader*, ed. Werner Sollors (New York: New York University Press, 1996), 52-66. Weber points out the subjective nature of ethnic identity, asserts its difference from kinship, and states that "ethnic membership does not constitute a group; it only facilitates group formation of any kind, particularly in the political sphere" (56). Roger M. Smith's essay ("Citizenship and the Politics of People-Building" *Citizenship Studies* 5, no. 1 [2001]: 73-96) offers a helpful sketch of the political processes behind the formation of ethnic identity and calls attention to the role of what he terms "constructive stories"—narratives utilized as political tools in shaping ethnic consciousness (73).

12. The 1990s war in the former Yugoslavia is perceived by many as a continuation of the unresolved conflicts devastating the region during World War II.

13. Glenny, *Fall of Yugoslavia*, 169.

14. Regarding the crimes against humanity committed by the various factions in the war, see Peter Maass, *Love Thy Neighbor: A Story of War* (New York: Alfred A. Knopf, 1997); David Rieff, *Slaughterhouse: Bosnia and the Failure of the West* (New York: Touchstone, 1995). On the vast use of rape as a weapon of war and ethnic cleansing during the conflict in Bosnia, see also Tom Post (with Alexandra Stiglemayer, Charles Lanr, Joel Brand, Margaret Garrard Warner, and Robin Sparkman), "A Pattern of Rape," *Newsweek*, January 4, 1993. See also Roger Thurow, "Bosnian Album: Snapshots of Suffering," *The Wall Street Journal*, August 12, 1992.

15. Glenny, *Fall of Yugoslavia*, 169.

the other's face forecloses its unavoidable demand for a shared future—for commitment to the common good.

Indeed, the shared image in the other's face (confronting, demanding, and summoning to responsibility for mutual safekeeping) points to the shared reality of human flourishing. It exposes the self-destructive/self-dehumanizing consequences of one's violence against the other and reminds the beholder that the pursuit of the common good begins with the recognition of and commitment to the stewarding of the common image. To paraphrase Emmanuel Levinas, the interface with the other is the moment of one's ethical awakening,[16] but also of one's anamnesis of origin and eschatological homecoming—becoming oneself *with* and *for* the other. Christian pneumatology makes the bold assertion that this teleological process is the cosmos-mending, hallowing, Christoforming work of the Holy Spirit, who opens our eyes to see the face of God shining through the opacity of otherness in the face of our fellow human and grasps us in the wonder of encounter.

In the startling surprise of the divine nearness mediated to us by otherness, the Spirit teaches the idols-shattering lesson that (in the famous apophatic statement of Saint Gregory of Nyssa) preconceived "Concepts [of God] create idols; only wonder can grasp anything."[17] Grasping and being grasped by wonder, one comes to the realization that wherever genuine forgiveness and reconciliation are found, wherever unconditional hospitality toward the ethnic, religious, political, cultural other (even the enemy) is practiced in uncompromised commitment to the other's flourishing, wherever infrastructure of unhindered access to life and (sociopolitical and economic) inclusion is built and sustained for all anthropic and nonanthropic others, this is the doing of the Spirit in/through the human community—the redemptive pneumatic, world-mending movement of the Creator within his creation. This movement is authenticated and enfleshed in/through Spirit-filled, Christified, hallowed human life, proclaiming the gospel (as a redemptive counternarrative to the violent, world-fracturing egocentrism of sin) and making God's love toward the other visible in the cosmos.

When, during the summers of 2011 and 2012, I traveled in Eastern Slavonia (the highly contested multiethnic and multireligious territory where the borders of today's Serbia, Croatia, and Bosnia come together), most streets

16. Emmanuel Levinas, "The Ego and Totality," in *Collected Philosophical Papers*, trans. Alphonso Lingis (Dordrecht: Martinus Hijhoff, 1987), 25–48, 30–34. For more on Levinas's thought, see chapter 1 in the present book.

17. Gregory of Nyssa, *Life of Moses*, Patrologia Graeca 44:374.

and buildings were still punctured by shrapnel holes, and the rich agricultural land of the region was marked by signs warning about mine fields. The shrapneled facades and deserted, death-seeded farmland were only the visible, exterior marks of a deeply traumatized and wounded society, tortured by restless memories of fratricide. Eastern Slavonia saw the bloodiest fighting during the war. The savage destruction of the city of Vukovar and the massacre of 260 Croat hospital patients (buried in a nearby mass grave) shook Croatia with an urge for revenge.[18] Yet this was also the one contested territory in the region that at the end of the war experienced a successful process of peaceful reintegration. Undoubtedly, there were many factors impacting and shaping the turbulent postwar transition. However, aware of religion's role in the early stages of the conflict—as a catalyst for nationalism-driven violence against the other—I was interested in the transformation/redemption of religion's agency during and after the war. Could religion be redeemed as "festival of life" and prayer as "jubilation over the joy of existence"[19] in a place where it had watered the seeds of violence and had reaped a harvest of death?

A 1993 report, following a visit to Serbia and Croatia by representatives of the Council of Churches for Britain and Ireland, notes particularly the peacebuilding contribution of the "often marginalized" minority churches in the region "who, under difficult circumstances continue to place the gospel call for forgiveness and reconciliation at the center of their lives."[20] Among them was the small (around seven hundred members) Pentecostal community of Eastern Slavonia, which despite its demographically insignificant size, became an important peacebuilding force within the region and an active contributor to the postwar development of civil society. The research's grounding presupposition was that, due to their historical neutrality in the conflict, the Pentecostals were uniquely positioned to provide safe space for societal healing and facilitate reconciliation among the warring (Orthodox, Catholic, and Muslim) factions.[21] The research involved conducting over

18. Mark Heinrich, "Eastern Slavonia Agrees to Join Croatia," *Independent*, November 13, 1995, https://www.independent.co.uk/news/world/eastern-slavonia-agrees-to-rejoin-croatia-1581721.html.

19. Phrases used by Jürgen Moltmann in depicting the origin of religion in his book *The Living God and the Fullness of Life* (Louisville: Westminster John Knox, 2015), 90–92.

20. "Churches Urged to Play Their Part in Ex-Yugoslavia," *Ecumenical Press Service*, February 22, 1993.

21. While becoming the central subject of a different project and remaining outside the parameters of the present monograph, this thesis was consistently reinforced/confirmed by the conducted interviews.

thirty interviews with representatives of non-Pentecostal confessions about the Pentecostals' peacebuilding agency. The community's remarkable stories of kenotic self-giving in commitment to the well-being and flourishing of all (witnessed and narrated by the religious others) surprise, captivate, confront, and inspire with their courage and simplicity. Their moral imperative bridges the challenging gap between faith and practice, enfleshing (in the days of war) love for God through love for the neighbor who has become the enemy. These stories are the catalyst behind the present book's thematic scope, and the readers who desire a preliminary glimpse through its contextual lenses will find some of them woven into the second half of the Epilogue—a brief semihagiographical tribute to the ecumenical Christian peacebuilding movement of Eastern Slavonia.[22] The movement, which contributed to the developing of a vast grassroots network of advocacy for and collaboration toward just peace, actively aided the successful postwar reintegration of the region.

Turning to the hagiographical genre in narrating the stories of the Christian peacebuilders in Eastern Slavonia (as the most appropriate conclusion of the book) is not accidental. When striving to depict saintly lives, most contemporary hagiographies rightly emphasize their kenotic ethos and eucharistic spirit, manifested in the extraordinary ability to transcend "the pull" of one's own ego[23] in altruistic self-giving for the flourishing of the anthropic and nonanthropic other. In this vein of thought, Lawrence S. Cunningham offers an insightful depiction of saintliness, which summarizes the inner drive of hallowed human life in its recovered capacity of being for others: "A saint is a person so grasped by a religious vision that it becomes central to his or her life in a way that radically changes the person and leads others to glimpse the value of that vision."[24] Indeed, the saints are people who have

22. As the report of the delegation to Serbia and Croatia of the Council of Churches for Britain and Ireland states, "within all religious traditions" there were people committed to the gospel mandate for forgiveness and reconciliation. "Churches Urged to Play Their Part in Ex-Yugoslavia," *Ecumenical Press Service*, February 22, 1993.

23. Andrew Michael Flesher, *Heroes, Saints, and Ordinary Morality* (Washington, DC: Georgetown University Press, 2003), 175.

24. Laurence S. Cunningham, *The Meaning of Saints* (New York: Harper & Row, 1980), 65. The author contrasts the story telling of the saints' lives with that of church history and depicts it as "Christianity from below rather than from above." As such, hagiography is much more "democratic" than conventional church history in its representation of the holy—it includes the lives of women, of the economically and politically disenfranchised, and "leaves room for the neurotic, the naïve, the unlovely as well as for the forceful and the attractive personality" (5).

caught a glimpse/a vision of God that in turn has caught them into itself and transfigured them through the agency of the Holy Spirit into the likeness of what they behold. Yet what is particularly significant in Cunningham's description is its emphasis on the broader socio-transformative capacity of saintly lives. As the saints have indwelled (and have been indwelled by) the life of God, so their lives can captivate others, leading them into the divine life. As the vision takes residence in the saint and transfigures him or her into its likeness, the saint becomes the embodiment of that vision for others, so that they also may see and taste the life of God and become its living image on earth. Thus, the life of the saint becomes not only a moral imperative for its addressees but a summoning into their theotic eschatological destiny, and Spirit-saturated means for their divinely ordained *theoformation*.

The socio-transformative capacity of the saints' lives as pneumatic embodiment of the world's eschatological future is further catalyzed by the ability of their Spirit-filled vision to inspire redemptive daydreaming and reenvisioning of the world. In view of this, reflecting on saintliness's subversive confrontation with the postlapsarian condition of the cosmos, Sallie McFague employs the notion of "wild space"—a term used by anthropologists to indicate "the peculiar insight into alternative ways of living that some people seem to have."[25] For McFague, "wild space," as "that part of each of us that doesn't quite fit into our conventional world,"[26] is what makes us strange/different/divergent. One's wild space is incubated in and nurtured by one's otherness, which could be experienced as physical (race, gender, visible disability),[27] cultural, sociopolitical, or economic marginality that forces the person to encounter reality as a minority, pushed to the fringes of a society that feels threatened, perplexed, or simply inconvenienced by difference. Wild space is, therefore, often nurtured by suffering—the suffering of societal exclusion and oppression, of loneliness and abandonment, of shattered relationships, of enduring the pain of broken body, mind, and heart. The wild space of saints often springs from wounds that have been surrendered to the Spirit, permeated by divine groaning for the ontological renewal of the cosmos, embraced and redeemed in the Spirit's enlivening presence, and transfigured into means of communion in solidarity with the suffering

25. Sallie McFague, *Blessed Are the Consumers: Climate Change and the Practice of Restraint* (Minneapolis: Fortress, 2013), 46.

26. Sallie McFague, "Epilogue: Human Dignity and the Integrity of Creation," in *Theology That Matters: Ecology, Economy, and God*, ed. Darby Kathleen Ray (Minneapolis: Fortress, 2006), 199–212 (206).

27. McFague, *Blessed Are the Consumers*, 47.

others, indeed, with all of creation (Rom 8:18–22).[28] Humanity's groaning in and with the Spirit is moved by the anamnesis of paradise and the longing for the eschatological wholeness of creation.[29] As a "paradise-haunted creature"[30] living between memory and hope, the human being strives to change the world in recollection-fueled assurance of its possible otherness. As giver of dreams and visions, which bridge the suspense between origin and eschaton, the Spirit teaches humanity to imagine, to ask for,[31] but also to enact a different world. This Spirit-nurtured restless expectation of God's future for creation confronts and discredits all political projects attempting to cement the world's fractured present stage as its immutable future condition. For McFague, humanity's wild space—its mode of difference—is precisely where this Spirit-induced prophetic interface between present and future takes place, yearning for change and springing forth into viable socio-transformative action.

This is why the saints often appear as *holy misfits* whose lives challenge the conventional flow of the surrounding culture, for they see themselves, the others, and the world otherwise, through the eyes of the Spirit, illuminated by the light of the adventing kingdom. Yet, as McFague asserts, precisely this uncomfortable (often socially disadvantaging and marginalizing) perspective "suggests that alternatives are possible."[32] This pneumatic opening of the possibility of reenvisioning the relation to the other offers a

28. McFague asserts Simone Weil's disturbing and frightfully beautiful statement that "The extreme greatness of Christianity lies in the fact that it does not seek a supernatural remedy for suffering but a supernatural use for it." See McFague, *Blessed Are the Consumers*, 58.

29. McFague, "Epilogue," 207.

30. McFague, "Epilogue," 207.

31. McFague, "Epilogue," 207.

32. McFague, *Blessed Are the Consumers*, 47. In its capacity to facilitate an alternative vision of the world and induce social transformation, McFague's notion of "wild space" resonates with John Paul Lederach's articulation of "the moral imagination." See John Paul Lederach, *The Moral Imagination: The Art and Soul of Building Peace* (New York: Oxford University Press, 2005), ch. 2. For Lederach, a defining characteristic of the moral imagination is "the capacity to give birth to something new that in its very birthing changes our world and the way we see things" (27). The moral imagination sets in motion the bringing about of possibilities that are hard to imagine in current circumstances and opens space for "the creative act to emerge" and to birth forth the nonexisting and the unimaginable (38). It springs off "something rooted in the challenges of the real world" and, in reference to peace building, has to do with the capacity "to generate constructive responses and initiatives that, while rooted in the day-to-day challenges of violence, transcend and ultimately break the grip of those destructive patterns and cycles" (29). Ultimately, for Lederach, transcending violence is "forged by the capacity to generate, mobilize, and build the moral imagination" (5).

prophetic critique of the cultural, sociopolitical and economic exclusion of the other—a critique that comes in the compelling power of embodiment. Indeed, the undeniable socio-transformative persuasion of saintliness resides precisely in the fact that it tangibly presents God's future for the world in the encounter with a transfigured human life "*lived according to a new vision*."[33] The saints' radically incarnational "practice of wild space"[34] becomes the paradigm of moving "from knowing the good to actually doing it."[35] Therefore, the wild space of a hallowed human being becomes the location from which the Spirit starts the world's redemptive mending as the wild space itself springs out of one's uniqueness/difference. The Spirit gardens difference and catalyzes its socio-transformative power in healing the postlapsarian fractures of creation. One of the lessons of socio-transformative pneumatology is that it takes difference to make harmony—this is the lesson of Pentecost. As Moltmann asserts, its imperative for the Christian community is "not just to proclaim the gospel of God's love, but also to live it in community"[36] with the other. Indeed, Pentecost reveals that God has opened his future for the other, and the Spirit (who enfleshes that future in the human *socium*) demands the same from all flesh. The Spirit of Pentecost condemns the spirits of racism, sexism, tribalism/ethnocentrism, and nationalism as manifestations of sin's fracturing and antagonizing of the human community. Pentecost announces God's judgment upon these social pathologies and upon all attempts for their religious justification: they have no future, for in the divinely ordained relational sacramentality of the cosmos there is no future/no eschaton without the other. At Pentecost (as well as in the transfigured economic life of the post-Pentecost community), the Spirit reveals *the sacrament of the other*,[37]

33. McFague, *Blessed Are the Consumers*, 47.

34. McFague, *Blessed Are the Consumers*, 77.

35. McFague, *Blessed Are the Consumers*, 53–54.

36. Moltmann, *Living God and the Fullness of Life*, 152.

37. In his biographical essay on Mother Maria Skobtsova (Saint Maria of Paris), Michael P. Plekon uses the phrase "the sacrament of brother/sister" as a hermeneutical key to understanding Mother Maria's theology and tireless benevolent work for the needy. (See Michael P. Plekon, *The World as Sacrament: An Ecumenical Path toward a Worldly Spirituality* [Collegeville, MN: Liturgical, 2016], 35–49. See also footnote 31 in the epilogue of the present book.) Maria Skobtsova is an atypical saint—a brilliant, strong, and complex woman with a difficult life (having endured twice the pain of divorce and the devastation of the deaths of her three children). When Bishop Evlogy tonsured her (after the end of her second marriage), he told her that "the world and its suffering people will now become her monastery." Mother Maria lived and died fulfilling this commissioning mandate, enfleshing daily her love for God through love toward the fellow human. While in her theological works she offers eloquent

even the enemy (as in ethno-religious conflicts and protracted, violent territorial disputes), and the essentiality of loving them as the means of loving communion with God. Thus, the consequent Spirit-saturated daily commensality of the Pentecost community (giving shared access to life for all according to each one's need) is uplifted as the continuation of the eucharistic table. It makes the gospel visible and tangible by paradigmatically bridging the gap between faith and practice and unveiling the church as the eschatological future of the cosmos—the living icon of the triune life enfleshed by the Spirit in the redeemed human community and destined to circumscribe all that exists into its cosmic *sobornost*[38] (pneumatic conciliarity).

The capacious polyphony of the eschaton vibrates in the many tongues of Pentecost's radical inclusion of and hospitality toward the other.[39] Therefore, as Amos Yong asserts, the miracle of the day of Pentecost is "not the end but the redemption of history."[40] The Spirit's kenotic self-sharing with the other "produces the apocalyptic affection . . . that binds people, even enemies, together and makes forgiveness possible." Forgiveness and reconciliation are possible "because the Spirit enables the speaking and understanding—indeed, confession—of many tongues."[41] Yet the tongues of Pentecost are inseparable from the Spirit's Christoforming/Christifying incarnational work in redeemed humanity and relentless eschatological priming of all creation toward its theotic communal destiny. As Yong points out, Pentecost is not only for societal but for cosmic renewal and reconciliation—"of the earth and all its creatures."[42] Therefore, Pentecost's communion in/of the Spirit is "a fellowship of all flesh," providing a pneumatological justification for "a democracy of the commons,"[43] which circumscribes all of creation in life-giving pneumatic consensus.

---

articulation of love toward the needy as the bridge between Christian faith and practice, she also sharply critiques the monastic life of her time (with its pursuit of "holiness in isolation" from the world and an "unhealthy obsession with rules and details of tradition"). She also condemns the subordination of the Russian Church to any rulers and governments (from Peter the Great to the Soviet regime) or national political interests.

38. For an extended reflection on the complex notion of the church's *sobornost* (often translated as "conciliarity" or "catholicity"), see chapter 1 in the present book.

39. See Daniela C. Augustine, *Pentecost, Hospitality, and Transfiguration: Toward a Spirit-Inspired Vision of Social Transformation* (Cleveland, TN: CPT, 2012).

40. Amos Yong, *In the Days of Caesar: Pentecostalism and Political Theology* (Grand Rapids: Eerdmans, 2010), 342.

41. Yong, *In the Days of Caesar*, 342–43.

42. Yong, *In the Days of Caesar*, 343.

43. Yong, *In the Days of Caesar*, 345.

In light of these assertions, the present volume offers a theological vision of the common good based on the Spirit's Christoforming agency in the life of redeemed and ontologically renewed humanity, recovering its eucharistic nature as a priestly communal being and emphasizing (in continuity with its underlying Christology) that to be truly human means to be for others.[44] In this embodied journey of growing into Christlikeness, the Spirit empowers humanity to discern anew the meaning of creation, both as God's living household (depicting all life as a gift of unconditional divine hospitality) and as cosmic liturgy—a eucharistic sacrament unfolding within the immediacy of the divine presence. This socio-transformative vision teaches humanity to see the world as created to be shared with the other—as means of communion with God and both the anthropic and nonanthropic neighbor and, therefore, as a pedagogy on becoming like God (in his perichoretic love, enacted in self-giving to the other). This renewed (and renewing) vision becomes the foundation for constructing a theological ethic of planetary flourishing in/through commitment to a sustainable communal praxis of a shared/common future with the other and the different.

The project unfolds in four major chapters. The first one is dedicated to the articulation of the book's overarching pneumatological vision of pursuing the common good. The second offers an application of this vision in examining the causes of violence against the other and searching for a viable antidote to its distorting iconoclasm. Chapter 3 carries the vision's application further to the realm of economics, highlighting that all material human existence has a spiritual base and uplifting the sacramental life of the church as pedagogy on disciplining human desires toward a reverent consumption (thus nurturing an embodied resistance to the all-commodifying drive of unrestrained consumerism with its devastating communal and ecological consequences). The fourth chapter applies the book's vision to the experience of forgiveness and reconciliation, highlighting the creative artistry of the Spirit's reconciling agency and pondering the challenges of "forgiving the unforgivable" as well as the pressuring (global, regional, and national) demands of practicing "legislated forgiveness." Finally, the epilogue illustrates the book's vision by drawing on the hagiographical genre(s) and highlighting

44. As a theological ethics project in pneumatological key, the volume's primary focus is on the Spirit's redemptive transformation of the horizontal relationship between human beings as well as between humanity and the rest of creation. Yet, while not explicitly designated in separate sections within the text, the chapters' constructs arise out of the distinct weaving of the book's underlying Christology, cosmology, anthropology, and ecclesiology.

the moral imperative of saintly lives amidst a concrete living community. As previously noted, seizing on the interviews and testimonies collected during my field research in Eastern Slavonia, this concluding segment of the work portrays also the ecumenical peacebuilding efforts of the Christian community in the region by offering an account of its shared communal life that enfleshes the Spirit's movement through kenotic/self-giving human agency toward bringing about the flourishing of all others.

While constructed as a theological ethic of the common good through distinctly pneumatological lenses, the book engages the reader in an interdisciplinary dialogue—cross-pollinating its construct with insights from political philosophy, sociology of religion, economics, and environmental rsearch, as well as forgiveness/reconciliation and peacebuilding studies. Its point of departure resides in pneumatological anthropology and ecclesiology, uplifting the centrality of the church's liturgical life as foundational for cultivating her *in-Spirit-ed* socio-transformative agency for the life and flourishing of all creation.

Chapter 1

From the Common Image to the Common Good

In his 1989 book *Creating a Just Future*, Jürgen Moltmann locates the reasons for the current global ecological, political and socioeconomic crisis, within distorted perceptions of God's image and their reflective mirroring by human society within the cosmos to the detriment of all creation. In light of this beckoning assertion, he proposes that the profound socio-transformative change needed to cure the dehumanizing and ecologically devastating effects of modernity's ethical visions must begin with a renewed gaze at the image of the triune God—with rediscovery and inspired imaging of the divine community of love.[1] Moltmann's brief book (first published in the year that marked the collapse of the Eastern Bloc) reads as a manifesto against the madness of civilizational self-extermination, culminating in the Cold War's nuclear proliferation race (and its present threat amidst global political tensions and economic uncertainties).

In an era dominated by fear of the ideological (including religious) other and a rampant competition for an ever-shrinking world with limited natural resources, the text provokes distressing questions about humanity's prospects for survival. Has modern society aborted its own future by refusing to take responsibility for the present and for the well-being of the next generations through uncompromised commitment to sustainable economic development, unceasing peacebuilding and faithful stewardship of creation? Have narrow national and regional interests, ruled by the "trinity" of power, prosperity, and security at the expense of others, distorted so irreversibly our vision and understanding of the self and the world that we have lost sight of the deep, organic continuity between our flourishing and that of others?

1. Jürgen Moltmann, *Creating a Just Future: The Politics of Peace and the Ethics of Creation in a Threatened World* (London: SCM, 1989), 54–56.

Have we been blinded (by fear of the other and anxiety over scarcity) to the truth that there is no security and well-being for us without security and well-being for the other (for the ethnic, racial, cultural, religious, ideological, and nonanthropic other),[2] that authentic flourishing depends on mutuality since (in the words of Sallie McFague) "relationality" is "the hallmark of creation"?[3] Has the worship of unrestrained, self-indulging consumerism (coined with fervent religious justification of savage, devouring "dominion" over nature) left any place for genuine human community and the pursuit of a planetary common good? Moltmann's concise answer is painfully sobering—if there is any future left for society that "future is repentance."[4] Yet amidst this call to metanoia, his work vibrates with visionary anticipation of a cosmic shalom—of comprehensive flourishing for all of God's creatures, illuminated by a new (trinitarian) epistemology of love and undergirded by an "ethic of the common life" in a global community of justice and inclusion of all (both anthropic and nonanthropic) others.[5]

For Moltmann, the return to the image of the triune God, essential for the mending of our own humanity as well as of our common home, planet earth, is an outcome of the Spirit's renewing, socio-transformative work within the redeemed community—the church—the fellowship of the ones whose eyes have been open to see and ears to hear. The Christian is to see the world anew and know it otherwise, through the glorious, illuminating vision of the divine face. Therefore, the community of faith is humanity resensitized by the Spirit to the divine presence within the cosmos, to God's nearness that fills creation and sustains the breath of all that lives (Job 32:18; 34:14–15). The church is the community of the ones who have seen the face of God (Jesus Christ) and have been empowered by the Spirit to image it in the world through self-giving, unconditional love for God and neighbor. Moltmann's vision of world-mending centers on this new, in-Spirit-ed, relational epistemology of love in knowing the self, the other and the world—the active, creative love of the communal God poured out by the Holy Spirit into redeemed humanity and embodied by the ontologically renewed, reconciled covenantal community. As the author states, "We always know something else only in so far as we love it, and in this love can allow it to be wholly itself."[6]

2. Moltmann, *Creating a Just Future*, 46.

3. Sallie McFague, *Blessed Are the Consumers: Climate Change and the Practice of Restraint* (Minneapolis: Fortress, 2013), 197.

4. Moltmann, *Creating a Just Future*, 15.

5. Moltmann, *Creating a Just Future*, 47, 61.

6. Moltmann, *Creating a Just Future*, 60.

In light of this assertion, the remainder of the present chapter offers a reflection on the Spirit's Christoforming work in humanity's ontological renewal as essential for the healing of the world. It begins by turning to the pneumatic hallowing of human life as the embodied bridge between faith and the practice of the common good, articulated and enacted in the Christified lives of the saints. The text proceeds with a brief "exegesis" of the Eastern Orthodox icon of creation and its undergirding "theology of the face," highlighting the event of the Incarnation, through which the world beheld God's face in the face of Jesus of Nazareth. The chapter continues with exploring some of the ways in which redeemed humanity images the Trinity within the cosmos, and concludes with reflecting on the significance of Pentecost in establishing the church as the visible icon of the Trinity on earth.

From Belief to the Practice of the Common Good

The divine triune communal love that speaks the world into existence and sustains it with its very breath is manifested in redeemed humanity: in its Christoformed, kenotic longing for all others to live and have life to the fullest (John 10:10), for (as stated by Arthur McGill) love "is the communication of life"—the creative activity through which "life is passed from one person to another, from one community to another."[7] Therefore, love, as the new way of knowing, according to Jürgen Moltmann, is not for "dominion" but for "participation"[8] in the cosmic community of the Spirit. The Spirit of God, "poured out on the whole creation," brings forth and sustains "the unity and community of all creatures with one another and with God."[9]

7. Arthur McGill, *Sermons of Arthur C. McGill: Theological Fascinations*, ed. Daniel Cain (Eugene, OR: Cascade, 2007), 1:80. Quoted in McFague, *Blessed Are the Consumers*, 167.

8. Moltmann, *Creating a Just Future*, 60. Moltmann's language is, undoubtedly, theotic (as well as enotic and kenotic), resonating well with Eastern Orthodox anthropology, soteriology, pneumatology and doctrine of creation. In her kenotic theology, Sallie McFague reflects on the Eastern Orthodox soteriology by discussing its description and summary in the terms *kenosis*, *enosis*, and *theosis*, and highlights the embodiment of their meaning in the life of Jesus Christ as "the face of God" on earth. Thus, Christ's self-emptying on behalf of the other (kenosis), the union of the divine and human will in his being, or rather the submitting of the second to the first (enosis) and the moral transformation/ascent of human nature toward the divine likeness in "union with God" (theosis) define the intentionality and action of Jesus of Nazareth and the way to God—the way of becoming fully human. See McFague, *Blessed Are the Consumers*, 188.

9. Moltmann, *Creating a Just Future*, 57.

The "cosmic Spirit" is the "common bond," the living presence that holds all things together as "the ground and source of all that does not live of itself but from, with and in others."[10] Therefore, life together in pursuit of the common planetary good that circumscribes the flourishing of all God's creatures is possible only in, with and through the Spirit and her work of renewing the image of God within the cosmos (which coincides with understanding and discerning of the world as a living sanctuary of the divine presence).

In this vein of thought, Moltmann highlights the need of "a new, Christian 'natural theology', not so much for the sake of God as in earlier times as for the sake of nature and its worth"[11] and insists that if we "find the 'traces of God' in the nature of our environment, then we can discover the 'image of God' in ourselves."[12] Orthodox theology describes this journey as nothing less than becoming *like* God through the Spirit's sanctifying, Christoforming work within the human community. Therefore, the journey to the common good is the journey toward becoming fully human (becoming Christlike); it is the creature's ascent to theosis.

Often theologies which justify unrestrained exploitation and destruction of creation perceive the first human beings, placed by God in the garden of Eden, as a perfect, complete project (the very crown of creation) for which all exists and over which they are given unquestionable dominion. Differing from such views, Eastern Christianity understands the first Adam as a "good" (Gen 1) unfolding creation, an ongoing project, whose telos is the final/last Adam—Jesus Christ. This is the project of growing in the freedom of divine love toward all that exists, the totality of creation; it is the free-willed journey toward the likeness of God, in which humanity is transfigured by the Spirit in a perpetual, glorious ascent of partaking in and making visible (within the materiality of the world) the divine communal life of the invisible God. This transfiguring work of the Spirit takes place though bringing about the embodiment/incarnation within the human community of the Word that has spoken the world into existence—a pneumatic movement that weaves and sustains the essential continuity and community between humanity and the rest of creation (itself being materialized words spoken forth by the eternal Word).

In light of this pneumatological anthropology, it is not accidental that many of the Eastern church fathers differentiate in their works between

10. Moltmann, *Creating a Just Future*, 58.
11. Moltmann, *Creating a Just Future*, 77.
12. Moltmann, *Creating a Just Future*, 78.

the terms "image" and "likeness" in relation to humanity's ontology and vocation within the cosmos.[13] Their theological vision depicts these terms as reflective precisely of the transfiguring movement from prototype to telos, from potentiality to actualization, while magnifying the redemptive tension between divine grace and human responsibility as an intended pedagogy on becoming like God. Therefore, the image is often portrayed as the full God-given potentiality for attaining the likeness, while likeness, understood as theosis culminating in union with God, is seen as the vocation and destiny of human existence.[14] In the ontological brokenness of the fallen world, the spiritual ascent toward theosis is experienced as "a journey into God"[15] through the sanctifying/Christoforming work of the Holy Spirit who transfigures humanity from glory to glory (2 Cor 3:18), making it a partaker of the divine nature (2 Pet 1:4). Indeed, theosis is Christlikeness (the likeness of God in human flesh), and since Christ is the visible image of the invisible God (Col 1:15) in the material cosmos, to be truly human is to be Christlike.[16] Yet theosis is experienced as ontological renewal and healing that engulfs not only humanity but all of creation in life-giving union with the Creator. This all-permeating cosmic healing involves free-willed, Christoformed, Spirit-empowered human agency. Therefore, humanity's vocation is engraved from the beginning in its ontology. The first Adam represents the communion of heaven and earth, as the union of matter and spirit—of the visible and invisible, the created and uncreated.[17] Adam stands within the world as a microcosm which is to unite the creation to the Creator until the entire world is transfigured into a cosmic, ecclesial macroanthropos—a destiny actualized in the cosmic Christ as the last Adam.[18] Since from the

13. Timothy Ware, *The Orthodox Church* (New York: Penguin, 1997), 219–21; Vladimir Lossky, *The Mystical Theology of the Eastern Church* (Crestwood, NY: St. Vladimir's Seminary Press, 1976), 114–21.

14. Christoforos Stavropoulos, "Partakers of Divine Nature" in *Eastern Orthodox Theology: A Contemporary Reader*, ed. Daniel B. Clendenin (Grand Rapids: Baker, 1995), 183–92 (183–84).

15. Sarah Coakley, *God, Sexuality, and the Self: An Essay 'On the Trinity'* (New York: Cambridge University Press, 2013), 19. Indeed, Christ is the one truly theotic human being, manifesting the fullness of theosis as human life transfigured by and luminous with its union with God—a human life making the invisible God visible within the cosmos, tangibly involved in its mending for the flourishing of all created.

16. Bartholomew I, Archbishop of Constantinople and Ecumenical Patriarch, *Encountering the Mystery* (New York: Doubleday, 2008), 132.

17. Dimitru Staniloae, *The Sanctifying Mysteries*, vol. 5 of *The Experience of God: Orthodox Dogmatic Theology* (Brookline, MA: Holy Cross Orthodox Press, 2012), 4.

18. For Vladimir Lossky, the church (as the communal body of Christ) is destined to

beginning, the last Adam is the ontological telos of the first Adam and of all creation, and his communal body, the church, is to circumscribe all existence (both terrestrial and celestial) into union with the Creator, then not the first Adam but the church as cosmic, Christoformed community is the crown of creation—the destiny of all existence. To paraphrase the Shepherd of Hermas, she is the goal for which the world exists.[19]

The path toward attaining the likeness of God demands cooperation and alignment of the free human will with the divine will. It unfolds as an empowering pedagogy on becoming like God by choosing to love and will like him. It is a call to one's continual Christic transfiguring through sanctification of personal will and desires, in fasting from oneself on behalf of the other as expression of incarnated love toward God and neighbor. Because Christoformed love is a free and voluntary response to God's call to humanity, the freedom of human will in the image of God is a prerequisite for attaining the divine likeness. As Vladimir Lossky states,

> To be what one must in loving God, one must admit that one can be the opposite; one must admit that one can revolt. The resistance of freedom alone gives sense to the union. . . . This freedom comes from God: it is the seal of our divine participation, the masterpiece of the Creator.[20]

---

engulf the cosmos, reuniting it with God. Lossky states, "The church is the center of the Universe, the sphere in which its destinies are determined. All are called to enter into the church, for if man is a microcosm, the church is a *macro-anthropos*, as Maximus says. It increases and is compounded in history, bringing the elect into its bosom and uniting them to God. The world grows old and falls into decay, while the church is constantly rejuvenated and renewed by the Holy Spirit who is the source of its life. At a given moment, when the church has attained to the fullness of growth determined by the will of God, the external world, having used up its vital resources, will perish. As for the church, it will appear in its eternal glory as the Kingdom of God." Lossky, *Mystical Theology of the Eastern Church*, 178. Dimitru Staniloae, also utilizing the language of Saint Maximus the Confessor (*Mystagogy*, ch. 7, Patrologia Graeca 91:684C–685A) depicts the human being as a *microcosm* and the world as a *macroanthropos*, and emphasizes human agency in the process of gathering all creation into union with God. Staniloae, *Revelation and Knowledge of the Triune God*, vol. 1 of *The Experience of God: Orthodox Dogmatic Theology* (Brookline, MA: Holy Cross Orthodox Press, 2005), 4–6.

19. Shepherd of Hermas, Vision 2, ch. 4, http://www.earlychristianwritings.com/text/shepherd.html.

20. Vladimir Lossky, *Orthodox Theology: An Introduction* (Crestwood, NY: St. Vladimir's Seminary Press, 2001), 72.

Therefore, it takes one will to create humanity, but two to sanctify it. Or in the words of Lossky, "A single will to rise up the image, but two to make the image into a likeness."[21]

As Christoforos Stavropoulos points out, the Holy Spirit is "the main and essential beginning" of humanity's sanctification,[22] the One who applies what is objectively accomplished in Christ to the life of the individual believer and the community of faith, forming Christ's body on earth as the communal icon of God. Echoing Saint Athanasius, Lossky asserts that God became flesh so that humanity may receive the Holy Spirit[23]—become pneumatized. Therefore, Pentecost is not merely a continuation of the Incarnation or its sequel. It is its result and purpose as the inaugural event of the Spirit's sanctifying work in humanity.[24] As such, Pentecost is the beginning of the "last things" for it is the event of unveiling the church—the end of creation—amidst the present.

In light of this understanding of theosis, Christians (as the ones on whom the Spirit has poured himself) are those who through the Spirit's illuminating and transfiguring work have responded to the divine call (mandate) to humanity to become Christ-(God in flesh)-like by following and imaging within the world Christ's kenosis (emptying themselves for the sake of others, Phil 2:7) and *enōsis* (submitting their human will to the divine will, Luke 22:42) until they are fully filled with his life, and no longer they but he lives in them (Gal 2:20). According to Sallie McFague, one can discern this movement of the Spirit within the Christoforming journey of the saints, whose stories depict salvation not as "the atonement of an angry, all-powerful" deity, but as a "fourfold process of responding to the call of God to empty the self of its false, egotistic attempt to ground one's life in oneself so that we may, like Jesus, become the face of God for others."[25] The fourfold process toward saintliness that McFague summarizes in her 'hagiography' of three modern saints (John Woolman, Simone Weil, and Dorothy Day), whose lives become a living icon of Christ and a prophetic negation of injustice toward the other, is her proposal for engendering a redemptive, socio-transformative movement from belief to action. Thus, according to McFague, the process of imaging God in the struggles of daily

21. Lossky, *Orthodox Theology*, 73.
22. Stavropoulos, "Partakers of Divine Nature," 188.
23. Lossky, *Mystical Theology*, 179.
24. Lossky, *Orthodox Theology*, 85.
25. McFague, *Blessed Are the Consumers*, 159.

life unfolds in the following stages of radical incarnationalism in solidarity with the suffering of others:

> 1. Experiences of "voluntary poverty" to shock middle-class people out of the conventional model of self-fulfillment through possessions and prestige, and into a model of self-emptying, as a pathway for personal and planetary well-being. . . . 2. The focus of one's attention to the needs of others, especially their most physical, basic needs, such as food. . . . 3. The gradual development of a "universal self," as the line constituting one's concern (compassion or empathy) moves from its narrow focus on the ego . . . to reach out further and further until there is no line left. . . . 4. A new model of the universal self operates at both the personal and public levels, for instance in the planetary rules: (1) take only your share; (2) clean up after yourself; (3) keep the house in good repair for those who will use it after you.[26]

Yet when we look at the lives of the saints, it seems that these stages unfold not so much as a distinct, ascending sequence but as interwoven, somewhat simultaneous developments within the kenotic movement toward Christoformation, or in McFague's terms, toward the formation of "the universal self." It is hard to establish when the saint transitions from life in solidarity with the suffering of others (motivated by moral/religious convictions) to incarnated Christic selfhood—a human life so "enlarged"[27] by the Spirit that it becomes a sanctuary not only for the immediate other (the known neighbor), but the distant, anonymous, unknown others (anthropic and nonanthropic). The life of the saint becomes a living reflection of the incarnate, crucified, and risen God, in whom all creation is joined both in its present suffering and future glory.

McFague rightly suggests that the Christoforming transition from belief to action to transfigured/sanctified (universal) self is not accomplished "primarily through reason . . . but through emotion, getting inside someone else's skin," being able "to *feel* with any creature."[28] As the author asserts, "For these folks, nothing less than the world was their body."[29] In light of this assertion, reflecting on the deep biological interdependence of life and

26. McFague, *Blessed Are the Consumers*, xii–xiii.
27. McFague, *Blessed Are the Consumers*, 117.
28. McFague, *Blessed Are the Consumers*, 112.
29. McFague, *Blessed Are the Consumers*, 111.

creaturely well-being, McFague states that the "strange" religious statement "that in order to find your life you must lose it is not a paradox or a mystery: it is simply a description of what science is telling us as well—we are universal selves. The main difference between the saints and the rest of us is that they actually acknowledge this and live by it, while we do not."[30]

The saints' profound, all-engulfing, empathy and compassion, uncompromisingly material in addressing the physical lack and suffering of others, is an incarnation of the spaciousness of God's unconditional love that seeks the flourishing of all his creatures. Therefore, in an age obsessed with personal rights and self-indulging desires, the lives of the saints stand out as a countercultural model of societal and planetary flourishing—one of recognizing the world as a hallowed sanctuary, filled with the divine presence, in which all life unfolds as deeply and organically interconnected/synchronized worship of the Creator. The Spirit opens human eyes to see the cosmos as a temple and life as a divine liturgy and urges redeemed humanity to embrace its vocation as a worshiping creature so that the world may live life to the fullest. It is impossible to cultivate an authentic eucharistic society committed to a reverent way of being in the world without this sacramental vision of shared creation. This transformed in-Spirit-ed way of knowing and seeing is essential for cultivating a common life of ascetic and kenotic restraint, in reverent consumption and sustainable, just economic practices that take seriously one's summoning by the Spirit into the divine liturgy. This life of daily worship unfolds in the tedious smallness of the mundane, magnifying and examining every thought, act, and word amidst resensitized awareness of the divine presence and putting aside all that does not communicate to others God's embodied love.

In the lives of the saints, this illuminated perspective of the world turns to the fellow human with "the eyes of the crucified Christ"[31]—paying close attention to the immediate, instant physicality of the suffering other—of his or her dehumanizing poverty and ecological deprivation, political oppression and marginalization, crippling sickness, effacing loneliness, and frail mortality. Seeing through the eyes of the crucified Christ means making visible the suffering of the other amidst a world blinded by political rhetoric of personal rights versus shared well-being, a world that refuses to accept responsibility for the suffering of the fellow human and the rest of creation, justifying it as self-afflicted and well deserved. To use the words of Pope Fran-

30. McFague, *Blessed Are the Consumers*, 112.

31. John Woolman, quoted by McFague (*Blessed Are the Consumers*, 177).

cis (from his homily on the occasion of Mother Teresa's canonization), the saints become the voice of the destitute, the oppressed, the forgotten "before the powers of this world, so that they might recognize their guilt for the crime of poverty" and exclusion "they have created."[32] Perhaps the prophetic protest of the saints' lives against the selfish indifference and self-righteous judgmentalism that dismisses any human responsibility to be one's "brother's keeper" could be summarized by the words of one of Dostoevsky's characters in *The Brothers Karamazov*: "everyone of us is responsible for everyone else in every way, and I most of all."[33] While some may dismiss this assertion as "stretching" social responsibility "beyond the limits of sense,"[34] it expresses something of the burden felt by those who are enlarged by the Spirit to embrace the entire cosmos on their journey toward Christic (or in McFague's language "universal") selfhood.

Seeing through the eyes of the suffering, self-emptying Christ—the icon of love's kenosis for the life of the world—enables the saints to discern his face in that of the suffering other (Matt 25:31–46). Thus, in the paradox of faith, illuminated by the vision of God's face, the eyes of Christ (in his radical self-identification with "the least of these") look at us through the eyes of the hungry, the sick, the naked, the homeless, the imprisoned. Their summoning gaze moves the saints to radical ascetic and kenotic action of imaging God to the world so that it may regain its humanity. Yet this imaging means living his life in following the pattern of the Incarnation through the leading and empowerment of the Holy Spirit (the agent of the Incarnation). Therefore, the saints offer their bodies to Christ in a radical choice of self-identification with those in whom he has chosen to see himself. Their lives become a living extension of Christ taking upon himself the poverty and misery of "the least of these" and cosuffering with them amidst their alienating, dehumanizing neediness and destitution, thus affirming their human dignity. Through the lives of the saints the invisible are seen, the silenced are heard, the unloved are cherished as beloved, the lonely

32. Pope Francis, *Homily for the Canonization of Mother Teresa*, Holy Mass and Canonization of Blessed Mother Terese of Calcutta, St. Peter's Square, September 4, 2016, http://en.radiovaticana.va/news/2016/09/04/homily_for_the_canonization_of_mother_teresa_full_text/1255727.

33. Jonathan Sacks, *To Heal a Fractured World: The Ethics of Responsibility* (New York: Schocken, 2007), 116. Fyodor Dostoevsky, *The Brothers Karamazov*, (Mineola, NY: Dover, 2005), 261. Words spoken by the very ill Markel, brother of Father Zosima, in a conversation with their mother.

34. Sacks, *To Heal a Fractured World*, 116.

are embraced in community, the homeless are sheltered in unconditional hospitality, the powerless are empowered to do likewise in sharing their life with others.

Since the church is the community of the saints (the ones who have been baptized in the body of the resurrected Lord and summoned by the Spirit unto Christlikeness), to see the world through the eyes of Christ, living in ascetic and kenotic solidarity with the suffering other and mirroring the face of God within the world, becomes the vocation of each Christian. Therefore, as Pope Francis states,

> Just as the Lord has come to meet me and has stooped down to my level in my hour of need, so too do I go to meet him, bending low before those who have lost faith or who live as though God did not exist, before young people without values or ideals, before families in crisis, before the ill and the imprisoned, before refugees and immigrants, before the weak and defenseless in body and spirit, before abandoned children, before the elderly who are on their own. Wherever someone is reaching out, asking for a helping hand in order to get up, this is where our presence—and the presence of the Church which sustains and offers hope—must be.[35]

Moltmann's and McFague's assertions of the Spirit's sanctifying presence within the community of faith, empowering men and women to face each other with the face of God in harmonious pursuit of the common good, resonates not only with the Eastern Orthodox understanding of theosis but also with the notion of *sobornost*. *Sobornost* (often translated "catholicity" and "conciliarity")[36] is a complex idea and an overarching theme within Orthodox ecclesiology. Reflective of the communal essence of humanity (the creature created in the image of God as a triune community), the ecclesial principle of *sobornost*, in the words of Bishop Kallistos Ware, constitutes the life of the church as "living and organic unity which reconciles the conflict-

35. Pope Francis, *Homily for the Canonization of Mother Teresa*.

36. For the origin and meaning of the word, see Todor Subev, "The Nature and Mission of Councils in the Light of the Theology of Sobornost," *The Ecumenical Review* 45, no. 3 (July 1993): 261–70 (esp. 262–64). For the development and articulation of the notion of *sobornost* in the work of Aleksei Khomiakov, considered the first Orthodox theologian to think systematically about ecclesiology, see Kallistos Ware, "*Sobornost* and Eucharistic Ecclesiology: Alexei Khomiakov and His Successors," *International Journal for the Study of the Christian Church* 11, nos. 2–3 (May–August 2011): 216–35.

ing claims of freedom and obedience."[37] Todor Subev describes *sobornost* as the "vision of the church as a great 'council,' gathered from all over the world by the Holy Spirit," the ecclesia's internal "principle" of "spiritual Christian unity and communion," marked by "the unique harmony of faith, love and freedom which grow by the grace of God."[38] In a rich reflection on the essence of *sobornost*, Subev remarks,

> Sobornost is the heart of catholicity and conciliarity. It emphasizes catholicity as harmony of truth and life achieved by the union of each with all, and conciliarity as the principle and expression of the inner catholicity of the body of Christ, as the consensus of faith held by the whole people of God.[39]

Yet the church's *sobornost* stretches both horizontally and vertically across time and space.[40] Therefore, *sobornost* does not run just to the extremities of the world, joining redeemed humanity in a given generation, but in a transgenerational fusion of past, present, and future. Further, it apprehends within its reach both heaven and earth—the church terrestrial and celestial, visible and invisible, the faithful known and unknown in the one community of saints, worshiping together with the angels and archangels, cherubim and seraphim, and the rest of creation (Ps 19). Therefore, Subev concludes that, finally, "sobornost should be seen in the perspective of the kingdom of God as a force and a process of gathering the universe together, to redeem time and space, by the power of love."[41] The author points out that "the basic factor" for the harmonious unity within the "sobornaia church" "is saintliness and self-renouncing love" and asserts Vladimir Solovyov's claim that "such a Christian communion can radiate freedom, concord and common life in secular society."[42]

The idea of *sobornost*, in its cosmic span, resonates (though in a small way) with Sallie McFague's call for a new mark of the church—"ecological catholicity"—that spreads beyond the human community to embrace the

37. Ware, "*Sobornost* and Eucharistic Ecclesiology," 219.

38. Subev, "Nature and Mission of Councils," 263.

39. Subev, "Nature and Mission of Councils," 264.

40. Ware, "*Sobornost* and Eucharistic Ecclesiology," 224. Ware offers a beautiful quotation by Alexei Khomiakov on the comprehensive, cosmic reach of *sobornost* across time and space, in heaven and on earth, and into eternity.

41. Subev, "Nature and Mission of Councils," 264.

42. Subev, "Nature and Mission of Councils," 265–66.

rest of creation.[43] Engaging Simone Weil's and Teilhard de Chardin's insistence on a broader definition of catholicity that views the whole planet as God's household and takes seriously the organic, "interdependent relations" between human beings and "all other life-forms," McFague points to the Incarnation as "giving us permission to love the world" and the assignment to figure out what that means in our daily life.[44] In light of the Incarnation, as McFague asserts, ecological catholicity "is not a minor addition to the marks of the church: it is central to its mission to preach good news to *all* creation,"[45] gathering the cosmos into its telos—the incarnate, resurrected Christ.

The Memory of a World Illuminated by the Divine Face[46]

Humanity is a restless, homesick creature, deeply imprinted with and haunted by the primordial memory of Eden as the lost home for which it has been created—the memory of shalom as harmonious wholeness in communion with God and neighbor (both anthropic and nonanthropic). It is the memory of unlimited access to life that is shared by all of God's creatures in the tangible immediacy of the Creator's presence. This memory of human (and cosmic) flourishing is the anamnesis of life shaped by seeing God's face and recognizing it in the face of the other as in oneself—a tridirectional mirroring of the meaning and destiny of being human; standing without fear before the eyes of God, in a transparent openness toward the other, an

43. Sallie McFague, *A New Climate for Theology* (Minneapolis: Fortress, 2008), 33–35.

44. McFague, *New Climate for Theology*, 34. Reflecting on the incarnation, McFague states, "One of the most distinctive characteristics of Christianity is that God is *with us* in the flesh. . . . Jesus Christ is the paradigm, the explicit good news, that we are not alone on the earth and that we do not belong somewhere else. God is not antiflesh or antiworld; in fact, just the opposite; the incarnation says that God is the one in whom we live and move and have our being *as* fleshly, earthly creatures. God does not despise the world; God loves the world and expects us to as well."

45. McFague, *New Climate for Theology*, 34.

46. This section of the book and the one entitled "Making the Divine Community Visible in the Cosmos" contain expanded, revised versions of segments which originated in my essays "Image, Spirit and *Theosis*: Imaging God in an Image-Distorting World," in *The Image of God in an Image Driven Age: Explorations in Christian Anthropology*, ed. Beth Felker Jones and Jeff Barbeau (Downers Grove, IL: InterVarsity, 2016) and "Creation as Perichoretic Trinitarian Conversation: Reflections on World-Making with Robert W. Jenson," in *The Promise of Robert Jenson's Theology*, ed. Stephen Wright and Christopher W. Green (Minneapolis: Fortress, 2017).

openness built into the very fibers of human ontology's communal reality as sacramental imaging of the trinitarian life within the created cosmos.

In its creaturely essence of representing within the creation the material embodiment of the divine communal life, humanity is to exhibit the communion of matter and spirit in a perichoretic movement of love toward God and neighbor. Thus, according to the memory of paradise, the human being does not image the Trinity on its own, nor just within the parameters of one's relationship with the fellow human—God appears as the third (or rather the first) person of the communal dynamic that sustains the essence of authentically human ontology. In the sacred meaning of the cosmic time sequence, the relationship with the Creator precedes the relationship with the fellow human and the rest of creation. As it is eloquently depicted by the Eastern Orthodox icon of creation, the very first face that humanity sees, while coming forth from the earth through the divine creative agency, is the face of its maker. Through the theology of the icon, beholders understand that they are seeing together with Adam the face of God, which (in a perspective illuminated by revelation) they have come to recognize as the face of Christ, the only face of the Creator that humanity has seen, manifested by the enfleshed creative Word in the face of the last Adam (1 Cor 15:45). As in a mirror, the first Adam sees his face in the countenance of the last Adam. The icon makes its theological point crystal clear—God and humanity have something in common—something expressed in the theological symbolism of the divine face. The uncreated, eternal God shares his face with the created, finite human being. He gives his face to both Adam and Eve so that (individually and collectively) they may become his icon within the cosmos as the image of the Creator imprinted within a creature. Thus, the depositing of the divine image within the human being becomes the mystical mark of humanity's priming for communion and community with God and with one another—a communion that through the agency of the Holy Spirit makes one a partaker in the divine communal life and nature. On the other hand, matter becomes the means of communion between humanity and the rest of the created cosmos as humanity's participation in the shared created nature. Thus, in the first Adam, the icon of the uncreated image and created matter meet together in a communion destined to encapsulate the likeness of God's life within the embodied human life amidst the created world. This is the human destiny of theosis realized and fulfilled in the last Adam—the fullness of deity dwelling in bodily form (Col 2:9), as the communion of matter and Spirit, of the uncreated eternal Word and the enfleshed human existence (John 1:1, 14).

While the Orthodox icon of creation is not concerned with exhausting the complexity and depth of the divine image's meaning and essence within humanity, it makes some important theological assertions. First, it reminds the viewer that "the image" represents the full potentiality for the "likeness"; humanity is made to be like its maker in its intersociality and relation to the rest of creation. Second, both male and female share exactly the same image, and thus, the same potentiality of becoming like God. Third, both Adam and Eve are made to stand face-to-face first with God before they face each other; their fundamental orientation is to be first and foremost toward him. Thus, before seeing the face of the anthropic other—the face of shared human nature outside of the singularity of the self—humanity sees the face of God as the origin of its self-understanding and self-recognition. In the loving affirmation of this face, the human creature is to recognize its true meaning and destiny—its beginning, essence, and telos. By learning this face and its interaction with the cosmos, humanity is to learn its own vocation within the created world as the image of God. Therefore, the relationship to the other creature (anthropic and nonanthropic) becomes functionally predetermined and shaped by one's relationship with the Creator. Human life becomes mirroring the life of God amidst the created cosmos.

The progression of the image emerges from the fundamental interface with God toward turning one's face to the fellow human by following God's own example in movement and orientation. The human being realizes that it is to be a *prosōpon* (face or countenance) turned toward the other in the freedom of encounter, "looking into their eyes and allowing them to look into ours."[47] It realizes its social nature by following God who turns his face toward the other in willingness to share himself with them in communal life. God shares himself with humanity by raising humanity into his own image; now in turn humanity is to learn to share itself with the other, for the image is social and visibly manifested in the communal encounter with the other person. When humanity learns to share the face of God and live out its embodied openness and vulnerability in an orientation toward and for the other, the human being becomes like God in relation to all of the created cosmos, treating it with loving care of nurture and protection. In that communal imaging of the divine face, humanity lives the life of Eden as peace, as life to the fullest.

The tridirectional mirroring of the divine image depicted in the primordial life of Eden points to its social/relational nature within creation. It

47. Bartholomew I, *Encountering the Mystery*, 132.

establishes that, to be truly human, humanity has to stand in communion with both God and the fellow human. When one of these two communicants is absent, when one of these fundamental relationships is broken, the human identity is threatened by dehumanization. The theology of the face seems to present the possibility of sustainable humanness only through a continual standing face to face with God, for only then can one face the other and the rest of the world in a way consistent with the meaning and vocation of being human. Therefore, the icon depicts humanity's fall as turning away from the face of the Creator toward the world and making the world an end in itself, thus substituting the creation for the Creator. The icon makes the theological assertion that all sin is, in a way, a form of idolatry.

The significance of the theology of the face is reflected also in the Eastern Orthodox iconographic depiction of saintly lives. The faces of the saints, while being distinctly different, are all intentionally reminiscent of the face of Christ, the prototype and telos of humanity. The icons depict humanity transfigured in theosis together with all of creation. The recapturing of the divine face in the faces of the saints articulates holiness as the visible and tangible presence of God in a human life that has been transfigured by the Holy Spirit into Christlikeness. Therefore, the liturgical incorporation of the saints' icons could be understood not merely as recognizing the presence of and communing with the "great cloud of witnesses" (Heb 12:1) but also as being summoned by the divine face into an encounter with one's telos and vocation within the cosmos—Christ himself in his mystical communal body. Standing face to face with the icon, one is faced with his or her true, healed human ontology, with the meaning and purpose of being human. Looking at the icon becomes pedagogy on discerning the face of God in the fellow human that, in turn, humanizes the communicant. Therefore, believers are instructed to look at the face, especially of the icon of Christ during confession, standing eye-to-eye with it—neither looking from above nor from below, neither from a posture of superiority nor of inferiority, for both would distort the image of God in the other and therefore in oneself.

The icon is a depiction of the renewed creation summoned in the last Adam and made once again luminous with the beauty of restored communion between heaven and earth.[48] The halo becomes "an iconographic

48. Leonid Ouspensky, "The Meaning and Content of the Icon," in *Eastern Orthodox Theology: A Contemporary Reader*, ed. Daniel B. Clendenin (Grand Rapids: Baker, 1995), 33-63 (58).

device, an outward expression of holiness, a witness of the light"[49] of the world, Jesus Christ (John 8:12), taking up its residence in redeemed humanity. Through sanctified humanity, the entire cosmos is once again illuminated. Therefore, objects in icons "do not project shadows."[50] Light becomes the very background of the icon, permeating everything. Leonid Ouspensky points out that, as the image of sanctified humanity, "the icon represents the reality which was revealed in the transfiguration on Mount Tabor."[51] Thus, the liturgy during the Feast of the Holy Face sings forth this proclamation: "Having illuminated the human image which had grown dark, O Creator, thou didst reveal it on Mount Tabor . . . and now bless and sanctify us, O Lord, who lovest mankind, by the brightness of thy most pure image."[52] In a way, all icons point to the event of the Incarnation.

Creation, Incarnation, and Redemptive World-Mending

As Alexander Schmemann remarks, the icon is "a witness, or better still, a consequence of the unification of the divine and the human, of heaven and earth, that has been accomplished in Jesus Christ. All icons are in essence icons of the Incarnation."[53] The Incarnation of the eternal Word makes the face of the invisible God visible in the countenance of ontologically renewed humanity—Jesus Christ—the beginning of the new creation (Col 1:15). Therefore, any reflection on the divine image and its reflective imaging in the cosmos by the community of saints must begin with a look at the embodiment of the Word (both in the first and in the new creation).

The Embodied Word and the Healing of the World

It takes the Word to heal the fractured world, traumatized by the consequences of the fall. This conclusion is not surprising. Indeed, according to the creation account of Genesis (echoed in the poetic prologue of John's Gospel), the divine Word is in the very fibers of the world and as such unveils creation's origin

49. Ouspensky, "Meaning and Content of the Icon," 53.
50. Ouspensky, "Meaning and Content of the Icon," 62.
51. Ouspensky, "Meaning and Content of the Icon," 43–44.
52. Ouspensky, "Meaning and Content of the Icon," 44.
53. Alexander Schmemann, *The Eucharist: Sacrament of the Kingdom* (Crestwood, NY: St. Vladimir's Seminary Press, 1987), 20.

and destiny—from the Word to the Word, from the Spirit to the Spirit, from eternity to eternity. The world, therefore, points back to the Word (Ps 19:1–6) and, as Dimitru Staniloae asserts, becomes a witness and sign of the Word, bearing within itself the Creator's divine presence and teleological intent.[54] Therefore, matter has a spiritual origin, content, and purpose that are indispensable from its design. The cosmos is filled with the Word's imprint, which identifies not only its authorship, but also its ownership by God. Therefore, the "cosmos is like a book, and the Bible is like the cosmos: both consist of words, *logoi*, which, though diverse,"[55] have come forth as the loving, kenotic self-sharing of the eternal Logos. To paraphrase Saint Maximus the Confessor, while remaining beyond the totality of contingent, created things ("that can be known in relation to other things"), in the revelatory parallelism of creation and Scripture, the One Logos is many *logoi*, and the many *logoi* are One.[56] The Logos holds all things together (Col 1:17) as they are drawn and providentially guided toward him in one grandiose, teleological movement navigated by the Spirit toward the eschaton, where creation finds itself pneumatized and united to its Creator (as its telos in theosis).

In the midst of this Logos-made world, humanity comes forth as the special creature in which matter, as embodied Word, and Spirit, as the animating and life-giving breath of God, commune within a living, sacred space, organically connected to the entire cosmos. Indeed, ontologically, the first Adam represents the communion of heaven and earth, as the mystical unity of matter and spirit—of the visible and invisible, the created and uncreated. Thus, according to Staniloae, the human being appears last within the divine creative act "as a kind of natural link (*syndesmos*) between the extremities of the whole" so that on behalf of the cosmos he or she may maintain and fulfill "the all-encompassing mystery that is the union of God with creation" and that may be "the conscious and willing means through which God maintains and fulfills this union."[57] Therefore, it is not accidental that

54. Dimitru Staniloae, *The World: Creation and Deification*, vol. 2 of *The Experience of God: Orthodox Dogmatic Theology* (Brookline, MA: Holy Cross Orthodox Press, 2005), 21.

55. Andrew Louth, "From Doctrine of Christ to Icon of Christ: St. Maximus the Confessor on the Transfiguration of Christ," in *In the Shadow of the Incarnation: Essays on Jesus Christ in the Early Church in Honor of Brian E. Daley, S.J.*, ed. Peter W. Martens (Notre Dame: University of Notre Dame Press, 2008), 260–75 (269).

56. Saint Maximus the Confessor, *On the Cosmic Mystery of Jesus Christ* (Crestwood, NY: St. Vladimir's Seminary Press, 2003), 57.

57. Dimitru Staniloae, *The Sanctifying Mysteries*, vol. 5 of *The Experience of God: Orthodox Dogmatic Theology* (Brookline, MA: Holy Cross Orthodox Press, 2012), 4.

the human being is placed within the Garden of Eden as into a proto-holy-of-holies, an "archetypal sanctuary"[58] built by God where he dwells within creation, communing with humanity and through the human being, with the entire cosmos.

As a sacral image of God within the cathedral of the universe, humanity is placed in paradise with the mandate to unite to it all creation, so that the entire cosmos may become a paradise,[59] until all of creation becomes holy of holies. This all-engulfing, teleological movement toward cosmic transfiguration is to flow from the actualized human destiny in theosis which involves the internalization of paradise (the appointed place for communion with the Creator as a God-made sanctuary) until humanity presents itself as a sanctuary for God. Thus, "always carrying paradise"[60] in him or herself, the human being is to take it wherever he or she goes and mold the world into its likeness through creative, cultivating activity. The procreation of humanity becomes an organic, God-ordained vehicle toward the actualization of this telos. The human being is commanded to be fruitful, to multiply and populate the earth (Gen 1:28), for the globe is to be covered with the living, embodied communion of matter and Spirit engraved into human ontology until the entire world has become a sanctuary for the divine presence. This calling presents the priestly agency of the human community to all of creation toward its eschatological gathering in union with the Creator. Human agency is, therefore, essential for this profound transformation of the cosmos into paradise, because the theosis of humanity is the condition for the theosis of the rest of creation.

By being made to inhabit the world (as materialized Word), humanity (itself an embodied/enfleshed Word, filled with the Spirit) is destined to abide within the Word's material, embodied form and live according to it. To the extent to which humanity internalizes and lives out the world-creating Word, it dwells in harmony with the fellow human and the rest of creation. Humanity is made to inhabit the Word as its home, and to be a vocal, embodied, enacted Word which has become itself a home/tabernacle for the Spirit within the created cosmos. Indeed, the last Adam, Jesus Christ, is the very purpose and destiny of the first Adam as the theosis of the human

58. Gordon J. Wenham, "Sanctuary Symbolism in the Garden of Eden Story," in *Proceedings of the Ninth World Congress of Jewish Studies* (Jerusalem: World Union of Jewish Studies, 1986), 19.

59. Lossky, *Orthodox Theology*, 74-75.

60. Lossky, *Orthodox Theology*, 74.

hypostasis, for he is the Word made flesh and indwelled by the Spirit as a living temple, filled to its limits with "the fullness of deity" (Col 2:9).

Creation as materialized Word becomes home for humanity and for human creativity and freedom (as attributes of the divine image within the creature). That freedom (indispensable from the reality of being human) becomes the subversive point of risk, vulnerability, and volatility within the project of creation.[61] Humanity is created with the full potentiality to choose a way other than the way of the Word and to go against its own ontology in a self-destruction that engulfs the entire created order.[62]

Since a world made by the Word can be mended only by the Word, in the conditions of the fall the Torah is given to Israel for the sake of the world and the healing of the cosmos. After all, the Torah is not just a cultural reality, and its study is not a mere activity of cultural transmission. The Torah is life and, therefore, it is the ultimate medicine for a perishing world traumatized by its mortality, for it "is stronger than death."[63] The Torah is to find its healing enfleshment within the human community and overflow from there into the entire cosmos. Thus, according to Rabbi Jonathan Sacks, the Hebrew Bible is concerned not just with "salvation" but also with "redemption"—the first being understood in terms of "the soul in its relationship to God," the second highlighting society "as a vehicle for the divine presence."[64]

61. The rabbis searched for answers to the question of how the omniscience of God can be reconciled with the creation of humanity, knowing in advance the violence and injustice that this creature will introduce into the universe. Sometime their answers (or rather narratives and interpretations) sound distant, puzzling, even dreadful for the Christian understanding of God as just, loving, and companionate redeemer. (See, for example, the words of Rabbi Judah recorded in the Babylonian Talmud, Sanhedrin 38b.) Yet, as Rabbi Sacks insightfully points out, "More than we have faith in God, he has faith in us. We are here because he wanted us to be, free because the Master-of-all made space for our freedom. . . . However lost [we are], he does not cease to believe that one day we will find our way back to him. For in his world he has given us the map, the guide, the way of return. That is the theology of responsibility" (Sacks, *To Heal a Fractured World*, 200).

62. Christian cosmology (contrary to pantheistic sentiments) carefully guards the uniqueness of the world that organically proceeds from God's creativity yet remains other than its Creator. Human freedom (free human will) epitomizes this otherness and depicts the process of divine world-making as a self-sacrificial respacing of God's omnipresence in order to create a home for the other—an act of unconditional hospitality *par excellence*. See Daniela C. Augustine, *Pentecost, Hospitality, and Transfiguration: Toward a Spirit-Inspired Vision of Social Transformation* (Cleveland, TN: CPT, 2012), especially ch. 2.

63. Emmanuel Levinas, *Beyond the Verse: Talmudic Readings and Lectures* (London: Continuum, 2007), 45.

64. Sacks, *To Heal a Fractured World*, 33.

God abides amidst his people—within the sacred space of redeemed relationships between fellow humans where heaven descends on earth. In light of this understanding, Sacks offers a moving reflection on the risks and the message contained in the divine instructions for the creation of the most holy item in the tabernacle—the ark of the covenant. While the covenantal law forbade making an image of anything created, God commanded the placement of two cherubs over the ark. "Their faces were turned to one another" (Exod 25:20). As Sacks reminds the reader,

> *It was between the cherubs that God spoke to Moses.* The message of this symbol was so significant that it was deemed by God himself to be sufficient to outweigh the risk of misunderstanding. *God speaks where two persons turn their face to one another* in love, embrace, generosity, and care.[65]

The therapeutic transfiguring of the world requires human agency. It takes a Spirit-filled, renewed/redeemed/ontologically healed humanity, bonded by the Torah in a covenantal community, whose life has become a healing, incarnate Word, applied as a balm to the wounds of a broken world. Thus, redemption demands the incarnation of the eternal Logos (and its consequent corporal extension within the human community) through the agency of the Holy Spirit.

No doubt, the culmination of the scriptural model of socio-transformative world-mending through the embodiment of God's Word is epitomized in Christ. He is the beginning of the *eschata*—the coming of the new creation. This time the creative order is reversed: while in the Genesis account of cosmologic emergence, humanity appears as the final interlocker of all created things, in the eschatological order of redemption, the new Adam is the first fruit, the beginning of the new creation. The event of Christ fulfills the purpose of the cosmos, and thus, the biblical narrative outlines an essential theological symmetry, highlighting the deep familiarity in the appearance of the new, binding together the essence of the first and the last creation. In the beginning of each is the Word (John 1:1; Col 1:15–16), which is to become flesh (to be materialized in the cosmos), and nothing that comes into existence appears apart from it. Yet the Word is not just the beginning but also the end ("the Alpha and Omega"—Rev 1:8)—the goal of all creation is for Christ (the incarnated Word) to be "all in all" (1 Cor

65. Sacks, *To Heal a Fractured World*, 54.

15:28). In the revelatory essence of the Incarnation, the Word becomes flesh as "the type and symbol of himself,"[66] unveiling his purpose in the cosmos, by self-interpretation through self-application upon the totality of human existence.

In the eschaton, the world is gathered in the Word from which it has proceeded while maintaining its otherness, and at the center of this cosmic transfiguration stands the redeemed human community—the communal body of Christ in which the entire creation finds its redemptive summoning. The redemption of humanity is not just reconciliation with God; it is transfiguration into his likeness (with one's freedom preserved) expressed in love for God and both the anthropic and nonanthropic neighbor. The end is the communal embodiment of the Word in the ontologically renewed human *socium*, for it takes a human community to image within the cosmos the divine protocommunity of the Trinity. Thus, in the mystery of redemption, the church as the Spirit-saturated Body of Christ—the communal, corporal reality of the incarnate Word—is unveiled as the goal of creation since the beginning. God creates the world as home for humanity (a home made by his very being and essence as Word) so that humanity may make (or rather be) a home for God on earth (a home for his Word, where he is all in all). Thus, the church is conceived by the Spirit as God's dwelling place on earth—until the entire world finds home in it (or rather in him), until the world becomes a church—a sanctuary for all of God's creatures. This is a vision of a healed world realized in the theosis of the church. This redemptive transfiguring is a transition from being an unaware beneficiary of divine grace (in God's providential care for his creatures) to becoming an active, intentional embodiment of the divine hospitality within the cosmos: a transition to internalization of the Word until one becomes its living extension in the world. It is a healing mirroring of the divine likeness in home-building for the other.

The Embodiment of the Word in the Last Adam

The opening lines of the Epistle to the Hebrews (1:1–2) depict the embodiment of the divine Word as God's "homily" to humanity par excellence, unveiling Christ as the singular telos of the church's kerygma—the performative word of God that goes forth in the midst of the communion of the

66. Saint Maximus the Confessor, *Ambigua* 10.31c, Patrologia Graeca 91:1165D.

saints"[67] in the proclamation of the gospel, transfiguring humanity into the likeness of the last Adam. Therefore, the Word's embodiment in the Son is not just the content of the divine message; it is its very purpose for humanity. As Christ takes residence in ontologically renewed humanity making it God's consecrated temple on earth, the "homily" actualizes its telos. Likewise, the proclaimed gospel, as the word about the Word made flesh, searches for its incarnation by the agency of the Spirit, calling forth into being its communal body and indwelling it with the divine communal life until the hearers become the message. In them, the Spirit makes the Word's presence tangibly apprehensible as in living epistles (gospel) of Christ, "written not with ink, but with the Spirit of the living God, not on tablets of stone, but on tablets of human hearts" (2 Cor 3:3), for as Robert W. Jenson states, the gospel "wants to be as visible as possible."[68] As the life of Christ becomes incarnate in the community of faith, it becomes a visible word. As Jenson insists, "Whatever else a disembodied word could be, it could not be a word of or to God."[69] The "God of the gospel does not merely have a word for us, he is his Word . . . he is his self-communication"[70]—an assertion pointing to the divine protocommunal Trinitarian essence. If "God is the Word he speaks; and the word he speaks is an embodied Word," then it is imperative to undertake a theological journey into the event of the Word's enfleshment as the unveiling of its telos.

The prologue of John's Gospel (John 1:1–3, 14, 18) highlights the teleological continuity and synthesis between the first and the new creation, the first being illuminated within the revelatory light of the Christology in the Gospel's account.[71] Both creations have their origin in the Word and, as this special title[72] of the second person of the Trinity indicates, through

67. J. V. Fresko, "Preaching as a Means of Grace and the Doctrine of Sanctification: A Reformed Perspective," *American Theological Inquiry* 3, no. 1 (January 15, 2010): 35–54 (35).

68. Robert W. Jenson, *Visible Words: The Interpretation and Practice of Christian Sacraments* (Minneapolis: Fortress, 2010), 32.

69. Jenson, *Visible Words*, 28.

70. Jenson, *Visible Words*, 32.

71. Hans Urs von Balthasar, *The Word Made Flesh*, vol. 1 of *Explorations in Theology*, trans. A. V. Littledale and Alexander Dru (San Francisco: Ignatius, 1989), 47–48. Von Balthasar insists on Christology as the beginning of all Christian theology and therefore as the lenses through which we are to understand all other forms of God's self-disclosure, including his revelation in creation. Therefore, Christology (and not cosmology) is to bring out "the cosmic presuppositions that the incarnation of the Word implies" (47).

72. Raymond E. Brown, *The Gospel According to John I–XII: A New Translation with Introduction and Commentary*. The Anchor Bible 29 (Garden City, NY: Doubleday, 1966), 32. The

them God has spoken to humanity in self-sharing, unveiling the beginning and telos of the cosmos as gathered within the divine reality. Therefore, the encounter with the Word-made-cosmos and the Word-made-flesh is an interface "with revelation itself."[73] Thus, as Saint Athanasius exclaims in his reflection on Eph 3:17–19, "The Self-revealing of the Word is in every dimension—above, in creation; below, in the Incarnation; in the depth, in Hades; in the breadth, throughout the world. All things have been filled with the knowledge of God."[74]

The event of the Incarnation brings forth the Word of God as his revelatory self-sharing *par excellence*. As Francis J. Moloney asserts, "to gaze on the incarnation of the Word" is to see "the revelation of the divine in the human story."[75] For indeed, this Word-made-flesh in the person of the only begotten Son is the visible icon of the invisible God (Col 1:15) and while no one has seen the Creator, the incarnate Word has "explained him" (exegeted him) (John 1:18). Therefore, the Incarnation could be understood as an act of the Word's self-interpretation and self-proclamation. In Christ the living Word unveils the meaning and telos of its self-sharing in the law and the prophets by applying to the reality of human communal existence its very own substance, articulated implicitly within the fibers of creation and inscribed explicitly on tablets of stone. As God chooses to speak to humanity through the Son[76] (Heb 1:1–2), the medium becomes the message, translating the content of divine self-revelation into the multidimensionality of human life. The Word takes upon itself the materiality of the cosmos in the totality of the human hypostasis and tabernacles among the human community

author expounds on the assertion that this title points to the second person of the Trinity as "being destined to speak to humanity."

73. Rudolf Karl Bultmann, *The Gospel of John: A Commentary* (Louisville: Westminster John Knox, 1971), 42.

74. Saint Athanasius, *On the Incarnation* (Crestwood, NY: St. Vladimir's Seminary Press, 1996), 44.

75. Francis J. Moloney, S.D.B., *The Gospel of John*, Sacra Pagina 4 (Collegeville, MN: Liturgical, 1998), 39.

76. In relation to an exposition of John 1:14, see Brown (*The Gospel According to John I–XII*, 32), who asserts that "if the Word became flesh, it was not only to be encountered but also to speak," as well as D. A. Carson (*The Gospel According to John* [Leicester: Inter-Varsity and Grand Rapids: Eerdmans, 1991], 127) and Moloney (*Gospel of John*). Moloney states: "the Word enters the human story. The preexistent Word, so intimately associated with God (vv. 1–2), now enfleshed, can be the communication and revelation of God in the human situation, where he now dwells" (38). See also F. F. Bruce, *The Gospel of John: Introduction, Exposition and Notes* (Glasgow: Pickering and Ingles, 1983), 40.

as the new temple on earth, full to its limits with the divine presence[77] (an assertion that John 2:19–22 makes through the words of Jesus, "Destroy this temple, and in three days I will raise it up"[78]). Therefore, the Incarnation could be understood also as the very purpose and "climax of creation and covenant," of Torah and temple. In the words of N. T. Wright, "Wisdom, God's blueprint for humans, at last herself becomes human. The Shekinah glory turns out to have a human face."[79] The last Adam as the restored full communion between heaven and earth, between matter and Spirit, manifests in his very being the ontological renewal of the cosmos and its reconstitution as a temple of the divine presence, locating God's ultimate home/sanctuary on earth within humanity itself. Therefore, according to Saint Maximus, the Incarnation "provided another beginning (*archē*), a second nativity (*genesis*)"[80] for human nature and the rest of creation, unveiling the grace of God as being "effective to deify" the entire universe[81] in the cosmic Christ. The last Adam circumscribes the totality of creation in order to present it to the Father redeemed and renewed in the glorious eucharistic liturgy of his very birth, death, resurrection, and ascension, through which he offers his life for the life of the world, overturning the effects of the curse and conquering death and the grave.[82]

The embodied Word stands within the cosmos as a new holy of holies and a new Sinai where humanity is brought into a new covenant with its Creator (Heb 8:8–13). Yet Christ is also the fulfilment of the old covenant—of the law and the prophets (Matt 5:17), for he holds in his very being the beginning and the end of all that exists (Rev 21:6). Perhaps no other scene of Jesus's life depicts more explicitly the incarnate Word as God's new sanctuary on earth (and new Sinai) than the gospel account of the transfiguration (in Matt 17 and Mark 9). In a vivid textual parallel to Moses's ascent up the mountain (Exod 24:15) into the visible theophany of the divine presence, and

77. On Jesus as the replacement of the old tabernacle, see Brown, *Gospel according to John I–XII*, 32–33.

78. On the association between the temple and Jesus's earthly body, see also T. Desmond Alexander, *From Paradise to the Promised Land* (Grand Rapids: Baker Academic, 2012), 235.

79. N. T. Wright, *The Challenge of Jesus: Recovering Who Jesus Was and Is* (Downers Grove, IL: InterVarsity, 1999), 120. Wright also reflects on Jesus as the "one-man Temple-substitute" in "Jesus' Self-Understanding," in *The Incarnation*, ed. Stephen T. Davis, Daniel Kendall, S.J., and Gerald O'Collins, S.J. (New York: Oxford University Press, 2002), 47–61 (57).

80. Saint Maximus, *On the Cosmic Mystery of Jesus Christ*, 135.

81. Saint Maximus, *On the Cosmic Mystery of Jesus Christ*, 100.

82. For more on the renewing and unifying work of Christ, see Lossky, *Mystical Theology of the Eastern Church*, 136–37.

later the descent of the *shekinah* upon the finished tabernacle (Exod 40:34) and the temple (1 Kgs 8:10–11), permeating the human-made sanctuary with God's glory, Mount Tabor is engulfed by the cloud of the divine nearness (Matt 17:5). The apostles' New Testament eyewitness of this glorious event is joined by that of Moses and Elijah, symbolizing the Old Testament witness of the law and the prophets (Matt 17:3). They all behold the eternal Word–embodied as the true temple and filled with the radiant glory of the uncreated heavenly light. The brilliance of the *shekinah* breaks through the veil of Christ's human flesh, clothing it with the divine energies (which brought forth all that exists) and illuminating the cosmos (Matt 17:2). The revelation of Mount Tabor summons those of Mount Sinai and Mount Carmel unveiling Christ as their telos. He stands *within* the created order as "a new cosmic Adam"[83] drawing all things together into himself.

Indeed, in the Incarnation, the earthly body of Christ becomes also the veil of the temple making the eternal Word tangible and visible as the messenger and the message become One and the same. As Margaret Barker insightfully states regarding the veil's function in the ancient tabernacle, as "the boundary between earth and heaven . . . the veil was matter which made visible whatever passed through it from the world beyond the veil. Those who shed the earthly garments, on the other side of the veil, were robed in garments of glory."[84] In other words, they become pneumatized. The event of the Incarnation depicts the Word coming forth from the holy of holies not through the mediation of the priest or the prophetic message, but passing itself through the veil and entering the cosmos clothed with its materiality. This is an act of the Word's self-translation and self-application to the substance of the created world. Thus, the old patristic assertion of the Incarnation's necessity for the sake of humanity's telos in theosis could be explained as God passing through the veil and becoming human so that, in reverse, the human being can pass through the veil and become deified through his or her pneumatization. Through the agency of the Spirit, the Word becomes flesh so that the flesh (saturated by the Spirit) may become a living Word. In Christ, human flesh enters the holy of holies through its communion with the Spirit, making humanity partaker in the divine nature

83. Lossky, *Mystical Theology of the Eastern Church*, 137.

84. Margaret Barker, "Beyond the Veil of the Temple: The High Priestly Origin of the Apocalypses," Presidential Address to the Society for Old Testament Study, Cambridge, January 1998, first published in the *Scottish Journal of Theology* 51, no. 1 (1998), http://www.marquette.edu/maqom/veil.html.

(2 Pet 1:4). Thus, as depicted by the visual theology of the annunciation's iconography, Mary receives the message of the archangel while holding needle and thread, ready to start working on making the new veil for the temple.[85] As she receives God's Word and submits her life to his will, she herself becomes a temple of the divine presence in which God weaves the veil of the Word's earthly body through the agency of the Spirit.

The ontology (and vocation) of humanity, embodied in the first Adam (male and female—Gen 1:27) before the fall, is that of a community of priests in the cathedral of the cosmos, bearing the image and growing into the likeness of the communal Trinity amidst the material world. Adam's priestly function as a mediator between heaven and earth is engraved in his very being. He is a Word made flesh through the agency of the Spirit—formed from the earth as spoken-forth Word and animated by the divine breath—but also as an enacted Word within the universe that preserves its harmony and wholeness. Thus, his priestly function is to keep the cosmos gathered and abiding in the Word; it is the mission of keeping the Word (and the boundaries placed by God within the structure of the world) and passing that calling and sacred knowledge from generation to generation for the life of the world. For as Philo states, the Word of God is "the first beginning of all things, the original species or the archetypal idea, the first measure of the universe."[86]

Being the true living temple and thus, the intended telos of the cosmic sanctuary, the last Adam stands within the universe as the embodiment of its right measurement according to which all is to be judged, renewed and sustained. As such, he is also the new high priest in the cosmic cathedral, joining in his very being heaven and earth, the visible and the invisible, bringing all that is before God in an act of worship expressed as total and utter realignment of the world with the Word, of the will of the creature with that of the Creator (Mark 14:36). In him the world stands whole, healed and theotic (united to God) through his redemptive unconditional hospitality, for (in the words of Saint Athanasius) "the renewal of creation has been wrought by the Self-same Word Who made it in the beginning."[87]

85. The icon's theology merges Luke's nativity account with oral tradition reflecting some of the assertions made in the Infancy Gospel of Saint James that, together with some other young girls, Mary was chosen to work on making/repairing the Jerusalem temple's veil.

86. Philo, *Questions and Answers on Genesis* 1.4, *The Works of Philo*, *Early Jewish Writings*, http://www.earlychristianwritings.com/yonge/book41.html.

87. Saint Athanasius, *On the Incarnation*, 26. For more on human ontology before the fall, see chapter 3 in the present book.

In the Incarnation, the eternal Word that spoke matter into existence reunites with matter so that the ontological relation between Creator and creation may be redeemed in the eschatological reality of the cosmic Christ. As Alexander Schmemann asserts, "In the world of incarnation nothing neutral remains, nothing can be taken away from the Son of man."[88] Therefore, the Incarnation claims all of reality as a subject of theological inquiry and faith praxis, and becomes the fundamental hermeneutical key to understanding its true meaning and purpose. Embodiment and particularity become essential dimensions of revelatory theological substance, and the body is depicted as the place of divine revelation and encounter *par excellence*.[89] As Anthony Godzieba points out, "In light of the incarnation and the resurrection of Christ, 'being,' 'presence,' 'representation,' and especially 'body' have a positive character, a sacramental intensity, and an eschatological intentionality that is not obscured by their finitude."[90] "Embodiment thus becomes a fundamental theological principle," joining the truth with its faith enactment, and theological anthropology and ethics become "fundamental theology." Indeed, in the theological ethics of the Incarnation, "the embodied enactment of the values" of God's kingdom "is critical to their claim to truth."[91]

The truth of the Incarnation insists on the particular as being "constructive . . . essential and indispensable" to its reality. In Christ who is the truth dwelling in the human community, knowing the truth is transitioned from the realm of cognition to the realm of embodied interpersonal encounter—thus, being human becomes critical for a truth that is to be revealed "among human beings."[92] Yet being truly human demands radical sociocultural, ethnographic, linguistic, geographical, historical particularity. Thus, the Word becomes flesh not as a "generic, one-size-fits-all"[93] human being but in the

88. Alexander Schmemann, "The Missionary Imperative in the Orthodox Tradition," in *Eastern Orthodox Theology: A Contemporary Reader*, ed. Daniel B. Clendenin (Grand Rapids: Baker, 1995), 195–210 (201).

89. Anthony Godzieba, "'Stay with us . . .' (Lk. 24.29)—'Come, Lord Jesus' (Rev. 22.20): Incarnation, Eschatology, and Theology's Sweet Predicament," *Theological Studies* 67 (2006): 783–95 (791).

90. Godzieba, "'Stay with us . . . ,'" 792.

91. Godzieba, "'Stay with us . . . ,'" 791.

92. Lieven Boeve, "Resurrection: Saving Particularity: Theological-Epistemological Considerations of Incarnation and Truth," *Theological Studies* 67 (2006): 795–808 (805).

93. As John Meier famously remarks, "The Word became truly flesh insofar as the Word became Jewish. No true Jewishness, no true humanity" ("The Present State of the 'Third Quest' for the Historical Jesus: Loss and Gain," *Biblica* 80 [1999]: 459–87 [486]).

concreteness of the true humanity of a first-century Jew in Palestine under Roman occupation. The eternal Logos unveils the divine reality in the far-too-particular humanity of the Son of God and not despite of it. As Lieven Boeve points out, "For Christians, therefore, God's manifestation in Jesus Christ forms the hermeneutical key to the particular and contingent."[94] By encompassing all concrete dimensions of authentic humanness, the embodied Word designates the totality of human existence as a sacred space for an encounter of the divine presence. The Logos takes upon itself the entirety of humanness in both its particularity and universality in order to redeem it. As the Greek patristic tradition affirms in the words of Saint Gregory of Nazianzus,

> For that which he [Christ] has not assumed he has not healed; but that which is united to his Godhead is also saved. If only half Adam fell, then that which Christ assumes and saves may be half also; but if the whole of his nature fell, it must be united to the whole nature of him that was begotten, and so be saved as a whole.[95]

In the Incarnation, the great scandal of metaphysics,[96] time, space and matter are sanctified and sanctioned as instruments of grace in the consecration of the cosmos. The Word becomes flesh, taking upon itself cosmic matter—its "first and primal revelation"[97] through embodiment—and magnifies its sacramental capacity to reveal God by "being thoroughly itself."[98] If the cosmos is a temple and a sacrament spread upon the canvas of time, then its primary function is as a space for encounter and means of communion with the divine presence (and all of its elements are to serve this purpose since all of creation itself is destined for a "complete union with God and

94. Boeve, "Resurrection," 805.

95. Saint Gregory of Nazianzus, *Epistle* 101 (To Cledonius the Priest against Apollinarius).

96. Lossky, *Orthodox Theology*, 91.

97. Zachary Hayes, O.F.M., "Christology-Cosmology," *Spirit and Life* 7 (1997): 51.

98. Michael J. Himes and Kenneth R. Himes, "The Sacrament of Creation: Toward an Environmental Theology," *Commonweal* 117 (1990): 45–46. Engaging the assertions made by these authors and reflecting upon Thomas Aquinas's teaching of a relationship of participation existing between God and creation, Gloria L. Schaab asserts: "While participation in divine being and the sacramental principle come to full focus in the Incarnation with Jesus himself as the preeminent sacrament of God, this preeminence should serve to validate rather than derogate divine revelation through the sacrament of creation" ("Incarnation as Emergence: A Transformative Vision of God and the Cosmos," *Heythrop Journal* 54, no. 4 [July 2013]: 631–44 [640]).

rest in his fullness"[99] through the pneumatization of matter). Therefore, as Dionysius Areopagite states, "The Good returns all things to itself. . . . Each being looks to it as a source, as the agent of cohesion, and as an objective. . . . All things are returned to it as their own goal. All things desire it."[100] The Incarnation's assertion of the world's sacramental essence infuses existence with anticipation of meeting God in the simplicity of everyday life—in the concreteness and particularity of time and space, in the limitation and transience of matter, in the demands and complexities of communal and family relationships, in the repetitive and mundane tasks of world- and home-building, in work and in rest, in the totality of human existence from the cradle to the grave.

As intensification of sacramental potential, the Incarnation (as well as the resurrection) sanctions all aspects of human life as means of grace toward theosis and affirms their goodness. Therefore, the incarnation is a powerful anti-gnostic statement, affirming the innocence of matter, victimized through the violent consequences of the fall of humanity (Rom 8:19–22). The conditions of the curse have antagonized matter as a part of creation torn by and infused with violence against the other.[101] The first Adam is responsible for the curse that permeated creation and caused its consequent suffering and distortion. The last Adam—Jesus Christ—sets free from the curse not only humanity, but also the rest of creation. Creation anticipates this redemption at the birth of the Savior and celebrates together with heaven the grace of God in the mystery of the Incarnation as the ontological renewal of humanity and, with it, of the entire cosmos. Those who are present hear angelic choirs and see heavenly fireworks, a "travelling" supernova, followed by wise men making their pilgrimage to the newborn king (Matt 2:1–2, 9–11). Poor shepherds and their flocks witness the cosmic event that unites heaven and earth in the fragile body of an infant (Luke 2:8–20). The cosmos welcomes the Creator in anticipation of its own welcome into life eternal.

Through the Incarnation, matter participates in the drama of redemption with its culmination in the passion of the Christ. Thus, in his broken,

99. Staniloae, *World*, 19.

100. Dionysius Areopagite, *Divine Names* 4.4, Patrologia Graeca 3:700A–B.

101. In Genesis 3:14–19, the articulation of the curse outlines this all-permeating violent conflict with the other in the struggle of the woman against nature in the pain of childbearing, the man against the woman in fight for domination, the man against nature in the resistance of the earth to give him the fruit of his labor, one creature against another in the battle between the woman's seed and the snake.

crucified body matter is subjugated to torture and death so that it may overcome death. In the last Adam, matter's innocence is met with the moral purity of the Son of Man who, while tempted in all things, still remains without sin (Heb 4:15). Thus, death has no power over him and his material body. His incarnation, crucifixion, and resurrection overcome the consequences of humanity's fall and exhaust the power of sin and death (1 Cor 15:26).[102] The triumph of redemption culminates in the resurrection in which the Spirit welcomes matter out of death into eternal life. Matter's possibility of life in eternity is contingent on divine hospitality for only God is eternal (noncontingent, without beginning and end). Thus, matter experiences eternity only as a gift of divine welcome in which God shares his life with the other so that they may have life eternal.

Redemption and sanctification, as intersocial enterprises of divine grace, point to human identity as a complex social construct of relationships to the other. Therefore, the way of redemption becomes the journey of recapitulating all of these relationships back into the restored ontological communion between humanity and God as the ultimate other. As humanity is reconnected to the One who is life itself (eternally and fully), the divine communal reality overtakes the complex tapestry of human intersociality, saturating, healing, and redeeming all until the life of God becomes the life of redeemed humanity—the perichoretic trinitarian life in a human communal form.

In light of this, it is impossible to think about redemption as a socially disembodied personal experience. Instead, it should be understood as the process of bringing all social relationships that comprise human identity within the presence of God—within the fellowship of the communal Trinity. Christ's incarnation makes this redemption possible by birthing forth the embodied reality of the eternal Logos as the-Word-in-relationships, as the-Word-applied to the totality of human social existence. This is an extension of the hospitality of God, who has not quarantined himself away from human life, but has taken it upon himself, sanctifying and redeeming it in his own divine communal reality.

Thus, in the scandalous particularity of the Incarnation, Jesus the Christ (the Savior of the world) is born not only a Palestinian Jew, but also as someone's son, and grandson, brother and cousin, teacher to his followers who are both male and female, young and old, slave and free, tax collectors and Roman soldiers, synagogue leaders and Pharisees, Jews and gentiles, poor and rich. He heals their broken bodies and spirits, opens their eyes,

102. Stavropoulos, "Partakers of Divine Nature," 188.

illuminates their minds and hearts, and nurtures them with words of eternal life while multiplying on their behalf bread and fish, extending to them the fellowship of the social Trinity. The embodied Word applies itself to the complexity of human relationships in order to heal the human sociality (fractured by the fall) and infuse it with God's shalom.

Through the Incarnation of the eternal Logos that shared itself with humanity in the giving of the Torah, Jesus Christ becomes also Scripture applied to the totality of human life with its all-encompassing social relationships. As the enfleshed application and fulfillment of the law and the prophets, he stands among the human community as the concrete embodiment of their mandate for unconditional hospitality as justice for the other. He alone is/has the "words of eternal life" (John 6:68) needed to redeem and restore human intersociality and transfigure it into an embodiment of the divine likeness of the triune communal life within human society as radical equality, freedom, and justice for all. Among this all-encompassing self-application of the incarnated Word to human life, the gospels highlight Christ's powerful, authoritative reinterpretations of the law's prescribed relationships to strangers, gentiles, women, children, the poor, the oppressed, the marginalized, the excluded. They all enjoy unconditional divine hospitality in his acts of benevolence as healing, forgiveness, acceptance, and inclusion. They are all welcomed into the kingdom of God and experience its advent within their own life as redemption, restoration, wholeness, and community. As Jesus visits the homes of sinners and fellowships with tax collectors, prostitutes, and gentiles, salvation comes to their households (Luke 19:1–10)—they welcome the kingdom and in return are welcomed by it.[103] God makes them part of his household and sits them around his table making them beneficiaries of divine hospitality; he becomes their home.

Making the Divine Community Visible in the Cosmos

John Meyendorff describes the Eastern Orthodox understanding of theology as "*internal* vision, which requires ascetic . . . communal effort, an effort made within the community of saints."[104] It depicts the meaning of human

103. Regarding Jesus as a recipient of hospitality in the accounts of Luke-Acts, see Amos Yong, *Hospitality and the Other: Pentecost, Christian Practices, and the Neighbor* (Maryknoll, NY: Orbis, 2008), 100–103.

104. John Meyendorff, "Doing Theology in an Eastern Orthodox Perspective," in *Eastern*

existence as an unceasing liturgical askesis expressed in communal striving toward tangibly depicting the protocommunal trinitarian life in and through the daily life of the human community. In and through the Spirit, humanity is to become what it beholds: the visible, living iconography of the invisible God in the cathedral of the cosmos.

Imaging God as Communion of Otherness and Unconditional Hospitality

Humanity's imaging of the trinitarian protocommunal life starts with a vision of God as communion of otherness, as mystery of unity and difference, demanding humanity's reflective, perpetual respacing on behalf of the other so that they may freely be and become. It is enacted in the consecrated, sacramental effort of fasting from oneself, as an expression of one's free choice to decrease in order for God to increase in their being until the divine presence saturates the totality of his or her life. Transfigured by this in-Spirit-ed askesis into a living home and sanctuary of the divine presence, the human being becomes a reflective, liturgical image of the Creator Trinity speaking forth into existence the cosmos (out of nothing) and hosting it within its own (kenotic and ascetic) communal self as an act of generous, unconditional, divine hospitality. In a way, in its willingness to welcome God in oneself, the human being is "enlarged" by the deifying Spirit and enabled to extend unconditional, loving hospitality to the entire cosmos circumscribed in the Creator. Thus, in becoming a living temple of the divine presence, humanity finds itself reflecting the divine "spaciousness" and love for the other and the different from oneself. In the sanctifying work of the Spirit, making humanity partaker of the divine nature, love for God becomes love for his entire world, and the creature experiences and manifests the likeness of the Creator as perfect love for the whole of creation (both anthropic and nonanthropic). Thus, embodying the life of the Spirit, one finds him or herself apprehended into the trinitarian communal life. Striving to recapture the image, one is captured by it.[105]

The Holy Spirit catches up not only humanity but the whole created realm into the life of God. Yet, while the Spirit strives to bring all the cosmos

Orthodox Theology: A Contemporary Reader, ed. Daniel B. Clendenin (Grand Rapids: Baker, 1995), 79–96 (87).

105. As Sarah Coakley points out, the work of the Holy Spirit is "incorporative" and "reflexive." It is to incorporate humanity into the trinitarian communal life, as well as to work "reflexively" in believers, "in the circle of response to the Father's call"—the call to be transfigured in the divine likeness (*God, Sexuality, and the Self*, 111).

into a life-giving communion with the triune, communal God, the Spirit's love (in the words of Sarah Coakley) "presses not only outwards to include others, but also inwards (and protectively) to sustain difference between persons, thus preserving a perfect and harmonious balance between union and distinction."[106] Thus, translating and incarnating the mystery of the triune life within the material cosmos, the Spirit fosters communal unity while gardening and celebrating otherness. Each collapse of unity into uniformity, of distinction and conversational polyphony into a repressive monologue that mutes the voice of the other, each flattening of polychromatic otherness into monochromatic homogeneity grieves the Spirit and distorts the divine face imprinted upon the human community. It defaces the image in a violent rejection of the other, in a totalitarian imposition of the self upon the world via a centrifugal marginalization and exclusion of difference. Therefore, for John D. Zizioulas, the fall could be understood in terms of giving the self "ontological priority over the Other."[107]

Humanity's call to theosis, as summoning in Christlikeness, is a call to otherness. This call, proceeding from the ultimate other, is the foundational event of human existence, the constitution of what it means to be truly human.[108] It is a call to Christ's otherness engraved in human ontology as its origin and telos, and as full potentiality to become like the other while retaining one's distinct otherness. The first Adam turns his face away from the other into himself, resigning his vocation to love God in loving and caring for his world as a liturgical reflectivity of the triune image; the last Adam restores in his redemptive embrace of the other the ontological communion of otherness constituting the calling and telos of the first Adam.

The biblical account of the tower of Babel rearticulates the communal dimension of humanity's drama first enacted in the garden of Eden. It depicts humanity's turning away from its vocation to the other and concentrating its creative energies into a monolithic, homogenizing attempt at self-deification. Therefore, by deconstructing that, God creates the conditions for initiating authentic human community through bringing forth and securing the presence and voice of the other and establishing the communal necessity of diversity in unity (Gen 11:7–8). The new accomplishment of human community after Babel demands accepting the other and making space for them in oneself through the effort to learn their language.

106. Coakley, *God, Sexuality, and the Self*, 24.

107. John D. Zizioulas, *Communion and Otherness* (New York: T&T Clark, 2006), 43.

108. Zizioulas, *Communion and Otherness*, 42.

Indeed, the image of Babel represents an antipode to the image of God. It depicts human creativity as a distorted imaging of the divine creative act. It juxtaposes the two creative acts (divine and human) as the contrast between inclusion and exclusion of the other. The creation of the world *ex nihilo* is an act of divine love expressed as radical respacing of the trinitarian protocommunal life in welcoming and hosting the existence and conversational inclusion of the other. Indeed, this is what love *is* and *does* as the ultimate act of freedom.[109] Love has the extraordinary creative capacity (to use the words of Hannah Arendt) to "insert a new world into the existing world"[110] between two persons. Love, as the most generous and spacious relationship to the different than oneself, is a hospitable sanctuary for the presence and flourishing of others, for it knows not the distorting/destructive oppression of fear, jealousy, envy, suspicion, competition, or rage (1 John 4:18, 1 Cor 13). Love (and, therefore creation itself) is inclusion and empowerment.[111] Love makes family out of strangers, creates space for them at the table, empowering the voice of the other and securing their access to life, justice, and flourishing. Therefore, the bringing forth of creation can be understood as movement of love in an internal act of *praktikē*—of the Trinity's loving askesis and kenosis. On the one hand, in an ascetic expression of self-giving love, God fasts from himself in order to create within his eternal omnipresence space and time[112] for the existence of the other. In a gift of unconditional hospitality, the protocommunal Trinity becomes the immediate dwelling place of the other as the very environment in which they live and move and have their being (Acts 17:28). On the other hand, God (being self-sharing love and life itself) pours himself forward into the existence of the other through the kenosis of the Word and the Spirit so that the creature may come to be (as materialized *logoi* spoken by the *Logos* and animated by the Spirit who circumscribes them in the self-giving, life-sustaining generosity of love).

109. Lossky, *Orthodox Theology*, 71–72. Lossky discusses the freedom of love in the context of humanity's ontology, created in the image of God as "a free responsible being" summoned to the supreme vocation of deification—"that is to say, to become by grace in a movement boundless as God, that which God is by His nature." As Lossky asserts, that is "a movement of love."

110. Hannah Arendt, *The Human Condition* (Chicago: University of Chicago Press, 1998), 242.

111. The notion of creation as empowerment is prominent in Jonathan Sacks's inspiring work *To Heal a Fractured World*, ch. 2.

112. Continuing his reflection on the roominess of God, Jenson states "God as Father, Son and Spirit can make room in himself for others, and the room that he makes is our created time. The opening of that room is the act of creation" (Robert W. Jenson, *Systematic Theology*, vol. 1. *The Triune God* [New York: Oxford University Press, 1997], 226).

Thus, in the act of creation, we see the Trinity as an ascetic community of self-sharing with the other: this is the materialization of God as love—a communal life of radical hospitality (*philoxenia*) marked by unconditional love for the other, the different, the absolute stranger, all the while sustaining their uncompromised otherness.

Yet creation, as inclusion and empowerment of the other, is also summoning them to the responsibility to do likewise—to love in the likeness of the Creator. As the very fruit and cosmic expression of the divine reality of love, humanity is created to be an icon of the Trinity on earth and to exhibit the same communal life marked by askesis (self-fasting) and kenosis (self-sharing) in relation to the fellow human and the rest of creation. Humanity is placed amidst the cosmos as a priestly, eucharistic, communal reality, in order to serve as an agent/mediator of the world's transfiguration into the likeness of God's communal life until the divine community becomes all in all.

Since humanity is created in the image of and for the likeness of God, from the beginning the spirit of askesis is to be cultivated in the human being through abstention from some of the fruit of the world (Gen 3:2–3) for the sake of communion with God and nature. The priestly vocation of humanity involves the eucharistic discernment of the world as a divine gift of substance and beauty for the sake of cultivating a community of shared life with the other—with God and (the anthropic and nonanthropic) neighbor. This discernment necessitates growing in love (in the divine likeness) through unceasing covenantal commitment to differentiating between one's needs and desires, and sanctifying the latter through the theocentric, deifying movement of worship as *theoformation* (or rather *Christoformation*) in and through the Holy Spirit.

In the first chapter of Genesis, we see God creating within the divine communal self not only an opening for the possibility and flourishing of the other but also building a home for them.[113] Yet within the teleology of the cosmos, God creates within himself home for humanity so that, in turn, humanity may learn to image the trinitarian communal life by welcoming God within itself and presenting its own being as a home for the divine presence. Ultimately, the eucharistic nature and pedagogical goal of the cosmos, intended to cultivate humanity in the divine likeness, is to transform all

113. For an exposition on God as an architect building and furnishing a house, see John Dominic Crossan, *God and Empire: Jesus against Rome, Then and Now* (New York: HarperOne, 2007), 51–52.

everyday work of world-making into a home-building for the other. Human creative labor becomes a priestly sacramental enactment of God's love for his creation—the very love which hosts the cosmos in self-sacrificial nurture and care for all creatures and demands the same of humanity as a faithful stewardship of God's household.

The poetry of the Fourth Gospel's prologue fuses together the visions of the divine creative act as both unconditional hospitality for and a loving communal discourse with the other. It depicts the act of cosmic creation as proceeding from the Word that speaks it forth while being turned toward God (*pros ton theon*) (John 1:1).[114] The orientation of the creative speech is not directed outside the divine reality, but rather remains in the inner communion of the Trinity itself. Thus, creation takes place within the perichoretic intimacy of the trinitarian life. If the creation of the world is an outcome of a loving communal conversation made visible through the *poiēsis* of divine creativity, then its transformation into a sanctuary for the divine presence (via creative, in-Spirit-ed, human agency) cannot be accomplished by other means. It takes an intentionally dialogical human community, bringing together its polyphonic cultural and ethnographic diversity into a constructive conversational unity that images the divine life in active, creative consensus of world-making as home-building for the other and as sanctuary-carving for the life and flourishing of all God's creatures. The conversational inclusion of the other in a dialogical community is essential for the possibility of building a common future. It opens the door to envisioning a world of multidimensional unity of oneself with the other while preserving each one's distinctiveness. Respacing one's right to speak for the sake of creating space for the voice of the other presents the possibility of shaping a future of harmonious diversity, of sociocultural unison within the challenging landscape of a pluralistic world. Indeed, nothing less would be sufficient to image within the cosmos the communal life of the Creator Trinity as multiplicity of consubstantial hypostasis, joined in harmonious, conversational oneness of world-making as liturgical askesis in unconditional hospitality for the other.

In light of this, if Babel is both a conversational exclusion of the other and a refusal to welcome them in communion, the event of Pentecost constitutes its overturning by the kenosis of the Spirit upon the believers. Pentecost is the antidote to the age-old temptation to employ Babel's blueprint in hu-

114. On the significance of the preposition *pros*, see Carson, *Gospel according to John*, 116; and Moloney, *Gospel of John*, 35.

man cultural world-making. The event of Pentecost marks this embodiment of the divine spaciousness within the redeemed human community. Indeed, Pentecost could be understood as the event of the last Adam's (Christ's) incarnation through the agency of the Holy Spirit within the communal body of the first Adam, illuminated by faith.[115] Since Christ is the visible icon of the invisible God (Col 1:15), "the perfect Eucharistic Being,"[116] Pentecost marks the ontological renewal of the image of God within the human community. The Spirit's kenosis transforms the 120 persons in the upper room into Christ-bearers and a living extension of his resurrected body on earth. Sergius Bulgakov refers to the event of Jesus's miraculous conception as "the Pentecost of the Virgin."[117] The Holy Spirit descends upon Mary in response to her willingness and readiness for service (Luke 1:38) and transforms her into an instrument of God's Word becoming flesh amidst humanity (John 1:14). The freedom of her will is essential for welcoming God in this response of unconditional hospitality ("may it be done to me according to your word," Luke 1:38), for the incarnation of the Word has to be a free act of love (the beginning of the new/renewed creation is to echo God's divine creative act in the beginning of all beginnings). In the breathtaking vision of the Incarnation's mystery, as depicted by the words of the resurrection dismissal *Theotokion*, Mary's womb "became more spacious than the heavens" for she carried in it her Creator, the one who hosts and sustains the cosmos. In a similar manner, as the Spirit descends upon the disciples on the day of Pentecost, Christ is conceived in them and they are empowered (Acts 1:8) toward Christlikeness (the likeness of God in flesh). Individually and corporately, they become *theophoros* (God-bearing) and bear forth (as an embodied gospel) the one who is the light and life of the world, the one who summons all of creation in his redemptive cosmic embrace as the origin and telos of existence. At Pentecost the church (the communal body of Christ) is born as a home for the world, an ecclesial cosmic last Adam destined to circumscribe not only the entire globe but also join the terrestrial and celestial creation in an all-engulfing movement of worship toward union with the Creator. This

115. For more on the ecclesiological significance of the event of Pentecost, see my work *Pentecost, Hospitality, and Transfiguration*.

116. Alexander Schmemann, *For the Life of the World*, 38. Schmemann states, "He alone is the perfect Eucharistic Being. He is the Eucharist of the world. In and through this Eucharist the whole creation becomes what it always was to be and yet failed to be."

117. Sergius Bulgakov, "The Virgin and the Saints in Orthodoxy," in *Eastern Orthodox Theology: A Contemporary Reader*, ed. Daniel B. Clendenin (Grand Rapids: Baker, 1995), 65–75 (67).

is precisely the world's destiny depicted in John's eschatological vision of the church as the bride of the Lamb—the city of God—a transcontinental, global holy of holies, a cosmic home for the divine presence that hosts all that lives, a sanctuary that has covered the earth with God's glory (Rev 21–22).[118]

The event of Pentecost offers a paradigmatic vision of the incarnation of God's self-giving hospitality in the community of the believers as an extension of Christ's body on earth. The outpouring of the Spirit manifests God's ascetic respacing and kenotic self-sharing in welcoming all nations under heaven (Acts 2:5), through submitting his Word to the form and sound of their ethnic tongues (v. 6). Therefore, the proclamation speech of the faith community on the day of Pentecost embraces the language of the other in a gift of divine hospitality. The Spirit invites all humanity to make its habitat in the intersociality of the Trinity. It is an initiation of dialogue by respacing oneself and creating conditions for conversational inclusion of the other. It is a gesture of welcoming all foreigners, aliens, strangers literally on their own terms.

Imaging God in Prayer and Human World-Making

The divine act of creation unfolds before the eyes of its enthralled witness—heaven itself with its entire host. Heaven hears and sees the materialization of the triune perichoretic discourse as harmonious "visible words"[119] within the *poiēsis* of the cosmos cascading under the carving flow of the uncreated divine energies. The melody of creation takes its corporeal form amidst the unceasing worship of the angels who sing for joy at its grand unveiling (Job 38:4–7), understanding that they themselves are an outcome of God's loving, kenotic self-sharing in Word and Spirit. Thus, creation unfolds as a divine liturgy performed by God himself before heaven's worshiping host in the cathedral of the universe. Within the liturgical choreography of the perichoretic trinitarian movement, each creature comes forth (in the words of Robert Jenson) as a "word of obedience and worship"[120]—as a communal response to the summoning self-proclamation of the uncreated, eternal

118. For more on the city of God in relation to divine hospitality, see my book *Pentecost, Hospitality, and Transfiguration*, especially 67–69 and 133–38.

119. See Augustine, *Tractates on the Gospel of John* 80.3, http://www.newadvent.org/fathers/1701.htm.

120. Robert W. Jenson, *Systematic Theology*, vol. 2. *The Works of God* (New York: Oxford University Press, 1999), 8.

Word. Therefore, by virtue of being "visible words," the whole world could be understood as a sacrament enacted by the Creator in the grandiose liturgical cosmogony of creation.

Amidst the divine liturgy performed by God in the act of creation, humanity is summoned into existence as the special creature made to hear the Word's calling and respond to it in prayer: the creature whose ontological actualization is to be attained through partaking in God's communal discourse, within the conversational communion of the divine nature (2 Pet 1:4). In light of this, the understanding of the world as a sacrament resonates with Robert Jenson's interpretation of the image of God in humanity as "consisting in the action of prayer."[121] For Jenson, "God's ritual word to us" is "sacrament," but "sacrifice" as "embodied prayer" is our ritual word to God.[122] Therefore, human life before the Creator is "an antiphony of God's word to us and our word to God; and the whole antiphony is both audible and 'visible.'"[123]

Indeed, in its priestly and liturgical essence as *homo adorans*, humanity is to offer an unceasing intercession on behalf of the world, taking it in prayer before its Creator. Therefore, the act of intercessory prayer mirrors, in a way, the Trinity's sustaining, providential work in creation—the work of the Word and the Spirit for the life of the world according to the will of the Father. Intercession is an act of one's respacing on behalf of the other, a form of self-fasting and hospitality for the different from us. It is caring for their well-being and striving to provide them with what is needed but lacking for their flourishing. Intercession embraces the pain and brokenness, the struggles and hopes of the other, making place for them in one's words, thoughts, and embodied life in the world and carrying them in one's very being before the face of the Creator. Intercessory prayer is making time and space for the other within one's life and being. Further, to pray for the other is to bring them up, to make them spoken of and heard of within the trinitarian communal conversation now extended to the creature called to become *theoumenon*[124]—to be deified. Therefore, prayer could be seen as imaging both the divine askesis and kenosis constituting God's creative act; yet it is also reflective of the Trinity's ongoing providential care for all of

121. Jenson, *Works of God*, 68.

122. Jenson, *Works of God*, 59–60.

123. Jenson, *Works of God*, 59.

124. Saint Gregory of Nazianzus spoke of humanity as *zoon thoumenon*—"an animal that is being deified" (*Oration* 38.11).

creation. This understanding asserts prayer as pedagogy on becoming like God—as a divinely ordained means of communion with the Creator and a way of partaking in the divine nature toward pneumatization in theosis. It teaches humanity how to image the life of the Trinity by acquiring a "eucharistic spirit" and an "ascetic ethos."[125] To be capable of prayer means (in the words of Bartholomew I) that we "have the capacity to offer the world back to God in thanksgiving, and it is only in this act of offering that we become genuinely human and truly free."[126] Yet in accordance with the trinitarian communal image in humanity, this true freedom is "never solitary but always social."[127] Therefore, freedom "is expressed as encounter"—facing the face of God and being its mirror for the other, allowing them to see themselves in this reflection and be liberated to be truly human.

Being created to partake in the divine communal discourse of world-making as "intertrinitarian love,"[128] implies humanity's creative capacity as well as a sense of open-endedness, spontaneity, and freedom within the clear teleology of the world's becoming. According to Jenson (echoing Saint Augustine), "the freedom by which we as persons participate in the divine life is the very Spirit that evokes all life, all the dynamic processes of creation."[129] He further asserts that in Scripture "all the dynamics of the created world, the events in which it constantly becomes what it was not yet, are understood to represent the creative actuality of the Spirit."[130] Therefore, the universe is "an omnipotent conversation that is open to us"[131]: an openness that makes prayer meaningful, for the Spirit's hospitality extends to us the freedom to speak up, discuss, plead, and even argue, confronting the condition of the world and addressing the communal Creator in "faith and trust" for its mending.[132]

Prayer responds to the openness of possibilities sustained within the Spirit's spontaneity and freedom. Therefore, Paul instructs the believers to pray without ceasing (1 Thess 5:17), and this perpetual life as prayer and prayer as life is to take place "at all times in the Spirit" (Eph 6:18). Yet in the reality of prayer as a pedagogy on becoming like God, the ultimate goal of

125. Bartholomew I, *Encountering the Mystery*, 118.

126. Bartholomew I, *Encountering the Mystery*, 132.

127. Bartholomew I, *Encountering the Mystery*, 132.

128. Staniloae, *World*, 18.

129. Jenson, *Works of God*, 42.

130. Jenson, *Works of God*, 43.

131. Jenson, *Works of God*, 44.

132. One can recall, for example, the passage of Gen 18:17–33 depicting Abraham's inclusion in the divine discourse and his intercessory pleading on behalf of Sodom and Gomorrah.

all the openness and freedom gardened by the Spirit within the fibers of the world is humanity's *theoformation*. Prayer does not change God and the telos of creation; it changes us into the divine likeness. Prayer is joining the Spirit's intercession for the healing of the cosmos and partaking in her "groanings too deep for words" (Rom 8:26). For "we do not know how to pray," but we can enter into and entrust ourselves to the intercessory movement of the Spirit "who helps our weakness."

Indeed, prayer as world-mending becomes a divine-human partnership—breathing, speaking, groaning, and moving with, in, and through the Spirit. Yet this seems to be true in relation to all human creativity. Prayer is more than laboring alongside God in world-mending. In the freedom of the Spirit, prayer becomes also creative world-making, speaking forth future beauty and hope within the cosmos. It is a consecrated, cultic, creativity that mirrors the divine creative discourse back toward the communal Creator, thus transforming the "Let there be . . ." into "Lord, let there be . . . ," fully conscious of its dependence on the divine creative agency.

Since prayer (as part of human ontology) is more primordial than belief,[133] we can think of human, creative world-making as an antiphony—a responsive prayer of the paradise-haunted, homesick creature, longing for the beauty and harmony of its origin within the divine presence. As Bartholomew I points out, "Beauty is a call, beyond the here and now, to the original principle and purpose of the world."[134] Therefore, not only creation itself but also human creativity is a means of communion with the Creator—it is a prayer, an offering to God, an act of worship. Thus, in the postfall conditions of the world, human creativity is marked by the tension between the deep-seated primordial memory of paradise and the struggle to forget God[135] and compensate for his absence with the gratification found in human civilization itself. Reflecting, therefore, on Genesis 4:22 and the life of the descendants of Cain as "the first citizens, the inventors of arts and techniques," Lossky states that the "arts here appear as cultural, not cult, values; they are a prayer that is lost since it is not addressed to God."[136] "The beauty they raise up closes back on itself to enchain" humanity "with its magic."[137] As cult and culture part their ways within human world-making,

133. Harvey Cox, *The Future of Faith* (New York: HarperOne, 2010), 5–6.
134. Bartholomew I, *Encountering the Mystery*, 28.
135. Lossky, *Orthodox Theology*, 86.
136. Lossky, *Orthodox Theology*, 87.
137. Lossky, *Orthodox Theology*, 87.

art (being a form of language itself) retains its essence as a means of communion with the other.

It is not accidental that the first creative act of humanity recorded in the biblical narrative demands the agency of speech. As the divine speech brings forth the genesis of all creation, so is human speech to inaugurate humanity's inspired, liturgical imaging of the divine creativity within the cosmos. Yet this creativity remains located in the communal dynamics of collaborative dialogue between humanity and God. In the naming of the animals, Adam speaks forth words as an act of completing through their meaning what God has created. The human being adds its *logoi* to the *logoi* spoken forth by the one eternal *Logos*. Thus, human language as creation "coincides with the very being of things."[138] Adam can name the animals because of the deep organic connection between humanity and the rest of God's creatures, for the human being rises from the earth as a hypostasis and continuity of "the terrestrial cosmos." Thus, as Lossky points out, Adam knows the animals "from within; he specifies their secret . . . poet as he is priest, poet for God."[139]

If human creativity in prayer and cultural productivity is to mirror the divine creative act and facilitate the transfiguration of humanity into the likeness of the Creator, then language is essential to its actualization. Alongside the entire created cosmos, language presents itself as a means of eucharistic communion between humanity and God and between human beings themselves in the process of their theoformation. Its essence is explicitly communal, for language manifests itself only when shared with the other. Therefore, the purpose of language unveils itself as the means of bonding all of humanity into one polyphonic speech community,[140] into a creative discourse, cultivating the cosmos toward its eschatological gathering into the one incarnate Word that is to be all in all—a vision actualized by the Spirit in the event of Pentecost.

Reflecting on language's communal essence and its ability to create a foundation for shared life, Levinas states:

> Language is universal because it is the very passage from the individual to the general, because it offers things which are mine to the

138. Lossky, *Orthodox Theology*, 69.

139. Lossky, *Orthodox Theology*, 69.

140. As Jean-François Lyotard reminds us, the translatability of language points to the fact that all human beings are called to one speech community ("The Other's Rights," in *On Human Rights*, ed. S. Shute and S. Hurley [New York: Basic, 1993], 140–41).

> Other. To speak is to make the world common, to create a commonplace. Language does not refer to the generality of concepts, but lays the foundation for a possession in common. . . . The world in discourse is no longer what it is in separation, in the being at home with myself where everything is given to me; it is what I give: the communicable, the thought, the universal.[141]

In Levinas's beautiful and compelling ethic, the nakedness of the other's face (along with language as a common good) summons us with the demand to recognize the shared nature of the world. The fact that the other exists questions one's own sense of "joyous possession of the world" and the inevitability of one's inalienable property rights over it.[142] The demanding gaze of the other—the gaze of hunger and destitution searching for our conscience, calling it unapologetically to responsibility, demanding to be recognized in giving—this gaze for Levinas "is precisely the epiphany of the face as a face." Therefore, "[t]o recognize the Other is to recognize hunger. To recognize the other is to give."[143] Yet, in a way, this recognition begins with what Levinas terms (in his essay "The Ego and Totality") "the first thought." At a primordial level, living beings take themselves to be a totality, being "ignorant of the exterior world."[144] In the dialectic between interiority and exteriority of personal identity, the first thought begins "with the possibility of conceiving freedom external to" one's own.[145] This process takes place at the relational boundaries between us and others. Levinas reflects on the reality of moral myopia resulting in an innocent violence toward the other.[146] Human beings may recognize injustice when they see it, yet remain completely blind to their contribution to injustice in the world. Subjects cannot recognize, from within the interiority of innersubjectivity, their failure to live up to their own moral code. The appearance of the first thought, therefore, is the moment of the birth of conscience, or of ethical awakening. Yet the goal of conscience is to summon the human being to responsibility for the condition of the world and dispel the anonymity of

141. Emmanuel Levinas, *Totality and Infinity: An Essay on Exteriority* (Dordrecht: Kluwer, 1991), 76.

142. Levinas, *Totality and Infinity*, 76.

143. Levinas, *Totality and Infinity*, 75.

144. Emmanuel Levinas, "The Ego and Totality," in *Collected Philosophical Papers*, trans. Alphonso Lingis (Dordrecht: Martinus Hijhoff, 1987), 25–48 (30–34).

145. Levinas, "Ego and Totality," 28.

146. Levinas, "Ego and Totality," 39.

his or her contribution to the ecological, economic, and political crisis depriving the world of its flourishing.

In the words of Mikhail Bakhtin, "language, for the individual consciousness, lies on the borderline between oneself and the other."[147] Therefore, knowing the language of the other is integral to knowing the other's reality. Applying Bakhtin's notion of dialogical *heteroglossia* to the reality of the divine creative act, we can think of it as a discourse that creates a multidimensional unity of oneself with the other while preserving the distinctiveness of each one.[148] Therefore, the divine trialogue speaks the world into existence as a living, organic continuity of interconnected histories unfolding into the story of the trinitarian communal life. Since language is a historically charged reality, dialogical unity with the other involves participation in the story of the other. However, this cohabitation of the story of the other provides, at the same time, another perspective on one's own language and story.[149] The individual is able to see him or herself through the eyes of the other. In light of this, language, as means of communion between humanity and God, necessitates the mutual cohabitation of the communicants' stories. Therefore, as Staniloae points out, the opening words of Genesis, "in the beginning," "indicate the first union of the eternity of God with time."[150] It is "the first moment of the dialogue between the God who has come down to creation and the creation which is beginning along its path through time."[151] No doubt, the incarnation of the eternal Word in the person of Jesus Christ represents the culmination of this process. In it the story of God indwells the human story, carrying it back into the redemptive dialogical communion of the divine life.

147. Mikhail Bakhtin, "Discourse in the Novel," in *The Dialogic Imagination*, ed. Michael Holquist (Austin: University of Texas Press, 1981), 259–422, here 293. See also Maria Teresa Morgan, "Tongues as of Fire: The Spirit as Paradigm for Ministry in a Multicultural Setting," in *The Spirit in the Church and the World*, ed. Bradford E. Hinze (New York: Orbis, 2004), 106–25, here 107.

148. Bakhtin, *Dialogic Imagination*, 293, 282.

149. Bakhtin, "Response to a Question from Novy Mir Editorial Staff," in *Speech Genres and Other Late Essays*, trans. Vern W. McGee, ed. Caryl Emerson and Michael Holquist (Austin: University of Texas Press, 1986), 1–7. See also James P. Zappen, "Mikhail Bakhtin," in *Twentieth-Century Rhetoric and Rhetoricians: Critical Studies and Sources*, ed. Michael G. Morgan and Michelle Ballif (Westport, CT: Greenwood, 2000), 7–20.

150. Staniloae, *World*, 9.

151. Staniloae, *World*, 10.

Pentecost and the Church as the Icon of the Trinity on Earth

The breathtaking iconostasis of the church at the Theological School of Halki holds among its iconographic treasures a magnificent icon that articulates the very foundation of Orthodox ecclesiology—an intricate piece devoted to the Holy Trinity. The upper portion of the icon narrates the story of the visitation of Abraham by the three divine guests at the oak of Mamre (Gen 18:1–15). Since no one has seen God (John 1:18), this is the only visual articulation of the Trinity that is considered canonical by the Eastern Orthodox tradition. The lower portion of the icon is subdivided into a triptych depicting the New Testament witness of the trinitarian mystery through three distinct theophanic scenes recorded in Scripture. On the left, we see the depiction of Jesus's baptism in water by John the Baptist—the public trinitarian witness to the identity of the Son through the audiotheophany of the voice of the Father, and the visual theophany of the Spirit descending as a dove upon the Messiah. On the right, we see the icon of the transfiguration on Mount Tabor as an articulation of "the humanity of the Son, manifesting forth that deity which is common to the Father and the Spirit."[152] This time the event depicts the private New Testament witness of the inner circle of disciples joining the Old Testament witness of the law and the prophets symbolized by Moses and Elijah (Matt 17:3). The witnesses see the uncreated divine energies piercing through the veil of the Son's humanity, illuminating the cosmos, while hearing the voice of the Father (authenticating Jesus as the Christ) and being immersed in the all-engulfing cloud of the Spirit. In the center of the triptych, however, we see the icon of Pentecost—the event of the transfiguration of the community of faith into Christ's communal body on earth, empowered by the Holy Spirit to do the will of the Father. This is the event in which the church is established as the image of the Trinity on earth. Little wonder that the Orthodox tradition celebrates the day of Pentecost as the festival of the Trinity.[153]

If the church is an image of the Trinity, she is also the image of the Holy Spirit. Yet the Spirit descends upon the community of faith, bearing witness not of himself but of the Son (John 15:26). He comes in the name of the Son in the way the Son comes in the name of the Father. This is why Saint John Damascene states that "The Son is the Father's image, and the Spirit the Son's."[154]

152. Lossky, *Mystical Theology*, 243.

153. Lossky, *Mystical Theology*, 239.

154. Saint John Damascene, *An Exact Exposition of the Orthodox Faith* 1.13, http://www

The Holy Spirit, however, does not have his image made visible in another divine person (or hypostasis). Yet the event of Pentecost made the invisible Spirit visible in the Spirit-saturated community of faith. If the Old Testament "proclaimed the Father openly, but the Son more obscurely" and the gospels reveal the Son plainly, but the Spirit dimly,[155] Pentecost presents the church animated and empowered by the Spirit as his clearly manifested image on earth. The charismatic dynamic of the church makes the invisible Spirit visible and tangibly communicated in the unity of the saints' diversity. They are the ones who have been empowered toward Christlikeness—living together the life of the triune God as their very own life. Therefore, the two distinct dimensions of the Spirit's presence, the communal and the eschatological,[156] become clearly visible in the Pentecost inauguration of the church as his image on earth. Pentecost ushers in the unfolding of the *eschata* evoking the prophetic fusion of time and eternity as the "last days" erupt into the present and become its time-transcending substance. Yet this eschatological vision is the one of the Spirit-saturated community with its radical egalitarian catholicity and democratized polyphony of prophetic utterance.

The "likeness of God" is not a distant mirroring of the divine image; it is the fullness of a communion and community with the Creator through the incorporating and transfiguring work of the Holy Spirit. A community that images the Trinity in the cosmos is marked by recognition of, and commitment to, humanity's irreducible consubstantiality and equality, and depicts the divine life in perichoresis as unceasing movement of covenantal love between all members of the community—love that is manifested in justice for the other as unconditional access to life and human flourishing, while sustaining their otherness intact. Rabbi Jonathan Sacks states that society is faceless, but community "is society with a human face," the face of God made visible in the covenantal loving-kindness between its members. Only when we discover God's image in ourselves by learning to discern it in others, are we capable of building a "human and humanizing" society.[157]

.orthodox.net/fathers/exacti.html. As Lossky states, "The divine Persons do not themselves assert themselves, but one bears witness to another" (*Mystical Theology*, 160).

155. Gregory Nazianzen, *The Fifth Theological Oration. On the Holy Spirit* 26, in Cyril of Jerusalem and Gregory of Nazianzen, Christian Classics Ethereal Library (http://www.ccel.org/ccel/schaff/npnf207.iii.xvii.html).

156. John D. Zizioulas, *Being as Communion: Studies in Personhood and the Church* (Crestwood, NY: St. Vladimir's Seminary Press, 1995), 131.

157. Sacks, *To Heal a Fractured World*, 54.

God abides amidst his people, the new human community, within the redeemed relationships between fellow humans. There, in the tridirectional mirroring of the face, heaven descends to earth. Thus, according to the Decalogue, redemption takes place in the sacred space between each human being and the other (God and neighbor) and is experienced as healing of relationships that rehumanizes society and mends the broken world.

On the day of Pentecost, the church is established as the visible, embodied communal theophany of the invisible divine protocommunity. Thus, in her mystical union with God in the Spirit-saturated human community, the church becomes the telos of all of creation and stands within the present as the embodiment of the world's future in which God is all in all (1 Cor 15:28). The Pentecost's kenosis of the Spirit transforms the corporate body of Christ into the communally embodied temple of the divine presence within the cosmos (2 Cor 6:16; Eph 2:19–22), destined to be the vehicle through which God extends his redemptive hospitality to all of creation. The Spirit births forth the church so that the entire cosmos may become a church—a eucharistic communion of heaven and earth in the union of God and his world: this is the breathtaking, glorious future of humanity in the likeness of God.

Chapter 2

From the Iconoclasm of Violence to Love as the Life of the New Creation

Political philosophy[1] has offered different proposals regarding the causes of violence (some more pessimistic than others), seeing them as rooted

1. The social sciences have also given various answers to the question about the origins of violence—ranging from biological/medical issues such as hormonal disbalance to psychological and social problems such as humiliation, sociopolitical, economic, ideological, and cultural oppression. More recently, clinical psychology has offered insights on the causes of violence that seem rather optimistic against the background of the deterministic Freudian assertion of aggression as a primal, inner drive toward death and self-destruction (*thanatos*) that can be (occasionally) misplaced when diverted from the self to others. (Originally, Freud tried to explain all manifestations of human behavior as flowing from a primal life drive, which he termed "*eros*." In his later work, however, he developed the idea of the death drive, manifesting itself as a counterforce to *eros*. (See his book *Beyond the Pleasure Principle* [London: Hogarth, 1920].) James Gilligan suggests that violence is triggered at the intersection of concrete (known) biological, psychological, and social factors, and can be approached as a medical condition that is diagnosable, treatable, and, most importantly, preventable (Gilligan, *Violence: Reflections on a National Epidemic* [New York: Vintage, 1996], 24). Further, the complex, polyvalent relation between violence and religion (religion being depicted both as a culprit and a restrainer of violence) has long preoccupied theorists (especially in light of the past few decades' global surge of religions and religiously justified violence—a development that caught by surprise many of modernity's prophets of secularism). Thus, for example, one cannot overlook René Girard's influential and disturbingly fascinating correlations between violence and ritual sacrifice. Girard states that if "sacrifice resembles criminal violence . . . there is, inversely, hardly any form of violence that cannot be described in terms of sacrifice" (1) and that religion "shelters us from violence just as violence seeks shelter in religion" (24). He suggests that while having certain "functional and mythical differences," the institutions of vengeance, sacrifice, and legal punishment "are essentially the same"—"they tend to adopt the same types of violent response in times of crisis" (25). According to Girard, sacrifice is both the symptom of communal violence and the means by which society attempts to cover and deflect it. He proposes that the "minor catharsis of the sacrificial act is derived from the major catharsis circumscribed in collective murder" and that ritual sacrifice is based on a double

in a broad spectrum of ideological, political, and economic processes. Thus, for example (from his seventeenth-century perspective), Thomas Hobbes famously depicts violence as inherent in human nature (correlated to natural law) and positioning each human being in perpetual war with all others—a war motivated by competition, diffidence, and striving for glory.[2] Hobbes paints a grim depiction of human life unfolding in a perpetual stage of uncertainty, "solitary, poor, nasty, brutish and short," overshadowed by a "continual fear, and danger of violent death."[3] Carl von Clausewitz's military theory, on the other hand, perceives violence as a political tool of statecraft, famously defining war as the mere continuation of politics by other means.[4] Engels's political economy discusses it as an accelerator of economic development when (in light of Marx's historical materialism) there is an internal contradiction between the forces and the mode of society's production.[5]

---

substitution—the first being of the substitution of one member of the community for all; the second, the substitution of a person from outside the community (the ritual victim) for the original one who has been chosen from within (the surrogate victim) (102). See his work *Violence and the Sacred*, trans. Patrick Gregory (Baltimore: Johns Hopkins University Press, 1979).

2. Thomas Hobbes, *Leviathan (Or the Matter, Form and Power of a Commonwealth Ecclesiastical and Civil)* (New York: Simon and Schuster, 1962), 99. Hobbes's famous statement on the causes of conflict and subsequent violence is as follows: "So that in the nature of man, we find three principal causes of quarrel. First, competition; secondly, diffidence; thirdly, glory. The first, maketh men invade for gain; the second, for safety; and the third, for reputation. The first use violence to make themselves masters of other men's persons, wives, children, and cattle; the second, to defend them; the third, for trifles as a word, a smile, a different opinion, and any other sign of undervalue, either direct in their person, or by reflection in their kindred, their friends, their nation, their profession, or their name" (99–100).

3. Hobbes, *Leviathan*, 100.

4. Carl von Clausewitz, *On War* (Princeton: Princeton University Press, 1984), 87. Examining the realities of the state's institutional violence against its population, Michel Foucault famously reverses Clausewitz's aphorism. Foucault questions if politics are not the continuation of war with other means and concludes that the role of political power is to perpetually "reinscribe" force within "institutions, economic inequalities, language and even the bodies of individuals" as a "silent war" taking place under the surface of society. Foucault concludes: "War is the motor behind institutions and order. In the smallest of its cogs, peace is waging a secret war. To put it another way, we have to interpret the war that is going on beneath peace; peace itself is a coded war. We are inevitably someone's adversary." (*Society Must Be Defended*, ed. Mauro Bertani and Alessandro Fontana, trans. David Macey [New York: Picador, 2003], 48–51).

5. Engels, *Herr Eugen Dühring's Revolution in Science*, part 2: "Political Economy," ch. 4: "Theory of Force (Conclusion)" (https://www.marxists.org/archive/marx/works/download/pdf/anti_duhring.pdf). Reflecting on this internal contradiction as having the potential to trace the path to a revolution, Engels states: "But where—apart from cases of conquest—the internal state power of a country becomes antagonistic to its economic development as at a certain

Reflecting on some of political philosophy's classical formulations on the causes of violence, Hannah Arendt points to their apparent inadequacy within the context of the Cold War era[6] with its aggressive proliferation of weapons of mass destruction. Arendt states that now, tragically, "instead of war being 'an extension of diplomacy (or of politics, or of the pursuit of economic objectives),' peace is the continuation of war by other means—is the actual development in the techniques of warfare."[7] Utilizing Nigel Calder's prophetic insights on the future development of warfare,[8] Arendt predicts, in a way, (almost fifty years ago) the unsettling volatility of today's global village (particularly in light of the recent escalation of terrorist threats). Reflecting on the potential sociopolitical outcomes of the development of biological, chemical, and nuclear weapons, she forecasts the "complete reversal in the relationship between power and violence, foreshadowing another reversal in the future relationship between small and great powers." Therefore, Arendt states:

> The amount of violence at the disposal of any given country may soon not be a reliable indication of the country's strength or reliable guarantee against destruction by a substantially smaller and weaker power. And this bears an ominous similarity to one of political science's oldest insights, namely that power cannot be measured in terms of wealth, that an abundance of wealth may erode power, that riches are particularly dangerous to the power and well-being of republics.[9]

---

stage occurred with almost every political power in the past, the contest always ended with the downfall of the political power. Inexorably and without exception the economic development has forced its way through—we have already mentioned the latest and most striking example of this: the great French Revolution." Continuing his critique of Dühring while insisting on the historical essentiality of revolutionary force, Engels concludes: "To Herr Dühring force is the absolute evil; the first act of force is to him the original sin. . . . That force, however, plays yet another role in history, a revolutionary role; that, in the words of Marx, it is the midwife of every old society pregnant with a new one, that it is the instrument with the aid of which social movement forces its way through and shatters the dead, fossilized political forms."

6. While traditionally the Cold War has been associated with the period from the end of World War II until the fall of Communism in 1989, some see the present-day intensification of the conflict between the United States and Russia over the military and humanitarian crisis in Syria as a resurgence of Cold War realities.

7. Hannah Arendt, *On Violence* (New York: Harcourt, 1970), 9.

8. Nigel Calder, ed., *Unless Peace Comes* (New York: Viking, 1968) (particularly his essay "The New Weapons").

9. Arendt, *On Violence*, 10.

Arendt refuses to accept the traditional equating of power with violence and offers extensive definitions of the terms in light of their relationship to each other within broader sociohistorical frameworks. She describes power as "corresponding to the human ability not just to act but to act in concert." Therefore, power "is never the property of an individual; it belongs to a group and remains in existence only so long as the group keeps together."[10] Violence, on the other hand, "is distinguished by its instrumental character"[11] and "like all means, it always stands in need of guidance and justification through the end it pursues."[12] Arendt concludes that while power is "indeed of the essence of all government . . . violence is not."[13] Power (as peace) is an end in itself and, "being inherent in the very existence of political communities," it does not need justification; "what it needs is legitimacy." In contrast, violence, according to Arendt, "can be justifiable, but it will never be legitimate."[14] As she points out, the "extreme form of power is All against One, the extreme form of violence is One against All."[15] Therefore, power and violence are each other's "opposites"—"where the one rules absolutely, the other is absent." In other words, violence "appears where power is in jeopardy"[16]—it "comes into play where power is being lost" (as in Soviet Russian tanks overrunning the peaceful protests of the 1968 "Prague Spring," or the desperation of weakened British imperialism, manifested in

10. Arendt, *On Violence*, 44.

11. Arendt, *On Violence*, 46.

12. Arendt, *On Violence*, 51. As Arendt remarks later in the text, the danger of violence "will always be that the means overwhelm the end." She continues by stating: "The practice of violence, like all action, changes the world, but the most probable change is to a more violent world" (80).

13. Arendt, *On Violence*, 51.

14. Arendt, *On Violence*, 52. In all fairness, it has to be noted that Arendt is not trying to equate violence with evil (nor is she ideologically committed to unconditional nonviolence), but to stress that violence "cannot be derived from its opposite," namely power. Yet she emphatically states that while violence can destroy power, "it is utterly incapable of creating it" (56). Further in her work, Arendt points out that violence often springs from rage, which can be "irrational and pathological, but so can every other human affect." She states that it is enormously tempting to resort to violence when confronting outrageous events because of its inherent immediacy and swiftness, and that in some situations "the very swiftness of a violent act may be the only appropriate remedy" (63), "the only way to set the scale of justice right again" (64). Yet her definitions of power and violence, as well as the depiction of their reciprocity, are intriguing and insightful, and serve well the argument for commitment to the common good as a remedy for violent outbursts against the ideological other.

15. Arendt, *On Violence*, 42.

16. Arendt, *On Violence*, 56.

the 1919 Amritsar massacre).[17] Arendt's provocative conclusion deserves further attention (beyond the limited scope of the present work), particularly her proposal that it is not correct to think of "nonviolence" as the opposite of "violence," that the opposite of violence is power as harmonized communal consensus manifested in constructive action for the benefit of all. In this sense, authentic power (as an antidote to violence) is a shared participatory reality, actualized in the active pursuit of the common good. Thus, violence results from the disintegration of communal consensus and abandonment of mutual commitment to shared flourishing, ending in violation of the social contract.

Perhaps then (in light of the preceding discussion in chapter 1), we can think of the Spirit-created *sobornost* that starts from the redeemed human community (and is destined to circumscribe the entire cosmos into the self-giving divine love) as the ultimate form of authentic sociopolitical power and, therefore, as the absolute opposite of the iconoclasm of violence. Thus, the antidote to violence is Spirit-saturated human community that welcomes the world in the spacious hospitality of the triune embrace, in shared life and flourishing for all creation. The cure to violence is humanity living a Christoformed life together in the power of the Spirit—it is the life of Pentecost.[18]

In light of this assertion, the remainder of the present chapter will proceed by taking a look at the Genesis account of the first fratricide in view of the iconoclasm of violence against the other. It will continue further with examining Scripture's correlation between violence and sibling rivalry over limited goods, and will conclude with discussing the biblical call to responsi-

17. Arendt, *On Violence*, 53. Arendt states: "To substitute violence for power can bring victory, but the price is very high; for it is not only paid by the vanquished, it is also paid by the victor in terms of his own power."

18. As Nicolas Berdyaev points out (*Philosophy of Inequality* [Sofia: Prozoretc, 1995]), only the Spirit creates a brotherhood and sisterhood that are a realization of true freedom—as freedom in Christ. In the Christ-centered spiritual togetherness (*sobornost*) there is no "mechanical equality" (115). There is also no contradiction and difference between "a right and an obligation" (113). As noted in chapter 1, the *sobornost* of the faith community is the work of the Spirit, who translates the communal life of the Trinity within the community of believers, making possible sharing life with the other in all of its wholeness. The personal freedom in the Spirit's *sobornost* does not contradict the freedom of the other, for it is not based on competition for the limited resources of material reality. It is based rather on the eternal and infinite reality of divine love and grace. In this divinely initiated and infused *sobornost*, the hospitality of God is incarnated in the community of Christ as a gift of the Spirit, a gift of freedom to the other to be and to become.

bility for the fellow human, flowing from an uncompromised commitment to shared life in covenantal community of comprehensive equality, justice, and peace.

Genesis's First Account of Fratricide in Light of the Iconoclasm of Violence

As articulated in the previous chapter through the "exegesis" of the Orthodox icon of creation, commitment to the common good starts with recognition of the common image of God and its mutual reflection in the relationship with the other. Looking first at the divine face before turning one's eyes toward the face of the fellow human is pedagogy toward recognizing the face of God in the other and treating them accordingly. Learning to share the divine face (as recognition of shared humanity) becomes the foundation for mutual flourishing in a shared world. In light of the human communal vocation to be the icon of the trinitarian protocommunity within the cosmos (through the tridirectional mirroring of the divine face between oneself, God, and neighbor), violence against the other becomes violence against (the one who bears) the face of God—an iconoclastic negation and denial of the divine face in its incarnate proximity. The iconoclasm of violence distorts the common image and rejects its summoning demand toward the common good. The intrinsic value of human life, the sacredness of its liturgical presence amidst creation as a visible icon of the invisible God, is denied by violence against the other. Yet, according to the theology of the face, the violent refusal to recognize the other's humanity results in one's own effacing and dehumanization. In contrast, recognizing the face of God in the face of the other, as a liturgical anamnesis of paradise, translates one's relationship to the fellow human into means of communion with God (Matt 25:31–46).

Since the relationship to the other becomes a sacred replica of one's social/communal encounter with the Creator, as 1 John 4:20 states, a person cannot claim that they love God and hate their brother/sister—such a statement immediately renders them a liar. If "God is love" (1 John 4:16), then love for the other makes the invisible God visible as an embodied proclamation of humanity's Christoformed telos—"because as he is, so also are we in this world" (1 John 4:17). The life of God, as love for the other streaming into the cosmos through the consecrated, Spirit-indwelled human community, transfigures humanity's communal life into a living icon of the Trinity, offering itself for the life of the world as an antidote for the toxic pathology of violence. Contrary to this socio-transformative world-mending capacity of love, Scripture points to hatred and anger as violent negation of the other, as murdering the fellow human in one's heart—an act of rejecting God's future for creation by imagining the world as a better place without the other. Thus, 1 John 3:15 states that everyone who hates his brother is a murderer (*anthrōpoktonos*).[19] In the first of the six minor precepts (Matt 5:21–48), the Decalogue's ethical radicalization within the context of the Sermon on the Mount, Jesus strikingly parallels anger with murder.

> You have heard that it was said to those of ancient times, "You shall not murder"; and "whoever murders shall be liable to judgement." But I say to you that if you are angry with a brother or sister, you will be liable to judgement; and if you insult a brother or sister, you will be liable to the council; and if you say, "You fool," you will be liable to the hell of fire. (Matt 5:21–22)

Undoubtedly, Jesus's audience did not miss the allusion to the biblical account of the first premeditated murder of one human being by another—the primordial fratricide depicted in the story of Cain and Abel (Gen 4:1–16).[20] It is not accidental that the Genesis narrative of the first violent act

19. On the New Testament use of *anthrōpoktonos*, especially in reference to the story of Cain's fratricide, see John Byron, "Slaughter, Fratricide and Sacrifice: Cain and Abel Traditions in 1 John 3," *Biblica* 88, no. 4 (2007): 526–35.

20. The story of Cain and Abel presents a number of hermeneutical challenges that have preoccupied many Jewish and Christian thinkers throughout the ages, producing a plethora of different interpretations. For a helpful overview of the inherent grammatical ambiguities in the biblical account of the first murder and the related hermeneutical struggles, see John Byron, *Cain and Abel in Text and Tradition: Jewish and Christian Interpretations of the First Sibling Rivalry* (Leiden: Brill, 2011). See also Karolien Vermulen, "Mind the Gap: Ambiguity in the Story of Cain and Abel," *Journal of Biblical Literature* 133, no. 1 (Spring 2014): 29–42. On contemporary studies regarding the use of the story as a rhetorical device in the New Testament, see Tom Thatcher, "Cain and Abel in Early Christian Memory: A Case Study in 'The New Use of Old Testament in the New,'" *The Catholic Biblical Quarterly* 72, no. 4 (October 2010): 732–51. As Angela Y. Kim points out, "expansions and reworkings of biblical text by ancient interpreters generally arise from perceived peculiarity" within the narrative. The author identifies two particular problems in the story: the first one being theological in nature "since it concerns God's seeming capriciousness in the rejection of one sacrifice and not of the other," and the second as existing on a narrative level, in relation to "the lack of a murder motive" in the story, since there is no mention of an open hostility between Abel and Cain. Kim offers an overview of the ways in which the rabbinical and patristic traditions treated these problems by asserting interpretive content in the story in order to provide a motive (e.g., envy, jealousy,

against the human other gravitates around the thematic nuancing of "the face." Cain becomes consumed by burning anger against his brother and his own countenance/face "falls" (v. 6). Anger deforms the "engravement" of God's face upon Cain—distorts the distinct mark of his humanity. The icon of God "falls" down amidst the cosmic sanctuary as anger's iconoclasm desecrates creation (the prototemple) with its dehumanizing intrusion, culminating in violence against one's brother. The trespassing iconoclasm of murderous anger effaces God from his icon on earth rendering him once again invisible, thus, obscuring the divine (omni)presence. God's fatherly warning to Cain against anger asserts human responsibility for guarding one's attitude toward the other against sin's distortion of the divine image in oneself by obscuring the ability to recognize it in the face of the fellow human. The divine instruction reveals both the freedom and the mandate for sustaining one's humanity by choosing to resist and "master" (v. 7) sin's

---

sibling rivalry, struggle for "limited good") in order to redirect attention away from the potential perception of God as a capricious or unjust deity. See Angela Y. Kim, "Cain and Abel in the Light of Envy: A Study in the History of Interpretation of Envy in Genesis 4.1-16," *Journal for the Study of Pseudepigrapha* 12, no. 1 (2001): 65–84. Rein Nauta's theological reflection on the psychology of Cain's act of fratricide introduces an intriguing reading of the story, proposing that its seemingly meaningless violence depicts the choice of replacing shame with guilt ("Cain and Abel: Violence, Shame and Jealousy," *Pastoral Psychology* 58, no. 1 [March 2009]: 65–71). Nauta describes shame as "the narcissistic affect *par excellence*. All the once, one's self-image and the image one wants others to believe in is proven false. Such shame cannot be managed or controlled" (66). Abel witnesses the shame of his brother at the rejection of his sacrifice—a witness that has to disappear together with the painful memory of the rejection. "For it was Abel's glance that determined the inescapability of Cain's worthlessness" (66-67). Nauta points out that, in contrast to shame, guilt "presupposes freedom: a choice between what should be done and what has been done, between duty and desire." Shame, on the other hand, "is related to the feeling of being wronged." "Guilt always concerns the violation of rules designated to protect the common good." The author suggests that when "one is overwhelmed by shame, guilt seems the lesser of two evils" (66). He states that "Cain would rather be actively guilty than passively ashamed. Guilt reduces the universal to the partial: guilt implies punishment and possibly forgiveness, guilt can make life better" (67). Further, commenting on the traditional interpretations of Cain's act as a result of envy, Nauta suggests that perhaps Cain is not envious but jealous (69). He states, "In envy, one is envious of what another, in one's eyes unjustly, possesses. . . . Jealousy can perhaps be understood as a helpless attempt to excuse the one who unexpectedly and suddenly gives his love to somebody else by attributing that dramatic loss to the power of the intruder. Lethal hate for the intruders expresses the continual love for the original love object." In light of this assertion, Nauta concludes that Cain is consequently marked by God not only to protect him against revenge, thus putting an end to further violence, but also "as an expression of compassion for the injured heart at the core of fratricidal tragedy" (69).

temptation. Neglecting to embrace the cathartic promise of God's warning word, Cain refuses to recognize and take responsibility for the resident evil in his heart. Instead, he externalizes and projects that evil upon the other (God and fellow human), thus, justifying violence against them. Cain's anger toward God as the ultimate other is translated into anger and violence toward the immediate other. The murder of Abel is not just an extermination of a competitor for divine favor (as access to life), but also an act of rage and defiance against the Creator. "If you prefer blood (of animal sacrifices), here you go, I will give you some blood (the blood of your Abel)."[21] This is rebellion against the inherent sociality of humanity as a creature, against one's humaneness' dependence on the reciprocal, relational imaging of the divine face. Here once again, as in the story of Adam and Eve in the garden of Eden, sin manifests itself as a claim to autonomy/independence and ontological primacy over the other, bending the human being inward into itself (its own self-indulging desires) and away from the summoning encounter with the other's face.[22]

The horror of the story is intensified by the context of cultic sacrifice. The surrounding narrative of worshiping God deeply disturbs the reader, pointing to the fact that a religious act of devotion (religion itself) does not protect against the incubation and nurture of evil in one's being. As Gerhard von Rad states, "The terribleness of Cain's sin lies in the fact that it does not catch him in a condition of separation from God, i.e., where he forgets himself in human life, but precisely at the point where he lifts his hands to God, at the altar."[23] The story magnifies the danger of excusing/justifying violence against the other by its cultic sacramentalization. For as the history of

21. John Byron discusses the use of *sphazō* ("to slay," "to slaughter") in 1 John 3:12 in light of its occurrences in the LXX as well as in the works of Philo of Alexandria and Josephus, pointing to the common connotation of ritual sacrifice. The author highlights one of the interpretations of Cain's murder of Abel offered in Genesis Rabbah 22.8, which states: "R. Azaria and R. Jonathon in R. Isaac's name said: Cain had closely observed where his father slew the bullock [which he sacrificed, as it is written], *And it shall please the Lord better than a bullock* (Ps. 69:32), and there he killed him: by the throat and its organs." See "Slaughter, Fratricide and Sacrifice," 531-35.

22. The graphic image of "*incurvatus in se*" was famously utilized by Luther in his metaphoric depiction of fallen human nature. "Our nature has been so deeply curved in upon itself because of the viciousness of original sin that it not only turns the finest gifts of God in upon itself and enjoys them . . . indeed, it even uses God himself to achieve these aims, but it also seems to be ignorant to this very fact" (Martin Luther, *Lectures on Romans*, vol. 25 of *Luther's Works* [St. Louis: Concordia, 1972], 291).

23. Gerhard von Rad, *Genesis*, trans. John Marks (Philadelphia: Westminster, 1961), 105.

religion has taught us, projecting one's thirst for the blood of the other upon God serves as justification of crimes against humanity in the name of God.[24]

The drama of the narrative contrasts the dreadful sacramentalization of violence against the other with the sacramental openings for divine grace toward humanity's redemptive restoration and renewal. Standing before God's face, however, Cain dismisses the opportunity for confession and penance—the opportunity for his rehumanization—"lifting up" and imaging once again "the face" of God upon the face of the earth. He spills Abel's blood and buries his brother's face in the ground, covering the image (and his crime) together with the image-bearer, while denying responsibility for its disappearance. As von Rad points out, God's first summoning to responsibility of fallen humanity in the garden of Eden through the question "Where are you?" (Gen 3:9) now appears as a social question: "Where is your brother?" For, responsibility before God "is responsibility for the brother"[25] (and sister)—for the fellow human. The cold callousness of Cain's refusal to take responsibility depicts the original epicenter of violence whose aftershocks engulf human history in the chilling, transepochal echo of "Am I my brother's keeper?" (Gen 4:9) The question haunts us with its desensitization toward violence and injustice against the other. As De La Torre points out, this is "the very first ethical question" humans ask God—"a question that will take the rest of Genesis, if not the rest of the Bible, to answer."[26] Yet it is clear that God's answer to Cain's sarcastic, rhetorical question is an emphatic "yes": we are accountable before God for the well-being of the other. The story reminds the reader that all murder is fratricide, for (within the human family) we are all siblings; we are brothers and sisters and "are ultimately consigned for

24. There is no doubt that the visions of God articulated by various religions are reflected by their undergirding social fabric. They translate into sets of values that inform the shaping of society on interpersonal, communal, and broader structural (including formalized institutional) levels. As Miroslav Volf points out, however, religions (and this surely includes their visions of God) are not monolithic or static. They are multidimensional, complex cultural constructs that continually interact with the surrounding environment (cultural, political, economic), including the presence of other religions. Therefore, their propensity toward justice or injustice, toward violence or peace, is not disentangled from political and socioeconomic circumstances and interests. See Miroslav Volf, *Flourishing: Why We Need Religion in a Globalized World* (New Haven: Yale University Press, 2015), 183–86. Perhaps we can think then of the evocation of religions for the moral legitimization of both violence and peace (depending on concrete political agendas) as projecting back on God the image of society itself.

25. Von Rad, *Genesis*, 102.

26. Miguel A. De La Torre, *Genesis* (Louisville: Westminster John Knox, 2011), 96.

each other's safekeeping."[27] God has given us to one another as cosharers in the gift of life so that we may understand that there is no flourishing without the other, that our good is an outcome of theirs, that the good of the other is my good, that good is what is shared—what is held in common. Therefore, the story of Cain ends with God's judgment on fratricide. As Gerhard von Rad states, this judgment is more terrible than the punishment in Genesis 3 of the first couple; it is something "that cannot be made good again," for the earth, humanity's "maternal basis of life, has drunk a brother's blood." Since earth is a home for humanity made to be shared with the other, now "the earth has no home" for Cain.[28] The one who defaces the immediate other is banished from the face of God—the face of the ultimate other that he must reflect—and from "the face of the earth" (v. 14). Cain becomes a fugitive, wandering east of Eden, in the land of Nod—in "the land of restlessness,"[29] "away from the face of the Lord" (v. 16) in whose presence is rest and shalom. Cain is homeless. Yet his homelessness appears in the moment in which the earth swallows Abel's blood (v. 11) because, in the arresting words of Miroslav Volf, "belonging is home, and home is brother, who is no more."[30]

The killing of Abel as an extermination of competition (in a rage against God and negation of the fellow human) could be interpreted also as an attempt to conceal one's own degradation, exposed in the face of the other's humanity.[31] Instead of searching for his reflection in the face of the

27. Naomi H. Rosenblatt and Joshua Horwitz, *Wrestling with Angels: What the First Family of Genesis Teaches Us about Our Spiritual Identity, Sexuality, and Personal Relationships* (New York: Delacorte, 1995), 57.

28. Von Rad, *Genesis*, 106.

29. Von Rad, *Genesis*, 104. Here von Rad points to the possible etymology of Nod in the Hebrew word *naôd*, meaning "fugitive."

30. Miroslav Volf, *Exclusion and Embrace: A Theological Exploration of Identity, Otherness, and Reconciliation* (Nashville: Abingdon, 1996), 97.

31. The biblical text does not offer a moral portrait of Abel. The juxtaposition of the brothers' characters appears in the history of interpretation as a consequent assertion of content within the story in an attempt to fill in the blanks and compensate for Abel's silence in the face of Cain's rage. Yet Rein Nauta sees in Abel's silence the narrative's inherent protest against meaningless violence and the elevation of the paradox of "a victory won by denying the competition" ("Cain and Abel," 68). De La Torre discusses the text's silence regarding "the motivation for bringing sacrifices to a God who has not requested any." He points out that the type of sacrifice "is not important"; what matters is one's faith and the content of one's heart. After quoting Isa 1:11, 13, 16–17, emphasizing God's insistence on uncompromised justice (and not sacrifices) as the only thing he has required from humanity, De La Torre states: "It seems as if God rejected Cain's offering because Cain chose not to live faithfully by choosing to do justice. Instead, he set up religion and offered religiously" (De La Torre, *Genesis*, 95). Continu-

fellow human as an icon of the divine face, illuminating and exposing the content of his own heart,[32] Cain effaces the other and, with that, the need for stewarding his own humanity for the sake of the integrity and flourishing of God's creation. He refuses to take responsibility for the common planetary good. The story reveals the difficult/inconvenient truth that the struggle for the common good starts and has to be won first within the human heart; apart from that no social contract, no legal coercion would guarantee sustainable, communal flourishing in uncompromised commitment to mutual "safekeeping."

Undoubtedly, however, the Christian imagination contrasts the temptation of Cain with that of Christ (Luke 4:1–14; Mark 1:12–13; Matt 4:1–11)[33]—the visible icon of the invisible God (Col 1:15), the quintessential antipode of Cain—the one who emerges victorious from his temptation in the wilderness (clothed in the power of the Spirit, Luke 4:14) and offers his life on behalf of the fellow humans so that they may live and regain their humanity. It seems that the story of Christ's temptation starts where Cain's ends—in the wilderness. It is not accidental that the Gospel of Mark's account highlights the urgency of this inaugural event of the messianic mission. "Immediately" after descending upon Christ in the baptismal waters of Jordan at the public unveiling of Jesus's messianic identity (Mark 1:10–11), the Spirit leads him to be tempted in the wilderness (v. 12). The Spirit starts its world-mending with exposing, confronting, and sanctifying human desires. There, in the estranged solitude of the wilderness, following the movement of the Spirit, the last Adam recapitulates in himself the first Adam (the totality of being human), renewing human ontology and vocation within the cosmos. The new creation has to start with redeemed and hallowed human desire that does not devour the world by making it an end in itself, but turns instead to the Creator and finds in him its true destiny in contentment and shalom

ing the emphasis on social justice, De La Torre asserts that when God asks, "What have you done with your brother? The question reveals God's preferential option for those abused and murdered—then and now. Those made invisible so that the few can enjoy their privilege are still important to God. God continues to ask those who are privileged: What have you done to your sisters and brothers? Those who live on your margins? Those who die dispossessed for your benefit? Their cries continue to rise up to God's ear" (97).

32. See the section entitled "The Memory of a World Illuminated by the Divine Face" in chapter 1 of the present book.

33. There are three direct, interpretive references to Cain in the New Testament: Heb 11:4; 1 John 3:12; Jude 11. On the contrast between Cain and Christ in 1 John, see Byron, "Slaughter, Fratricide and Sacrifice," 528, 531.

with God and neighbor. As the misplaced/misdirected longing of the first Adam brought the curse and shut the gates of Eden before the face of humanity, so they are reopened before the face of the last Adam—the new, complete humanity (with sanctified affections, imagination, and desires), drawing creation unto himself as the visible icon of the invisible God. In the wilderness, where once Cain was banished away from the face of God, the Son of Man faces heaven and earth ("the wild beasts, and the angels," Mark 1:13)[34] with the face of their Creator and joins them once again in worship of the one and only God. In Christ, humanity regains its priestly function as *homo adorans*, and worships by joining the proclamation and the enacted embodiment of the Word (the union of orthodoxy and orthopraxy, which stands in vivid contrast to Cain's refusal to embrace and embody God's word to him). The incarnate Word that has spoken the cosmos into existence comes out of the wilderness in the power of the Spirit (Luke 4:14) in order to heal and enliven the broken creation. Christ, the one wholly human being, steps forth from the domain of Cain's homelessness in order to bring humanity home—within the embrace of the fellow human, before the face of God in the face of the other—the place where God makes all things new.

Therefore, in his reflections on the assertion of Mark 1:13 that Jesus was with the wild animals, Richard Bauckham rightly suggests that the text could be interpreted as pointing to the inauguration of the messianic age of cosmic peace and reconciliation. The last Adam ushers in the overturning of the curse in restoration of paradise, for (unlike the first Adam) he has resisted Satan and while tempted in all things has remained without sin (Heb 4:15). As Bauckham states,

> The peace with wild animals belongs to this Messiah's righteous reign. Mark's account of Jesus' baptism (1:9–11), in which he is anointed with the Spirit (Isa 11:2) and addressed as God's Son (Ps 2:7), identifies him as this Davidic Messiah, who therefore inaugurates the messianic ages not only by overcoming Satan, but also by establishing the messianic peace with wild animals. Against the background of the Jewish eschatological expectation, the latter has a real significance

34. For a brief overview of alternative interpretations regarding Mark 1:13, see Charles A. Gieschen, "Why Was Jesus with the Wild Beasts (Mark 1:13)?" *Concordia Theological Quarterly* 73, no. 1 (January 2009): 77–80. See also A. B. Caneday, "Mark's Provocative Use of Scripture in Narration: 'He Was with the Wild Animals and Angels Ministered to Him,'" *Bulletin for Biblical Research*, no. 9 (1999): 19–36.

> in its own right. It is not simply a symbol of Jesus' victory over Satan or of his inauguration of the age of eschatological salvation. Peace with wild animals is actually one aspect of eschatological salvation.[35]

In contrast to the brevity of Mark's account of Jesus's temptation, the detailed narratives offered by Matthew and Luke[36] seem to depict Satan's three provocations as targeting the three dimensions of the messianic identity. The *prophetic dimension* is met with the urging to break one's vow before God (in this case, the act of fasting in pointing to the Creator as the one true source and telos of life, in whom alone there is wholesomeness and contentment for creation) and turn instead to the self, driven (as in the American dream) by the lure of self-sufficiency in pursuit of prosperity. In his response, Jesus quotes Deuteronomy 8:3 (with reference to the manna in the wilderness), affirming that life (and well-being) proceeds from God himself as its author and sustainer. Thus, the food of the Son, according to John 4:34, is to do the will of the one who has sent him,[37] "and to accomplish his work"—a statement central to the prophetic mission. John P. Meier suggests an alternative understanding of the text—as the tempter inviting the Messiah to use his sonship in order to perform an economic miracle—providing sustenance without existing natural resources (turning stones into bread). Is not the messianic expectation of a world plagued by starvation and poverty, amidst limited resources, rightly hoping and searching for a political and economic Savior?[38] Is not feeding the poor and summoning humanity to political and economic responsibility for "the least of these" also an essential part of the prophetic vocation? Yes, indeed;

35. Richard Bauckham, "Jesus and the Wild Animals (Mark 1:13): A Christological Image for an Ecological Age," in *Jesus of Nazareth: Lord and Christ—Essays on the Historical Jesus and New Testament Christology*, ed. Joel B. Green and Max Turner (Grand Rapids: Eerdmans, 1994), 3–21, there 19–20. Bauckham states further, "For us, Jesus' companionable presence with the wild animals affirms their independent value for themselves and for God. He does not adopt them into the human world, but lets them be themselves in peace, leaving them their wilderness, affirming them as creatures who share the world with us in the community of God's creation" (20).

36. Notably, the narrative of Luke's Gospel reverses the order of the second and third temptations.

37. On the connection with John 4:34, see D. A. Carson, *Matthew: Chapters 1 through 12*, The Expositor's Bible Commentary (Grand Rapids: Zondervan, 1995), 113.

38. John P. Meier states that "this may hint at a temptation" for Jesus to misuse his sonship to his own advantage and exchange it for the role of "a political and social Messiah by feeding a hungry mankind" (*Matthew* [Wilmington, DE: Michael Glazier, 1990], 30).

however, the prophetic summoning to socioeconomic justice always points to the one who alone gives and sustains life, in whom life finds its meaning and telos, and before whom, therefore, we are accountable for sharing this life with fellow humans so that they may flourish. In light of this assertion, while religions strive for the eradication of starvation and poverty (stirring the world's consciousness to responsibility for the other's well-being), their main challenge to market-driven globalization is, in Miroslav Volf's words, "to issue an effective reminder that, as Jesus said, 'life is more than food' (Luke 12:23)—and that only when that is so does the food itself acquire deeper meaning and thus can be more richly enjoyed."[39]

Continuing further, the temptation narrative depicts the *priestly dimension* of the messianic calling being confronted with the urge to test and manipulate one's access to life, divine favor, and protection. It is not accidental then that in the Gospel of Matthew the tempter takes Jesus to the "pinnacle" of the temple in Jerusalem, the visible location of the priestly vocation. As Meier points out, here the devil shows that he, too, can quote Scripture (Ps 91:11–12) "for his purpose," and the temptations quickly "turn into a rabbinic debate on the nature of true sonship."[40] Jesus responds with Deuteronomy 6:16 ("Do not put the Lord your God to the test, as you tested him at Massah"), revealing his duty and authority as high priest to interpret, teach, and live the Word rightly, in the obedience of embodied proclamation. Finally, the *royal dimension* is challenged by the lure of a shortcut to absolute power and dominion (over the kingdoms of the earth) through idolatry—worshiping Satan (the fallen creature) instead of the Creator. The tempter presents the seduction of power as wrapped in the promise of Scripture (Ps 2:6–8): Has not God stated that he will give the Messiah the nations as an inheritance (v. 8)? The King of kings puts an end to the debate, exercising his God-given authority over both the terrestrial and celestial creation and commanding Satan to leave while responding with Deuteronomy 6:13—an uncompromising call to monotheism. As the tempter leaves, the angels arrive and, in Meier's vivid depiction, "the mount of temptation becomes the mount of paradise."[41]

As most commentators agree, the narratives of Jesus's temptation in the wilderness (after forty days of fasting) appear as a direct contrast to Israel's temptations during its forty years of wandering in the wilderness of

39. Volf, *Flourishing*, 51.
40. Meier, *Matthew*, 30.
41. Meier, *Matthew*, 31.

Sinai. Thus, David Hill asserts that "Jesus triumphs over the temptations to which Israel succumbed in the desert, and takes upon himself the destiny of Israel to carry it to its fulfillment."[42] In a way, the gospels depict Jesus as "the true Israel."[43] Yet one cannot avoid the association of this triptych with the ever-present temptation for the church (the communal body of Christ) to betray her prophetic, royal, and priestly identity for the lure of prosperity, protection (security), and power.[44] The temptation in the wilderness is depicted as an invitation to utilize God's Word as a means toward achieving one's personal ends—satisfying one's own immediate needs, longings, and desires (a practice common to various "prosperity" forms of Christianity, exported from the West around the world).[45] The response of Christ, the incarnate Word, is refusal to view the world as an end in itself and to reduce the written Word to a mere utility in the pursuit of this end. Instead, while pointing to the need for redemption and sanctification of human desires, he proclaims in word, act, and being the Word as the world's all-summoning telos—the Word in its living, redemptive embodiment. In his rejection of the tempter, Christ—the light (John 1:9), life (John 14:6), and peace (Eph 2:14) of the world, enacts the new creation, fusing together the ontological renewal of humanity with that of the entire cosmos. He comes out of the wilderness in the power of the Spirit as the beginning of a new world and clothes with it, on the day of Pentecost, his communal body, the church, so that she can carry the reality of this newness to the uttermost limits of creation.

42. David Hill, *The Gospel of Matthew*, New Century Bible Commentary (Grand Rapids: Eerdmans, 1981), 99. The author points out that there are three biblical themes from which the gospels draw in shaping the temptation narrative: Israel's temptations in the wilderness, the parallelism between Jesus and Moses, and "the protection of God given to the hero of Ps. 91."

43. Meier, *Matthew*, 29.

44. For example, the merging of Christianity with civil religion on its quest of regaining its lost cultural influence "through political means" is reflective of the church's temptation to exchange her prophetic social marginality for the lure of political power and economic affluence. See Miroslav Volf, *Public Faith: How Followers of Christ Should Serve the Common Good* (Grand Rapids: Brazos, 2011), 77–78.

45. The prosperity gospel, which functions as an ideological platform of global neoliberal capitalism, is an example for such utilization of the Word as transcendental ("magical") means to worldly ends. See Daniela C. Augustine, "Pentecost and Prosperity in Eastern Europe: Between Sharing of Possessions and Accumulating Personal Wealth," in *Pentecostalism and Prosperity: The Socio-Economics of Global Renewal*, ed. Amos Yong and Katy Attanasi (New York: Palgrave Macmillan, 2012).

Scripture's Correlation between Violence and "Limited Goods"

Where does Scripture locate the origins of violence as communal discord and disintegration of covenantal bonds? Angela Y. Kim's insightful essay "Cain and Abel in the Light of Envy" points out that the biblical narratives of sibling rivalry and the phenomenon of envy surrounding "key heroes of Israel's history" follow a general pattern. They begin with the availability of limited (or perceived as insufficient for all) good(s), leading to violent conflict over these goods between brothers (or other family members) that eventually finds temporary resolution in physical separation (as in the cases of Abraham and Lot, or Jacob and Esau), which in its final, irreversible form is the death of one (or many) of the rivals (as in "the case of Cain and Abel, Abimelech and the 70 brothers, and Amnon and Absalom").[46] The author also highlights the conclusions of current sociological studies indicating that the violent propensity of struggles over limited good(s) is "aggravated" by the close proximity of the rivals.[47]

Locating the origin of violence against the other in the fight for survival amidst conditions of limited goods and anxiety over scarcity can be traced also to the theological undercurrents of the Genesis narrative of the curse. The Bible depicts the curse as manifested in the wreckage of essential, life-giving relationships, leading to their deformity into violent, often lethal enmity. Thus, the brokenness of creation proceeds from the disrupted relationship between humanity and God (between creature and Creator) and permeates all other organic relational bonds that outline human identity: between the man and the woman (as conflict with the fellow human), between the serpent and the human being (as enmity between the anthropic and nonanthropic creatures), between humanity and the earth itself (as clash of human civilization and nature, articulated in terms of humanity's grueling agricultural toil and the earth's continual resistance to cultivation, Gen 3:14–19). In the midst of this relational brokenness, Adam and Eve's banishment from Eden and its unlimited access to life (symbolized by the tree of life in the center of the garden, Gen 3:22–24)[48] could be understood

46. Kim, "Cain and Abel in the Light of Envy," 66.

47. Kim, "Cain and Abel in the Light of Envy," 66.

48. See Walter Vogels, "The Tree(s) in the Middle of the Garden (Gen. 2.9; 3.3)," *Science et Esprit* 59, nos. 2–3 (2007): 129–42, there 129. Reflecting on the symbolism of the two trees in the middle of the garden, Vogels states: "The two trees in the middle of paradise are indeed in the middle of our human existence: life and knowledge. They are two divine attributes and therefore the deepest and most sacred human desires" (141).

as "unplugging" humanity from the tangible immediacy of the presence of God, who alone is life eternal. Indeed, the possibility of matter's life in eternity is completely contingent on divine hospitality for only God is eternal (noncontingent, without beginning and end—a living home/habitation for all creation—Deut 33:27). Thus, matter, including the human body, experiences eternity only as a gift of divine welcome in which God shares his life with the other so that they may have life eternal. Excluded from Eden and separated from the source of life (God himself), humanity acquires (metaphorically speaking) an "expiration date"; its "life battery" starts to run out and human death appears within the material cosmos as an unavoidable, time-bound reality manifested in the gradual deterioration and disintegration of matter and reflected symbolically in the accounts of humanity's progressively shortening lifespan.[49] Thus, the warning of Genesis 2:17,[50] unfolding in the midst of the once harmonious cosmos, could be viewed as a death sentence that human beings now share with their world until all of creation stands subjugated to the consequences of humanity's free moral choice (Rom 8:20–21). Yet we can understand the meaning of Genesis 2:17 also in relation to the immanence of death residing within human behavior inconsistent with humanity's ontology and purpose. In this sense the appearance of death may be seen also as a pointer to the end/the dissolution of true human ontology as result of the fall's[51] breaking of the essential com-

49. In his book *The Mystery of Christ: Life and Death* (Crestwood, NY: St. Vladimir's Seminary Press, 2006), John Behr states that while the "privileged position" of the first humans, being "closer to the source of life than their descendants," is reflected in their longevity, "it is after the Flood, not the expulsion from Eden, that the human life span decreases dramatically" (81). The author also notes that in the text of Genesis the word "sin" is not used to describe "the deed of Adam and Eve," nor words such as "transgression" or "rebellion." The first occurrence of "sin" in the Genesis account is in relation to the story of Cain and Abel (in Gen 4:7 the term appears in God's warning to Cain) (79). Behr also points out that the Old Testament seems to regard mortality as natural. He states: "In the Old Testament, death is not ubiquitously seen as a curse or a punishment for sin." In fact, good death (as that of Abraham—in a ripe old age, surrounded by multiple generations of heirs) is viewed as a blessing (81). Yet Christology transforms our perspective and understanding of death, a theme that is revisited later in this section.

50. For an engaging study of Gen 2:17 and the interpretive issues presented by the passage's contrast to Gen 3:3–4 (God's warning and the serpent's statement regarding it), see R. W. L. Moberly, "Did the Interpreters Get It Right? Genesis 2–3 Reconsidered," *Journal of Theological Studies* 59, no. 1 (April 2008): 22–40.

51. John Behr insightfully points out that many of the Eastern church fathers did not use the vocabulary of "fall." He states that we tend to treat the fall as having resulted "in an accidental alteration in the life of creation" as an outcome "solely of free human will." Yet

munal relationships constitutive of human nature in the image and unto the likeness of the Trinity. In the conditions of the fall, the human being (as originally intended to be by the Creator) is no more: it has ceased to exist, has died and needs to be re-created/resurrected/redeemed/renewed.

It is not accidental then that Scripture articulates salvation (as ontological healing and renewed access to life) in terms of restoration of the essential ontological communion with God and neighbor in the perichoretic mutuality of Christic (self-sacrificial, self-giving) love for the other (Matt 22:37–40). In light of the depiction of sin as *incurvatus in se*, redemption is experienced as restored communal human identity that "uncurves" one's life upward toward a renewed interface with the other. Redemption is manifested in humanity's metanoic turning away from the self-centeredness of sin that approaches the other only in a predatory way as means for survival and self-indulgence, to sharing one's life with the other on a Christoforming journey of becoming human—regaining one's communal being in continual interface with the other. This uncurving is the creation-mending work of the Spirit, who convicts "the world concerning sin" (John 16:8), renews and sanctifies (1 Pet 1:2) humanity (including its sociopolitical imagination, its dreams, longings, and desires), and pours the love of God into the human heart (Rom 5:5), enabling it to image once again the divine communal face with and for the other. Redeemed life becomes a continual, pneumatic, liturgical anamnesis of God's face, practiced through the ongoing commitment to its discernment in the face of the fellow human, striving to provide for

---

church fathers spoke about the free choice of Adam and Eve in terms of "turning away from contemplating the Word" (Saint Athanasius), "misusing their God-given capacity for spiritual enjoyment" and moving toward the creation rather than the Creator (Saint Maximus the Confessor). The author also highlights the striking assertion of Saint Irenaeus that humanity was created in order to be saved, understanding salvation fundamentally in terms of attaining Christlikeness (78). In light of this, John Behr proposes that the only time period described in Genesis that "has something in common with the customary picture of the Fall is the period before the Flood" when the earth is saturated with violence. "The Lord saw that the wickedness of humankind was great in the earth, and that every inclination of the thoughts of their hearts was only evil continually. . . . Now the earth was corrupt in God's sight, and the earth was filled with violence" (Gen 6:5, 11) (81). Behr states that while mortality is not viewed as unnatural in the Old Testament, "Violent death does not occur at the will of God and, as such, is unnatural and ungodly. The ungodliness of the violent man, and of violence itself, is a theme which runs throughout the Old Testament, and into the New Testament in important ways" (82) (*Mystery of Christ*, 78–82). While the term "fall" is used in the present book in its traditional understanding, Behr's assertions of the ungodliness of violence and violent death are relevant to the present study on the iconoclasm of violence.

him or her what is needed but lacking for their flourishing (Matt 25:31–40). Christian life becomes the liturgical recapturing and enacting of the memory of Eden's shalom within the living communal memory of Christ as our peace (Eph 2:14).

As already noted in chapter 1, the fall impairs the vision and understanding of the other as a corecipient of the gifts of life, creation, and community, and reduces the fellow human from cocelebrant of creation's divine liturgy to a competitor for the world's limited material resources—for access to life. Since, according to the primordial memory of shalom, peace is not simply the absence of violent conflict in an idyllic cosmos but access to life in communion with the other (God and neighbor), salvation involves a renewed vision of God, the fellow human, and the world—a vision that fosters community and solidarity of shared life (including material resources) in pursuit of planetary flourishing. The postlapsarian distortion of humanity's vision leads to replacing the eucharistic sharing of the world with a frantic, unrestrained devouring amidst intensifying fear of scarcity and violence over limited goods.[52] The essence of access to life shifts from relational encounter to self-indulging consumption, from fellowship and communion to competition for survival of the fittest. Undoubtedly, while experiencing deterioration and decay, the world still represents in itself life (conserved) in the form of matter, energy, and natural resources. Yet, apart from the Creator, this life is also limited and subject to expiration.[53] From that first tragic bite in the garden of Eden (the moment in which humanity turns toward the creation instead of toward the Creator, searching for a shortcut to satisfy its ontologically given desire toward attaining the likeness of God),[54] the hu-

52. For further discussion of the eucharistic nature of creation in the generosity of the Spirit, see chapters 1 and 4 of the present book.

53. The bleak current prognosis on availability of natural resources for sustained economic growth intensifies the urgency to develop new paradigms of relationships with our ecosphere within the ongoing human cycle of production and consumption. See John E. Tilton, *On Borrowed Time? Assessing the Threat of Mineral Depletion* (Washington, DC: Resources for the Future, 2003), as well as his article "Depletion and the Long-Run Availability of Mineral Commodities," *Mining, Minerals and Sustainable Development* 14 (March 2001). This is a publication of the International Institute for Environment and Development, available online at: http://www.iied.org.

54. See Daniela C. Augustine, *Pentecost, Hospitality, and Transfiguration: Toward a Spirit-Inspired Vision of Social Transformation* (Cleveland, TN: CPT, 2012), 40–42. There I propose that the story of the fall in the garden of Eden could be viewed as a narrative of humanity's free choice to reject God's way toward attaining his likeness and take, instead, a "pseudo short cut" toward fulfilling its destiny in theosis. The desire of Adam and Eve to become like God

man being starts frantically and violently "eating" its way into the world. It ingests the world in order to live (becoming, in a way, what it eats: a creature having its limits in the limitations of its world, its end in the end of matter). Faced with its own finiteness and dependence on the limitations of creation, humanity becomes territorial, possessive, and greedy, desiring more of the world, which progressively decreases before its very eyes. This degenerative change in humanity's relation to nature seems to be inevitable; the human being has become dependent on the world (instead of on God) for its survival, desperately contingent on a limited resource for life amidst multiple competitors struggling to lay hold of it. Obsessed with the world's finiteness, humanity misdirects its God-given hunger for communion with the divine presence. The creature tries to satisfy its bottomless hunger for the infinite Creator by consuming the finite creation. As Alexander Schmemann sums it up, "Man is a hungry being. But he is hungry for God. Behind all hunger of our life is God. All desire is finally a desire for Him." In his sin-impaired vision of creation, humanity forgets that all "that exists is God's gift" intended to make human life "communion with God." It is, in Schmemann's breathtaking words, "divine love made food, made life" for humanity.[55]

In the conditions of the fall, consuming the world becomes a daily struggle to postpone death, the inevitability and nearness of which become a mark of postlapsarian reality. The fall's inherent pathology is manifested in the tragic irony of humanity's self-destructive relationship to the world. The human being turns against the world—the only thing that now stands between its survival and death—and devours it in a desperate attempt to stay alive, thus destroying its very lifeline. In a dreadful twist of fate, humanity consumes life unto death. Since the life conserved within the creation can be prolonged and multiplied (to some extent) only through cultivation, humanity tries to subdue and colonize nature in order to extract its life more efficiently. The violent conquest of nature exposes further the limits of material existence and the inevitability of death as natural resources run out, land becomes infer-

---

(Gen 3:5) is a God-given ontological impetus reflecting their purpose as creatures. Yet there is only one way for the creature to become like the Creator—the Creator's way of participation in his life, until the life of the deity becomes the life of his creation. There is not a shortcut or a magical fruit that can spring this likeness into one's being. It takes life in covenantal communion with God as a perpetual surrender of one's existence on earth to the divine telos; as an incarnational enactment of his will in the human being, until the human being becomes an extension of God's life on earth.

55. Alexander Schmemann, *For the Life of the World: Sacraments and Orthodoxy* (Crestwood, NY; St. Vladimir's Seminary Press, 1963), 14.

tile, and the environment (together with the human body) suffers abuse and sickness through pollution and indiscriminate greedy exploitation.[56] Perhaps the growing metamorphosis of agricultural land into desert (resisting cultivation and surrendering itself to the noninhabitability of wildness)[57] could

56. Perhaps the despair produced by the limitations of matter and energy in the face of the ever-growing consumption needs of human civilization is best articulated in the dark inevitability of cosmic finitude spelled out by the second law of thermodynamics. Contemporary to its discovery in the second half of the nineteenth century, the philosopher Henri Bergson famously termed it "the most metaphysical of the laws of physics since it points out without interposed symbols, without artificial devises of measurements, the direction in which the world is going" (*Creative Evolution* [New York: Cosimo Classics], 265). The law confirmed that the earth's reserves of energy and natural resources are limited, a discovery that had far-reaching sociopolitical, economic, and ecological consequences. (See Kiril Neshev, *The Philosophical Postmodernism* [Sofia: Filvest, 1997], 7–9.) The rising awareness of the finiteness of energy and natural resources fueled further the fierce competition for more of the world, driving forth the neocolonial imperialistic expansions of the Western, North Atlantic economies at the expense of (what is termed today) the majority world. The subsequent unrestrained extraction of life from the countries numbered within this geopolitical category left their economies crippled for many decades while increasing the disparity between them and the North Atlantic West, sabotaging their economic development and keeping in perpetual poverty much of humanity around the globe. The devastating ecological effects of the frenzied consumption of natural resources through indiscriminate greedy practices of extraction from creation brought about environmental devastation and escalating health problems. Greed mandated shortcuts to economic prosperity that were not only detrimental to the ecospheres of multiple already impoverished communities, but also caused the defacing of creation, altering the environmental aesthetics of generations as once paradise-like mountains, forests, and gardens were transformed into slums, toxic waste dumps, and uninhabitable wilderness. Consider, e.g., the practices of mountaintop removal in the Appalachians, deforestation in the Amazon region, overexploitation of agricultural lands, extracting the waters of natural wetlands, and building heavy industry (which produces toxic residue within its environment) on fertile lands of traditionally agrarian communities. See Peter Jacques, "Ecology, Distribution, and Identity in the World Politics of Environmental Skepticism," *CNS Journal* (September 2014), http://www.cnsjournal.org/wp-content/uploads/2014/09/Jacques.19.3.Sep_.08.pdf.

57. International news continually presents distressing reports on the growing pandemic of desertification of once fertile agricultural land around the globe. See, e.g., *Reuters*, June 18, 2014, http://www.businessinsider.com/r-a-quarter-of-indias-land-is-turning-into-desert-minister-2014-18. The news agency quoted India's environment minister's statement that about "a quarter of India's land is turning to desert and degradation of agricultural areas is becoming a severe problem . . . potentially threatening food security in the world's second most populous country." For over forty years, the United Nations has engaged in active study and program implementations to stop or at least slow down the phenomena of desertification (The final documents of its 1977 conference can be found at http://www.ciesin.org/docs/002-478/002-478.html). On June 17, 2016, the World Day to Combat Desertification, the UN listed the following most common causes for the loss of agricultural land through its rapid decline

be seen through sympathetic, ecotheological lenses not just as an expression of the curse but as creation's protest in self-defense against its devastation by ruthless, greedy exploitation. Perhaps this is nature's symbolic refusal to share itself with abusive and ungrateful humanity. Perhaps it is an expression of creation's despair and longing for shalom, Sabbath, and healing, which seem to be attainable only by expelling humanity out of its embrace until the human community attains its final Christlike form through the redeeming, sanctifying work of the Spirit—that of the children of God (Rom 8:21). Perhaps this is creation's groaning in birth pangs.

Kiril Neshev suggests that the nineteenth-century discovery of the finitude of the universe (and the subsequent intensification of the predatory exploitation of the global ecosphere, causing its further devastation) has led, in the words of Jürgen Habermas, to "the exhaustion of utopic energies."[58] As Habermas points out, "the function *of utopian thought* with its exuberance seems to be opening alternatives for action and margins of possibilities that push beyond historical continuities."[59] Humanity's utopian energies fuel the sociopolitical imagination toward envisioning the world otherwise, stimulating creative, transformative engagement within the present and framing hopeful openings for the arrival of the *novum*.[60] Therefore the exhaustion of

into desert/wilderness: 1) the tree and plant cover that binds the soil is removed, which occurs when trees and bushes are stripped away for fuel wood and timber, or to clear land for cultivation; 2) animals eat away grasses and erode topsoil with their hooves; 3) intensive farming depletes the nutrients in the soil (http://www.un.org/en/events/desertificationday/background.shtml). The document cited the following gloomy statistics from the latest UNCCD Brochure: "2.6 billion people depend directly on agriculture, but 52% of the land used for agriculture is moderately or severely affected by soil degradation. Land degradation affects 1,5 billion people globally. Arable land loss estimated at 30 to 35 times the historical rate. Due to drought and desertification each year 12 million hectares are lost (23 hectares/minute), where 20 million tons of grain could have been grown. 74% of the poor (42% of the very and 32% of the moderately poor) are directly affected by land degradation globally" (http://www.unccd.int/Lists/SiteDocumentLibrary/WDCD/DLDD%20Facts.pdf).

58. Neshev, *Philosophical Postmodernism*, 8.

59. Jürgen Habermas, "The Crisis of the Welfare State and the Exhaustion of Utopian Energies," in *Jürgen Habermas on Society and Politics: A Reader*, ed. Steven Seidman (Boston: Beacon, 1989), 285.

60. Habermas correctly points out the historical record of post-Enlightenment suspicions and negativism toward utopic thought and asserts that its hopeful socio-transformative impulses were not reaffirmed until the twentieth century, when such thinkers as Ernst Bloch and Karl Mannheim purged "the term 'utopia' of its association with 'utopianism'" and rehabilitated it "as a legitimate medium for depicting alternative life possibilities that are inherent in the historical process itself" ("Crisis of the Welfare State," 285–86).

utopic daydreaming coincides with foreclosing the possibility of imagining an alternative (better) future, reducing the horizons of human creativity (in world-making and world-mending) to mere maintenance of the present. This is a desperate, futureless stage of existence, with deep-reaching demoralizing consequences for the pursuit of a planetary common good in solidarity with others. It exacerbates the loneliness and alienation of one's struggle to postpone death within a finite world, intensifying violent competition for survival and hostility toward the anthropic and nonanthropic neighbor. Apart from the Spirit's generous, hospitable spaciousness that enlarges humanity (cultivating it as a eucharistic, communal being), society's anxiety about scarcity, driven by the undergirding fear of death, faces the other as an unwelcomed intruder into a desperately finite, claustrophobic world. This distorted vision of the other (desensitized to the Spirit's groaning for the renewal of creation and blinded by moral amnesia of the divine face) eventually justifies the logic that, due to nature's material limitations, it is unavoidable for one's life to become a function of another's death. Driven by a malformed instinct of self-preservation, humanity faces the other not in the sacramental call to communion, but in the dehumanizing iconoclasm of violence. The face of the other is no longer a summoning encounter unto life eternal, but a marker of potential competition for life within the drama of the universe's temporality and finiteness. The one who was made to be cosharer in the gift of life has become associated with the nearness of death. In light of humanity's communal nature, however, the destruction of the other is nothing less than self-destruction; as one acts in predatory effacement of the other, one ceases to be truly human.

As previously noted, the last Adam overturns the consequences of the curse bringing healing to the ontological relationships that constitute humanity, delivering them from "the tyranny of sin"[61] through the sanctifying power of the Holy Spirit. Yet in him also death itself is overcome and transfigured into a passage unto life eternal through the Spirit's resurrecting presence within the redeemed humanity (Rom 8:11) even on this side of the eschaton. As John Behr asserts, the Holy Spirit dwells within Christians now, "preparing them for the resurrection"; for the "resurrectional life of Christ begins, this side of the grave, in the life of continual dying to this world."[62] Therefore, the sanctifying (Christoforming) work of the Spirit within believ-

61. John Behr, *The Mystery of Christ: Life and Death* (Crestwood, NY: St. Vladimir's Seminary Press, 2006), 98.

62. Behr, *Mystery of Christ*, 100.

ers results in their embodying (amidst the present age) the resurrected life of the age to come. The resurrection starts (as enacted in the public liturgical proclamation of water baptism, Rom 6:3–4a) by dying and being buried with Christ in order to experience in him "newness of life" (Rom 6:4b) in the true freedom intended by God for humanity—the freedom to be and to become truly human, to be Christlike. Being "crucified with Christ" (Rom 6:6) delivers humanity from the fear of death in all of its forms (including one's anxiety about scarcity, or striving to enslave, exploit, and lord over others out of fear that otherwise they will lord over oneself); for fear of death underwrites the pathology of violence against the fellow human and the rest of creation.[63] In fact, all fear is to be "exorcised" from human life by the divine love now poured through the Spirit in believers' hearts (Rom 5:5). In the famous statement of 1 John 4:18, there is "no fear in love; but perfect love casts out fear . . . and the one who fears is not perfected in love." The very next verse points to the mirroring reciprocity of this redemptive, liberating love, articulated in the beautiful simplicity of the proclamation, "we love, because he first loved us" (v. 19).

The ethical implications of this statement point to our responsibility for building community with the other (including the alien/stranger whose coming and presence we fear—a fear of violent death and of insufficient, limited goods). We have to love them first before they learn to love us; we have to extend to them the spaciousness and sanctuary of love before they can mirror it in reciprocity to us, before we can weave together community of shared life. The passage summons the readers back to their humanity (to a renewed life of mutual, covenantal responsibility for the other in free-willed imaging of the divine face) and sobers them up with the assertion that the only cure for anxiety about scarcity and all other forms of fear of death is not prosperity, power, and security but love. Love is the ultimate form of freedom that makes space for the other in a finite world, by making space for God (who is love) in oneself. The epistemological assertion of 1 John 4:7–8

63. In his philosophical reflections on the fear of death in relation to slavery and freedom, Nikolai Bardyaev states: "Fear and slavery are cancerous in their consequences. If the human succeeds to overcome the slavish fear, he[she] will stop killing. The human being sows death out of his [her] fear of death. Lordship always needs to murder. Lordship always feels fear, and because of that needs to murder. It does not want to fight with death" (my translation). Nikolai Berdyaev, *Slavery and Freedom* (Paris: YMCA, 1939), 209. The relationship between fear of death and violence against the fellow human and the rest of creation is explored further in the next section of this chapter.

depicts love toward the fellow human as the manifestation of one's ontology as child of God (birthed by him), whose life has become a living extension of the divine communal life as love for the other. "Beloved, let us love one another, because love is from God; everyone who loves is born of God and knows God. Whoever does not love does not know God, for God is love." Love is the fundamental form of the new creation and its life in and with God, the fruit of the indwelling Spirit (Gal 5:22), the perfected, organic continuity (that shall not pass away, 1 Cor 13:8–13) between the present and the eschaton as the life of God enlivening the renewed human community. As Karl Barth states, love "is the one form of Christian action which does not require and is not subject to transformation of absorption into another, higher and future form."[64] Or as Troeltsch famously exclaims, it is "the power of this world which already as such is the power of the world to come."[65] Love is, therefore, the perfection which has come as Christian maturity—the believer's Christoformation (1 Cor 13:10–11).

Indeed, death in Christ is the death of the old humanity and the resurrection of the new so that the believer may confidently say: "I have been crucified with Christ; and it is no longer I who live, but it is Christ who lives in me" (Gal 2:20). This is not simply new life; it is *the one who is life itself* (John 14:6) indwelling human existence and making all things new (Rev 21:5). Yet

64. Karl Barth, *Preaching through the Christian Year: A Selection of Exegetical Passages from the Church Dogmatics* (Grand Rapids: Eerdmans, 1981), 255. Barth makes this statement in the context of his exegesis of 1 Cor 12 and 13 where he reflects on the charismatic gifts of speaking in tongues and love—on the living continuity between the *charism* of the Spirit and the character of Christ. He states that "it is possible to speak with tongues (as enabled by the Holy Ghost) and yet not to have love but to omit all self-giving to God and one's neighbor." Yet at the end it is "love alone that counts"—for that love is Christ within redeemed humanity—the hope of glory (Eph 1:18). When tongues, together with the rest of the charismatic gifts, fulfil their telos, they shall cease (1 Cor 13:8), but their telos—love itself—shall remain. In a similar line of thought, Raniero Cantalamessa concludes that in "the final analysis, love makes one identical with [like] the Giver of the charism himself, the Holy Spirit, and the Giver is surely preferable to his gifts" (*The Mystery of Pentecost*, trans. Glen S. Davis [Collegeville, MN: Liturgical, 2001], 51). Cantalamessa utilizes Saint Augustine's correlation between 1 John 4:8 ("God is love") and Rom 5:5, which asserts that when the Holy Spirit pours the love of God into someone's heart, he pours himself (*The Trinity*, Fathers of the Church 45, trans. Stephen McKenna [Washington, DC: Catholic University of America Press, 1963], 495–96). Cantalamessa reaches also for Thomas Aquinas's argument defining charity/love as sanctifying grace and pointing out that it unites the believer directly to the end, which is God, while the charism has a rather instrumental character, leading/pointing to this end (*Summa Theologiae*, vol. 30, trans. Cornelius Ernst [London, UK: Blackfriars, 1972], 141–43).

65. Quoted by Barth in *Preaching through the Christian Year*, 255.

this newness of life does not involve just human spirituality. Scripture does not speak about Christ's (and the believers') resurrection only in the spiritual sense, for he "rose bodily from death" and ascended into heaven to sit at the right hand of the Father.[66] When the paschal troparion triumphantly and joyously proclaims, "Christ is risen from the dead, trampling death by death, and to those in the tombs bestowing life"—this is an announcement of the good news to the entire cosmos, circumscribed through Christ's incarnation, death, and resurrection into the newness of his life. This includes also the physicality of the human body and the materiality of the earth from which it was taken. Therefore, not only the Incarnation but also the resurrection and the ascension are manifestos of God's redemptive love for his creation in all of its vulnerable, fragile, finite materiality. This is why, despite its hopeful expectation of the resurrection, Christianity takes death very seriously, viewing it (at worst) as "catastrophe"[67] and (at best) as a temporary emergency that finds its resolution in the eschaton (through the resurrection).

Yet the eyes of faith, illuminated by the Spirit, see both life and death in this world as teleological sacramental movements intended to lead the believer toward Christoformation. As John Behr asserts, both creation and salvation, "the appearance of human nature and the vanquishing of mortality by immortality, belong to the same economy," which has as its final purpose "the original divine intention of fashioning the creature made from mud into the image and likeness of God."[68] Therefore, both life and death are redeemed as tools in the hands of God toward fulfilling his creative project—bringing forth a wholesome human being—humanity that lives the life of Christ. Inspired by Saint John of Damascus's description of death as "marvel" and "mystery that befalls us," Behr points to the liturgical use of the word "mystery" as a designation of "sacrament." In the sacrament of Christ, even human death attains sacramental dimension toward redemptive union with the Creator.

Reflecting further on the role of death's mystery within the divine economy (in light of Saint Irenaeus's theological assertions), John Behr highlights three important points. First, he notes that the "temptation for human beings is to think that the life they have is theirs by nature,"[69] not understanding that their every breath depends entirely on God's uncondi-

66. Behr, *Mystery of Christ*, 99.
67. Behr, *Mystery of Christ*, 100.
68. Behr, *Mystery of Christ*, 95.
69. Behr, *Mystery of Christ*, 102.

tional hospitality. According to Behr, therefore, death has an educational role to play, "enabling humans to experience to the uttermost their weakness and mortality in their apostasy from God, the only Source of life, so that they might therefore hold ever more firmly" to him.[70] Further, the author proposes that death's second role is as "the means of limiting the reign of sin." He states that if "death has come into the world as a result of sin (Rom 5:12), in reverse, death can also be seen as a restriction to sin." The final aspect to the mystery of death within the divine teleology, according to Behr, is to see it in eucharistic terms. "The life in death, begun by dying to sin in baptism as a "likeness" of Christ's death (Rom 6:5), finds fruition in the eucharistic self-offering of the Christian in his or her own bodily death in witness to Christ."[71] This was and is the experience of the church throughout the ages in embracing martyrdom.[72] The saints willingly sowed their bodies bringing forth the harvest of the church,[73] witnessing to the new Christo-formed life, vibrating in their earthly vessels—a life over which death does not lord in fear. Yet, saturated by the Spirit as living sanctuary of the divine presence and incarnational continuity of Christ's life on earth, their bodies often remained incorruptible even on this side of the eschaton—a reoccurring phenomenon which continues to defy scientific explanation, leaving the world in unsettling wonder before sanctified human life. Indeed, they were human beings fully alive.[74] As John Behr points out, for the saints, dying a Christlike death was following their Lord in the journey of becoming truly human.[75] The author's Christology offers an illuminating reflection

70. Behr, *Mystery of Christ*, 104.

71. Behr, *Mystery of Christ*, 105.

72. For a brief overview of the historical development and transformation of the church's theology of martyrdom, see Timothy Ware (Bishop Kallistos of Diokleia), *The Orthodox Church* (New York: Penguin, 1997), 14–15.

73. Tertullian famously states in chapter 50 of his *Apology*: "The oftener we are mown down by you, the more in number we grow; the blood of Christians is seed" (http://www.newadvent.org/fathers/0301.htm).

74. Saint Irenaeus famously states that "the glory of God is man fully alive" (*Adversus Haereses* 4.20.7).

75. Behr, *Mystery of Christ*, 105–6. The author brings the examples and theology of martyrdom of Saints Ignatius and Irenaeus. For example, he quotes Ignatius's famous words to the Christians in Rome, asking them not to interfere with his martyrdom. See *Letter to the Romans*, ch. 4 (available at http://www.newadvent.org/fathers/0107.htm). Ignatius states: "I write to the Churches, and impress on them all, that I shall willingly die for God, unless you hinder me. I beseech of you not to show an unseasonable good-will towards me. Allow me to become food for the wild beasts, through whose instrumentality it will be granted me to

on the gospels' account of Jesus's death on the cross in light of the divine act of creation of humanity that starts with the carving from the earth of the first Adam and ends with the death and the returning to the earth of the last Adam. Behr states:

> When Christ said "It is finished" (Jn 19.30), he is not simply declaring that his earthly life has come to an end, but rather the work of God is now "fulfilled" or "completed." The divine economy, that is the whole plan of creation *and* salvation, told from this perspective, culminates at this point. The work of God spoken in Genesis, creating "the human being" [*anthrōpos*] in our image and likeness" (Gen 1:26–27), is completed here: as Pilate said a few verses earlier, "Behold, the man [*anthrōpos*]" (John 19:5). The work of God is complete, and the Lord of creation now rests from his work in the tomb on the blessed Sabbath. By himself undergoing the Passion as a man, Jesus Christ, as Son of God and himself God, fashions us *into* the image and likeness of God, the image of God that he Himself is (Col. 1:15).[76]

The Call to Responsibility for the Other amidst a Violent World

Defacing God from the cosmos, the iconoclasm of violence desensitizes humanity to the divine presence and its call to responsibility for the fellow human and the rest of creation; it numbs human conscience to the suffering and pain of the world and justifies the brutality of aggression, alienating hostility, and war as civilizational norms.[77] Religion has been implicated as an ideological culprit in humanity's desensitization to and sacramental-

---

attain to God. I am the wheat of God, and let me be ground by the teeth of the wild beasts, that I may be found the pure bread of Christ. Rather entice the wild beasts, that they may become my tomb, and may leave nothing of my body; so that when I have fallen asleep [in death], I may be no trouble to anyone. Then shall I truly be a disciple of Christ, when the world shall not see so much as my body."

76. Behr, *Mystery of Christ*, 107–8.

77. Against these assertions of the normalcy of war as a civilizational device, John Dominic Crossan proposes that our particular hermeneutical lenses, shaped and focused by cultural dynamics and anticipations, search for and read into Scripture justifications for violence against the other by noting an ambiguity within its depiction of God as both violent and nonviolent. Crossan's proposal is that "*the Christian Bible presents the radicality of a just and non-violent God repeatedly and relentlessly confronting the normalcy of an unjust and violent civilization*" (*God and Empire: Jesus against Rome, Then and Now* [New York: HarperOne, 2007], 94).

ization of injustice, oppression, and violence.[78] Thus, within the turbulent context of revolution-shaken nineteenth- century Europe, Marx famously describes religion as "opium for the masses"[79]—a potent ideological sedative that numbs the suffering of the proletariat afflicted by violent economic exploitation and demobilizes its revolutionary energies that might otherwise be directed toward just sociopolitical transformation. As history teaches us, religions can be coopted by political systems toward both just and unjust causes, and their sacred texts utilized for the defense of violence, exploitation, and oppression as well as for the promotion of equality, justice, and peace.[80] Yet history has also made clear that not only religions (with their supposed irrationality), but also the militantly religious zeal of atheism (as an intellectual/ideological negation and expulsion of the divine presence from society on the basis of reason), can tranquilize humanity to the systemic affliction of suffering and injustice and dismiss the human conscience as a neurotic obstacle to civilizational (cultural and scientific) progress. The absence of God relativizes the suffering or the extermination of the other until it becomes an acceptable part of human existence, reducing life to a competition for evolutionary survival; it normalizes and justifies political and economic violence against the other for the sake of social expediency. By demythologizing religious notions of life's sacredness and demystifying its phenomenology as a biological process, atheism's modernist veneration of science and technological development as vehicles for social salvation strips away much of the ethical ambiguity surrounding scientific advance-

78. See the content in footnote 1 of the present chapter regarding René Girard's work *Violence and the Sacred*.

79. Karl Marx, "Introduction," *A Contribution to the Critique of Hegel's Philosophy of Right*, http://www.marxists.org/archive/marx/works/1843/critique-hpr/intro.htm.

80. See Volf, *Flourishing*, 183–94. Volf gives an insightful analysis of the notable ambiguity of religions in their propensity toward both violence and peace, justice and injustice. He discusses the arguments of both the critics and the defenders of religions' social role and proposes a viable explanation for religions' apparent ambiguity. For an intriguing engagement of the relation between religion and violence/war (in defense of religion), see Stanley Hauerwas, *Approaching the End: Eschatological Reflections on Church, Politics, and Life* (Grand Rapids: Eerdmans, 2013), 120–38. Also, in relation to the defense of religion, see William Cavanaugh, *The Myth of Religious Violence: Secular Ideology and the Roots of Modern Conflict* (New York: Oxford University Press, 2009). Examining the role of religion within the historical context of Europe, Cavanaugh points out that religion is a cultural/ideological construct that accompanied the creation of the nation-states, the existence of which was justified by ascribing it a messianic purpose, saving old Europe from religious violence (114).

ment and eliminates moral obstacles to further explorations. After all, in the words of Dostoevsky, "without God and the future life . . . everything is permitted."[81]

For decades, during Communism's militant atheist reign in Eastern Europe, one of the regime's most powerful dissident critiques was embodied in the life of the Christian community. Its relentless faith in the coming of God and the inevitability of his kingdom (as comprehensive sociopolitical reality of justice, equality, and freedom in shalom) was a potent prophetic judgment against Communism's triumphant self-identification with the future of the world as representing the very end of the historical process. The Christians' daily covenantal commitment to love one another and their atheist neighbors was a courageous revolutionary action against the Communist state's carefully crafted, skillfully maintained culture of betrayal, suspicion, spying, and collaboration against the other.[82]

Responding to Marx's claim for religion's systemic desensitization toward injustice, Rabbi Jonathan Sacks affirms the socio-transformative potency of Scripture, stating that its monotheist faith

> is not acceptance but protest, against the world that is, in the name of the world that is not yet but ought to be. . . . The Bible is not a metaphysical opium but its opposite. Its aim is not to transport the believer to a private heaven. Instead, its impassioned, sustained desire is to bring heaven down to earth. . . . To imitate God is to be alert to the poverty, suffering and loneliness of others. Opium desensitizes us to pain. The Bible sensitizes us to it.[83]

81. Fyodor Dostoevsky, *The Brothers Karamazov*, trans. Richard Pevear and Larissa Volokhonsky (San Francisco: North Point, 1990), 589.

82. See Daniela C. Augustine, "Pentecost and Prosperity in Eastern Europe: Between Sharing of Possessions and Accumulating Personal Wealth," in Amos Yong and Katy Attanasi, eds., *Pentecostalism and Prosperity: The Socio-Economics of Global Renewal* (New York: Palgrave Macmillan, 2012), 189–212.

83. Jonathan Sacks, *To Heal a Fractured World: The Ethics of Responsibility* (New York: Schocken, 2005), 27–28. The author emphasizes the restlessness of Judaism in the face of injustice (inspired by the passion and poesis of the prophetic message and articulated in the teaching of the sages) and concludes that the Bible is God's call to human responsibility (28). He asserts that "Judaism is not a religion that reconciles us to the world. It was born as an act of defiance against the great empires of the ancient world, Mesopotamia and Egypt, which did what he accused all religions of doing—sanctifying hierarchy, justifying the rule of the strong over the weak, glorifying kings and pharaohs and keeping the masses in place . . . it was in and as the voice of social protest that the Biblical imagination took place" (18).

The Bible is a radically dissident text that scrutinizes and critiques all forms of imperial consciousness with their ideological justifications of sociopolitical and economic oppression (and its roots in fear of the other). It destabilizes empires by proclaiming the inevitability of their end. It denounces any form of injustice introduced by institutional or private pursuits of political power and economic benefit at the expense of the other in a world created by a just God. Scripture's dissident edge culminates in the direct, subversive message of the prophets. As Walter Brueggemann points out, the "prophetic imagination" effectively deconstructs the arguments of "dominant imagination as a practice that cannot give life because it fails in truth-telling."[84] Truth is terrifyingly insurrectionary for imperial rule and is systematically counteracted by ideological propaganda purposed to secure the status quo in perpetuity by construction of appropriate civil/political religions.[85] After all, the dialectic of liberation from all forms of systemic oppression is summed up in the words of Christ: "You shall know the truth and the truth shall set you free" (John 8:32).[86] A truth-telling God who hears the cry of the oppressed and is moved by their suffering to radically liberating action (Exod 2:23–24; 3:7–8) is not a sedative for the affliction of injustice, but a threat to all tyrannical regimes.

84. Walter Brueggemann, *The Practice of Prophetic Imagination* (Minneapolis: Fortress, 2012), 42.

85. Civil religions merge God and empire/emperor (or God and country in the conditions of the nation-state) in a way that lends divine sanction to the political oligarchy and its actions. Sacralizing secular authority asserts its eternal/nontransient establishment by fusing earthly and divine interests. It develops appropriate liturgies (often mimicking the liturgical patterns of popular religious cults), holy days and festivals that display the undisputed power of the rulers and form the moral imagination of the citizens in a way compliant with the imperial political interests. (For an insightful "exegesis" of secular liturgies, including those of civil religions, see James K. A. Smith's *Desiring the Kingdom: Worship, Worldview, and Cultural Formation*, vol. 1 of *Cultural Liturgies* [Grand Rapids: Baker Academic, 2009], ch. 3). Yet civil religions have served the formation of important civic virtues, essential in sustaining the commitment to the common good as promoted by the civil contract. (See Martha C. Nussbaum's *Political Emotions: Why Love Matters for Justice* [Cambridge, MA: Harvard University Press, 2015].)

86. Even Marx could not disagree with this insurrectionary principle of biblical revelation; it resounds within his insistence that the birth of the proletariat's revolutionary consciousness proceeds from the illuminating, liberating effect of the truth regarding its conditions of economic exploitation and oppression. In chapter 4 of *The Communist Manifesto*, Marx and Engels articulate the truth that has to be grasped by the proletariat through the assertion that in the revolution the workers "have nothing to lose but their chains. They have a world to win" (http://www.marxists.org/archive/marx/works/1848/communist-manifesto/ch04.htm).

As was already pointed out, Scripture's uncompromising commitment to justice for the other is visible in the conspicuous inclusion of the social covenant (the constitution of just relationship to the fellow human) within the Decalogue (Exod 20:1–17). Making the just relationship to the other an indispensable requirement for fulfilling the divinely instituted covenant between God and his people illuminates the vital scriptural correlation between divine grace and human responsibility. It establishes the law as divine pedagogy in learning to recognize God's face in the face of the immediate other. The relationship to the other is part of the relationship with God. Making place for the other by fasting from oneself (from one's self-indulging desires) is making place for God in the world; it is transfiguring the human community into a home for the divine presence—"because we have learned to honor the image of God that is humankind"[87] and not to have other gods (money, power, ideological influence, lust, etc.) or to make idols of temporal created things (Exod 20:3–5) to which we sacrifice the other. The covenant is designed to transfigure humanity into the likeness of God (and thus fulfill its creaturely destiny derailed by the fall)—for we worship what we love and become like what we worship. Thus, the ultimate expression of worship is "to keep the way of the Lord by doing righteousness and justice" (Gen 18:19) being his active, embodied extension in healing a hurting world.

The Decalogue reveals God's righteousness and justice as built within the fibers of the cosmos, as a materialization of the divine presence in a world created in the generous hospitality of God as a home for the other. Redemption is expressed in the social enfleshment of justice as the ontologically renewed relationship to the other[88]—a relationship that presupposes equality—the equality of the divine face imprinted upon all humanity. Thus, the law is for all who live in a land marked by the visibility of God's presence in the face of the other; all stand equal before it: young and old, male and female, the Jews and the foreigners living among them. The promised land is the land of equality that brings justice and peace, a land where the ways of the Lord are kept as doing righteousness and justice. In these redeemed relationships between fellow humans, God makes his dwelling place on earth.

Indeed, the Bible (in the words of Jonathan Sacks) is a call to responsibility and as such is addressed to free moral agents. As noted in chapter 1,

87. Sacks, *To Heal a Fractured World*, 28.

88. Emmanuel Levinas, *Totality and Infinity: An Essay on Exteriority* (Dordrecht: Kluwer, 1991), 87.

creating humanity as a free moral agent is, undoubtedly, a risk; it is the risk of love, but it is also the inherent mark of human responsibility. Freedom is responsibility—without freedom of personal choice for action or inaction, one is not responsible for the drama and pain within the surrounding material existence. Yet freedom is a responsibility *in community*, for, as Bartholomew I asserts, according to the trinitarian communal image in humanity true freedom is "never solitary but always social."

> We are only free if we become a *prosōpon*—to use the Greek word for 'person', which means literally 'face' or 'countenance'—only if we turn towards others, looking into their eyes and allowing them to look into ours. To turn away, to refuse to share, is to forfeit liberty. Freedom is expressed as encounter.[89]

Affirming the relationality of freedom, Jürgen Moltmann contrasts the notion of "freedom as dominion/lordship" (in light of the common definition of freedom emerging from political history) with "freedom as community." He states that as a "sign of a patriarchal culture," "freedom as lordship" is "a one-sided relationship of a subject to objects" (typical of the feudalist social construct). Contrary to the one-sidedness of this relationship, the bourgeois revolution uplifted freedom as "the autonomous self-determination of every individual over his or her own life and abilities," which "is limited only by the freedom of" others in an act of mutual recognition and respect of individual autonomy. Yet Moltmann proposes that there is a better and more organic alternative to this society "of free and solitary individuals: The Lonely Crowd,"[90] namely, a society characterized by communal relationships of "mutual and alternating social representation" in which "people are there for one another" because they share life together.[91] For Moltmann, in "these representative relationships people take over responsibility for each other; and ever since New Testament times these relationships have been known in the Christian tradition as *love*." He identifies this communal ethos as "*communicative freedom*," in which

89. Bartholomew I, Archbishop of Constantinople and Ecumenical Patriarch, *Encountering the Mystery* (New York: Doubleday, 2008), 133.

90. Jürgen Moltmann, *The Living God and the Fullness of Life*, trans. Margaret Kohl (Geneva: World Council of Churches, 2016), 112–13.

91. Moltmann, *Living God and the Fullness of Life*, 113.

> the other person is not a restriction of my freedom, but an extension of it. In mutual participation in the life of other people, individuals become free beyond the boundaries of their individuality. That is the social side of freedom. We call it solidarity. In a community of this kind individuals become persons. An individual is ultimately indivisible, but a person emerges through participation and communication with other people, that is to say, in community.[92]

Following Nietzsche, Moltmann defines personhood in terms of the free human being's ability to promise and to keep one's promises, of building sustainable, trustworthy "networks of promises" that represent "the political paradigm of a free society." Therefore, a "free society is not an accumulation of independent individuals; it is a community of persons in solidarity—a community of 'care and share.'"[93] Yet in continuity with his theological process, Moltmann does not limit this solidarity (as an outcome of the humanizing replacement of the old rules of dominion/lordship) only to human society but extends its reality of shared communal freedom to the rest of creation. He concludes: "Freedom as harmony will be the watchword once competition is replaced by cooperation, and a mutual give and take with nature comes into being, which will serve the common survival of all."[94] As has been already noted, this cosmic, communal perichoresis of shared life in harmonious freedom—*freedom as love*—is the work of the Spirit, for "where the Spirit of the Lord is, there is freedom" (2 Cor 3:17). Through the Spirit we partake in the freedom of the trinitarian communal life and human communal freedom becomes an in-Spirit-ed vehicle of God's socio-transformative presence within the world. Therefore, as Moltmann insists, freedom is experienced as active, *creative expectation* of "the things God has promised with the resurrection of Christ."[95] This is living "here and now" in the Spirit's continual priming of humanity for (and weaving it into) the sociopolitical reality of "the new heaven and earth" (Rev 21:1), making

92. Moltmann, *Living God and the Fullness of Life*, 113.

93. Moltmann, *Living God and the Fullness of Life*, 114.

94. Moltmann, *Living God and the Fullness of Life*, 114.

95. Moltmann, *Living God and the Fullness of Life*, 115. Moltmann points out that for the Christian "faith does not live solely in love" but also in hope, which is "not a waiting or a matter of 'wait and see'" but an active, creative anticipation of God's promised future. His notion of human freedom as a creative, active reality develops in engagement with Hannah Arendt's depiction of "freedom as the ability to begin" something new (articulated in *Viva Activa oder vom tätigen Leben* [Stuttgart: Kohlhammer, 1977], 168).

its life visible within the creative, life-making (and life-sharing) freedom to *love and hope* for all.[96] This is freedom as communal transfiguration into the likeness of God. Through the Spirit's enlivening presence, the human community is apprehended into the trinitarian communal life, until "all of us, with unveiled faces, seeing the glory of the Lord as though reflected in a mirror, are being transformed into the same image from one degree of glory to another; for this comes from the Lord, the Spirit" (2 Cor 3:18). Freedom of life in the Spirit (as creative world-making and world-mending love and hope) urges the community to responsible action here and now, as Moltmann insists in his compelling prose:

> The person who hopes for the realm of freedom will desire liberation from political repression and economic exploitation here and now. The person who hopes for righteousness and justice of the new earth will respect the earth here and now, will develop reverence for earthly life, and will resist its exploitation and destruction. The person who hopes for eternally living life will be already seized here and now by this "unique, eternal, glowing life," and will make life live wherever he or she can.[97]

Precisely because freedom is responsibility with and for the other—responsibility for the common good—it is a terrifyingly demanding condition of being in the world. Freedom is breathtakingly empowering, but also frightening reality.[98] It is perpetually accompanied by the temptation of

96. The pneumatic connection between freedom and hope for others is also traceable (though in a different form) in the work of Karl Barth. See his *Dogmatics in Outline* (New York: Harper & Row, 1959), 139. According to Barth, living the life of the Spirit (as the life of Christ in humanity) is marked by the gift of eucharistic, responsible freedom—by gratitude for Christ's work and faithful stewardship of his gospel. Yet Barth adds another sign to these manifestations of new life in the Spirit, namely, a transformed vision of and relationship to the fellow human, experienced as the gift of freedom "to hope the best for all." This triptych of unceasing gratitude, faithful responsibility, and hope for all others saturates and sets apart "the Christian way" of life. Yet this life is not self-sustainable in its beautiful otherworldliness—it fully depends on the perpetual self-giving of God to humanity—on the ever-coming of the liberator Spirit. In the words of Barth, "We must therefore every day and every hour pray *Veni Creator Spiritus* in listening to the word of Christ and in thankfulness. That is a closed circle. We do not 'have' this freedom; it is again and again given to us by God."

97. Moltmann, *Living God and the Fullness of Life*, 115.

98. In his seminal book *The Fear of Freedom* (London: Routledge Classics, 2001), Erich Fromm discusses the complex psychology of humanity's autonomy/freedom, analyzing the

abandonment or denial of one's free moral agency in the face of responsibility, especially in the aftermath of irreversibly tragic outcomes from one's free choices, or the overwhelming sense of helplessness amidst the ever-summoning-to-responsibility brokenness of the world. This primordial temptation is clearly articulated in the Genesis narrative of the fall. The text offers a depiction of the world's structural intentionality, marked with God-established boundaries (Gen 2:16–17) that have been transgressed by humanity with the full knowledge of their existence and of the consequences of ignoring them.[99] The first human instinct in the face of responsibility (as the mark of freedom) is denial (Gen 3:8–12). As the man blames the woman and the woman in turn points to the serpent as the guilty perpetrator, ultimately humanity (the creature) projects its guilt onto the Creator ("one of *your* creatures that *you* have placed in my life made me do it"). The accusation puts God on trial as the suspected author of evil within the structures of the world. This refusal of responsibility is a dangerous perversion of the divine revelation of God and his creation; it implies that both the Creator and his world are imperfect/deficient/evil. If humanity is created in the image and destined for the likeness of *this* God, there is no hope for redemption, no expectation of deliverance. This distorted perspective forecasts evil as an

---

sixteenth-century context of the Reformation (with its rise of the individual) and that of Nazi Germany in twentieth-century modernity. He points to the overwhelming feeling/awareness of one's smallness, helplessness and aloneness in the midst of the world, due to the separation/disconnection of the individual from the broader entities within which he or she found identity, meaning, and belonging prior to the Reformation period (e.g., in his or her organic continuity with nature and community). The author reflects on the ambiguity of freedom as well as on the psychological and social mechanisms of "escape" from one's helplessness and alienation that may result in choosing to surrender (escaping) one's freedom and social responsibility.

99. Lee Roy Martin suggests, however, that "within the narrative world of Gen 2–3, the first humans had not seen death; therefore, they would have been incapable of fully understanding it" (personal e-mail exchange and prior conversation). For more interpretations of the passage, see John H. Walton, *Genesis*, The NIV Application Commentary (Grand Rapids: Zondervan, 2001), 174–75; and Walter Brueggemann, *Genesis*, Interpretation: A Bible Commentary for Teaching and Preaching (Atlanta: John Knox, 1982), 47–49. Brueggemann draws a striking parallel between the theme of Gen 3:1–7 and Dostoevsky's *Crime and Punishment*, stating: "What had been a story of trust and obedience (chapter 2) now becomes an account of *crime and punishment* (3:1–7). In brief limits, the dynamics are not unlike those of Dostoevsky. There is a strange slippage between the crime and the punishment. The torture of Raskolnikov is in seeing what is not there, in hearing voices and imagining threats. The power of guilt takes on its own life. It works its own destruction. Death comes, not by way of external imposition, but of its own weight" (49).

inescapable aspect of the created order—an inherent, incurable, fatal sickness in the fibers of creation—sickness unto death. Such an argument is also a convenient justification for consequent evils committed by humanity; it is an expedient dismissal of any responsibility for one's moral choices and actions. Thus, as Rabbi Sacks observes, "the depth and originality" of this primordial story "is not that Adam and Eve sinned (sin is rarely original) but its insight in the psychodynamics of self-deception. . . . They deny personal responsibility"[100] and through that deny their freedom as moral agents. This is an act of negating their identity as creatures imprinted with the image of God—an act with profound sociopolitical implications regarding the realities of war and violence against the other in the world.

Externalizing evil from oneself by projecting it onto others through resisting personal responsibility (blaming others for one's own failures) alienates humanity from God and neighbor and breaks down the ontological relationships that define humanness (and humanize us as creatures). It creates hostility and violent tension between oneself and the other that can escalate into hatred, leading toward the demonization and eventually, in the politically expedient moment, even to the scapegoating of the other. Reflecting on the sources of violence, Charles Taylor highlights the externalization of evil as an essential component within the mechanisms of unleashing violence against the other.[101] Even when hatred is kept subviolent and contained through restraints stipulated by and enacted according to the social contract, its latent morbidity may be manifested in various forms of social exclusion and the pathology of systemic alienation of individuals or entire groups of people (as in cases of categorical violence).[102] Scapegoating

100. Sacks, *To Heal a Fractured World*, 137. The author offers the following definition of sin reflective of Judaism's interpretation of the Gen 3 narrative: "A sin is an act in the wrong place, a failure to honor the boundaries and constraints that form the deep structure of the universe. It is a failure to engage in *havdalah*, the cognitive act of knowing the difference between one thing and another and what belongs where." He illustrates this notion by asserting that, for example, desiring "to make their home in heaven the builders of Babel failed to honor the distinction between man and God" (143).

101. Charles Taylor, "Notes on the Sources of Violence: Perennial and Modern," in *Beyond Violence: Religious Sources of Social Transformation in Judaism, Christianity, and Islam*, ed. James L. Heft, S.M. (New York: Fordham University Press, 2004), 15–42, there 19–23.

102. See Taylor, "Notes on the Sources of Violence," 15. The author defines "categorical violence" in terms of being "exercised against whole categories of others, people therefore that one may never have known or been in contact with." Taylor points to "violence wrought against a scapegoat minority or phenomena as ethnic cleansing or genocide," as well as "the events of September 11, 2001." On the practice of social exclusion as categorical (sub) violence,

sacralizes violence, giving it the aura of cathartic expelling/exorcising of evil out of the social fabric.[103] In the face of turbulent public discontent at the social outcomes of a given political/economic system, scapegoating can be utilized as sacred killing (within the "liturgies" of the ruling powers) that diverts the people's attention from the realities of systemic evils and temporarily subdues the urgency of the demand for justice, but also relieves free moral agency from the obligation to take responsibility for the conditions of injustice.[104] Scapegoating sustains the sacral mythology of power (both in

---

see 32–35. Examples of subviolent exclusion are the Roma ghettos built during communism throughout the countries in Central Europe and the Balkans. The ethnic Roma population was kept in isolated territory on the fringes or outside of the city limits often behind high walls. Even today, many of these ghettos are deprived of basic infrastructure (as canalization and running water). While the Roma intentionally maintain their indigenous ways of life and resist cultural integration within the larger society, their state-imposed isolation in the ghettos further deepens their sociopolitical and economic marginalization. Despite recent efforts to bring about the demarginalization and comprehensive social inclusion of the Roma minority through an international initiative known as the "Decade of Roma Inclusion 2005–2015" (partnership between the governments of twelve European countries), little progress has been made. (See the Declaration and other relevant documents of "Decade of Roma Inclusion 2005–2015" at http://www.romadecade.org/ and there at http://www.romadecade.org/about-the-decade-decade-in-brief#)

103. Taylor, "Notes on the Sources of Violence," 19–20. Taylor outlines the mechanism of scapegoating in dialogue with the work of René Girard, particularly *Le Bouc émissaire* (Paris: Grasset, 1982) and *Je vois Satan tomber comme l'éclair* (Paris: Grasset, 1999), and John Keegan, *A History of Warfare* (London: Hutchinson, 1993). Taylor, therefore, describes three possibilities leading to designating some as targets and justifying the violence against them. 1) "The mechanism of sacrifice," as articulated by Girard: starting in "mimetic rivalry," threatening "to dissolve society"; followed by "forging a unity out of everyone-minus one, the victim"; restoring the "general peace" at the expense of the victim. 2) The "scapegoating mechanism," which for Taylor is not identical with the mechanism of sacrifice: starting with catharsis—"expelling evil" with the assertion that "what has been expelled concentrates all evil in itself"—while venting "holy rage"; once again, as in the previous case, achieving unity with a sense of "solidity" or "firm allegiance." Finally, 3) Finding an external enemy/target and waging war against them, thus, limiting internal damage. Here Taylor engages Keegan's argument that, initially, war was also "ritualized."

104. The so-called "Vuzroditelen Process" ("Process of Rebirth") in Bulgaria's recent history, aiming at the cultural assimilation of the ethnic Turkish minority and the Pumaks (ethnic Bulgarians who converted to Islam during the centuries of Ottoman rule), could be viewed as an example of scapegoating executed by the country's Communist government in order to divert the population's attention away from their grievances and the potential escalation of social discontent. The "Process of Rebirth" culminated in these minorities' forced exodus from Bulgaria during the spring and summer of 1989, just months before the fall of Communism. In 2010, the Bulgarian Parliamentary Committee on Human Rights and Religious Freedom

totalitarian as well as in democratic forms of government) by the promise that after the elimination of "the enemy" (external, as in war, or internal, as in ethnic cleansing), the evil will dissipate and life will be delivered from suffering and injustice.

Many atrocities committed against humanity have been (and are being) justified as sacred, cathartic killings in the name of God and country via the mechanisms of categorical violence.[105] The rhetoric of xenophobia (as fear of the other/the stranger in our midst) forecasts all religious, ethnic,

---

approved a declaration condemning the communist regime's actions toward forceful assimilation of the country's ethnic Turkish and described the expulsion of 360,000 Turks in 1989 as a form of ethnic cleansing (Sofia News Agency, "Bulgaria MPs Move to Declare Revival Process as Ethnic Cleansing," Novinite.com [February 11, 2010]).

105. The terrifying drama of categorical violence is illustrated by the pogroms against Jews and Gypsies throughout European history, the tribal genocides in Rwanda and Kenya, the reoccurring violence against Christians in Nigeria, Somalia, and throughout countries in the Middle East, the massacres of Muslims by Hindus, and the mass graves in Bosnia and Croatia (during the 1990s war), the reality of terrorism as a new global pandemic, but also by the mass extermination of the ideological other and the socioeconomically different during the French and the Bolshevik revolutions and the Chinese Cultural Revolution. It is important to note that there is no consensus in political science regarding the causes of categorical violence/genocide. Scott Straus, however, helpfully identifies five clusters of theories. The first "revolves around intergroup animosity and disintegration" and sees genocide as rooted in "preexisting pejorative mass beliefs and discriminatory institutional practices" of social exclusion and marginalization, which further reinforce long-existing hatred, distrust, fear, and dehumanization between groups. The second cluster focuses on the characteristics of political regimes, stating that genocide "is possible when power is concentrated in the hands of few decision-makers," when there is a history of political repression of alternative political ideas, and when a political system and civil society lack the checks and balances that restrain extreme measures. The third cluster emphasizes the catalyst effects "of stress and upheaval" during traumatic periods of hardship, which are consequently channeled toward blame and scapegoating of a particular group within society. Within this cluster falls also the claim that in "periods of great change and uncertainty" populations are more accepting of "extreme policies." The fourth cluster "places ideology at the center of analysis" and insists on the need to understand "the political imaginary" (e.g., racial utopias, nationalist projects, etc.). The fifth cluster looks into the "strategic origins of genocide" in the empirical connection between genocide and war (e.g., seeing genocide as "an extension" of modern warfare). See Scott Straus, *Making and Unmaking Nations: War, Leadership, and Genocide in Modern Africa* (Ithaca, NY: Cornell University Press, 2015), 3–5. After analyzing the strengths and deficiencies of the existing theories, the author endorses "a synthesis" between the ideological and strategic arguments (33). One may be interested also in Manus I. Midlarsky's work *Origins of Political Extremism: Mass Violence in the Twentieth Century and Beyond* (New York: Cambridge University Press, 2011). The author's research focuses particularly on the significance of "ephemeral gain" and "mortality salience" (when combined together) as causes of political extremism and violence.

cultural, ideological otherness as potentially threatening to the integrity, stability, and "purity"[106] of the social fabric and the communal well-being. The externalization of evil into a group of people demands the division of the world into "us" and "them"; it requires (in Charles Taylor's terms) the existence of "a contrast case"[107]—the appearance of the other as moral opposite that personifies evil. The constructed contrast between oneself and the other helps define and consolidate the identity of the crusaders for societal purification, "but also defines evil, failing, lapse" as an outside reality embodied within the accused demographic group.[108] Thus, the process of scapegoating promulgates the fragmentation of society through the contrasting and alienating rhetoric of logocentric binaries[109]—good and evil, right and wrong, pure and impure—in which the privileged positive meaning is ascribed to the executors of social cleansing, and the negative to the blamed other. Justification of scapegoating often demands a distorted vision of the other constructed through their systemic defacement and dehumanization until they are projected as the antipode of everything good, dignified, virtuous, and holy. The villainization of the other as a social plague provokes the collective imagination toward the possibility of their extermination, awarding it the status of a sacred moral duty.

The dehumanizing distortion of scapegoating is based on a dangerous inversion of the realities of good and evil, of redemption and social healing, in order to justify the extermination of the other. Since (according to the Decalogue) redemption is a communal affair and there is no redemption without the other, the hallowing of the other's murder becomes the very act of jeopardizing the possibility of redemption: there is no hope of healing between oneself and the other, no hope of recapturing the memory of paradise and seeing the face of God in the face of the other, no future in the

106. As Charles Taylor notes, "when the Girardian scapegoat mechanism defines the outsiders as operating inside," they are seen as "polluters" ("Notes on the Sources of Violence," 20).

107. Taylor, "Notes on the Sources of Violence," 20. Taylor points out that "a contrast case" does not have to always be seen as representing "a vital threat" and can involve "distant people with whom there is no real contact," in which case the contrast construct "can be relatively harmless, although it can license terrible cruelty on contact." He gives as examples the *conquista* and the slave trade.

108. Taylor, "Notes on the Sources of Violence," 20.

109. In his famous work *Of Grammatology*, Jacques Derrida defines "logocentrism" as "the metaphysics of phonetic writing," which is "nothing but the most original and powerful ethnocentrism," "imposing itself upon the world," controlling the concepts of writing, science, and the history of metaphysics (*Of Grammatology*, trans. Gayatri Spivak [Baltimore, MD: Johns Hopkins University Press, 1998], 3–4).

likeness of God. Therefore, denial of personal responsibility for the evil manifested in society and its devastating effects upon creation is detrimental to the future of humanity. Conversely, admitting and accepting one's responsibility for the condition of the world is the beginning of redemption. Taking responsibility for the consequences of one's actions, words and thoughts opens the door to repentance (the entry into personal transformation) without which there is no renewal/healing of the self and of one's relationships to the anthropic and nonanthropic other.[110] Repentance is the beginning of change within one's outlook toward oneself, the other, and the world. It illuminates the myopic human vision of time-compressed material existence with the sobering realism of the Spirit's time-transcending, liberating truth, focusing the lenses of understanding the condition of the world, and sharpening the critical edge of prophetic discontent through the foresight of eschatological hope.

Repentance diverts from the human instinct to blame the other, externalize evil, and thus kindle conflicts between oneself and fellow humans (capable of escalating into scapegoating and physical violence against the other). Therefore, repentance (as taking social responsibility for the brokenness of the world and the intentional depletion of the other's access to life) aids the ending of strife, hatred, oppression, exploitation, bloodshed, and aggression against the other. As such, repentance is a building block of a just society—a society of equality and peace as access to life for all.

Internalization versus externalization of conflict—understanding that the fundamental struggle one leads in the world is located within oneself and not in the relational space between the self and the other—has, indeed, profound socio-transformative effects, as well as an empowering and liberating personal dimension. As Jonathan Sacks remarks,

> Once we locate the cause of our condition within ourselves, rather than 'out there' in external factors beyond our control, we enlarge the scope of human freedom. Responsibility is the negation of learned helplessness. It is a great weight to carry. But the alternative is heavier still.[111]

110. For an insightful engagement of the therapeutic and socio-transformative effects of repentance in relation to personal transformation and the healing transformation of the role of memory, see Max Scheler's chapter "Repentance and Rebirth," in *On the Eternal in Man*, trans. Bernard Noble (Hamden, CT: Archon, 1972).

111. Sacks, *To Heal a Fractured World*, 187.

The socio-transformative effects of repentance (and assuming responsibility for the pains of the world) point to the concern about nurturing and sustaining a culture of penance, forgiveness, and mutual covenantal accountability. Repentance highlights the need to move beyond the obligations of the political contract toward the intentionality of civil covenant that is "predicated on active interpersonal responsibility."[112] It denies the luxury of indifference, apathy, noninvolvement, or self-indulgence at the expense of the other's well-being and summons us to give an account for our participation in the wounding and curing of the world. Life in a civil covenant retracts from the cultural norms of individualism and consumerism idolized by contemporary Western society (as an enactment of the antisocial, dehumanizing effects of elevating the idea of personal autonomy over against the interpersonal, social reality of being human). The awakening of communal consciousness demands, in the words of Desmond Tutu, a spirituality of transformation that takes seriously the well-being of all members of society, including political opponents, former oppressors, present economic exploiters, abusers, torturers, and enemies.[113] When this spirituality finds its incarnation in a covenantal moral society, it contributes to the building of what Vaclav Havel has termed "the moral state"[114] (outside of which democracy remains an impossible project)[115] and assures the existence of "politics as the practice of morality."[116] This covenantal spirituality becomes the soil in which peace and well-being shared with the fellow human grow and flourish gardened by the Spirit.

Christianity has emphasized for centuries the ascetic discipline of penitent life and its significance for personal and corporate social transformation. A life lived from the perspective of "one's knees" protects against both the errors of overspiritualization and underspiritualization of evil in an attempt to avoid personal responsibility. While keeping in mind that, indeed, the striving for the healing of the world is not a fight "against flesh and blood" and that there are real and present "spiritual forces of wickedness in the heavenly places" (Eph 6:12), repentance insists on looking first of all at the fight in one's own "flesh" (in one's heart and mind)—the cradle of dreams

112. Sacks, *To Heal a Fractured World*, 115.

113. Desmond Tutu, *The Rainbow People of God* (New York: Doubleday, 1994), esp. ch. 6.

114. Vaclav Havel, "Politics, Morality, and Civility," in *The Essential Civil Society Reader: Classic Essays in the American Civil Society Debate*, ed. Don E. Eberly (New York: Rowman & Littlefield, 2000), 396.

115. Havel, "Politics, Morality, and Civility," 391–402, there 401.

116. Havel, "Politics, Morality, and Civility," 397.

and desires (Rom 7:5–25). Repentance entails confessing that systemic evils are an outcome of our choices; that poverty and exploitation are produced by our greed and lust. It provides the self-critical lenses that can facilitate not only the correction and "purification" of one's social imagery (and corresponding ethic) but pave the way to reconciliation with the other once designated as enemy.[117]

As was noted in the previous sections of the present chapter, Scripture emphatically places the roots of redemptive cosmic transfiguration in sanctification of one's will and desires by setting one's mind on "the things of the Spirit" and walking in his ways (Rom 8:5–8). This transfiguring journey involves the awakening of human responsibility as the Spirit stirs human conscience and exposes the hidden motives of the heart. This is why the pedagogy of becoming like God, as the essence of redemption, is expressed in a distinct Spirit-driven movement within the biblical narrative: in the words of Sacks, "*from acts done by God for the sake of human beings, to acts done by human beings for the sake of God.*"[118] This movement encompasses both Old and New Testaments; God delivers his people from oppression and sets them free so that they may choose his way and be transfigured in his likeness, in order to change/mend the world. The Acts of the Apostles is the culmination of this movement. Those who through the agency of the Spirit have become a living extension of the incarnate Christ, the way of God made flesh in their personal and communal life, become (in the power

117. Irvin Greenberg ("Religion as a Force for Reconciliation and Peace: A Jewish Analysis," in *Beyond Violence: Religious Sources of Social Transformation in Judaism, Christianity, and Islam*, ed. James L. Heft, S.M. [New York: Fordham University Press, 2004], 88–112) reflects on the socio-transformative potency of repentance within the context of interreligious conflicts and dialogues. He points to the importance of "self-criticism as a foundation" for building pluralist political systems without falling into moral and cultural relativism (109). Notably, Greenberg identifies repentance as "one of the most powerful forces that drives faith not only to correct its own errors but to reconcile one religion with another" (110). As a Jewish scholar involved in the Jewish-Christian dialogue after the Holocaust, he lifts up the example of Christians taking responsibility for the Holocaust and the effects of this act upon the credibility and impact of Christianity's message. Thus, Greenberg states: "Out of repentance, Christians have self-critiqued, repudiated supercessionism, and fought to clarify or eliminate anti-Jewish stereotypes. They have labored to reduce and neutralize texts of terror and exclusion. In the process, they have made Christianity into a far more morally effective faith. They have moved it from being a privileged sanctuary of hatred to being a true gospel of love—even to Jews" (109). While the present section discusses repentance in relation to social responsibility, chapter 4 revisits the significance of repentance within the context of forgiveness and reconciliation.

118. Sacks, *To Heal a Fractured World*, 157.

of the Spirit, Acts 2) world changers—they shake and move the world (Acts 17:6) toward its transfiguration.

In light of this destiny that demands the mobilizing of human agency, the Torah, and all of Scripture, is a call to responsibility[119] —the Word of God summoning humanity back into "the Way" (Acts 22:4) to healing the relationship with the other and the rest of creation. Essentially, this is healing of one's relationship with God for, according to the Decalogue's logic, a sin against the other is a sin against God himself. It locates evil in the interiority of personal desires, in the life of the mind and the heart. There, in one's innermost being, starts the transfiguring of the entire cosmos. Internalizing the Word, one becomes his embodiment participating in the redemptive reordering of the world according to God's Word: this is an intentional participation in the renewal of creation.

David's prayer of repentance in Psalm 51 is most instructive in this process of renewal. It starts with pleading for mercy in recognition of God's lovingkindness and compassion in blotting out humanity's transgressions (vv. 1–2); it continues with confession—taking responsibility for the perpetrated evil (v. 3) and recognition that the sin committed against the other was/is, indeed, a sin against God (v. 4—"Against you, you alone, have I sinned, and done what is evil in your sight, so that you are justified in your sentence and blameless when you pass judgement"). The second half of verse 4 asserts once more human responsibility by uplifting the righteousness of God and thus (contrary to Adam and Eve) pronouncing him innocent of evil. Verses 5 and 6 follow with a recognition of the fallen human condition and of God's will for inner transformation of the human being through the illumination of liberating truth (v. 6: "You desire truth in the inward being; therefore teach me wisdom in my secret heart"). The psalmist's desperate cry for renewal (vv. 7–12) is permeated by confidence in God's ability to purify one's longings and desires and to cleanse the intentions of the heart (the core of one's being) in the redeeming power of forgiveness and sanctification. Verse 13 crowns the passage with the assurance—"Then I will teach transgressors your ways, and sinners will return to you"—the one who has been forgiven and renewed in the pathways of righteousness becomes an instrument of God's healing presence in the world. The "ways of the Lord" now pour forth from the person's heart enacted as righteousness and justice toward the other. This is an embodied Torah and its transformative power is

119. Sacks, *To Heal a Fractured World*, 28. This is one of the main underlying arguments in Sacks's book.

contagious for the human *socium*; it becomes the pathway on which others come to God and find life.

Therefore, knowing the Torah is keeping it (or rather living it out); knowing God is doing his will as an enfleshed love for the other. Hearing the divine Word and doing it becomes the criteria for belonging to the true family of God (Luke 8:21). Keeping the Word charts the pathway out of death into life eternal (John 8:51). Thus, the earnest prayer of the psalmist is "Keep my steps steady according to your promise [your Word]" (Ps 119:133)—in the pathway of righteousness that is life more abundant. In reverse, Scripture implies that "the destruction of creation flows from the disobedience of Torah."[120] Thus, Hosea 4:3 describes a staggering ecological devastation; "the land mourns, and all who live in it languish; together with the wild animals and the birds of the air, even the fish of the sea are perishing." God unveils the reason for this environmental catastrophe; it has come to pass because "there is no faithfulness or kindness or knowledge of God in the land" (Hos 4:1). Instead of learning and enfleshing the ways of the Lord in lovingkindness and justice to the other, humanity has engaged in a perpetual cycle of violence and bloodshed (Hos 4:2). Therefore, with some risk of overstretching the implications of rabbinical teaching, one can conclude that hatred and violence against the other are violence against the whole world. While the Talmud reinstates this staggering conclusion, it does not stop there but contrasts it with an empowering statement of hope: "Whoever destroys a soul, it is considered as if he destroyed an entire world. *And whoever saves a life, it is considered as if he saved an entire world.*"[121]

Both Judaism's and Christianity's uplifting of the sacredness of each human life and insistence on the realization that each human being shares in the collective responsibility for the condition of the world, translate also into their outlook toward social transformation: "Change a life, and you begin to change the world."[122] Such a view offers a relief from the helplessness that may overwhelm the individual moral agent in the face of the world's all-

120. Walter Brueggemann, *The Practice of Prophetic Imagination* (Minneapolis: Fortress, 2012), 35.

121. Mishnah, Sanhedrin 4:5; Babylonian Talmud, Sanhedrin 37a. Irvin Greenberg comments on the second section of this talmudic statement in light of the first one out of "the three fundamental dignities of the image of God," namely, infinite value, equality, and uniqueness. He states that since each individual (as the image of God) has infinite value, by saving him or her, "one has saved an infinity" ("Religion as a Force for Reconciliation and Peace," 95).

122. Sacks, *To Heal a Fractured World*, 72.

engulfing brokenness and suffering. Through this empowering optimism, the one who despairs at the global challenges of escalating poverty, death, disease, violence, oppression, and ecological disasters, can find hope and courage to keep striving for the mending of the world one step at a time (one act of righteousness and justice, mercy and love, at a time). This outlook toward socio-transformative human agency offers also a cure for the moral myopia in relation to the needs of one's immediate neighbors, often obscured by the anonymous generality of the overwhelming, ever present demands for global justice. Changing the world begins with transforming the circumstances of our immediate other—extending to them the hospitality of God, respacing ourselves on their behalf in Godlikeness, seeking to provide what is needed but lacking for their flourishing. The face of the other, the always unique,[123] irreplaceable image of God, becomes for us the face of the world crying out for justice as access to life and flourishing. This is how the world is transfigured one person, one life at a time. In this dialectic of social transformation, change originates with us both as agents of change and as changing agents; we can change the world if we can first change ourselves and see the other otherwise.[124] For the Christian, this transformation is nothing else but becoming a living extension of Christ, the incarnate Word, amidst a desperately needy world.

As the human community becomes home for the Word, all creation finds itself at home with God. The glorious eschatological passage in Isaiah 11:1–9 illustrates this biblical assertion. The Messiah, upon whom the Spirit of the Lord rests (v. 2: "the spirit of wisdom and understanding, the spirit of counsel and strength, the spirit of knowledge and the fear of the Lord"), will establish God's comprehensive justice on earth (vv. 4–5), bringing about the healing of creation manifested as all-permeating peace.

> The wolf shall live with the lamb, the leopard shall lie down with the kid, the calf and the lion and the fatling together, and a little child shall lead them. The cow and the bear shall graze, their young shall lie down together; and the lion shall eat straw like the ox. The nursing child shall play over the hole of the asp, and the weaned child shall put its hand on the adder's den. They will not hurt or destroy on all my holy mountain; for the earth will be full of the knowledge of the Lord as the waters cover the sea. (Isa. 11:6–9)

123. Greenberg, "Religion as a Force for Reconciliation and Peace," 95.

124. Rabbi Jonathan Sacks, *The Politics of Hope* (London: Vintage, 2000), 269.

This is a breathtaking vision of the future of the world saturated with the knowledge of God—a world from which the Word cannot be squeezed out, for it has become organically present as the essential structure of one's relationship to the other. This is an enchanting glimpse of the redeemed and healed cosmos. This redemptive transfiguring of finite, cosmic material existence, brought within the infinity of the Spirit's life, is a reversal of the curse. It puts an end to death and suffering and culminates in healing of the relationships between humanity and the rest of creation, as well as between all nonanthropic creatures. There is no more bloodshed and one's existence is not sustained through consuming the other—one's life is no more a function of another's death. This is a restoration of paradise in the generous hospitality of the divine presence.

Equality, Justice, and Peace

If the human community is created to be the icon of the triune God within the material cosmos, its life is to be marked by consubstantiality, coequality, and perichoresis expressed in loving kenosis and askesis. Without the visible presence of these markers, human communal ontology breaks down and with it the world in and for which it is organically created. The presence of the divine image in each human being regardless of gender, age, race, ethnicity, and religion, becomes the foundation of social equality that finds its expression in comprehensive justice, which, in turn, leads to omnipresent peace manifested as access to life for all. Thus, reflecting on societal justice and planetary flourishing, Jürgen Moltmann suggests that

> the old saying, *Fiat justitia pereat mundi*—'let justice be done though the earth perish'—is assuming deadly righteousness and justice. But if righteousness is supposed to create peace and life, the saying ought to run *Fiat justicia vivat mundi*—'let justice and righteousness be done so that the earth may live'.[125]

Indeed, the realities of equality, justice, and peace cannot be separated from one another. They are organically and functionally correlated as one becomes the prerequisite of the others.[126] This indivisible continuity is most

125. Jürgen Moltmann, *Ethics of Hope* (Minneapolis: Fortress, 2012), 164.

126. For an exploration of the relation between justice, forgiveness, and peace in the pursuit of the common good, see chapter 4 in the present book.

explicitly articulated in the Old Testament. Reflecting on its radical preoccupation with justice for the other, Levinas remarks,

> The Torah is transcendent and from heaven by its demands that clash, in the final analysis, with the pure ontology of the world. The Torah demands, in opposition to the natural perseverance of each being in his or her own being (a fundamental ontological law), concern for the stranger, the widow and the orphan, a preoccupation with the other person.[127]

The God of the Torah equates righteousness with justice for the poor, the oppressed, the disenfranchised (Deut 10:17–18; 16:19–20). This notion transcends abstraction and culminates in the demand for economic justice through concrete instruction for sharing one's access to life with the fellow human. The text of Deuteronomy 24:17–22 outlines an economic program that cultivates covenantal communal consciousness of responsibility for the other's well-being and commitment to distributive justice for the poor (summed up in the famous triad of "the alien, orphan, and widow,"[128] thus including the immigrant, the stranger, the ethnically and religiously other) while protecting their dignity.

> You shall not deprive a resident alien or an orphan of justice; you shall not take a widow's garment in pledge. . . . When you reap your harvest in your field and forget a sheaf in the field, you shall not go back to get it; it shall be left for the alien, the orphan, and the widow, so that the Lord your God may bless you in all your undertakings. When you beat your olive trees, do not strip what is left; it shall be for the alien, the orphan, and the widow. When you gather the grapes of

127. Emmanuel Levinas, *In the Time of the Nations*, trans. Michael B. Smith (London: Athlone, 1994), 61.

128. For an overview of the meaning and significance of this triad in the Old Testament, see Mark Sneed, "Israelite Concern for the Alien, Orphan, and Widow: Altruism or Ideology?" *Zeitschrift für die alttestamentliche Wissenschaft* 111, no. 4 (1999): 498–507. The author notes that the triad designates not simply the poor but those who are especially vulnerable in their poverty for they had no kin "to buttress them" and, therefore, had "to take their seats among the blind and lame who begged at the city gates." Sneed states that due to the "lack of kin network to support them" as well as the absence of "any kind of modern welfare system, these social categories were quite vulnerable to oppression (legal and illegal) and annihilation in ancient times" (500–501).

> your vineyard, do not glean what is left; it shall be for the alien, the orphan, and the widow. Remember that you were a slave in the land of Egypt; therefore I am commanding you to do this.

Indeed, the protection of human dignity is a fundamental concern of both the Mosaic law and the rabbinic tradition. An uninvited (not intentionally embraced as in ascetic practices) poverty humiliates and subjugates the person to degrading conditions of existence that could be partially alleviated by others' charity. While charity (in its conventional forms of monetary-giving or providing food, clothing, and shelter) temporarily breaks the cycle of suffering and want, it rarely offers long-term solutions. While it dignifies the giver, it may create a sense of helpless dependence in the recipient. While humanitarian relief is essential for economic interventions (and, as already observed, is a fundamental Christian mandate, Matt 25), the best form of charity to a healthy adult remains economic empowerment (inseparable from sociopolitical emancipation and demarginalization) through proper employment[129] and related infrastructural prerequisites, such as quality education and professional training, that permanently alleviate hunger and poverty and secure just financial compensation for one's labor.[130] Thus, the instructions of Deuteronomy 24:17–22 protect the dignity of the other by joining benevolence to their labor; all this takes place within the theological understanding that the only true owner of the land, and its fruit, as well as of one's life and personal possessions is God himself, and all in Israel stand equal before him (Lev 25:23–55). The Old Testament highlights charity as God's distributive justice, enacted on behalf of the needy via responsible human agency. The "ways of the Lord" are depicted as righteousness (*tsedaqah*, understood in terms of distributive justice) and justice (*mishpat*, associated also with retributive justice) (Gen 18:17–19), and humanity has to learn them in order to be transformed into his likeness. Thus, the psalmist writes, "I shall behold your face in righteousness; when I awake I will be satisfied, beholding your likeness" (Ps 17:15). Jonathan Sacks points out that the rabbinical tradition translated this verse as "I shall behold Your face through charity, and when I awake, shall be satisfied with Your likeness,"

129. Sacks, *To Heal a Fractured World*, 38.

130. Due to its limitations, the present paper cannot adequately engage the important issue of just pay; however, it could be anticipated that a just society would strive to establish/legislate a minimum wage that is at least equal to (and hopefully even higher than) the properly calculated living wage.

or "I, through charity shall behold Your face."[131] According to Sacks, this is not an unusual translation. *Tsedaqah* is virtually untranslatable because it joins two seemingly mutually exclusive notions—charity and justice, thus articulating a concept of charity as justice.[132] Since not the individual person but God is the owner of everything that exists, then charity is distributive justice. Therefore, (in light of Ps 17:15) charity is a transformative/transfiguring religious experience; it is enactment of the character and nature of God in the world; it is partaking in the divine nature that translates us into the divine presence face to face with our Creator—a redemptive, restorative interface as recollection of Eden in beholding the very countenance of God.

Uplifting the moral character of God, Scripture insists that he loves righteousness (*tsedaqah*—charity as distributive justice) and justice (*mishpat*—retributive justice) (Ps 33:5; 37:28). They are the foundation of his throne (his rule and authority in the universe) (Ps 89:14; 97:2) and "lovingkindness [*hesed*] and truth go before" him (Ps 89:14). When embodied by humanity, *mishpat* and *tsedaqah* become the pathway to redemption (Isa 1:27), and God seeks to cultivate them within his people. Thus, Isaiah 5:7 depicts Israel as the Lord's vineyard in which he looks for righteousness/charity and justice as the fruit of his likeness, but disappointed he finds only "bloodshed" and "a cry of distress." Israel is not fulfilling its destiny to image the Lord in the cosmos; instead they practice oppression and violence against the other (a concern that blazes in the heart of prophetic critique—Jer 22:13; Ezek 22:29; Amos 6:12). They have "committed robbery, and they have wronged the poor and needy and have oppressed the sojourner without justice"; the Lord has "searched for a man among them who should build up the wall and stand in the gap" before him for the land, that it may not be destroyed, but he has found no one (Ezek 22:29–30). No doubt, the hearer of these words is reminded of Abraham's intercession on behalf of Sodom and Gomorrah, a striking conversation with God that reasserts God's righteousness and justice in the midst of a dehumanized and violent world (Gen 18:17–33).[133] Yet

131. Sacks, *To Heal a Fractured World*, 41. There the author quotes the Babylonian Talmud, Baba Batra 10a.

132. Sacks, *To Heal a Fractured World*, 32. As Sacks observes, in the Western mind the two notions usually don't intersect. If a person gives money to another, the recipient is either entitled to it or not. In the first case, the act of giving the money is justice, in the second, charity.

133. Inspired by the concept of embodied righteousness as a bridge of intercession on behalf of the world, the Jewish mystical tradition speaks of *Lamed-Vav Tzadikim* (or *lamedvovniks*)—thiry-six righteous people because of whom the world continues to exist and is not destroyed. The most important characteristic that they all share is that they themselves don't

God's promise is to renew and heal his people and all the earth by joining (betrothing) them to himself in righteousness and justice, in lovingkindness and compassion (Hos 2:19). They will be one with their maker in theosis for his law will be internalized in them; it will be written on their hearts; it will become their new nature in God (Jer 31:33) and their actions will translate their ontological renewal into the world, bringing it into accordance with the very Word that has made it.

Indeed, Deuteronomy 24:17–22 is a remarkable text that together with such passages as Deuteronomy 15:7–11, as well as the entire scriptural segment dealing with the institution of the Jubilee (the return of ancestral lands to their original owners and a "year of release" of the slaves), charts (as established by the Torah) what could be seen as "an early form of welfare state."[134] Yet, as Rabbi Sacks observes, the uniqueness of this socioeconomic construct is that it did not depend on the state and was not sustained by its power, but "by moral responsibility and the network of obligations created by the covenant at Sinai."[135] The law, as pedagogy of moral formation in the life of Israel, was to shape and form the people of God as a society of equals and assure equal dignity for all. Thus, Henry George remarks,

> the great concern of Moses was with the duty that lay plainly before him; the effort to lay the foundation of a social state in which deep poverty and degrading want should be unknown—where men released from the meaner struggles that waste human energy should have opportunity for intellectual and moral development.[136]

---

know that they are counted in that number. This Jewish belief is based on a talmudic assertion that in each generation there are thirty-six righteous individuals who "greet the Shekhinah," the very presence of God (Sanhedrin 97b; Sukkah 45b). In relation to the hospitality that Abraham offered to God which preceded his intercession for the two cities and which the rabbis spoke of as meeting/greeting the *Shekhinah*, see the commentary on the related talmudic passages by Nancy Flam in "'Pass Not Away': Yearning for a Seamless Life of Connection," in *Jewish Mysticism and the Spiritual Life: Classical Texts, Contemporary Reflections*, ed. Lawrence Fine, Eitan Fishbane, and Or N. Rose (Woodstock, VT: Jewish Light, 2010), 3–14.

134. Sacks, *To Heal a Fractured World*, 34.

135. Sacks, *To Heal a Fractured World*, 34. As Sacks states, "The message of the Hebrew Bible is that civilizations survive not by strength but by how they care for the poor; not by power but by their concern for the powerless. What renders a culture invulnerable is the compassion it shows to the vulnerable" (37).

136. Henry George, *Moses: A Lecture*. This famous text was delivered originally as a lecture in 1878 in San Francisco and in 1884 in Dundee, Scotland. Consequently, the text was published multiple times by various publishers. (It can be found as a free source at http://www

Indeed, in both Jewish thought and early Christianity the notions of equality and justice are inseparable. Thus, in the words of Philo of Alexandria, equality is "the mother of justice" and justice is the "offspring" of equality.[137] No doubt, the theme of equality as the foundation for justice continued to preoccupy Jewish thought during the time of Jesus and the apostles and was translated into the early Christian ethos as evidenced by such noncanonical Jewish-Christian texts as the Sibylline Oracles.[138] The oracles forecast a stunning eschatological vision of equality and social justice:

> And equal land for all, divided not by walls or fences; more abundant fruits spontaneous shall then bear, and the course of life be common and wealth unapportioned. For there no longer will be poor nor rich, tyrant nor slave, nor any great nor small, nor kings nor leaders; all alike in common.[139]

As equality births justice, so justice bears peace. Thus, the oracles culminate in the proclamation of a transfigured world marked by the cessation of violence that encompasses the healing of all the earth as humanity's home:

> Nor sword nor uproar shall be on the earth; no more shall earth groan heavily and quake; nor shall war longer be on earth, nor drought, nor

.cooperativeindividualism.org/george-henry_moses-a-lecture-1878.html) The author asserts: "It is not the protection of property, but the protection of humanity, that is the aim of the Mosaic code. Its sanctions are not directed to securing the strong in heaping up wealth so much as to preventing the weak from being crowded to the wall. At every point it interposes its barriers to the selfish greed that, if left unchecked, will surely differentiate men into landlord and serf, capitalist and workman, millionaire and tramp, ruler and ruled. Its Sabbath day and Sabbath year secure, even to the lowliest, rest and leisure. With the blast of the jubilee trumpets the slave goes free, the debt that cannot be paid is canceled, and a re-division of the land secures again to the poorest his fair share in the bounty of the common Creator. The reaper must leave something for the gleaner; even the ox cannot be muzzled as he treadeth out the corn. Everywhere, in everything, the dominant idea is that of our homely phrase—'Live and let live!'"

137. For Philo, "the principle of equality" is the most important (praiseworthy) part of justice: "equality is a light which is never shaded" (*The Works of Philo Judaeus, Special Laws* 4, 42 [230]). (http://www.earlychristianwritings.com/yonge/book30.html)

138. For an inspiring theological engagement of the Sibylline Oracles, see Crossan, *God and Empire*, 78–82.

139. *The Sibylline Oracles*, book 2, 390–96, trans. Milton S. Terry (New York: Eaton and Mains, 1899), 20.

> famine, nor the fruit-destroying hail; but great peace shall be upon all the earth, and king to king be friend until the end of the age.[140]

These visions of social transformation affirm the indivisibility of political, economic, and ecological justice, and forecast the necessity of all three for the establishment of peace as access to life and healing of the cosmos. Lack of political justice breeds the conditions for economic exploitation and inequality. The same greed and self-indulgence that commodify the other and justify their savage exploitation underwrite the devastating exploitation of nature. As Moltmann remarks:

> There is a negative correlation between the social condition of human beings and their relationship to nature: if the exploitation of the work force is dominant in the social structures, then the relationship to nature will also be determined by exploitation of the earth's mineral resources. The exploitative relationship of the human being to nature will stop only if the exploitative relationship of people to one another stops too. Ecological justice will only be acquired at the same time as economic justice.[141]

In the wise and righteous structure of the universe are visible "the checks and balances" of divinely established limitations/boundaries that are not to be transgressed. Thus, ecological limits are placed on economic growth,[142] which in turn make terminal to both society and nature the unrestrained exploitation of one human being by another. Therefore, the law is given as the words of comprehensive justice (a verbalized expression of God's righteousness and providential care for creation) that articulate these limitations and bring the warning that the choice between their fulfillment or transgression makes all the difference between life and death, between a blessing and a curse (Deut 11:26), not only for the individual, but for his or her community and the rest of the world.

The divinely imposed guards/restrictions against economic and ecological injustice and social inequality built within the structures of the cosmos are made explicit within the (mandated by the law) liturgical life of Israel—a perpetual, living memorial of the original act of creation and its onto-

140. *The Sibylline Oracles*, book 3, 935–39.
141. Moltmann, *Ethics of Hope*, 221.
142. Moltmann, *Ethics of Hope*, 221.

logical renewal through redeemed human communal agency. The human communal covenant grafted within the covenantal communion with God uplifts the radically equalizing demands of the Sabbath (and the Sabbath year) extending rest to both the anthropic and nonanthropic creation as well as the elaborate instructions of the Jubilee along with the commands concerning giving every third year a tithe to charity for the needy, including the noncovenantal strangers and foreigners dwelling among the people of God. Therefore, nonidolatrous worship is manifested in the immediate communal effects of equality and justice as access to life for all of God's creatures.

It is not accidental that the New Testament summation of the law and the prophets is articulated in Jesus's teaching as love for God and neighbor. Love for God as the ultimate other is expressed in love for the immediate other and manifested as intentional, proactive care for their flourishing. Therefore, the love of God is experienced by the fellow human as a distributive justice. As John Dominic Crossan proposes, "justice and love are a dialectic" in which: "Justice is the body of love, love is the soul of justice. Justice is the flesh of love, love is the spirit of justice. When they are separated, we have a moral corpse. Justice without love is brutality. Love without justice is banality."[143]

Since distributive justice is inscribed in the very ontology of creation and is indispensable from its all-summoning destiny in union with its just Creator (accomplished through the socio-transformative pedagogy of communal, liturgical life), both the Old and New Testaments take a passionate stand against any attempt to use worship in order to avoid doing justice to the fellow human. Thus, the prophetic critique of Hosea 6:6 insists that God desires steadfast love and not sacrifice, "the knowledge of God rather than burnt offerings." This knowledge, evidenced as the living embodiment of the divine Word, prioritizes (in the words of Walter Brueggemann) "covenantal solidarity over cultic activity"; it seeks the well-being of one's neighbor as the fundamental form of worship in response to the recognition of the divine omnipresence in the world. Acts of distributive justice consecrate the human community and the rest of creation as a sacred space for encounter and communion with God; they unveil a renewed vision of the cosmos as a temple and of distributive justice as a sacramental practice that humanizes the human community, displaying (making once again visible) the divine image within the cosmic sanctuary. Undoubtedly, some of the strongest negations of the utilization of worship as a substitute for justice are found in

143. Crossan, *God and Empire*, 190.

the words of Isaiah, Jeremiah, and Amos. The famous text in Isaiah 1:14–17 shakes the reader with its uncompromising refusal to accommodate injustice under the cover of religious devotion:

> Your new moons and your appointed festivals my soul hates; they have become a burden to me, I am weary of bearing them. When you stretch out your hands, I will hide my eyes from you; even though you make many prayers, I will not listen; your hands are full of blood. Wash yourselves; make yourselves clean; remove the evil of your doings from before my eyes; cease to do evil, learn to do good; seek justice, rescue the oppressed, defend the orphan, plead for the widow.

The denial of justice to the needy is depicted as bloodshed, an act of premeditated violence against them. The blood of the fellow human cries out to God from the palms of the very hands lifted for worship in his presence, demanding divine intervention. Eventually, retribution comes as banishment from the land, for exile becomes the only way of cleansing it from the evil nested in its people. Thus, Jeremiah 6:20 reechoes the assertion that cultic activity will not compensate for the injustice done by Israel ("Your burnt-offerings are not acceptable, nor are your sacrifices pleasing to me") and proclaims the only conditions under which the divine verdict would be altered, for instead of burnt offerings, the Lord "delights" in "steadfast love (*hesed*), justice (*mishpat*) and righteousness (*tsedaqah*)"—the very marks of his own activity on earth (Jer 9:24) that the ones called by his name should also enact as the way of their worship-embodied life.[144] Therefore, Yahweh states,

> Amend your ways and your doings, and let me dwell with you in this place. Do not trust in these deceptive words: "This is the temple of the Lord, the temple of the Lord, the temple of the Lord." For if you truly amend your ways and your doings, if you truly act justly one with another, if you do not oppress the alien, the orphan, and the widow, or shed innocent blood in this place, and if you do not go after other gods to your own hurt, then I will dwell with you in this place, in the land that I gave of old to your ancestors for ever and ever. (Jer 7:3–7)

144. For a more in-depth reflection on Jer 9:24, see Brueggemann, *Journey to the Common Good*, 62–63.

Perhaps the strongest protest against concealed-in-worship injustice is found in Amos 5:21–24 (paraphrasing the divine discontent expressed in Isa 1:14–17):

> I hate, I despise your festivals, and I take no delight in your solemn assemblies. Even though you offer me your burnt-offerings and grain-offerings, I will not accept them; and the offerings of well-being of your fatted animals I will not look upon. Take away from me the noise of your songs; I will not listen to the melody of your harps. But let justice roll down like waters, and righteousness like an ever-flowing stream.

Using cultic activity as a compensation for the lack of justice is a perversion of the very essence of creation in which the glory of the Creator is (in Sallie McFague's beautiful paraphrase of Saint Irenaeus) "every creature fully alive."[145] Therefore, worship without justice is idolatry : it serves other gods (among which are greed, egoism, and self-indulgence), sacrificing before them the very life and well-being of the fellow human and the rest of creation. The gospels join the warning against such idolatrous distortion of God's world (and thus, of the very Word inscribed in its fibers and articulated in the law as the way to life) by asserting the impossibility of serving both God and "Mammon" (Matt 6:24; Luke 16:13). Matthew 15:5–9 and Mark 7:10–13 condemn worship without distributive justice as "invalidating" God's Word by the practice of religious traditions. The teaching of Christ, the embodied Word, recollects in these gospel passages the words of Isaiah 29:13: "these people draw near with their mouths and honor me with their lips, while their hearts are far from me, and their worship of me is a human commandment learned by rote."

The Synoptic Gospels' protest against the religious justification of injustice culminates in the so-called "cleansing of the temple" scene (recorded in Matt 21:12–16; Mark 11:15–17; Luke 19:45–46). This is a depiction of the Son of Man's prophetic act of reconsecrating "the house" of the Creator and its cultic function as a sanctuary for God's entire household (that includes "all the nations," Mark 11:17) and with it symbolically purifying all of creation (the cosmic temple) for its sacramental purpose—the indwelling of and communion with the divine presence. This radical gesture could be understood

145. Sallie McFague, *Life Abundant: Rethinking Theology and Economy for a Planet in Peril* (Minneapolis: Augsburg Fortress, 2001), 3.

as a symbolic summary and enactment of the first parousia's mission. Both the divinely constructed temple (cosmic creation)[146] and its human-made replica are to be places of safety, healing, and generous hospitality to God's creatures, but instead they have been usurped and permeated with systemic violence against the other through the practice of economic injustice. The use of religious authority to justify extortion and racketeering has reduced the temple to a "robbers' den." In light of this, John Dominic Crossan sees in this scene "a symbolic destruction of the Temple" based on the prophecy of Jeremiah 7:14: "I will do to the house which is called by My name, in which you trust, and to the place which I gave you and your fathers, as I did to Shiloh."[147]

This striking, deliberate act of the incarnate Word (previously spoken through the prophets) finds its conclusion in the healing of all "the blind and the lame" who come to him in the temple (Matt 21:14), thus embodying the restored purpose of the sacred structure as the location from where the healing of the entire cosmos is initiated. Indeed, as N. T. Wright observes, in this intense scene, Jesus reveals himself as the "one-man-temple-alternative"[148]—in him God has accomplished the telos of humanity (its renewed ontology) as a divinely constructed, living temple for his presence. There the poor and the needy find access to life more abundant.

No wonder the scene appears as a prelude to the passion of Christ. There is no other way to put an end to the world's violent brutalization except by absorbing it into himself and refusing to retaliate as his tortured, broken body engulfs all victimization of the other and his death swallows death and the grave. As all of his life, Christ's passion is a fulfillment of the Word and an authenticating illustration through embodiment of his teaching. (Indeed, in his life and death, the incarnate Word interprets and fulfills the proclaimed and written Word.)[149] Thus, the passion becomes an enactment of the last two of the six great precepts recorded in Matthew 5:38–45 and considered the foremost distinction of Christian ethics:

146. For more on creation as the first God-made sanctuary/temple and the temple in Jerusalem as its replica, see chapter 3 of this book.

147. Crossan, *God and Empire*, 133.

148. N. T. Wright, "Jesus' Self-Understanding," in *The Incarnation*, ed. Stephen T. Davis, Daniel Kendall, S.J., and Gerald O'Collins, S.J. (New York: Oxford University Press, 2002), 47–61, there 57.

149. Indeed, as Anthony Godzieba points out, "the embodied enactment of the values" of God's kingdom "is critical to their claim to truth." "'Stay with us . . .' (Luke 24:29)–'Come, Lord Jesus' (Rev. 22:20): Incarnation, Eschatology, and Theology's Sweet Predicament," *Theological Studies* 67 (2006): 783–95 (791).

> You have heard that it was said, "An eye for an eye and a tooth for a tooth." But I say to you, Do not resist an evildoer. But if anyone strikes you on the right cheek, turn the other also. . . . Love your enemies and pray for those who persecute you, so that you may be children of your Father in heaven; for he makes his sun rise on the evil and on the good, and sends rain on the righteous and on the unrighteous.

The paschal suffering of the Messiah is a decisive refusal to perpetuate the cycle of violence induced by humanity's sin in the world: refusal that culminates in forgiveness to the perpetrators (which, in the transepochal reality of Christ's crucifixion, extends beyond "Jewish religious cooperation with Roman imperial control"[150] to encompass all humanity). Thus, in its mystical essence of all-engulfing cosmic redemption, Christ's violent death on the cross marks the ultimate end of violence against the other and the beginning of peace as reconciliation with God and neighbor. The cross's salvific power points to the paradox of peace building, in which the victim is "the one who has the key to a real and fundamental reconciliation, because it is in the victim that Jesus Christ is present."[151] Thus, each act of forgiveness drives the cosmos to its eschatological telos of summoning in the cosmic Christ. If creation comes forth as means of communion with God and a Christoforming pedagogy, then forgiveness is anticipated by and "written into the structure of the universe."[152] As Teilhard de Chardin's breathtaking prose reminds us,

> One day, the Gospel tells us, the tension gradually accumulated between humanity and God will touch the limits prescribed by the possibilities of the world. And then will come the end. The presence of Christ, which has been silently accruing in things, will suddenly be revealed—like a flash of light from pole to pole. Breaking through all

150. Crossan, *God and Empire*, 132.

151. Emilio Castro, "Reconciliation," in *The Ecumenical Movement: An Anthology of Key Texts and Voices*, ed. Michael Kinnamon and Brian E. Cope (Geneva: World Council of Churches, 1997), 67.

152. Sacks, *To Heal a Fractured World*, 25. Reflecting on the pedagogical function of creation, Sacks points out that in the process of learning "we will stumble and fall, but only by so doing does a child learn to walk. . . . God asks us only to acknowledge our mistakes and to learn from them." Therefore, forgiveness is anticipated by and inscribed within the reality of creation's pedagogy.

> the barriers within which the veil of matter and the water-tightness souls have seemingly kept it confined, it will invade the face of the earth.[153]

Until that day when Christ will shine forth through the opacity of his creation, becoming visible to all, his indwelling presence is unveiled in courageous love for God and neighbor amidst a violence-plagued world: a love that forgives, refuses to hate or to become the enemy, cherishes the other with their hopes for the future, and fills the space between oneself and the fellow human with healing acts of lovingkindness.

153. Pierre Teilhard de Chardin, *The Divine Milieu* (New York: HarperCollins, 2001), 129–30.

Chapter 3

Recovering of Eucharistic Being in a Market-Shaped World

The world is a market! Hardly anyone would contradict this statement today. The process of globalization, as the technologically induced compression of time and space, has lent a true sense of omnipresence to Western neoliberal capitalism and its all-commodifying market logic. Global economic integration has insured that the entire world may share the devastating impact of each crisis engineered in the prosperous stock markets of the West by unholy trading and lending practices. Thus, in 2008 the global economy absorbed and "equitably" distributed the negative outcome of Wall Street's moral irresponsibility, making everyone pay for the greedy appetites of a few. It could be argued that every person in the world was/is subjugated in one way or another to the effects of this economic crisis (e.g., through the loss of "investments, retirement, college savings; a home lost to foreclosure or a job lost to cutbacks; or simply the increased debt burden"[1] of national governments as well as through the reduction of charitable giving toward international and domestic projects).[2]

Yet we are told that moral values are irrelevant to the market—that markets are morally neutral and navigated by scientifically assessable economic

1. Rebecca Todd Peters, "Examining the Economic Crisis as a Crisis of Values," *Interpretation* (April 2011): 154–66 (154).

2. In their 2012 book *Declaration*, Michael Hardt and Antonio Negri argue that "neoliberalism and its crisis have shifted the terms of economic and political life, but they have also operated a social, anthropological transformation, fabricating new figures of subjectivity." For example, the "hegemony of finance and the banks has produced *the indebted*" (9). As the authors state, being in debt "is becoming the general condition of social life" today (10). In a way, "*debtfare*" has become the substitute to *welfare*. Hardt and Negri assert that exploitation's primary manifestation today is not unequal exchange but debt, transforming the creditor-indebted relationship into a new master-slave mode of existence in which the poverty of the enslaved "is characterized primarily by the chains of debt" (13) (*Declaration* [Argo Navis Author Services, 2012]).

laws of production, consumption, and exchange. The claim of neoliberal economics is that everything can potentially be commodified and sold by the market, and that since the market is neutral, impersonal, and automatic it can function "without systems of justice based on natural law."[3] As M. Douglas Meeks points out, "the great fascination of the market is the assumption that we have finally found a way to organize mass human behavior without dominion, authority and coercion."[4] However, the father of neoliberal (or "neoclassical") economics, Adam Smith, utilized rather morally charged language in developing his political economy. He insisted that the common good is an eventual outcome of the personal pursuit of wealth and economic self-interest. Smith asserted the guidance of society by "the invisible hand" of divine providence in accomplishing the betterment of all while indulging individual interests and desires.[5] Other thinkers of the time affirmed Smith's idea that personal greed functions as a virtue in this model of market economy since its final end leads to a richer society as a whole.[6]

3. M. Douglas Meeks, *God the Economist: The Doctrine of God and Political Economy* (Minneapolis: Fortress, 1989), 38.

4. Meeks, *God the Economist*, 38.

5. Adam Smith, *The Theory of Moral Sentiments* (New York: Augustus M. Kelley, 1966), 304. In this particular work, Smith advocates a connection between human greed and divine providence in God's "care of the universal happiness of all rational and sensible beings" (210). For further reading on Smith's ideas about the function of self-interest, see his work *An Inquiry into the Nature and Causes of the Wealth of Nations* (London: William Benton, 1955). While a superficial reading of his work in economics may give an impression of a secular rationale in support of his analyses and corresponding conclusions, many researchers have suggested that we view Smith as a "life-long moral philosopher, who never casts aside his earlier concerns about human morality in his later pursuit of economic truths" (Kathryn D. Blanchard, *The Protestant Ethic or the Spirit of Capitalism: Christians, Freedom, and Free Markets* [Eugene, OR: Cascade, 2010], 57). Such an understanding of Smith necessitates keeping in dialectical tension his two main works, namely, *The Theory of Moral Sentiments* and *An Inquiry into the Nature and Causes of the Wealth of Nations*, and it assumes that the second text is somehow informed and shaped by the first. If this is true, "then Smith can be seen as promoting an economic model that is based on socially sanctioned ethical norms supported by appropriate and just social institutions" (Blanchard, *Protestant Ethic or the Spirit of Capitalism*, 57). Some authors go as far as to suggest that Smith is in fact a moral theologian and that his elaboration on the "invisible hand" is "his particular contribution to eighteenth-century theodicy" (Lisa Hill, "The Hidden Theology of Adam Smith," *European Journal of the History of Economic Thought* 8, no. 1 [2001]: 1–29 [22]). Hill articulates the various interpretations of the function of "the invisible hand" in Smith's work, e.g., lexical and metaphorical, critical and ironic, evolutionary Darwinian, theological assertion of divine providence, and others.

6. Munyaradzi Felix Murove, "Perceptions of Greed in Western Economic and Religious Traditions: An African Communitarian Response," *Black Theology* 5, no. 2 (2007): 220–43.

Neoliberal economics claim that profit and efficiency "are the end goals of any rational economy," yet deny the fact that these goals function as moral values in society "by guiding behavior and decision-making."[7] As Rebecca Todd Peters asserts,

> By establishing that economic theory does, in fact, privilege certain values, we are able to ask why these values are more important than justice, compassion, and environmental sustainability. Thus, we open up the possibility for the important conversation about what values ought to guide decision-making in economic theory and in the business community.

Awareness of the fact that economics are not morally neutral raises the important question regarding the legitimacy of the undiscerning marriage between Western Christianity and the neoliberal market economy. Christianity has lent its spiritual authority to the market—hallowing its values, partaking (often indiscriminately) in its commodifying practices, and benefiting by its mechanism of turning speculative promises into easy money. As William E. Connolly (Krieger-Eisenhower Professor of Political Theory at Johns Hopkins University) has observed, neoliberalism in America "lives off the larger cultural ethos within which it is embedded, without committing itself publicly to all aspects of it."[8] Neoliberalism feeds off

> the spiritual support of constituencies that claim that the market is divinely inspired, that state support of ecological and egalitarian practices constitutes an attack on the divine order, and that microeconomic experiments with the property form, consumption practices, and the work process assault American exceptionalism.[9]

The irony of joining the conviction of divinely ordained and guided capitalism with "the neoliberal faith in the market as nearly self-sufficient, self-equilibrating system" is that these are mutually contradictory ideas. While global society is now painfully aware that there is no such thing as a totally self-regulating market, the problematic union of these two convictions is

7. Peters, "Examining the Economic Crisis as a Crisis of Values," 160.

8. William E. Connolly, "Capitalism, Christianity, America: Rethinking the Issues," *Political Theology* 12, no. 2 (2011): 226–36 (228).

9. Connolly, "Capitalism, Christianity, America," 229.

further fortified through the assertion made by proponents of neoliberalism (e.g., Milton Friedman) that "because profit-making is the essence of democracy," any government that pursues stricter market-regulation policies "is being anti-democratic."[10] Paradoxically, however, as Robert W. McChesney has argued, the assertion of the "sacredness" of the market actually has had a demoralizing and deconstructive effect on the democratic process because it eventually depoliticizes the citizens. "If electoral democracy affects little of social life, it is irrational to devote much attention to it."[11] Therefore, regardless of change of governments, no essential change can be expected within the economic system. McChesney further insists that

> Neoliberal democracy with its notion of the market *über alles*, takes dead aim at this sector. Instead of citizens, it produces consumers. Instead of communities, it produces shopping malls. The net result is an atomized society of disengaged individuals who feel demoralized and socially powerless.[12]

Western Christianity cannot keep ignoring that both neoliberal economic theory and its application are morally charged, often in ways that stand in conflict with the foundational values of Scripture and Christian tradition.[13] Christianity cannot afford to be indifferent in the face of the comprehensive "objectivity" of the market that prioritizes profit over people and remains blind to the creation of a nonmarketable populace which is alienated from the cycle of production and consumption, by virtue of lacking market value. The weak, the young, the elderly, and the handicapped are among this "surplus"[14] humanity excluded from the bliss of market society.

While critically reexamining the moral values of neoliberal capitalism, Western Christianity could employ its own spiritual resources in reenvisioning the function of *oikonomia* within the global *oikos*—the planetary household—by summoning economics to moral responsibility and empha-

10. Robert W. McChesney, introduction to *Profit over People: Neoliberalism and Global Order*, by Noam Chomsky (New York: Seven Stories, 1999), 7-16 (9).

11. McChesney, introduction, 10.

12. McChesney, introduction, 11.

13. Peters, "Examining the Economic Crisis as a Crisis of Values," 156-58.

14. In his work, M. D. Meeks develops the concept of "surplus people" who do not fit in the logic and cycles of the market economy. See "The Church and the Poor in Supply-Side Economics," *Cities* 1 (Fall 1983): 6-9.

sizing the importance of moral and social values in economic development.[15] M. Douglas Meeks defines *oikos* as "access to livelihood."[16] For home

> is where everyone knows your name. Home is where you can always count on being comforted, forgiven, loved, and cared for. Home is where there is always a place for you at the table. And, finally, home is where you can count on sharing what is on the table.[17]

If we apply this poetic definition of home to planet Earth as the *oikos* of contemporary global society, we may conclude that almost two-thirds of the planet's population is homeless, for they live in poverty—in subhuman conditions with scarce access to livelihood.[18] As Daniel G. Groody remarks, when looked at from "below," "it becomes all the more evident that economic development in the global village has not always led to greater human development. Most of the world lacks the basic necessities for dignified human life."[19] Economic justice has become the central question of the *oikonomia* of the global village, and receiving justice is receiving "access to home."[20] The inadequacies of economic development are further highlighted by the growing awareness of the interdependence between ecological, economic and social sustainability. Therefore, concerns for economic justice have become closely linked with the demand for ecological justice as authors like Sallie McFague have identified nature as the "new poor" in the North Atlantic economies and called for its emancipation and inclusion in the planetary household.[21]

The Eastern European experience has proven that neither socialism nor capitalism holds the answer to solving issues of economic justice and sustainability in the world. As Nicolas Berdyaev asserts, both capitalism and

15. Bartholomew I, Archbishop of Constantinople and Ecumenical Patriarch, *Encountering the Mystery* (New York: Doubleday, 2008), 161.

16. Meeks, *God the Economist*, 33.

17. Meeks, *God the Economist*, 36.

18. For statistics on poverty in the global village, see Daniel G. Groody, "Globalizing Solidarity: Christian Anthropology and the Challenge of Human Liberation," *Theological Studies* 69 (2008): 250–68.

19. Groody, "Globalizing Solidarity," 258.

20. Meeks, *God the Economist*, 36.

21. Sallie McFague, "An Ecological Christology: Does Christianity Have It?" in *Christianity and Ecology: Seeking the Well-Being of Earth and Humans*, ed. Dieter T. Hessel and Rosemary Radford Reuther (Cambridge, MA: Harvard University Press, 2000), 29–45 (30). See also McFague's *Life Abundant: Rethinking Theology and Economy for a Planet in Peril* (Minneapolis: Fortress, 2001), 33–37.

socialism are ultimately motivated by individualism, and their displays of concern for the common good cannot be separated from this prioritizing of self-interest.[22] Both capitalism and socialism have substituted material means for the spiritual goals of life; both economic models are therefore unable to sustain authentic human rights and freedom (since these rights and freedoms represent high spiritual goals and have a spiritual origin).[23] Berdyaev points out that "the historical material force is a part of the spiritual historical reality" and that "the entire economic life of humanity has a spiritual base, a spiritual foundation."[24] Therefore, the spiritual root of economic injustice resides in the reversal of the natural hierarchism between spirit and matter, between spiritual and economic life, which manifests itself in the individualist inversion of social vision, and the secularization and fetishism of materialism and economics.[25] Economic individualism has substituted Mammonism for truth. "Economic Materialism," in turn, has declared the entire spiritual life of humanity "as being an illusion and a fraud,"[26] has obscured the spiritual nature of the world, demystifying it and depriving it of wonder. In view of this assertion, according to Berdyaev, "socialism is only a further development of the industrial capitalist system; it is the final celebration of its beginnings and a triumph of their universal spread."[27] Therefore, any expectation of social transformation that facilitates authentic human freedom and socioeconomic justice would demand a "revolution of the Spirit"[28] resulting in a renewed vision of the world that recaptures its spiritual identity and purpose. As Berdyaev points out, only the Spirit creates a brotherhood and sisterhood that are a realization of true freedom—as freedom in Christ. In this Christ-centered spiritual togetherness, or rather *sobornost*,[29] there is no "mechanical equality." There is also no contradiction and difference between "a right and an obligation."[30] Indeed, the *sobornost* of the faith community is the work of the Spirit, who trans-

22. Nicolas Berdyaev, *The New Middle Ages*, in vol. 2 of *Collected Works* (Sofia: Zachari Stoyanov, 2003), 515–607 (526, 530–31).

23. Berdyaev, *New Middle Ages*, 531–32; Berdyaev, *Philosophy of Inequality* (Sofia: Prozoretc, 1995), 113–15.

24. Nicolas Berdyaev, *The Meaning of History*, in vol. 2 of *Collected Works* (Sofia: Zachari Stoyanov, 2003), 299–514 (313).

25. Berdyaev, *New Middle Ages*, 531.

26. Berdyaev, *New Middle Ages*, 531.

27. Berdyaev, *New Middle Ages*, 531.

28. Berdyaev, *New Middle Ages*, 522.

29. For more on the concept of *sobornost*, see chapter 1 of the present book.

30. Berdyaev, *Philosophy of Inequality*, 115.

lates the communal life of the Trinity within the community of believers, making possible the sharing of life with the other in all of its wholeness. The personal freedom in the Spirit's *sobornost* does not contradict the freedom of the other, for it is not based on competition for the limited resources of the material world but rather on the eternal and infinite reality of divine love and grace. In this divinely initiated and infused *sobornost*, the hospitality of God is incarnated in the community of Christ as a gift of the Spirit, a gift of freedom to the other to be and to become.

On the day of Pentecost, the sociopolitical and economic reality of the kingdom of God is birthed in the womb of the church by the Spirit. What the Spirit creates is holy for it is the social form of the trinitarian communal life embodied within humanity—it is the life of the Holy God translated within the human *socium*. The economics of the Spirit transform the community of faith into God's household so that, in return, it may make the world into a home for all. The Spirit exposes the unsanctified nature of the market and reveals the sacredness of the world, created and given to humanity as a gift toward a holy communion with God and neighbor. In the last Adam humanity experiences the restoration of its ontological essence as a eucharistic being with a priestly mandate within the cosmos. This renewed ontology reunites economics with their spiritual foundations in the new Christlike consciousness of the believers.

Undoubtedly, Christianity can make a lasting contribution toward inspiring and building a new global economic ethos that prioritizes justice, compassion, and sustainability as guiding principles of economic management to the benefit of all God's creatures. After all, if attaining the likeness of God is the aim of the spiritual life, it means (as noted in chapter 1) that sanctification involves perfect "love for all of creation."[31] In light of the church's eschatological destiny of union with God in theosis, her fundamental social (and thus, also economic) program in the world should be the doctrine of the Trinity, of "God in communion, a social God."[32] As Bartholomew asserts, every form of human community "has as its vocation to become, each in its own way, a living icon of the Trinity."[33]

In light of the above, the remainder of the present chapter offers a theological reflection on some potential building blocks toward a new Spirit-inspired political economy. It highlights the reality of the world as eucha-

31. Bartholomew I, *Encountering the Mystery*, 94.

32. Bartholomew I, *Encountering the Mystery*, 133.

33. Bartholomew I, *Encountering the Mystery*, 133.

ristic sacrament, thus offering a vision of the cosmos that can motivate a politico-economic shift from the "sacred market" to a sacred world. The text examines the ontology and vocation of humanity (prior to the fall) as royal priests and stewards of the cosmos and takes a look at the correlation between Pentecost, holiness, and economics in the restoration of humanity's eucharistic priesthood in the world. Finally, the chapter offers an understanding of the Eucharist as pedagogy of disciplining desires and an antidote to the malformations of consumerism's secular liturgies.

The World as Eucharistic Sacrament

If the ongoing human project of world-making has its ontogenesis in God's infinite creative energies, then it is not accidental that human life unfolds into a procession of time organized into weeks as a perpetual memorial of the divine creative act. Each time segment of seven days becomes a cosmic echo of that event, resonating within the social fibers of the human community, casting forth all human life as a cultic replica of creation. God creates the world (nature and, arguably, the beginnings of culture) and gifts it to humanity, which in turn creates culture[34] by taking nature and adding to it its own life in the form of daily work illumined by creative imagination, which in a limited way recalls the divine creative act. The first seven days of the cosmic time-space continuum become the measure that marks all of time as its internal intentionality and driving principle. Thus, for the cycle of human productivity enwrapped in the liturgical anamnesis of everyday life, the experience of time appears as a sequence of six days of work

34. We have come to define culture as "what we make of the world." See Andy Crouch, *Culture Making: Recovering Our Creative Calling* (Downers Grove, IL: InterVarsity, 2008), 23. Therefore, many authors view nature as the creation of God and culture as the creation of humanity. See also Kathryn Tanner, *Theories of Culture: A New Agenda for Theology* (Minneapolis: Fortress, 1997), 28–29; and H. Richard Niebuhr, *Christ and Culture* (New York: Harper & Row, 1975), 32–34. Niebuhr concludes that "Culture is the 'artificial, secondary environment' which man superimposes on the natural. It comprises language, habits, ideas, beliefs, customs, social organization, inherited artifacts, technical processes, and values" (32). "The world so far as it is man-made and man-intended is the world of culture" (34). It could be argued, however, that if cultivation is the first, rudimentary stage of culture, the gateway to cultural creativity, then (according to the Genesis account) not only nature but also culture could be viewed as created (or, in the case of culture, at least initiated) by God, who not only brings the world into existence but performed the first act of cultivation, represented by the garden of Eden.

as worship culminating in the seventh day of "rest *as* worship."[35] This weekly movement creates a rhythm of life in which human world-making preserves the primordial memory of the cosmos emerging out of nothing as a materialization of the divine will under the bespeaking power of God's uncreated energies. Marked by the seven days of divine creation, weekly life becomes a liturgy that evokes the teleological procession of time and matter—from eternity toward eternity, from the Spirit toward the Spirit. In its sacramental substance, time guides the world toward its final consummation beyond its own boundaries into a new, never-ending "eighth day" that frames the gates of eternity—where the cosmos experiences "the gathering together and transformation of matter into spirit."[36]

This understanding of time and matter unveils the sacramental essence of the cosmos as being itself an exquisitely choreographed eucharistic liturgy intended to shape humanity into the likeness of the Creator. By participating in it, human beings learn solidarity with others in the shared cosmic nature that each one of them hypostatizes and yet all have in common. Therefore, as Dimitru Staniloae insightfully suggests,

> A separation of cosmic nature taken to the limit between human individuals is impossible. Too great or too unequal a separation of nature brings about war between persons and indeed war within human nature itself or else makes of the latter its slave. Precisely for this reason, everyone is able to contribute to the corruption not simply of a nature that belongs to himself [herself] personally, but also of that nature which belongs to all.[37]

Therefore, the God-given limitations of the material world are part of the intentional pedagogy of becoming like him—they press us to share life and grow spiritually out of selfishness into communal solidarity with others (striving for the common good), realizing that the only way matter can meet all existential needs is through the generosity of the Spirit. The liturgical nature of life as matter in communion with the Spirit is a pedagogical tool that teaches humanity to see the world otherwise—as a sacred space for an

35. John Dominic Crossan, *God and Empire: Jesus Against Rome, Then and Now* (New York: HarperOne, 2007), 54.

36. Dimitru Staniloae, *The World: Creation and Deification*, vol. 2 of *The Experience of God: Orthodox Dogmatic Theology* (Brookline, MA: Holy Cross Orthodox Press, 2005), 6.

37. Staniloae, *World*, 2.

encounter with the divine, as a cathedral where the life of God is seeded and gardened by the Spirit until it is fully grown into the materiality of the cosmos. This illuminated perspective cultivates human communal life of "work and sacrifice"[38] into an inspirited imaging of the Trinity's divine communal reality. It faces the limited resources of the world with the mandate for a new asceticism of surrender to solidarity in reverent consumption that gives to others "the possibility for development"[39] and flourishing. This is a mark of eucharistic existence that differentiates between the present stage of the world and its destiny in God and provides an antidote to the passions and desires that commodify the world by making it an end in itself.[40] A eucharistic consciousness nurtures a Godlike, self-sacrificial attitude for the life of the world (John 6:51). It shapes humanity into the form of Christ, who mends the world with his own life and offers it back to the Father whole, healed, and renewed.

As already articulated in chapter 1, in the act of creation, God gives the world to humanity in self-sharing as a gift of life so that humanity may, in turn, learn to share it with the other and the different. The world is a gift with a pedagogical function—helping humanity "grow spiritually"[41]—to grow in the likeness of God. This pedagogy (in the words of Staniloae) develops through the "dialogue of the gift" between the recipient and the giver, in which the world is to be continually received with gratitude and offered back to God in a gesture of self-sacrificial giving.[42] Therefore, since humanity does not have anything of its own to give to God, it learns to give back to the Creator from the creation (e.g., the tithe, the Sabbath). The greatest gift in this exchange is that of giving oneself, giving one's own life. This ultimate call to the likeness of God for humanity is communicated in God's self-giving in Christ.

38. Staniloae, *World*, 7.

39. Staniloae, *World*, 7.

40. Alexander Schmemann, *For the Life of the World* (Crestwood, NY: St. Vladimir's Seminary Press, 1983), 17.

41. Staniloae, *World*, 22.

42. Staniloae, *World*. "The paradox [of the return of the gift] is explained by the fact that the gift received and returned draws the persons close to one another to such an extent that the object of the gift becomes something common and comes to be the transparent means for the fullest communion between persons. And not only is the gift something common, but it is also increased through the life which the persons communicate to one another through the love manifested in the gift they make; in this way the persons give themselves as a gift, and through this giving they grow spiritually" (22). "The dialogue of the gift between God and the human person lies in the fact that each bestows himself upon the other" (23).

According to the paradoxical dialectic of the "complete dialogue of the gift,"[43] through the continual receiving and offering in return of the gift between two persons, they are drawn closer to one another until, in the words of Dimitru Staniloae,

> the gift becomes something common and comes to be the transparent means for the fullest communion between persons. And not only is the gift something common, but it is also increased through the life which the persons communicate to one another through love manifested in the gift they make; in this way the persons give themselves as gift, and through this giving they grow spiritually.[44]

Indeed, this logic affirms that the world cannot be kept for oneself—that it is made to be shared as a eucharistic communion with the other. Trying to keep the world for oneself—reducing it to a personal possession intended to satisfy one's own appetites and desires—distorts its meaning and purpose as a communion of matter and Spirit. Divorced from its spiritual dimension, the world is commodified and made an end in itself, and its material limitations are exposed together with the impossibility to satisfy the ever-present human demand for more of the world. As discussed in chapter 2, the realization that the world is not enough to satisfy the greed and self-indulgence of all persons causes alienation from and violence against the other, viewed now as a competitor for finite material resources. Being a pedagogy on becoming like God and a gift toward communion with him, the world becomes enough only when seen as having its origin, meaning, and end in God. The world is enough only when it is blessed and shared as a eucharistic gift with joy and gratitude, with the reverence of "liturgical askesis"[45] and self-giving for the life of the world.

43. Staniloae, *World*, 22.

44. Staniloae, *World*, 22.

45. For our purposes, "liturgical askesis" is understood as an act of *praktikē* (ascetic struggle) within the context of liturgy. As Margaret Pfeil asserts, *praktikē* takes place "as the Christian worshiper's graced and free response to God's gratuitous love celebrated in Christian liturgy. First, liturgical asceticism springs from and seeks to nourish the life of the Christian worshiping community, and second, it implies an eschatological horizon in which the ultimate telos of askesis consists in the fullness of life in God" ("Liturgy and Ethics: The Liturgical Asceticism of Energy Conservation," *Journal of the Society of Christian Ethics* 27, no. 2 [Fall/Winter 2007]: 27–149 [127–28]). As David Fagerberg states, if liturgy means "sharing the life of Christ" and "if askesis means discipline (in the sense of forming), then liturgical asceticism is the discipline required to become an icon of Christ and make his image visible in our faces"

Therefore, in its true nature, the world is given as a gift by God, so that it may draw humanity closer to him, but also that it may be shared by fellow humans as the means/element of full communion with the other, for when we gift it to the other, we are offering it back to God (Matt 25:31–46). Part of the Christoforming pedagogy of the gift is that we are to give to the other more than what we have received from God (Matt 25:14–30)—we add to the gift our very life in the form of creative work that increases the value of what we have received as nature (e.g., grain and grapes are transformed through the askesis of human work into bread and wine before being offered eucharistically to God). This makes our offering a sacrifice for the life of the other. We give from ourselves to the other, and as they receive this gift, we become partakers in their life. In a way, we receive the world from God, in order to join our life to it and offer it back to God in a eucharistic surrender to the form and content of his own communal life. In this offering, we become like God in flesh—we become like Christ—the perfect eucharistic being who through the Incarnation took into himself the world to the cross, "circumscribing all that have their origin in him"[46] in order to welcome them into his resurrection. Therefore, the world is intended to lead the human being toward God and the resurrection (life eternal) as a renewed life of partaking in the divine nature. As Staniloae remarks, "In this sense all things found in the middle between God and the human person call for the cross,"[47] through which humanity detaches itself from the gift in order to be united with the giver. "By returning to God the gift of nature transformed by the askesis of our work and through the imprinting of the cross," we sanctify the cosmos and refuse to continue making it an end in itself, thus also sanctifying ourselves. In doing so, we recognize our destiny in God and enact it in self-giving to the other. We become like him—we become holy with his communal holiness of shared life in self-giving love.

As already noted in chapter 1, the narrative of Genesis depicts God not only creating within the divine communal self a sanctuary for the possi-

("A Century on Liturgical Asceticism," *Diakonia* 31, no. 1 [1998]: 41). Liturgical asceticism "involves a contemplative awareness of the practices of the worshiping community as *leitourgia*, the work of the people of God at the service of the world" (Pfeil, "Liturgy and Ethics," 134). Traditionally, however, askesis is not understood only as the means of becoming like God, but as a mark of theosis (e.g., in the hagiographies of the saints). Askesis is imitation of God in Christlikeness, by applying the cross to the totality of one's life. Ultimately, it is fasting from oneself for the sake of the other, motivated by self-giving love.

46. Saint Maximus the Confessor, *Gnostic Chapters* 1.67, Patrologia Graeca 90:1108B.

47. Staniloae, *World*, 25.

bility and flourishing of the other, but also building a home for them.[48] He takes time in carefully crafting and furnishing this home according to the physical needs of his creatures so that they may truly have access to life more abundant. It could be argued that the unconditional hospitality of God in the act of creation culminates in the establishing of the Sabbath as a day of rest. Time is both an outcome of creation and the canvas on which God spreads the universe. Therefore, John Dominic Crossan invites us to consider that it is not humanity on the sixth day but the Sabbath on the seventh day that is the climax of creation, and that our "dominion" over the world is not ownership but stewardship under the God of the Sabbath.[49] Therefore, the eucharistic nature of the world as a shared communion with God and neighbor is clearly visible in the reality of the Sabbath. The seventh day is a day of rest for all of God's creatures. This is the day in which God gives humanity relief from its labor and commands it to do likewise to the other. Both the anthropic and the nonanthropic creation are to enjoy the unconditional care of God in the Sabbath rest, a gesture of all-encompassing cosmic hospitality provided by the divine host for his creatures. Yet this hospitality is justice, and the recipients of the divine welcome are to extend it to others as an act of "God's own distributive justice."[50] Therefore, Sabbath rest is commanded for one's entire household and all his or her dependents—sons and daughters, male and female servants, farm animals and livestock. The Sabbath is justice as radical equality, from which even the resident alien who lives in Israel is not exempt (Deut 5:14). The Sabbath logic as all-comprehensive justice of divine hospitality is further translated into the Sabbath Year and the Sabbath Jubilee. This is not just "rest *for* worship but rest *as* worship,"[51] in recognition of the ownership of God upon all creation, including time, and of the creatures' full dependence on the divine grace as hospitality.

Reflecting on the relevance of the Sabbath's inherent political theology for today's economic existence of perpetual exasperated weariness, Walter Brueggemann contrasts the never-ending slavish work under Egyptian imperial oppression with the covenantal freedom of Sinai's "economy of neighborliness."[52] Thus, the author depicts the socioeconomic and political

48. For an exposition on God as an architect building and furnishing a house, see Crossan, *God and Empire*, 51–52.

49. Crossan, *God and Empire*, 53.

50. Crossan, *God and Empire*, 54.

51. Crossan, *God and Empire*, 54.

52. Walter Brueggemann, *Sabbath as Resistance: Saying No to the Culture of Now* (Louisville: Westminster John Knox, 2014), 6.

significance of the divinely instituted Sabbath rest as an "alternative and resistance"[53] to the all-commodifying, restless anxiety and dehumanizing effects of market logic, exposing its life-distorting idolatry. In Brueggemann's words,

> YHWH is a Sabbath-keeping God, which fact ensures that restfulness and not restlessness is at the center of life. YHWH is a Sabbath-giving God and a Sabbath-commanding God. Israel, for that reason, is always again to re-choose between "life and death" (Deut. 30:15–20), between YHWH and "the gods of your ancestors" (Josh. 24:14–15), between YHWH and Baal (1 Kgs 18:21), between the way of Torah and the way of sinners (Ps 1). Sabbath becomes a decisive, concrete, visible way of opting for and aligning with the God of rest.[54]

Observing the Sabbath becomes a weekly liturgy, depicting the recovered trust between humanity and the rest of creation as rooted in the covenantal trust between the newly consecrated human community and the Creator. If (in the conditions of the fall) the curse manifests itself as enmity (and thus mistrust) between Adam and the land, now worshiping the God of Sinai in the Sabbath rest becomes a prophetic anticipation of the curse's overturning and creation's ontological renewal. It is a glimpse of a recovered Eden—of the world being once again a sanctuary, and life an act of worship to the life-giving and life-sustaining Creator. Therefore, as Brueggemann points out, Exod 34:21 states that the Sabbath should be kept "even in plowing time and in harvest time," placing the institution of covenantal rest "in the context of the productive, food-producing creation system in which human beings must participate." Yet they also must "trust the land," conforming their life "to the rhythms of creation."[55] In this way, the Sabbath resynchronizes (and heals the rift between) the anthropic and nonanthropic creation, instituting a new, just relationship between humanity and the earth. It constitutes covenantal ecological economics that correct distorted interpretations of humanity's "dominion" over creation by bringing in view the original context of Gen 1:26–28—worship of the one true God in the cathedral of the cosmos. Therefore, a godly relationship between humanity and the rest of creation can flourish only within the context of

53. Brueggemann, *Sabbath as Resistance*, 21.
54. Brueggemann, *Sabbath as Resistance*, 10.
55. Brueggemann, *Sabbath as Resistance*, 36.

a life (including work, production, and consumption) lived with reverent intentionality, as an unceasing worship of the Creator, marked by acute awareness of and attuned attention to the sacramentality of the cosmos and the unescapable nearness of the divine presence. Living life as a eucharistic liturgy centers human existence on God, realigning one's being in the world with the divine creative intent and cultivating resistance to the idolatrous social pathology of self-centeredness (including its manifestations in greedy exploitation of one's fellow human and the rest of creation under escalating anxiety of scarcity and blinding fear of the other). Recovered awareness of the world as a eucharistic gift summons humanity into its priestly service and responsible stewardship for the flourishing of all creation on this side of the eschaton.

Royal Priests and Stewards of the Cosmos in the Eucharistic Economics of the Spirit

As established in chapter 1, the ontology of humanity before the fall is that of a community of priests in the cathedral of the cosmos, bearing the image and growing into the likeness of the communal Trinity amidst the material world. As a priest before God, Adam stands as the embodiment of the cosmic communion of matter and Spirit, representing in his very being a sacrament in which the icon of the cosmos and the icon of God are united together as an evocation of the destiny of the world, where God is to be all in all (Eph 1:23). Thus, human ontology is to be the materialization of the sacred story of the world, joining together the primordial memory of its beginning with the anticipation of its eschatological unfolding in union with the Creator. In the words of H. A. H. Bartholomew I,

> The Word of God wanted to reveal that humanity participates in both worlds, namely in invisible as well as in visible nature. . . . Therefore, Adam was placed on this earth as a second world, a large world within a small world, like an angel that worships God while participating in the spiritual and material worlds alike. Adam was created to protect and preserve the visible world, while at the same time being initiated into the spiritual world.[56]

56. Bartholomew I, *Encountering the Mystery*, 96. Here Patriarch Bartholomew seems to find inspiration in John of Damascus, who states the following in his reflection on humanity

Indeed, humanity is created to participate in both worlds in order to unite them into a living communion. Yet Scripture preserves the reminder that both the material and spiritual components of humanity have their origin in God. Matter is spoken forth out of nothing by the Word as an act of the Creator's "self-limitation" in opening space for the existence of creation[57]—an image epitomizing the essence of God as love for the other and the different. Consequently, the earth/nature (in a way, following the example of its Creator) shares her material body with humanity so that the human body may rise from her under the craftsmanship of the divine creative energies. Further, the human spirit comes forth as the very breath of God—as his self-sharing with the other. Matter is indwelled with the divine presence as the human body becomes a temple of the Spirit on earth. Indeed, humanity is an outcome of the other's self-sharing (in askesis and kenosis)—it comes from the other and is to embody the gift of life as a shared communion with others. Therefore, humanity is placed amidst the cosmos as an anointed/Spirit-filled, priestly, eucharistic, communal reality, in order to serve as an agent/mediator of the world's transfiguration into the likeness of God's communal life until the divine community becomes all in all. This ontologically engraved human vocation involves the continual eucharistic discernment of the world as a sacrament toward cultivating a cosmic community of shared life and flourishing with the other—with God as well as with the anthropic and nonanthropic neighbor. Therefore, as Orthodox theologians have suggested, we can understand the "original sin" also in terms of humanity's rejection of its priestly vocation in the cosmos, forfeiting its eucharistic existence and reducing the world from a divine gift

---

and its destiny in theosis: "God then made man without evil, upright, virtuous, free from pain and care, glorified with every virtue, adorned with all that is good, like a sort of second microcosm within the great world, another angel capable of worship, compound, surveying the visible creation and initiated into the mysteries of the realm of thought, king over the things of earth, but subject to a higher king, of the earth and of the heaven, temporal and eternal, belonging to the realm of sight and to the realm of thought, midway between greatness and lowliness, spirit and flesh: for he is spirit by grace, but flesh by overweening pride: spirit that he may abide and glorify his Benefactor, and flesh that he may suffer, and suffering may be admonished and disciplined when he prides himself in his greatness: here, that is, in the present life, his life is ordered as an animal's, but elsewhere, that is, in the age to come, he is changed and—to complete the mystery—becomes deified by merely inclining himself towards God; becoming deified, in the way of participating in the divine glory and not in that of a change into the divine being" (John of Damascus, *An Exposition of the Orthodox Faith*, book 2, chapter 12, "Concerning Man," available at http://www.newadvent.org/fathers/33042.htm).

57. Jürgen Moltmann, *The Trinity and the Kingdom* (Minneapolis: Fortress, 1993), 59.

of encounter and communion with God and neighbor to a utility toward one's own self-indulgence, thus making it an end in itself. To proclaim the world as an end in itself is to deny its contingency on God and therefore its created essence as originating in him. By denying matter's causality in God, humanity commits the idolatry of substituting God with matter. "For what is an end in itself is also without a cause,"[58] and such is God alone. If the human being is created not only as *homo sapiens* or *homo faber*, but first and foremost as "*homo adorans*,"[59] as a priest standing in the center of the world in order to unify it with the fulfillment of its destiny, then humanity worships what it perceives as an end in itself and looks for its own fulfillment in it. As a worshiping creature, humanity is created with an inherent longing for a union with God—for its self-realization in theosis. The peculiarity of the dialectic of worship, however, is that we worship what we love and we become what we worship. Indeed, worship is a transfiguring pedagogy on becoming like God that accomplishes its aim through the intentional askesis of fasting from one's own misdirected desires, turned from the Creator to the created (from God to the world, thus making it an end in itself). Therefore, right worship (*orthodoxy*) is disciplining and reordering the affections so that the worshipers may learn to love and be loved rightly (*orthopathy*) until they themselves (their entire lives) become love—God's love for all his creation (*orthopraxy*). This is why humanity is instructed to love God with the entirety of one's being (Deut 6:5; Matt 22:37; Mark 12:30; Luke 10:27) so that it may worship him alone and therefore be transformed into his likeness—experience theosis. Thus, idolatry endangers humanity's destiny by forming it into the likeness of something else (something less) than God—something created rather than the Creator.

The *theoforming* (Christoforming) reality of worship is to enflesh within the human community the Trinitarian perichoretic life as unceasing movement of love for the other. It turns our face toward God in order to become once again his face for others. Indeed, worship rehumanizes us, makes us once again a *prosōpon*, "countenance," turned toward others as an encounter with divine love, striving to provide what is lacking but needed for their flourishing.[60] Therefore, the divine perichoretic reality enfleshed within the human community is manifested as *philanthrōpia* (self-giving as love for the fellow human—emphasizing the shared sameness of humanity) and *philox-*

58. Saint Maximus the Confessor, *Ambigua*, Patrologia Graeca 91:1072B–C.
59. Schmemann, *For the Life of the World*, 15.
60. Bartholomew I, *Encountering the Mystery*, 132.

enia (self-sharing in hospitality as love for the stranger—highlighting the unique, irreproducible otherness of each human being). As God's redemptive love turns humanity's face toward the other, he or she becomes an unavoidable encounter with the image of God as unapologetic summoning to priestly responsibility for the life of the world. Perhaps the earth's spherical form can be understood as providential underlining of the world's reality as a sacrament toward communion with the other. In the words of Immanuel Kant, the fact that the earth is a globe means that we cannot be "infinitely scattered, and must at the end reconcile ourselves to existence side by side"[61] with the other. Even when we turn our back to others and their need, the curve of the globe takes us on a journey back face to face with them, denying the possibility for infinite distance. The saving grace of God leads humanity back to the beginning, to the encounter of the face—the image of God facing itself in the other until a person sees him or herself in the fellow human as in a mirror and thus is capable to love the other as oneself (Lev 19:18; Matt 19:19). The human journey back to God becomes pedagogy of discerning him in the other. Apart from seeing God's image in the other, one cannot see God. Apart from loving the other, one cannot love God (1 John 4:20). Salvation becomes a way of seeing God disguised in the body and face of the other, despite his or her socioeconomic, cultural, ethnographic, racial, gender, and language otherness. Thus, discerning Christ in the other, even in his or her most distressful condition (Matt 25:31–46), becomes the Christoforming power in one's life that ultimately allows one to see God. Seeing Christ in the other makes one like Christ—makes one a renewed eucharistic being. Each human being stands in the face of the other, imprinted with the same ontological origin and telos—Christ himself—the beginning and the end of creation (Rev 21:6). In this sanctified/deified perspective, the face of the other meets us as the future of the world—as the full potentiality of the fullness of life more abundant in, with, and through God. Therefore, there is no future, no salvation, no world without the other.

As *homo adorans*, a worshiping creature, *the priest* ministering before God on behalf of the entire creation,[62] the human being is made to hear the divine Word and respond to it in prayer. Humanity's ontological actualization is to be attained through partaking (via priestly intercession) in God's communal discourse, carrying the world in itself (in its body, mind/

61. Immanuel Kant, *Perpetual Peace: A Philosophical Essay*, trans. M. Campbell (New York: Grand, 1972), 138.

62. Schmemann, *For the Life of the World*, 15.

thoughts, and heart/affections) before God, making it "spoken of" within the Trinitarian liturgy of world-making and (in the conditions of the fall) world-mending—thus becoming a communicant (partaker) of the divine nature (2 Pet 1:4), attaining theosis. However, the Word addresses humanity not only as a summoning to priestly intercession but, ultimately, as a call to its prophetic embodiment/incarnation in the human community. Actualizing its prophetic calling, the human being is not just to hear the Word but to enact it as a free-willed doer of the divine will, thus becoming the Word's living, embodied extension amidst the created order. In light of this assertion, Alexander Schmemann describes humanity's priestly and prophetic vocation as inscribed from *the beginning* within human ontology alongside the royal mandate for just stewardship of all creation.[63] Scripture articulates the essence of these three ontological dimensions of human vocation (the royal, priestly, and prophetic) as *charisms* of the Holy Spirit—as the Spirit's movement within the world in enactment (and embodiment) of the divine will through consecrated/anointed human agency. Therefore, from the beginning, humanity is created to move in and with the Spirit and to be an in-Spirit-ed, pneumatized sanctuary of God's breath (his living and enlivening presence) within the cosmos (Gen 2:7).

In this pneumatological anthropology, the three charismatic dimensions of humanity's vocation (royal, priestly, and prophetic) are inseparable from each other—Adam is a king only to the extent to which he is a priest and a prophet. As Schmemann asserts, we have to understand these dimensions in light of their Christic/Christoforming telos—there is "not kingship alone and not priesthood alone, but their belonging together as fulfillment of one in the other"—thus "royal priesthood."[64] Therefore, the power ("dominion") of humanity over creation is "fulfilled in *sacrifice*" and in "*sanctifying* the world, by 'making' it into communion with God"[65] as the Holy Spirit transforms human life itself into "a 'liturgy,' a service to God and communion with Him."[66] In light of this outlook to human ontology, to be human is *to be for others* so that they may flourish and live life to the fullest.

Since Christ is the visible icon of the invisible God (Col 1:15), "the perfect Eucharistic Being,"[67] Pentecost marks the ontological renewal of the image of

63. Alexander Schmemann, *Of Water and Spirit: A Liturgical Study of Baptism* (Crestwood, NY: St. Vladimir's Seminary Press, 1974), 95.

64. Schmemann, *Of Water and Spirit*, 95.

65. Schmemann, *Of Water and Spirit*, 96.

66. Schmemann, *Of Water and Spirit*, 97.

67. Schmemann, *For the Life of the World*, 38. Schmemann states, "He alone is the perfect

God within the human community. This Christoforming significance of Pentecost could be further magnified in perceiving the Spirit's outpouring as transference of messianic anointing from Christ to the community of believers. They become the anointed ones as a living extension of the Anointed One—of his life and mission. In a manner similar to that of Jesus's ministerial inauguration (Luke 3:21–22) in Jordan's baptismal waters, the Spirit of Pentecost descends upon his own—the incarnated Christ in his communal form—baptizing and empowering it for the fulfillment of its mission as a living, embodied gospel destined to cover the earth. Therefore, the prophetic, royal, and priestly dimensions of Christ's ministry become inseparable from the charismatic reality of his body, as the community of disciples is transformed into a royal priesthood and prophethood of all believers.[68] On the day of Pentecost, the communal body of Christ, saturated by the self-pouring of the Spirit, becomes the restoration of humanity's ontology and vocation according to God's original creative intent. The Spirit manifests the church as the new, anointed, cosmic *homo adorans*, ordained to circumscribe all creation in union with the Creator.

The Spirit-saturated community enfleshes the Trinitarian life in all aspects of its existence, including its *oikonomia*. In the words of Saint Gregory the Theologian, the first Adam "was destined to serve as a royal steward"[69] (*basileus oikonomos*—a royal economist) over creation. The economic and priestly responsibilities of humanity coincide in their purpose of labor in love for the life of the world, which is the household of God. Therefore, the economic management of the world is to be the *oikonomia* of household based on sharing the family resources for the equal benefit of all its members. It is no wonder that the ethos of household sharing becomes visible in the economics of the Spirit, embodied in the Pentecost-marked life of the Christian community.

Like the nonanthropic creation,[70] the economic model of Pentecost follows the pattern of sharing versus trading of goods and labor—it follows

---

Eucharistic Being. He is the Eucharist of the world. In and through this Eucharist the whole creation becomes what it always was to be and yet failed to be."

68. On the prophethood of the Pentecost Community through a Pentecostal perspective, see Roger Stronstad, *The Prophethood of All Believers*, JPTSup 16 (Sheffield: Sheffield Academic, 1999), 65–70. See also chapter 2 of the present book.

69. Bartholomew I, *Encountering the Mystery*, 96.

70. If we look closely at the function of creation within the economic process, we will notice a different form of economic participation that does not follow market logic. Creation is not compensated for its contribution—therefore it does not participate in the economic exchange, but follows a model of sharing itself (and its resources) with humanity. It follows the model of the self-sharing and hospitality of its Creator.

the pattern of the Creator's self-sharing. The communal composition of the Pentecost model moves from the socioeconomic predicament of the market to that of the household. The relationships of the household are not based on the amount of capital or possessions the members have, but on their family bonds. In contrast to the market, the household does not produce and maintain class structure. The social position of the members of the household is based upon family roles, and any privileges that pertain to these are appropriated within the understanding of a mutual calling to one another as a part of the same family. The members belong to one another: they are each other's brothers, sisters, mothers, children, etc. They are called together in a shared family identity. The family's wealth is the wealth of all its members, who share freely in its benefits. Household material possessions are utilized by the household members for the common benefit of the household unit. The well-being of the household as a whole guarantees the well-being of all its members. It is not accidental that the family table is the centerpiece of the household and its economic model. It symbolizes sharing of the fundamental necessities of life between equals in identity and purpose. The family is nurtured and sustained as its members break bread together and share possessions—they share life and make life together.

The community of Pentecost as the household of God exhibits this family-like pattern of sharing life, which also naturally includes sharing of possessions. Their identity as children of God, born into one family by the same Spirit, outweighs any particularities of gender, ethnicity, and economic class. It establishes instead the dynamic of the traditional family roles, including caregiving, nurture, protection, and provision for the needs of all.

The image of household summons to responsibility the members of the family of God to care also for creation and its needs, for indeed, God's household includes all creation. The well-being of the entire household demands this compassionate care within the context of the members', illuminated by the Spirit, recognition of their mutual belonging. Adam and the *adama* stand in unavoidable, organic continuity of shared well-being. Therefore, the suffering of the nonanthropic creation (through unrestrained, careless exploitation and pollution) leads inevitably to human suffering, endangering human health and denying access to life to entire communities (as well as to the unborn generations). On the other hand, the flourishing of the earth secures the symbiotic flourishing of humanity in a sustainable ecosphere of carefully nurtured and gardened common good. Since the world is a gift with and an inherent pedagogy for humanity's spiritual growth toward its Christic telos, then the faithful economic stewardship of creation and perpetual priestly intercession for its life and flourishing are not merely human responsibilities before God but a divinely ordained vehicle for humanity's ontological actualization as the anointed king, priest, and prophet upon whom the Spirit rests, the temple in whom God finds his home amidst the cosmos.

Therefore, the response to the other as an act of economic and social justice in Pentecost's communal economics is not an outcome of sociopolitical persuasion but of spirituality that extends one's participation in the life of God and his presence on earth in the community of faith. This spirituality prioritizes the needs and well-being of the other as indispensable from the well-being of the entire household, while exercising discernment between personal needs and desires and disciplining one's desires toward the likeness of God.

There is a sense of spontaneity in the communal sharing of possessions, manifesting the life of the invisible Spirit now made visible within the body of Christ.[71] The sharing of possessions is an external expression of the believers' renewed ontology. This is their way of being in the world as new humanity—the material enfleshment of their spiritual identity as a communal extension and continuation of Christ's own life on earth.[72] What they do is who they are—the resurrected Christ incarnated by the kenotic agency of the Spirit into the redeemed community. Their corporeal life, as the life of God within the human *socium*, follows a Trinitarian logic of perichoresis that translates itself in all aspects of human existence (including economics).

71. Martin Hengel, *Property and Riches in the Early Church* (Philadelphia: Fortress, 1974), 32.

72. The incarnationalist view of Pentecost for which I have argued in previous works also allows us to consider the possibility of looking at the remainder of Acts as rooted in Christ's extended presence on earth in his body. Therefore, if the Gospel of Luke represents the first volume of "all that Jesus began to do and teach" (Acts 1:1), the book of Acts can be seen as the second volume, outlining "the continuation and fulfillment of what Jesus did and thought." Matthias Wenk, *Community-Forming Power: The Socio-Ethical Role of the Spirit in Luke-Acts*, JPTSup 19 (Sheffield: Sheffield Academic, 2000), 242. The author points to the outpouring of the Spirit at Pentecost as a clear example that the ministry of Christ (the baptizer with the Holy Spirit) continues in Acts (243). He mentions also the passages of Acts 9:5, 10; 13:39; 7:55–56; 17:7; 18:10; 19:15; and 25:19 as indicative of Jesus's acting upon the disciples. Another example is the healing of the beggar in Acts 3:1–16, "presented as a continuation of Jesus' healing ministry (Acts 4:30)" (245). Beverly Gaventa's work also supports the view of the book of Acts as presenting a continuation of the ministry of Jesus. See her commentary *The Acts of the Apostles*, Abingdon New Testament Commentaries (Nashville: Abingdon, 2003), 34, 62–63.

For indeed, in the all-comprehensive reality of the Incarnation, nothing remains outside the reach of salvation, "nothing can be taken away from the Son of man."[73]

Therefore, if "possessions are symbolic expressions of ourselves because we both are and have bodies,"[74] then surrendering our possessions to Christ is redemptive, accepting of his identity (and of his body) as our own. The Eastern fathers of the church saw the image of God in humanity as incorporating the totality of the human being—of its spiritual and material existence.[75] Therefore, the likeness of God also cannot exclude the body and its material extension of possessions. Scripture continually emphasizes the reality of the body when articulating the mandate for sanctification (1 Thess 4:3–8; 5:23; Heb 9:13–14; Rom 6:19), and (as noted in chapter 2) the sanctifying work of the Spirit involves the totality of human existence with all its social and material expressions in actions, relationships, and desires.

Indeed, the eucharistic priesthood of the last Adam reestablishes the perichoretic economics of the Spirit within the community of faith. Yet this pattern of sanctified economic relationship to the other is also present in the earthly ministry of Christ, prior to his death and resurrection. The gospel narrative of the feeding of the multitudes reminds the reader of Christ as the perfect eucharistic being unveiling the economic manifestation of the embodied Trinitarian communal life on earth. What God has provided (bread and fish) is offered back to him in a liturgy of gratitude; it is broken to be shared with the other in a eucharistic meal, in which nature gives itself to the other in the elements of communion, blessed and multiplied by God himself to feed his household. He is the host of this banquet in which all who desire to partake are given access to life—not only to the children of Israel, but also to the gentiles, as in the feeding at the Decapolis (Mark 8:1–10)—where Christ offers "the bread of God's table to people of all nations."[76] They

73. Alexander Schmemann, "The Missionary Imperative in the Orthodox Tradition," in *Eastern Orthodox Theology: A Contemporary Reader*, ed. Daniel B. Clendenin (Grand Rapids: Baker, 1995), 195–210 (201).

74. Luke T. Johnson, *Sharing Possessions: Mandate and Symbol of Faith* (Philadelphia: Fortress, 1981), 40.

75. Vladimir Lossky, *Orthodox Theology: An Introduction* (Crestwood, NY: St. Vladimir's Seminary Press, 2001), 71; Christoforos Stavropoulos, "Partakers of Divine Nature" in *Eastern Orthodox Theology: A Contemporary Reader*, ed. Daniel B. Clendenin (Grand Rapids: Baker, 1995), 186.

76. Brian K. Blount, "The Apocalypse of Worship: A House of Prayer for All Nations," in *Making Room at the Table: An Invitation to Multicultural Worship*, ed. Brian K. Blount and Leonora Tubbs Tisdale (Louisville: Westminster John Knox, 2001), 21.

are all God's offspring—they are all his family. This is a radical transformation of humanity's vision of the world. Not as a place of savage competition for limited material resources, but as a household where one shares freely his or her life with the other. It is, indeed, the transformation of the world from a market into a home.

In the economics of the Spirit within the community of faith, there is no one needy among them (Acts 4:34). Classism is abolished by the radical equality of the Trinitarian perichoretic life, to which humanity stands emancipated as partaker of the divine nature (2 Pet 1:4). The Pentecost community, as an outcome of the socio-transformative work of the Spirit, becomes the embodiment of God's hospitality and self-sharing with the other within the present with its pending material needs (Acts 2:43–47). This divine hospitality is an all-inclusive justice. It reunites economics with their spiritual foundations in the new Christlike consciousness of the believers. The consequence is a new form of economic relationships, that is, relationships that embrace the other and provide for their need out of one's own resources. The result is "having all things in common" (v. 44) and sharing possessions as a visible material expression of the *oikonomia* of God's household. These new economic relations set the Pentecost community apart from the economics of the world. Thus, one encounters in the midst of the world the doing of the Spirit,[77] who has birthed the believers into the sociopolitical reality of God's kingdom and has transformed them into an extension of that reality on earth. The Spirit is the one who initiates and sustains the conditions that make this radical economic justice possible, for such justice is an outcome of one's act of worship in Spirit and truth. Therefore, as was proven by the Eastern-European Marxist experiment, the secularization of this vision is destined to failure.

Breaking bread together (v. 46), as both daily commensality and eucharistic celebration of the unity of Christ's communal body, becomes a symbolic centerpiece of living out the just sociopolitical reality of the kingdom within the household of God.[78] The architectural placement of the com-

77. Miroslav Volf, *Exclusion and Embrace: A Theological Exploration of Identity, Otherness, and Reconciliation* (Nashville: Abingdon, 1996), 228–29. For an extensive study on the spiritual mandate of sharing possessions, see Johnson, *Sharing Possessions*. The author discusses the topic also in relation to the event of Pentecost (21).

78. In her book *Of Widows and of Meals: Communal Meals in the Book of Acts* (Grand Rapids: Eerdmans, 2007), Reta Halterman Finger offers an in-depth study of the daily commensality of natural- and fictive-kin groups in first-century Palestine. She examines the passages in Acts concerning the economic life of the early Christians on the background of social economic practices of the day and from the contextual viewpoint of the poor (especially widows

munal dining table in the Eastern Orthodox monasteries is an intentional reminder and a symbolic enactment of this reality. The dining table is positioned in a way that presents it as an extension of the sanctuary's altar. Therefore, the daily commensality of the community is viewed as a continuation of its communion around the table of the Lord. Each table becomes the Lord's table, for he is the host that gives sustenance to all. His presence is invited, and the meal is offered and blessed in his name with gratitude in recognition of being a gift from God as "our daily bread" (Matt 6:11; Luke 11:3). Indeed, we are forever his guests. Yet this is also our family table—the table of our Father—and we are at home, for we are his children and members of his household. Here we all have accesses to life that is shared as a sacrament for the consecration of the entire cosmos. In a way, the daily communal commensality echoes the words of the eucharistic offering—"Thine own of Thine own we offer unto Thee on behalf of all and for all." Therefore, hospitality to the stranger (including unexpected dinner guests) is a monastic rule. No one is turned away, and the table becomes a liturgical anamnesis of Christ's feeding of the multitudes, anticipating the epiclesis of the Spirit that makes the world more than enough. In this prophetic anticipation (to use the words of Brueggemann), "the gospel of abundance overrides the claim of scarcity and invites to the common good."[79]

The Eucharist as Pedagogy of Disciplining Desires and an Antidote to Consumerism

The church's pneumatic sacramental life (as part of the new creation) proceeds from and points to the "sacramentality of creation itself"[80] before the fall. It unveils the liturgical character of the world's *beginning* and its eucha-

---

and their daughters, who were one of the most economically destitute demographic groups). She emphasizes the communal daily breaking of bread both as sharing between kin in a communal eating and a sacramental practice, which originated with the meals Jesus shared with both Jews and gentiles. Some authors have distinguished between the *koinōnia* in Acts 2:42 and the breaking of bread as between communal and eucharistic meals. However, it is the presence of Jesus Christ that transforms a meal into a Lord's Supper. Therefore, the sacramental nature of sharing the meal in the name of the Lord, in evocation of his presence in the unity of his body on earth in thanksgiving, is translated in both daily commensality and the Eucharist.

79. Walter Brueggemann, *Journey to the Common Good* (Louisville: Westminster John Knox, 2010), 32.

80. Alexander Schmemann, *The Eucharist: Sacrament of the Kingdom* (Crestwood, NY: St. Vladimir's Seminary Press, 1987), 33.

ristic reality and depicts its *telos* in the joining of heaven and earth, of the visible and invisible, of the material and the spiritual, gathering *all* creation in Christ, who is to be *all in all*. This very *telos* (in the words of Schmemann) "constitutes the essence and the purpose of the Church."[81] Therefore, the community of faith is the "manifestation and presence of the new and transfigured creation,"[82] the inbreaking of the age to come and the adventing of God's kingdom on earth. This is why the church in its essence and vocation is both "cosmic and eschatological,"[83] and so is her liturgy. In light of this assertion, redemption could be understood as renewal of the sacramental reality of creation (and life itself). As Schmemann states,

> Precisely in this *sacramental* understanding of the world is the essence and gift of that *light of the world* that permeates the entire life of the Church, the entire liturgical and spiritual tradition. . . . Sin is itself perceived here as a *falling away* of man, and in him of all creation, from this sacramentality, from the "paradise of delight," and into "this world," which lives no longer according to God, but according to itself and in itself and is therefore corrupt and mortal. And if this is so, then Christ accomplishes the salvation of the world by renewing the world and life itself as sacrament.[84]

The redemptive eschatological union of the ontologically renewed humanity with God in the cosmic Christ is articulated, anticipated, and experienced in the church's liturgical anamnesis.[85] This communal anamnesis of Christ (1 Cor 11:24–25) is not simply a mental recollection, but an enacted likeness. It is choosing "to be" and "to do" like him, becoming his extension on earth through the incarnational agency of the Holy Spirit. Through the body of Christ, heaven descends on earth and restores the unity of the Creator with his creation as the liturgical celebration translates the foretaste of the divine fullness of life in and through the Spirit-baptized *koinōnia*. Therefore, the eucharistic liturgy is an epicletic, pneumatically charged, socio-transformative event unfolding within the tension of "the already and

81. Schmemann, *Eucharist*, 19.

82. Schmemann, *Eucharist*, 21.

83. Alexander Schmemann, "Liturgy and Theology," in *Liturgy and Tradition: Theological Reflections of Alexander Schmemann*, ed. Thomas Frisch (Crestwood, NY: St. Vladimir's Seminary Press, 1990), 49–69 (57–58).

84. Schmemann, *Eucharist*, 34.

85. Pfeil, "Liturgy and Ethics," 136.

not yet," of anticipation and fulfilment, of the encounter between the present and the summoning otherness of its future.

As the focal point of the liturgical celebration of Christ's pneumatic oneness with his communal body, the Eucharist is also, in the words of M. Douglas Meeks,

> God's economic act par excellence in the household of Jesus Christ. In it is made present God's own self-giving, God's own economy by which God intends to make the world into a home.[86]

The Eucharist asserts the innocence of the nonanthropic creation, which comes to the table of God prior to the human community and welcomes it as the visible form of divine nourishment in the household of God. Through its inclusion within Christ in the event of the Incarnation, created matter enters redemptive participation in the life of the Trinity. In the materiality of the Son's body, matter is sanctified and sanctioned as an instrument of grace in the consecration of the cosmos.[87] Therefore, the Eucharist provides pedagogy of discerning and liturgical anamnesis of the ontological, soteriological, and eschatological interrelation between humanity and the rest of creation. It instructs us toward disciplining our desires in prioritization of the well-being of others and points us to the practice of liturgical asceticism of reverent consumption (1 Cor 11:27–34). Indeed, the Eucharist detoxifies us from the dehumanizing poisons of unrestrained consumerism and helps us build immunity toward its seductive lure. It cultivates the community of faith as a dissident force of resistance against the commodification of market logic and forms it as an incarnated critique of the utilitarian objectification of God's creation.

In the Eucharist, the Spirit reveals as transparent to Christ matter, space, and time and opens the believer's eyes to see the liturgical celebration as the convocation of both the anthropic and nonanthropic creation into one cosmic worshiping community. In his *Of Water and Spirit*, Alexander Schmemann describes the Eucharist as cosmic "joy" that "permeates all" that exists. As Schmemann states, the Eucharist is "the entire creation—its matter and its time, its sounds and colors, its words and its silence—that praises and worships God, and in this praise becomes again

86. Meeks, *God the Economist*, 45.

87. See Daniela C. Augustine, *Pentecost, Hospitality, and Transfiguration: Toward a Spirit-Inspired Vision of Social Transformation* (Cleveland, TN: CPT, 2012), 56–59.

itself: the Eucharist, the sacrament of unity, the sacrament of the new creation."[88] In *For the Life of the World*, Schmemann affirms that the Eucharist is best understood as "a journey or procession" "into the dimension of the Kingdom."[89] This journey begins when Christians leave their homes on Sunday morning, starting that symbolic procession from the present life into the life of the kingdom as the future of the world, gathered by the Holy Spirit in the *synaxis* of Christ's communal body. For Schmemann, in this journey "a sacramental act is already taking place," for the believers "are on their way to *constitute the Church*,"[90] being called out of the present world and transfigured by the Spirit into the world to come. Offering a spellbinding reflection on the cosmology of the Eucharist, George Theokritoff provokes the reader to see this processional journey in a new light and reexperience the liturgy with a renewed awareness not only of its all-engulfing reach through the epicletic omnipresence of the Spirit, who reveals (in the language of Saint Basel's liturgy) creation as the body of the incarnate God, but also of the celebratory participation as the offering of the entire cosmos. Analyzing the complex biological and chemical substances and processes that have to come together (including the intricate, synergistic choreography of nature and human labor) in order to produce the familiar elements of bread and wine, the author vividly depicts the beginning of the cosmic Eucharist's procession not as starting in the home (with humanity's journeying to the church building), but "in Creation—'*In the beginning*.'"[91] Thus, Theokritoff states:

> In the Eucharist we offer in this piece of bread and in this cup of wine, the entire Cosmos and every living creature including ourselves—everything from the tiniest particles of matter to the farthest reaches of space, as well as from the fruits of human labor in all places and all times. We thus come to see that the Eucharist is central to the Cosmos. And it is the Eucharist that enables us to recognize more clearly that the Cosmos is transparent to Christ, who shines through all matter.[92]

88. Schmemann, *Of Water and Spirit*, 118.

89. Schmemann, *For the Life of the World*, 26.

90. Schmemann, *For the Life of the World*, 27.

91. George Theokritoff, "The Cosmology of the Eucharist," in *Toward an Ecology of Transfiguration: Orthodox Christian Perspectives on Environment, Nature, and Creation*, ed. John Chryssavgis and Bruce V. Foltz (New York: Fordham University Press, 2013), 131–35.

92. Theokritoff, "Cosmology of the Eucharist," 133–34.

Therefore, the Eucharist points to a theological ethic of discerning creation not only as means of communion with God and neighbor, but as cocelebrant at the Lord's table. It involves recognizing one's well-being and flourishing as function and outcome of the well-being and flourishing of the totality of creation—of all anthropic and nonanthropic neighbors.

According to Walter Brueggemann, the Eucharist is a "replay of the manna narrative in the book of Exodus" and as such represents "a liturgical interpretive offer to reimagine the world differently," depicting the community of faith as a living embodiment of the rehumanizing journey "from *anxious scarcity* through *miraculous abundance* to a *neighborly common good*."[93] As in the communal partaking of the manna under the divine pedagogy of neighborliness in pursuit of shared flourishing, the Eucharist defies the fear of scarcity by teaching that taking more for oneself while leaving the fellow human hungry does not provide access to life (1 Cor 11:20–22) but condemns (even unto death) for not discerning rightly the body of Christ (vv. 27–34). As with the manna in the wilderness (the quintessential place of scarcity and deprivation), so also with the Eucharist (in a finite cosmos of ever-shrinking material resources) one lives life more abundant only when the world is offered in gratitude to God and shared with others, making sure that there is no one left hungry (v. 21). The Eucharist teaches us to take responsibility for the hunger and poverty of others, examining ourselves—our conscious or unintentional contribution to their economic depravity and marginalization—and to offer them access to the table, learning to "wait for one another" (v. 33), starting with the most vulnerable in the community (the orphans and the widows, the children and the elderly, the disabled, the economic migrants) until the needs of all are met. As a sacrament of the new creation, the Eucharist both depicts and cultivates within the new human community the economics of the Spirit. The shared life around the table of the Lord is to become paradigmatic for all human life—a sacramental enactment of the common good that hallows all dimensions of human existence, including its economics.

The Eucharist effectively deconstructs the logic of free-market consumerism, for (in the words of William Cavanaugh) as the individual partakes in the eucharistic elements, she "does not simply take Christ into herself, but is taken up into Christ. . . . The act of consumption is thereby turned inside out: instead of simply consuming the body of Christ, we are consumed by it."[94]

93. Brueggemann, *Journey to the Common Good*, 32.

94. William Cavanaugh, *Being Consumed: Economics and Christian Desire* (Grand Rapids: Eerdmans, 2008), 54.

As "we all partake of the one bread" (1 Cor 10:17), we stand as one body, for we have all become partakers of Christ, and in him of each other. Therefore, prioritizing one's personal desires over against the needs of others and consuming the other for one's own self-gratification within the body of Christ becomes devouring oneself.

The ultimate challenge of the eucharistic logic and pedagogy is that, by becoming the body of Christ, we "must become food for others."[95] Alexander Schmemann contemplates this extroverted missionary orientation of the Eucharist in reflecting upon the three liturgical movements of its celebration. It starts with a movement of ascent as the church is carried by the Spirit to heaven in "its entrance into the new eon."[96] The church experiences the fullness of the life of the community of the Trinity at the table of the Lord, and being filled and illumined by the divine presence, she is called to descend back to earth. This second movement of descent is part of her missiological identity, for unless the church reenters this world, there will not be "heaven on earth." Yet the church returns on earth for the sake of the world, and her final liturgical movement (animated by the Spirit) is from the interiority of the temple to the exteriority of all the world—even to its "uttermost" parts—the farthest, the darkest, the most different from us. Therefore, "the Eucharist transforms the church into what it is, transforms it into mission."[97] In fulfilling her calling, the church enters the cosmos as the living gospel in the body of Christ that gives itself daily to feed and heal a starved and broken world. Indeed, the Eucharist transforms the church herself into a sacrament for the life of the world.

It is not accidental that in many Eastern-European Pentecostal communities (under the influence of their Eastern Orthodox cultural roots), the eucharistic liturgy is followed by an agape feast. While the Eucharist takes place in heaven, the agape feast takes place on earth. It embodies the ultimate purpose of the eucharistic pedagogy—it is the life of heaven on earth captured by the household table of the family of God, where all share their resources and freely receive access to life, so that there is not a single one left hungry and needy among them. They are all children in their Father's house and equal beneficiaries of his loving homebuilding on behalf of all creation.

While ending with a feast, the eucharistic celebration is preceded by a time of intense prayer and fasting.[98] The commitment to a strict, preeucha-

95. Cavanaugh, *Being Consumed*, 55.

96. Schmemann, "Missionary Imperative," 200.

97. Schmemann, "Missionary Imperative," 200.

98. This, undoubtedly, is another aspect of the Eastern Orthodox cultural roots of these

ristic fast by many Eastern-European Pentecostals is an important dimension of their spiritual hygiene, cleansing themselves from blind submission to the urge for consumption and learning to differentiate between their legitimate needs and self-indulgent desires. The fast is practiced, therefore, as an ascetic struggle that helps the believers grow in spiritual maturity by strengthening their resistance to temptation. For these Pentecostal communities, embracing the fast translates into taking a stand against the demonic forces within the cosmos (and their manifestations in systemic evils, prompting the dehumanization and commodification of fellow humans)—an understanding developed in light of the gospel accounts of Jesus's temptation in the wilderness (but also in light of Jas 4:7—"Submit yourselves therefore to God. Resist the devil and he will flee from you"). As already discussed in chapter 2, Luke's and Matthew's accounts of Jesus's forty-day fast (and the subsequent spiritual confrontation with the devil) depict a profoundly epicletic event—it is an ascetic struggle that takes place in and through the leading and empowerment of the Spirit (Luke 4:1–2; Matt 4:1). In light of this assertion, for most Eastern-European Pentecostals, fasting (as other spiritual disciplines) is surrendering to the sanctifying/Christoforming work of the Spirit within the believer. Yet more than anything else, the eucharistic fast is perceived as a preparation in anticipation of encounter with the living God—a transformative moment, marked by both divine grace and the demand for human accountability/responsibility (an event in which the believer experiences blessing *and* judgment/discipline—both active expressions of the divine love, lifting humanity into an ascent from glory to glory, carving the believers into the likeness of God).

According to Alexander Schmemann, the relationship between the (pre)eucharistic fast and the eucharistic celebration reflects the church's liturgical "rhythm of expectation and fulfillment, preparation and 'presence.'"[99] In light of this assertion, he offers an insightful reflection on the differentiation and continuity between the eucharistic and ascetic dimensions of fasting, pointing to their gospel origins and theological significance in ecclesial life. As Schmemann asserts, the eucharistic fast is a preparation in expectation of the parousia, "of the second glorious advent of Christ, of

---

Pentecostal communities (particularly the preeucharistic fast and prayer vigil required by the Typikon). The length of the fast is up to each separate believer and may last from a day to over a week.

99. Alexander Schmemann, "Fast and Liturgy," *St. Vladimir's Seminary Quarterly* 3, no. 1 (Winter 1959): 2–9. (available at https://oca.org/reflections/fr-alexander-schmemann/fast-and-liturgy)

the fulfillment in which 'God shall be revealed as all in all.'"[100] This theological understanding is rooted in the Synoptic Gospels' record of Christ's response to the critiques of the Pharisees that his disciples do not fast: "The wedding guests cannot fast while the bridegroom is with them, can they? As long as they have the bridegroom with them they cannot fast. The days will come when the bridegroom is taken away from them, and then they will fast on that day" (Mark 2:18; cf. Luke 5:33; Matt 9:14). Therefore, the preeucharistic fast is an anticipation-pregnant vigil, unfolding in the suspense between the ascension and the second coming, keeping the church (the bride of Christ) alert and attuned into the Spirit's movement that gathers the world (and its history) in its eschatological future (for no one knows the day of the Lord's coming—Matt 24:42). The fast ends with the eucharistic celebration as with a wedding banquet, marked by the presence of the bridegroom. In the words of Schmemann, the "yearning" of the church for her Lord

> is now constantly fulfilled and answered in the sacrament of the Lord's Presence, in the Eucharistic banquet. . . . Thus, fasting and Eucharist form, so to say, two complementary and necessary poles of Church life, manifest the essential antinomy of her nature: expectation and possession, fullness and growth, eschatology and history.[101]

Yet, as Schmemann emphasizes, fasting has also a "second meaning, that completes" the eucharistic one—namely, the ascetic dimension, which (similar to the Eastern-European Pentecostal understanding) he depicts "as a fight against the demonic powers, as a method of spiritual life."[102] While he places the scriptural origins of the ascetic fast within the gospel accounts of Jesus's temptation in the wilderness (taking place after forty days of fasting),[103] Schmemann also asserts that the gospel makes a direct statement regarding the power of prayer and fasting as "the only means for a victory over Satan (Matt 17:21). For the advent of Christ not only fulfills the history of salvation, it is also the decisive moment in the struggle against Satan, who has become the 'prince of this world.'"

100. Schmemann, "Fast and Liturgy."
101. Schmemann, "Fast and Liturgy."
102. Schmemann, "Fast and Liturgy."
103. For an expounded reflection on the gospel accounts of Jesus's temptation in the wilderness, see chapter 2 of the present book.

Echoing the temptation of the first Adam, the temptation of the last Adam, in the wilderness, also starts with food. Therefore, Schmemann asserts that by abstaining from the essential "necessity" of food as a means of sustaining one's life, humanity (residing in the victorious Christ) finds out that it "lives not by bread alone" and willfully chooses fasting as

> a free return to the fulfillment of that commandment which Adam has transgressed. Accepting it, man again receives food as a Divine gift, food ceases to be a "necessity" and becomes the very image of the messianic banquet, for "eat in order to live" has become again "live in God."[104]

Indeed, this recovered freedom has profound social and environmental dimensions, for, in the words of H. A. H. Bartholomew I, "fasting underlines the dignity and value of everything and everyone." Fasting is "wanting less" while "recognizing the wants of others."[105] It is, therefore, an embodied recollection of "the hunger" and suffering of others and "a symbolic effort" to identify with them,[106] while striving (with one's material and spiritual resources) for the relief of their deprivation. Indeed, in its Christoforming spiritual depth, fasting is (as Bartholomew I explains) an act of love and compassion for others[107] and "a solemn reminder that everything we do relates to either the well-being or wounding of others."[108] This love and compassion extend to all creation, for fasting intensifies one's ecological awareness and longing for the healing of the cosmos. Affirming the totality of the material creation, fasting reminds us, as Bartholomew I points out, "that 'the earth is the Lord's' (Ps 24:1) and not ours to own, exploit, to consume or control. . . . It is restoring the primal vision of the world, as God intended it, and discerning the beauty of the world, as God created it."

Indeed, the fast sharpens the believers' spiritual vision, helping them to rightly discern not only creation as a divine eucharistic gift but also the communal body of Christ, and to partake in the Lord's Supper in a worthy manner (1 Cor 11:26–28). It opens their eyes to recognize Christ in the other and to embrace them as an organic part of the same family, as members

104. Schmemann, "Fast and Liturgy."
105. Bartholomew I, *Encountering the Mystery*, 82.
106. Bartholomew I, *Encountering the Mystery*, 84.
107. Bartholomew I, *Encountering the Mystery*, 82.
108. Bartholomew I, *Encountering the Mystery*, 84.

of the same household. The fast prompts the believers to examine their minds and hearts for any negation of Christ expressed as a negation of the other. Thus, the Eucharist liturgy includes private and public (individual and corporate) confessions and responsive articulation of forgiveness directed toward healing of one's relationship to the other—for a separation from them is a separation from Christ, from his communal body. Therefore, during the celebration of the Eucharist in some Eastern-European Pentecostal churches, the communicants take turns asking the congregation for forgiveness, and the body responds with a resounding, "We forgive you and may God forgive you!" The observer can easily discern in this exchange the liturgical influence of the Eastern Orthodox Forgiveness Sunday.[109] Indeed, each eucharistic celebration in these Pentecostal communities becomes a Forgiveness Sunday, magnifying the Eucharist as the quintessential sacrament of reconciliation.[110]

The Christoforming work of the eucharistic liturgy (with its preceding fast) cultivates in the believer the holiness without which no one shall see God (Heb 12:14). This social holiness that starts with discerning Christ in the other—even in his most radically different and unrecognizable appearance (Matt 25:31–46)—brings the believers face to face with God now, as they share possessions with others in benevolent actions toward those in need. Therefore, seeing the face of God in the face of the needy on this side of the eschaton brings them before his face in eternity as heirs of the kingdom prepared for them by the Father "before the foundations of the earth" (Matt 25:34).

Therefore, the Eucharist transforms the church into a "passage" to heaven, "from the old into the new, from this world into the 'world to come.'"[111] It teaches us, as Schmemann points out, that we were created as eucharistic beings,

> as celebrants of the sacrament of life, of its transformation into life in God. . . . We know that real life is 'eucharist', a movement of love and adoration toward God, the movement in which alone the meaning and value of all that exists can be revealed and fulfilled.

109. In the Eastern Orthodox liturgical calendar, this is the last Sunday prior to the beginning of the Great Lent.

110. The Eucharist as a sacrament of forgiveness and reconciliation is further discussed in chapter 4 of the present work.

111. Schmemann, *For the Life of the World*, 31.

This is a powerful antidote to the deformities of the free market's secular liturgies that have distorted our vision of the world. It is a redemptive recapitulation of humanity's economic life into God's economy of household.[112]

Holiness and Moral Economic Responsibility

As the Incarnation, so also Pentecost affirms the ontological relationship between matter and Spirit and opens the door to understanding "the material condition of others as a spiritual matter."[113] The economic paradigm of the Pentecost community affirms this understanding and outlines the social responsibilities of holiness as an extension of the life of the Spirit in human flesh. Saintliness manifests itself as serving the material needs of others with one's own possessions. Sharing possessions, therefore, becomes an expression of participation in the life of God and a materialization of shared spirituality.

Edith Wyschogrod offers the following identifier of sainthood:

> A saintly life is defined as one in which compassion for the Other, irrespective of cost to the saint, is a primary trait. . . . Their [the saints'] lives exhibit two types of negation: the negation of self and the lack of what is needful but absent in the life of the Other.[114]

Sallie McFague argues that personal material possessions can blind humanity from the material needs of others as being a spiritual matter. She asserts that "self-emptying, self-denial, allows us to see differently and hence to live differently . . . it is often the first step toward universal love of others, toward seeing others as valuable and all as interrelated."[115]

Viewed as self-denial on behalf of the others, the acts of sharing possessions stand among the gestures and images that summon our moral response through the hagiographies of the saints as imitators of Christ. Their

112. Schmemann, *For the Life of the World*, 34.

113. Sallie McFague, "Epilogue: The Human Dignity and the Integrity of Creation," in *Theology That Matters: Ecology, Economy, and God*, ed. Darby Kathleen Ray (Minneapolis: Fortress, 2006), 199–212 (209).

114. Edith Wyschogrod, *Saints and Postmodernity: Revisioning Moral Philosophy* (Chicago: University of Chicago Press, 1990), xxi. For more engagement of Wyschogrod's work, see the epilogue of the present book.

115. McFague, "Epilogue," 209–10.

redeemed humanity is defined not "by consumption but by kenosis" that flows out of "participation in the fullness of the Trinitarian life"—of mutual self-giving and receiving.[116] As the saints empty themselves in the body of Christ, they become his body on earth and are transfigured into his new humanity, taking the form and shape of their destiny and mission in Christlikeness. This imitation is interpreted as a fulfillment of the broader mission of the community of faith—the ministry of reconciliation (2 Cor 5:18). The peacemaking of the sons and daughters of God in this world is clearly not limited to the cessation of war and physical violence. It points to shalom of comprehensive justice that involves all humanity and the rest of creation. Therefore, the definition of peace also includes "providing the earth and its people with the basics of existence"[117] and thus affirming their dignity and identity as being part of our own common destiny.

The contrast between Pentecost's economics of the Spirit and the market logic of global economic neoliberalism exposes the profound need for the sanctification of humanity and its desires and points to the internal struggle of human consciousness when faced with the vision of the kingdom in the midst of the temptation and the promises of this world's economic systems. As Cavanaugh asserts, our temptation is to spiritualize our union and solidarity with the poor, the oppressed, and the suffering

> to make our connection to the hungry a sentimental act of imaginative sympathy. We could then even imagine that we are already in a community with those who lack food, whether or not we actually meet their physical needs. We might even wish to tell ourselves that our purchases of consumer goods do in fact feed others—by creating jobs. But we have no way of knowing if such jobs create dignity or merely take advantage of others' desperation. . . .[118]

Economics is a spiritual matter and an external expression of the individual and communal inner life. This is why poverty, as class-related reality, may be viewed as an outcome of a given spirituality that ushers and sustains economic models, which maintain and deepen disparities and further class division. This spirituality stands in contrast to the therapeutic measures in the old and the new covenants, aimed against further class dislocation

116. Cavanaugh, *Being Consumed*, 86.
117. McFague, "Epilogue,"209.
118. Cavanaugh, *Being Consumed*, 56.

and toward restoring moral economic and civic responsibility in society at large. The concept of Jubilee is one such striking example of the demand for a social covenant that executes economic justice and sustains human dignity. The forgiveness of debt and restoration of personal freedom are pointers to the spiritual destiny of the covenant people and their social bonds.[119]

The event of Pentecost induces an economic model of distributive justice as a witness of Christ's resurrected life in the Spirit-filled community (Acts 4:32–33). As Marcia Riggs states,

> corporate good requires sustainability. The means toward sustainability is the sharing of resources—that is distributive justice. Distributive justice means that all have the basics to survive and flourish.[120]

This model is based on reverent consumption, which shares the concern of well-being for all (Acts 4:34–35). Historically, Marxist thinkers have questioned the sustainability of this model and have identified the sharing of products without sharing the means of production as the primary reason for its decline and eventual disappearance.[121] The primary issue in the Acts account, however, is concerned with sustainability of unity, human dignity, and love as being the fundamental bonds of the Pentecost social covenant and tangible expression of the participation of the faith community in the communal life of the Trinity.

The pouring of the Spirit on all flesh gives a global dimension to the eschatological vision of Pentecost. All flesh is bonded together in and through the life of the Spirit and made participant in its socioeconomic reality. This globalized ethos is indispensable from the anticipation of the planetary spread of the kingdom of God—the reality of the life of God translated in the sociopolitical and economic dimensions of material existence on earth. This is a reality in which economics becomes an outcome and an extension of the divine life through the agency of the Holy Spirit. As such, economics is an extension of justice as the fundamental relationship to the other (things

119. For a study of the Jubilee theme in the Synoptic Gospels and its implication for ethics, see Sharon H. Ringe, *Jesus, Liberation, and the Biblical Jubilee: Images for Ethics and Christology* (Philadelphia: Fortress, 1985).

120. Marcia Y. Riggs, "The Globalization of Nothing and Creation Ex Nihilo," in *Theology That Matters: Ecology, Economy, and God*, ed. Darby Kathleen Ray (Minneapolis: Fortress, 2006), 141–53 (148).

121. Rosa Luxemburg, "Socialism and the Churches," *Marxist Classics*, http://www.newyouth.com/archives/classics/luxemburg/socialismandthechurches.html.

and beings). Through the Spirit, all flesh is brought into this comprehensive justice that realigns matter with its spiritual origin and purpose. This is a radical transfiguring of the fundamental relationships that construct the human *socium*—from material want and desires undergirding production and consumption in the context of anxious awareness of the depletion of material and energy resources, to spiritual life that permeates redemptively all material existence and translates it in the comprehensive shalom of the kingdom. This is life in the Spirit that is more abundant. It is life free from fear and competition for survival—a life in which there is a home for all (John 14:2).

While reflecting on the Old Testament idea of "the cities of refuge" (Num 35), Emmanuel Levinas makes the important observation that Western society—free and civilized—enjoys riches and privileges, often at the expense of the rest of the world, causing the suffering and deprivation of others (e.g., through neocolonial exploitation or through unrestrained consumption of "cheap" goods produced in sweat shops within the developing world). With ignorant innocence, we participate in manslaughter and act surprised when the anger of the world rages against us. In light of this volatile reality of our societal conscience, Levinas questions, "does not all this make our cities cities of refuge or cities of exiles?"[122] Perhaps this is why the arrival of the stranger in our midst makes us more anxious than ever—we are not sure whether they are "the avenger of blood." After all, driven by political and economic interests, we have continually lied to the rest of the world that the level of material prosperity, proudly advertised as "the American way" of life, can be made universal. Yet, though "the United States comprises only 5 percent of the world's population, we consume somewhere between 23 and 26 percent of the world's energy."[123] As James K. A. Smith observes, this way of life is destructive to creation and cannot be feasibly extended to others. It perpetuates "a system of privilege and exploitation," and the only way to continue enjoying it "is to keep it to ourselves."[124] While offering to the rest of the global dwellers empty promises of sustainable Western-style consumerism, the seductive glamor of the West rested for decades upon its arrogant claim for autonomy from the rest of the world and a guardianship of hu-

122. Emmanuel Levinas, *Beyond the Verse: Talmudic Readings and Lectures* (London: Continuum, 2007), 40.

123. James K. A. Smith, *Desiring the Kingdom: Worship, Worldview, and Cultural Formation*, vol. 1 of *Cultural Liturgies* (Grand Rapids: Baker Academic, 2009), 101.

124. Smith, *Desiring the Kingdom*, 101.

man freedom as unapologetic individualism that worships self-indulging desires at the expense of nature and human community. The current global economic and environmental crisis has shattered our self-delusions for autonomous existence and has summoned us to moral responsibility for the sickness and poverty of the world. Practicing benevolence as indulgences for our consumer addictions is not enough to mend a broken world. Global healing demands a global vision of the world as a sacrament shared with the other, as a communion with God and neighbor. This vision has to be coined with a eucharistic spirituality of priestly existence in the cosmos, marked by askesis and kenosis for the life of the world. This is a spirituality cherishing this world as God's household and a sanctuary in which all his creatures are to have access to life. For as the economics of the Spirit reminds us (in Sallie McFague's famous paraphrase of Saint Irenaeus), ultimately, "the glory of God is every creature fully alive."[125]

125. This is a paraphrase of Saint Irenaeus's statement, "the glory of God is man fully alive." The text continues: "moreover man's life is the vision of God: if God's revelation through creation has already obtained life for all the beings that dwell on earth, how much more will the Word's manifestation of the Father obtain life for those who see God" (*Adversus Haereses* 4.20.7). The paraphrase captures the spirit of the text and was made famous by Sallie McFague's writings, especially *Life Abundant*, 3.

Chapter 4

From Forgiveness to the Common Good in the Spirit's World-Mending

In his moving book *To Heal a Fractured World*, Rabbi Jonathan Sacks asserts that the prophets of Israel "were the first people in history to conceive of peace as an ideal."[1] Their eschatological vision of a reconciled cosmos, saturated in the divine shalom, was not simply extraordinary and otherworldly, it was "revolutionary"[2] for an age in which war and violence constituted normality (an understanding in political philosophy stretching all the way from antiquity into modernity).[3] For the ancient religious imagination, conflict was irretrievably "written into the structure of the cosmos."[4] Yet the prophetic promise of shalom seeded the new human community with dreams and longing for a transfigured world—a vision of societal flourishing, supposedly unattainable through human means but called into being by the creator Spirit—a glorious new world, yet utopically distant and unachievable on this side of the eschaton.

In light of this magnetic vision, the story of Israel speaks of a people carved from the present age and consecrated as the beginning of the age to come—the new human community, summoned unto stewardship of this in-Spirit-ed, hopeful daydreaming of God's future for humanity (indeed, for all of creation—Isa 11:6–9). Thus, amidst a violent, war-plagued present, Isaiah proclaims with stirring certainty the poetic otherness of Yahweh's looming peace: "they shall beat their swords into ploughshares, and their spears

1. Jonathan Sacks, *To Heal a Fractured World: The Ethics of Responsibility* (New York: Schocken), 98.

2. Sacks, *To Heal a Fractured World*, 99.

3. In the beginning of the Introduction to his book *The Invention of Peace* (London: Yale University Press, 2000), Michael Howard quotes Sir Henry Main's statement, "War appears to be as old as mankind, but peace is a modern invention" (1).

4. Sacks, *To Heal a Fractured World*, 99.

into pruning-hooks; nation shall not lift up sword against nation, neither shall they learn war any more" (Isa 2:4). This is a vision of an ontologically healed community, delivered from enmity. The text depicts this ontological renewal by asserting the restoration of humanity's vocation according to the Creator's original intent—imaging God and his unconditional care for all creation, while tending the earth in peaceful, harmonious coexistence with the other and extending (through creative human world-making) the proto-sanctuary of Eden until it covers the globe.[5] In its fallen stage, humanity has substituted its instruments for agricultural cultivation with weapons of war, making the world an end in itself (reducing it from means of communion with God and neighbor to a finite and ever-depleting resource for human survival) and distorting the other from cocelebrant of God's unconditional eucharistic hospitality into a competitor for limited access to life amidst escalating fear of scarcity and violence associated with the presence of the other. In Isaiah's vision, the weapons are transformed once again into tools for harvesting the fruits of the earth. In the poetry of the text, there is more than a dream of peace with the other in a recaptured paradise—there is a promise for harvest—a promise for abundant fruit of one's labor, a promise for restored communion not only between fellow humans but also between humanity and the earth, eradicating all strife against the anthropic and the nonanthropic other. This is, indeed, a vision of overturning the consequences of the curse—a promise of a redeemed, reconciled cosmos.

Later, Micah would quote this vision of eschatological peace, inserting it between what could be seen as his prologue and epilogue to Isaiah's prophecy. The prologue (Mic 4:1–3a) depicts the path toward the actualization of shalom as nothing less than global humanity's conversion into the "ways" of the Lord (4:2). The passage presents the nations streaming to "the mountain of the Lord," "to the house of the God of Jacob," so that he may teach them "about his ways" and they may learn to "walk in his paths" (4:2). They come to hear "the law" that "goes forth from Zion," "the word" of the Lord that sustains and mends the cosmos, enacting God's justice and delivering his judgment of the nations (4:3). This is a vision of the world transfigured by the knowledge of God and the embodiment of his word within the human community. Just peace becomes the evidence for this transfiguration. Indeed, Mic 4:1–3 depicts global flourishing in shalom as being a function

5. See Daniela C. Augustine, "The Liturgical Teleology of Human Creativity and the City of God as *Theosis* of Culture," *Cultural Encounters: A Journal for the Theology of Culture* 10, no. 2 (April 2015).

(or an outcome) of truth and justice, which flow from worship of and communion with the one true and just God. Here worshiping the Lord coincides not merely with knowing his law but "with walking in his paths." Therefore, Isaiah's glorious peace is that of humanity saturated by worship as its way of life, and being with the other.

The epilogue that follows extends further the description of Isaiah's vision, moving from the macrodimension of global peace (or the realm of international relations) to the microdimension of the individual human being and the reality of shalom in his or her everyday life. "[T]hey shall all sit under their own vines and under their own fig trees, and no one shall make them afraid; for the mouth of the Lord of hosts has spoken" (v. 4). The verse describes humanity delivered from the anxiety of scarcity and violent competition with the other. The world is once again more than enough for all, and there is no need to war against the fellow human for ever-shrinking material resources. What has made the world more than enough is the worship of God, transfiguring human life into a home for his Spirit and thus extending the divine generosity and hospitality to all creation. In the hospitality of the Spirit, residing within redeemed humanity, the fellow human and the rest of creation become one's co-communicants within the eternal eucharistic movement of grace.

In a way, the text's crescendo from the prologue to the epilogue articulates the eschatological prophetic vision of humanity's transition from reconciliation with God and neighbor to the covenantal commitment of peacefully sharing the world in upholding the common good. Yet it seems that biblical eschatology (not only in the Old but also in the New Testament) promises comprehensive, global peace only as an outcome of humanity's conversion in uncompromised worship to God. While reading Micah, one is reminded of John's apocalyptic vision of the new Jerusalem—the city of God—descending to earth as a transcontinental, global village that is in itself a temple, a holy of holies that has circumscribed the earth, saturating it with worship of the one true God. In this context, Rev 21:24–27 is often read as John's vision of the conversion of the nations:

> The nations will walk by its light, and the kings of the earth will bring their glory into it. Its gates will never be shut by day—and there will be no night there. People will bring into it the glory and the honor of the nations. But nothing unclean will enter it, nor anyone who practices abomination or falsehood, but only those who are written in the Lamb's book of life.

Naturally, the question that comes to mind is: could there be hope for cosmopolitan shalom (to echo Kant's language) without religious conversion? Could we live in lasting, sustainable peace and pursue the common good on this side of the eschaton with the religious and cultural other? Jonathan Sacks points out that while many religions praise peace and "decry conflict and war," they still engage in war and violence against their ideological opponents, for when they speak of peace, they mean peace on their own terms—peace as the comfort of sameness.[6] Yet in its claustrophobic, global compression of perpetual and unavoidable dwelling with the religious and cultural other, humanity's survival is faced with the challenge of peacebuilding as "*living with difference*"[7] between the present and the eschaton, while striving for comprehensive and sustainable flourishing of all amidst a shared planetary household. This present challenge is often further intensified by inerasable, transgenerational memories of conflicts and trauma,[8] associated with the other, that are often "cherished" as tribal/communal identity markers. To be is to remember; to forget is to refuse to be. Pursuing peace with the former enemy is viewed as betrayal of the communal identity sealed with the blood of its martyrs and innocent victims of violence and injustice.

Writing from the shadows of hallowed, restless memories of the Holocaust, Hannah Arendt lifts up *forgiveness* as the "possible redemption" for the irreversibility of the past and points to *promise* as "the remedy" for the "chaotic uncertainty of the future."[9] Humanity lives in the exasperating

6. Sacks, *To Heal a Fractured World*, 100. The author states: "Whatever the language in which it is couched, the argument tends to take this form: 'Our faith speaks of peace; our holy texts praise peace; therefore, if only the world shared our faith and our texts there would be peace.' Tragically, *this path does not and cannot lead to peace because it is predicated on the conversion of the world—to our religion or ideology conceived as a global truth or universal salvation. Peace such conceived is part of the problem, not of the solution*. That is why the prophets were right to envision peace not within historical time but at 'the end of days,' and even more to see this as the work of God, not humankind. The attempt to bring prophetic peace by human action creates not peace but war—what is often called 'holy war.' 'Holy war' is, I believe, unholy war, a desecration of the image of God in the name of God."

7. Sacks, *To Heal a Fractured World*, 101.

8. Reflecting on "intergenerational resentment" in its perpetuation of memories of conflict and "cherishing hope for revenge," Donald W. Shriver states, "the memory of past horrors prepares the ground for their repetition in the future" (*An Ethic for Enemies: Forgiveness in Politics* [New York: Oxford University Press, 1995], 67). In relation to memory and identity, see also Miroslav Volf, *The End of Memory: Remembering Rightly in a Violent World* (Grand Rapids: Eerdmans, 2006), 24–27.

9. Hannah Arendt, *The Human Condition* (Chicago: University of Chicago Press, 1998), 237.

suspense between past and future—often wishing to forget what it knows while fearing the inevitability of the coming unknown. In the perpetual tension between the irreversibility of past acts and the unpredictability of their future consequences, the possibility of movement from forgiveness to promise presents hope for peaceful coexistence with difference on this side of the eschaton in pursuit of the common good.

In light of this, the present chapter offers a theological reflection on forgiveness as opening the possibility of a common future with the other. The text finds its point of departure in highlighting the creative potentiality of forgiveness and the Spirit's agency toward its embodiment within the human community. The chapter proceeds further with discussing the intersections between forgiveness and the redemption of memory in relation to the church's sacramental life and concludes by reflecting on the difficult notion of forgiving "the unforgivable."

The Spirit's Artistry of Unconditional Forgiveness

Christian theology often articulates reconciliation as presenting the very "heart" of redemption[10] and unconditional forgiveness as the pathway to authentically reconciled cosmos.[11] The term "reconciliation" is utilized as an overarching expression of the Christ event and its embodied proclamation by the Christian community as a living gospel to a broken, traumatized by strife and violence world. The words of the apostle Paul recorded in 2 Cor 5:18–19 encapsulate a gripping theological summary of both God's redemptive, reconciling work in Christ and its translation into the praxis of the church as his communal body on earth:

> All this is from God, who reconciled us to himself through Christ, and has given us the ministry of reconciliation; that is, in Christ God was reconciling the world to himself, not counting their trespasses against them, and entrusting the message of reconciliation to us.

10. Karl Barth, *Church Dogmatics: The Doctrine of Reconciliation*, Church Dogmatics, vol. 4.1 (Edinburgh: T&T Clark, 1961), 3.

11. For an in-depth look into the essence of reconciliation in the Bible and Christian tradition, see John W. de Gruchy, *Reconciliation: Restoring Justice* (Minneapolis: Fortress, 2002), especially ch. 2.

"Not counting" the "trespasses" of others against them serves as a designation for the content and practice of forgiveness[12]—the initiating point of intersocial, communal healing, the act of opening space and time for the possibility of future with the other (even the enemy), for an authentic movement of hope-infused, shalom-building social change. Scripture locates the origin of this socio-transformative healing in God and his active, redemptive presence within the cosmos. Thus, the very possibility of forgiveness is inseparable from God's omnipresence—it is a manifestation of the divine communal life inbreaking within the human community (both covenantal and noncovenantal, Christian and non-Christian). Therefore, in its primordial depths, forgiveness is an act of the Spirit, vibrating within the world's fibers—an act of ontological healing and renewal of creation, overturning the curse's enmity between God's creatures. The Spirit's kenosis upon the broken world primes it for reconciliation with God and neighbor, stirring up the human conscience (the law of God written on the hearts of all human beings, regardless of their ethnic, religious, and cultural distinctives—Rom 2:12–16) toward imaging the Trinitarian protocommunal life. The Spirit empowers and magnifies the liberating voice of truth (John 8:32), both in the outcries of the victims and the confessions of the perpetrators, and mediates the embrace of the other toward inner and intersocial healing and freedom. Therefore, authentic forgiveness and reconciliation, wherever found, are manifestations of the Spirit's unceasing, redemptive, socio-transformative work of mending the world and transfiguring humanity into the likeness of its maker. Since one of the marks of the Spirit's work is the building of just, covenantal community,[13] the countercultural, counterintuitive nature of gifting forgiveness to the other makes the invisible Spirit visible and tangibly embodied within human communal existence. The Spirit renews the face of God in humanity and makes it visible in the face of the other. She clears our vision and gives us eyes to once again see the divine face engraved upon the

12. Desmond Tutu famously defines forgiveness as abandoning one's "right to pay the perpetrator" in his or her "own coin." Thus, forgiveness is a refusal to retaliate even when one could be justified or has the legal right to do so (*No Future without Forgiveness* [New York: Doubleday, 1999], 272). While this definition expresses in a rather limited way the reality of forgiveness by focusing only on its immediate practical manifestation, it still represents a good point of departure for the present study.

13. John D. Zizioulas, *Being as Communion: Studies in Personhood and the Church* (Crestwood, NY: St. Vladimir's Seminary Press, 1995), 131. Zizioulas points out that the Spirit's active work in the world is marked by two distinct dimensions—the communal and the eschatological.

countenance of the fellow humans. This healing of vision humanizes us; it is an actualization of society's rehumanization as a fundamental expression of the Spirit's community-building work in the world. For, in the words of Jonathan Sacks, community "is society with a human face"[14]—it is, therefore, a society facing the world with the face of God.

Rooted in God's omnipresence, and thus in the eschatological inevitability of divine justice, interhuman forgiveness does not exclude the presence of righteous discontent (and anger) within the victim's outcry for human justice[15] here and now—a plea for justice experienced as access to human flourishing and renewal of the divinely ordained "relation to the other"[16] on this side of the eschaton. As such, forgiveness does not eliminate (though it does not demand or depend on) the need for the perpetrator's repentance and penance as a movement toward his or her inner healing (without which intersocial restoration and true, just reconciliation are a mere impossibility).[17] Forgiveness refuses to be cheapened and reduced to a legalistic or a sentimental act of self-effacing,[18] nor does it excuse or enable

14. Sacks, *To Heal a Fractured World*, 54.

15. Jonathan Sacks offers a captivating insight from the Jewish tradition on the difference between divine and human justice. The very existence of justice is possible because of the existence of God, in whom it has its origin and essence. Therefore, human justice is rooted in divine justice. Yet divine justice is "justice from the perspective of the one who knows all, sees all, and considers all; the universe as a whole, and time as a whole, which is to say, eternity. But we who live in space and time cannot see from this perspective, and if we did, it would not make us better humans but worse . . . we would understand justice but *at the cost of ceasing to be human*." Sacks points out that God does not want us to cease being human; otherwise, he would have not created us. "We are not God" and will "never see things from his perspective. The attempt to do so is an abdication of the human situation." If we see the world as God does, then we may perceive that sometimes "bad is a necessary stage on the journey to the good" and capitulate our struggle against all forms of injustice, or as Sacks states, "that seeing heaven" may desensitize us to earth. Sacks concludes: "There is divine justice, but God wants us to strive for *human* justice . . . in this world, not in the next; from the perspective of time and space, not infinity and eternity. *God creates divine justice, but only we can create human justice*, acting on behalf of God but never aspiring to be other than human. This is why he created us" (*To Heal a Fractured World*, 22–23).

16. The allusion is to Emmanuel Levinas's definition of justice as "the relation to the other" (*Totality and Infinity: An Essay on Exteriority* [Dordrecht: Kluwer, 1991], 89).

17. For more on the importance of repentance and asking for forgiveness by the perpetrator, see Tutu, *No Future without Forgiveness*, 272–73.

18. Paul Tillich insists that unless the ethics of forgiveness are rooted in the message of divine forgiveness, "they are delivered to the ambiguities of justice, oscillating between legalism and sentimentality. In the holy community this ambiguity is conquered" (*Love, Power, and Justice* [New York: Oxford University Press, 1960], 121).

any form of oppression and victimization of the fellow human and the rest of creation. It is a deeply distressful, heavy burden—the Spirit's burden for the healing of the cosmos—for reconciliation, organic unity, and shalom of all God's creatures.

The act of forgiveness encompasses an ascetic struggle (fasting from oneself) for the sake of God's justice, which is experienced as nothing less than life to the fullest and ontological renewal of the world. The groans of the Spirit "too deep for words" (Rom 8:26) indwell the cries of the victims and the laments of the penitent perpetrators, transforming repentance, forgiveness, and reconciliation into a sacrament in which God's mystical presence transfigures the other before our very eyes, overturning their objectification, commodification, dehumanization, as well as their villainization/demonization. Forgiveness sees the image of God in the face of the torturer (beneath the mar of dehumanizing, self-indulging hatred of the other) and unveils their own victimization by the violent systemic evils of human civilization[19] while discerning their root in the postlapsarian brokenness of the world—brokenness that runs through the core of humanity. Forgiveness is a courageous act of reaching forth and "washing" the face of the other so they can see themselves for who they are created to be and have a chance of renewal toward the fulfillment of their ontological destiny. Through its moral courage,[20] forgiveness "rules out . . . malicious and vindictive vengeance that perpetuates the cycle of violence"[21] against the fellow human, refusing to partake in further destruction of God's creation and resounding the truth

19. On the "normalcy" of violence in the "barbarism" of human civilization, see John Dominic Crossan, *God and Empire: Jesus against Rome, Then and Now* (New York: HarperOne, 2007), ch. 1. One of the markers of liberation theologies of social transformation is the insistence that both the oppressed and the oppressor are victimized by the dehumanizing effects of systemic evils. In the words of Desmond Tutu, the oppressor is "dehumanized as much as, if not more than, the oppressed." Reflecting on the social pathology of apartheid, he states: "Our humanity was intertwined. The humanity of the perpetrator . . . was caught up and bound up in that of his victim whether he liked it or not. In the process of dehumanizing another, in inflicting untold harm and suffering, inexorably the perpetrator was being dehumanized as well" (*God Has a Dream: A Vision of Hope for Our Time* [New York: Image/Doubleday, 2004], 50).

20. For more on the political implications of forgiveness's moral courage, see Shriver, *Ethic for Enemies*, 67. Shriver describes "the moral courage of forgiveness" as "the facing of still-rankling past evils with first regard for the truth of what actually happened; with resistance to the lures of revenge; with empathy—and no excusing—for all the agents and sufferers of the evil; and with real interest on the part of the sufferers to resume life alongside the evildoers or their political successors."

21. De Gruchy, *Reconciliation*, 172.

that "our humanity depends on recognizing the humanity of others"[22] even in its most distorted form.

In light of this, it is not accidental that the Christian ethic of forgiveness (and its practice as a social sacrament toward communal healing) is magnified by Scripture as an essential "gospel imperative."[23] Christ instructs his disciples to forgive "seventy times seven" the trespasses of others against them (Matt 18:22). Indeed, this is a mandate for unconditional forgiveness. It does not demand or depend on the repentance of the perpetrator, thus refusing to be reduced to a calculated exchange or transaction of mutual benefits. It remains a true, undeserved, and unrepaid gift of grace—the world-mending grace of God finding its home in human beings and pouring forth itself from there into the rest of creation.

Understanding the peculiarity of unconditional forgiveness (as well as its healing, socio-transformative effects) could be aided by engaging Jacques Derrida's "impossible" notions of justice and "the gift" (as transcending all calculations and legal systematizations).[24] Derrida differentiates between "law" and "justice," defining the first "as the history of right . . . of legal systems . . . of the transformation of laws" and the second as "the impulse, the drive, or the movement to improve the law, that is, to deconstruct the law."[25] Justice is irreducible to the law ("to a given system of legal structures"), which makes it always "unequal to itself" (or "noncoincident with itself").[26] This is why the ever-present demand for justice remains the inner nugget of deconstruction within the law, perpetually calling for its further transformation (as well as adaptation and fine-tuning amidst shifting social conditions). The ongoing development of the law (and legal systems) is ceaselessly fueled by the reality of justice's irreducible uniqueness. Justice remains forever nonreplicable, nontransferable from case to case, from situation to situation, from one life story to another. This matchless particularity of justice proceeds from its relational character, for as stated in the brilliant simplicity of Emmanuel Levinas's famous definition, "justice is the relation to the other."[27] The irreducibility of justice to a normative regulation (to a law

22. Tutu, *God Has a Dream*, 50.

23. Desmond Tutu, *The Rainbow People of God* (New York: Doubleday, 1994), 222.

24. Jacques Derrida, "The Villanova Roundtable: A Conversation with Jacques Derrida," in *Deconstruction in a Nutshell: A Conversation with Jacques Derrida*, ed. John Caputto (New York: Fordham University Press, 1996), 3–28 (15–19).

25. Derrida, "Villanova Roundtable," 16.

26. Derrida, "Villanova Roundtable," 17.

27. Levinas, *Totality and Infinity*, 89. Reflecting on Levinas's definition of justice, Der-

and legal action) flows from the irreducibility of otherness to unification, systematization, and generalization. The uniqueness of justice as relationship between two persons springs from their individual personhood—from their own irreplicable, irreplaceable selves (with their personal narratives of life and death, love and pain, joy and brokenness, dreams and nightmares, friendships and betrayals, heaven and hell). This is why for Derrida the notion of justice implies "non-gathering, dissociation, heterogeneity, non-identity with itself, endless inadequation, infinite transcendence. That is why the call for justice is never, never fully answered. That is why no one can say 'I am just'. . . . That's why it's not a matter of calculation." But this also means that justice cannot be reduced to a system of "sanctions, punishments or rewards" and that if a judge wants to be just, he or she cannot be content with simply applying the law to a given case, but (in a way) has "to reinvent it"—"to reinvent in a singular situation a new just relationship."[28] Therefore, administering true justice is a creative, socio-transformative work of building conditions for mediating relational healing. In light of this assertion, as well as in view of the dialectic between justice and reconciliation as social/relational healing, forgiveness (as the first step toward reconciliation and "means of restoring justice") could be understood also as "a creative act" and its agents as "true artists."[29]

In this vein of thought, it would be helpful to consider Hannah Arendt's assertion that not only is forgiveness "the exact opposite to vengeance,"[30] but in contrast to revenge's automatic, predictable reaction to trespassing, "forgiving can never be predicted; it is the only reaction that acts in an unexpected way and thus retains . . . something of the original character of action."[31] In other words, forgiveness "acts anew and unexpectedly, unconditioned by the act which provoked it and therefore freeing from its consequences both the one who forgives and the one who is forgiven."[32] Forgiveness, therefore, is the only possible "redemption from the predicament of irreversibility,"[33] which marks the human act in general (and the act of

rida states: "Once you relate to the other as the other, then something incalculable comes on the scene, something which cannot be reduced to the law or the history of legal structures" ("Villanova Roundtable," 17).

28. Derrida, "Villanova Roundtable," 17.

29. De Gruchy, *Reconciliation*, 179.

30. Arendt, *Human Condition*, 240.

31. Arendt, *Human Condition*, 241.

32. Arendt, *Human Condition*, 241.

33. Arendt, *Human Condition*, 237.

trespassing against the other in particular). Indeed, forgiveness does not erase or reverse the world's past, does not obscure transgression, does not demean its consequences, does not commit it to amnesia. Instead, it gifts to the world a new beginning, reenvisions it in hope, redreams and re-creates it in freedom for oneself and the other. In its capacity to construct "out of nothing" a creative opening for new beginnings, forgiveness both echoes God's original creative act and images his redemptive initiation of the new creation while simultaneously embodying its eschatological reality in the midst of the present. As such, the otherworldly gift of forgiving joins together origins and eschaton, revealing that as cosmic telos, forgiveness coincides with love. Therefore, only love can truly forgive—the love that is the beginning and end of creation, the love that hosts the world sustaining its very breath in unconditional hospitality toward the other—that same love that through the Spirit finds residence within humanity and renews the world, carving space for the other, refusing to see one's well-being and future without them. Thus, John exclaims with confidence, "God is love, and the one who abides in love abides in God, and God abides in him" (1 John 4:16); we are capable of this love "because he first loved us" (v. 19).

For Arendt, "Love, by reason of its passion, destroys the in-between which relates us to and separates us from others." Indeed, love, the ultimate act of freedom, has the capacity to "insert a new world into the existing world"[34]—a world of fusion of the self with the other, a world in which the good is what we have in common—the common good. Yet in Arendt's political philosophy, this "unworldly" and "most powerful of all antipolitical human forces"[35] remains the rarest of realities—a temporary spell that cannot sustain a perpetual politic or ethic of forgiveness.[36] Nevertheless, she credits Jesus as "the discoverer of the role of forgiveness in the realm of human affairs"[37] and insists that the freedom in "Jesus's teaching of forgiveness is

34. Arendt, *Human Condition*, 242.

35. Arendt, *Human Condition*, 242.

36. This is why Arendt suggests "respect" as an alternative foundation for the practice of forgiveness. She states, "Yet what love is in its own, narrowly circumscribed sphere, respect is in the larger domain of human affairs. Respect, not unlike the Aristotelian *philia politikē*, is a kind of 'friendship' without intimacy and without closeness; it is regard for the person from the distance which the space of the world puts between us, and this regard is independent of qualities which we may admire or of achievements which we may esteem. . . . Respect, at any rate, because it concerns only the person, is quite sufficient to prompt forgiving of what the person did, for the sake of the person" (*Human Condition*, 243).

37. Arendt, *Human Condition*, 238.

the freedom of vengeance,"[38] of never-ending, reactive violence against the other. Arendt highlights the emphasis on human agency in Jesus's teaching on forgiveness and its radical demands in the gospel narrative. According to Jesus, it is not only God who has the power to forgive, but humans should do likewise. In fact, they should initiate the process, not simply as a form of imitation of God but because "if ye from your hearts forgive," God will do likewise (in reference to Matt 18:35 and Mark 11:25 [KJV]). This is a striking and illuminating reversal of mutual reflectivity—in the act of forgiving, humanity mirrors God, and God mirrors humanity, as human activity prompts divine action. Here human forgiveness becomes an essential link in the renewal of the cosmos. This macroperspective elevates the significance of personal responsibility for the mending of the world and highlights forgiveness as written in and vibrating throughout the very structures of the universe.[39] Therefore, the act of personal forgiveness carries the gravity and burden of responsibility for cosmic healing. This perspective guards against the temptation to reduce forgiveness to an instrument of personal therapy and refocuses it on its proper mission (function) for the life of the world within God's redemptive work in creation.

Since the reference to God's forgiving as reflective of ours occurs in the prepassion passages of the gospel narrative, this shift in emphasis from divine to human responsibility for interpersonal/relational healing is not surprising. Indeed, it challenges conventional Christian interpretations along the lines of "we have to forgive, for he first forgave us, thus, enabling us to forgive those who transgress against us." Yet more importantly, the shift to human responsibility in these passages points to Jesus's teaching as synthesizing the purpose and movement of both the Old Testament narrative and the broader reality of God's transepochal, redemptive activity in the cosmos. Not only the Hebrew Scripture but the entire Bible (Old and New Testament alike) is "God's call to human responsibility"[40] for the condition and mending of the world. For the Judaic tradition, this call involves the internalization and enactment of the Torah within the new human community, summoned to responsibility by the word of God and held accountable by the divine covenant. For Christianity, the process of cosmic renewal is initiated and sustained by humanity's free-willed incorporation in Christ—the embodied Word, the redeemer and healer of creation—and

38. Arendt, *Human Condition*, 241.

39. Sacks, *To Heal a Fractured World*, 25.

40. Sacks, *To Heal a Fractured World*, 28.

his indwelling presence within the believers through the Holy Spirit, resulting in an upward ascent of Christoformation, culminating in theotic union with the Creator.

The creative artistry of forgiveness is fueled by in-Spirit-ed prophetic imagination that empowers humanity to redream and reenvision the relationship with the other, refusing to embrace a future without them (or to imagine the world as being a better place void of the other). In the words of Desmond Tutu, there is "no future without forgiveness," but this also means that the future includes the perpetrator, the torturer, the enemy, and it demands a commitment to their well-being and human flourishing.[41] The radical inclusivity of such a future manifests the seemingly otherworldly (Christic) vulnerability of unconditional forgiveness and reconciliation as distributive justice in the midst of the present. The interface with the unexpected otherness of forgiveness is an encounter of the Spirit's transfiguring agency, birthing the world to come into the human community. Yet there is also a sense of familiarity in the encounter of this otherness, a feeling of nostalgia, of homesickness—a longing for the recovery of ontological human goodness, of the wholesomeness of creation, of home with the other in a reconciled cosmos—a longing for paradise as a shared good. Forgiveness is a return to the other as homecoming in a recovered Eden.

The otherworldly socio-transformative *poiēsis* of justice as world-mending through forgiveness toward reconciliation is inspired, indwelled, and hosted by the creator Spirit whose hovering presence becomes the incubator of the world's eschaton as all-engulfing peace and justice for God's creation. The Spirit conceives, cultivates, and births this future's embodiment within the community of faith—the collective body of ontologically renewed humanity (the body of Christ)—and primes/anoints it with his socio-transformative agency. Therefore, the Spirit-filled human community stands in the cosmos as the visible, enfleshed story of forgiveness and reconciliation with God and neighbor—the story of relational healing and world-mending, of transfiguring broken human communities into agents of hope for the redemptive renewal of the cosmos. Thus, the community of

41. See Tutu, *Rainbow People of God*, ch. 6. Tutu insists that building such a future demands a spirituality of transformation, which, in my own work, I ascribe to the socio-transformative agency of the Holy Spirit. Daniela C. Augustine, *Pentecost, Hospitality and Transfiguration: Toward a Spirit-Inspired Vision of Social Transformation* (Cleveland, TN: CPT, 2012).

faith—the corporate body of the resurrected Lord—is unveiled by the Spirit before the eyes of heaven and earth not only as the incarnation of the world's future (the communal Christ—the telos of creation) in the midst of the present, but also as the very "way" (John 14:6) toward its healing. The church in the power of the Spirit is revealed as the living gospel of the divine art of peacebuilding through distributive justice (as access to life) for the other. As such, she is the tangible manifestation of peacebuilding as homecrafting for the other and, therefore, of redemption as an outcome and extension of God's unconditional hospitality to all his creatures. In light of this revelation, the art of forgiveness as the pathway to comprehensive shalom refuses to pay the price for peace through sacrificing the life of the other (even that of the enemy) or through "sending them to hell" in order to eradicate the reality of hell on earth. The sterile security of ideologically supported, systemic extermination of the other (so tempting to imperial regimes as a strategy for social management) does not provide peace, for it precludes the possibility of redemption. There is no redemption and future without the other. For redemption is the human community's ontological renewal as an image of the Trinitarian protocommunity—the image of harmonious, perichoretic communion of otherness. Yet the fact that there is no redemption without the other is also clearly displayed by the strategic placement of the social communal covenant at the very heart of the Decalogue (Exod 20:3-17). It illuminates the relationship with the other as the location of breaking or fulfilling one's covenant with God—the location of experiencing condemnation or redemption.

In the complex, interconnected heterogeneity of creation resides the very pedagogy (and wisdom) of the impossibility of fullness of life without the other—the impossibility of existence as homogeneous uniformity. The very essence of creation, as multiplicity in harmonious codependent wholeness, negates all human attempts and calculations for engineering sociopolitical, cultural, and ecological redemption of the cosmos without the anthropic and nonanthropic other, and the rest of creation. Therefore, as we have learned from the current ecological crisis, the destruction (or savage exploitation) of the other results in our own self-destruction and dehumanization.

The socio-transformative artistry of unconditional forgiveness brings to mind another important category within the philosophy of Jacques Derrida—"the gift." Alongside his understanding of justice (which resonates with the Torah in its radical preoccupation with securing access to life and well-being for the other), Derrida's reflections on the gift lend some helpful insights concerning the practice of forgiveness as a social sacrament and civic virtue. According to Derrida, the gift is something that should never be recognized (or rather recognizable) as such and, thus, can never be "reappropriated." Therefore, it remains "unequal to gratitude, to commerce, to compensation, to reward."[42] As soon as the gift is acknowledged as such, as soon as gratitude is offered in recognition of and response to the gift, it is annulled and reduced to a mere transaction. According to Derrida,

> That is the condition the gift shares with justice. A justice that could appear as such, that could be calculated, a calculation of what is just and what is not just, saying what has to be given in order to be just—that is not justice. That is social security, economics. Justice and gift should be beyond calculation.[43]

Yet Derrida is also in a hurry to offer a clarification of his statement by asserting that rigorous calculation is, indeed, needed as an important part of the democratic life and political process; however, it has to be faced with a sober recognition of its limitations, of the reality that "there is a point . . . beyond which calculation must fail," for "a democracy or a politics that we simply calculate, without justice and the gift, would be a terrible thing, and that is often the case."[44] Indeed, this insight deserves consideration amidst the current struggles of democracy to offer a global platform for negotiating seemingly irreconcilable differences and to achieve the harmonization of humanity's cultural/ideological/religious polyphony toward a constructive conversation about its common good and planetary future. Derrida's "impossible" notions of justice and the gift are an invitation toward rethinking the democratic process and re-envisioning politics "otherwise"—as "a place of hospitality, the place for the gift."[45] In its essence, this is also an invitation for engaging in the creative act of homebuilding for the other and the practice of unconditional forgiveness as a gift of restorative justice able to transform conditions of protracted conflict and violence into locations of peaceful communal life with the other and the different.

42. Derrida, "Villanova Roundtable," 18.
43. Derrida, "Villanova Roundtable," 19.
44. Derrida, "Villanova Roundtable," 19.
45. Derrida, "Villanova Roundtable," 18.

Forgiveness and the Redemption of Memory

No doubt, the politicization of unconditional forgiveness is a controversial issue precisely because of the existing notion of "the unforgivable"[46] and of the possibility of manipulation and coercion of people (and communities) toward forgiving systemic abuse and injustice in order to avoid societal unrest induced by demands for social transformation. Indeed, if forgiveness is the key to reconciliation, then the possibility of peacebuilding rests at the hands of the victims. In light of this weighty reality and the assertion of unconditional forgiveness as a gospel imperative, Christian victims of violence, oppression, and exploitation around the world have been (at best) instructed (at worst—manipulated) to grant unconditional forgiveness to their abusers, while patiently enduring suffering and praying for the well-being of their enemies. Considered an essential dimension of authentic discipleship toward Christian perfection (as perfect love toward the unlovable), the ethical imperative of unconditional forgiveness highlights the victims' vulnerability in the face of unjust, dehumanizing power relations. Precalculated social manipulation toward individual and communal subjection to systemic injustice, shaming the victims into accepting the ongoing pathology of violence, sociopolitical repression, and economic exploitation, presenting it as civilizational/societal normalcy on this side of eternity—these are some of the ways in which the mandate for forgiveness has been utilized as a tool for perpetuating human-rights abuses.[47] As Rowan Williams points out, the church herself is often "unsure how to handle forgiveness . . . drowning it in a rhetoric of a forgiving and forgetting God,"[48] casting away the sense of real injury (and with it the demand for a just intervention) as being illusory. A "forgetting God"—is this not an absurdity in light of his omnipresent omniscience and witness to the thoughts and feelings hidden in the depths of the human heart, in the innermost being of his creatures, with all their capacity for good and evil? Is there true forgiveness without remembering? Is there true grace and mercy extended to the other in conditions of forgetfulness/of amnesia? If God forgets, can there be justice? Indeed, these are rhetorical

46. Jacques Derrida, "On Forgiveness," *Cosmopolitanism and Forgiveness* (New York: Routledge, 2007), 27–60 (32).

47. While de Gruchy addresses briefly the possibilities of manipulating forgiveness in the context of oppressive power relations (*Reconciliation*, 171–72), Derrida engages the subject in more detail in his important essay, "On Forgiveness," while reflecting on the realities of twentieth-century crimes against humanity (*Cosmopolitanism and Forgiveness*).

48. Rowan Williams, *On Christian Theology* (Oxford: Blackwell, 2000), 272.

questions. Justice has the duty to remember—to remember faithfully, for forgetting is betrayal not only of justice but of the possibility for relational redemption, societal healing and transformation. There is no forgiveness without memory, and Christian forgiveness is rooted in one all-engulfing memory—the suffering of the incarnate God. Elaborating on Williams's assertion, John de Gruchy reflects on the agonizing cost of forgiveness by stating:

> But if the crucifixion of Jesus means anything, it means that God had to descend into hell in order to redeem the world. Redemption could not come through a polite word of cheap grace, otherwise the words of Jesus from the cross—"Father, forgive them for they know not what they do"—would have been adequate on their own. Jesus would not have had to experience being forsaken by God, or endure death itself. This is why the ethics of forgiveness must be rooted in the message of divine forgiveness. . . .[49]

In the agony of forgiveness, one identifies with Christ's crucifixion, death and descent to hell for the sake of the other. Forgiveness is painful, for it cannot be generic and impersonal. It involves exposing one's unhealed wounds to reliving the hellish memory of afflicted suffering in hope of redeeming the offender. It recollects the degrading objectification of the offence, the defacing iconoclasm of violence, the dehumanizing oppression of commodification, the physical pain engraved in the psychosomatic recollections of the body with all its post-traumatic stress disorder and restless anxiety (a perpetual torture in which the exteriority of the trauma has transitioned to the interiority of one's being, where there is no escape, no retrieval, no rest). Forgiveness is the act of finding oneself in Christ, plunging into hell in order to plunder from it the soul of one's enemy, and as such is irretrievably grounded in refusing not to remember. Repressing the memory is forgetting the other—forgetting them in hell (and hoping that they will stay there)—a reality that love cannot bear.[50] Yet precisely because

49. De Gruchy, *Reconciliation*, 172-73.

50. Bishop Kallistos Ware, *The Inner Kingdom, Collected Works*, vol. 1 (Crestwood, NY: St. Vladimir's Seminary Press, 2000). The author quotes a moving conversation between Saint Silouan of Mount Athos (a twentieth-century Russian Orthodox monk) and a certain hermit who "declared with evident satisfaction, 'God will punish all atheists. They will burn in everlasting fire.' Obviously upset, the Staretz [Saint Silouan] said, 'Tell me, supposing you went to paradise, and there looked down and saw somebody burning in hell-fire—would you feel

it unfolds within the redemptive narrative of Christ's self-giving for the life of the world, unconditional forgiveness is experienced as the redemption of the one who forgives. For Christ not only descended to hell, he also ascended to heaven, catching in his own resurrection and ascension the resurrection and ontological renewal of all humanity (and with it the rest of creation—Rom 8). This divinely enacted plunder of hell's torture chambers is precisely how the theology of Eastern Orthodox iconography portrays the resurrection of Christ—the one who himself is the resurrection and the life (John 11:25). It captures the moment in which the uncreated energies of God burst forth as life eternal within the resurrected body of the Son of Man, "trampling death"[51] and the grave through his own death. Yet the redemptive depth of Christ's victory resides in the communal reality of his resurrection. He does not rise alone from the grave; it is not a solitary act—for in him all humanity is raised from the dead. The icon brings forth its central theological assertion by depicting Christ, in the very moment of the resurrection, as grasping in his hands the hands of Adam and Eve. They burst forth from the grave, pulled up into the victorious life of their incarnate Creator. His life becomes their life—the life for which they were created. In a way, the joint arms represent also the restored continuity between humanity's origin and telos—the resurrection welds together the broken link between the first and the last human being. This is a recapturing of paradise—a moment in which humanity stands once again conjoined with its Creator in a renewed tridirectional mirroring of the divine image within the life-giving (and life-sustaining) cosmic liturgy.[52]

Illuminated by the resurrection, forgiveness abides in "the creative space" "between memory and potentiality . . . pregnant with the unexpected."[53] This is a place where humanity encounters the transformative power of perfect love, casting out all fear (1 John 4:18) and renewing the vision of the other as a cosharer in a common future. From inside this creative tension between remembering and reenvisioning life together, one can face fearlessly the past, retelling his or her story (the trauma, the pain, the betrayal, the abandonment) within the story of Christ. There one can expe-

happy?' 'It can't be helped. It would be their own fault,' said the hermit. The Staretz answered him with a sorrowful countenance. 'Love could not bear that'" (194).

51. As it is proclaimed in the Easter troparion (already quoted in chapter 2): "Christ is risen from the dead, trampling death by death, and to those in the tombs bestowing life."

52. See chapter 1 in the present book.

53. John Paul Lederach, *The Moral Imagination: The Art and Soul of Building Peace* (New York: Oxford University Press, 2005), 149.

rience the healing of memory and be empowered "to remember rightly."[54] This is the redemptive "place of narrative, the art of restorying"[55] where the healed memory becomes a building block of a new future. As John Paul Lederach states, "to restory" is "to find the narrative that gives meaning to life and ongoing relationships."[56] "But it is also to live in the permanency of risk, for the journey between what lies behind and what lies ahead is never fully comprehended nor ever controlled. Such a space, however, is the womb of constructive change, the continuous birthplace of the past that lies before us."[57] There, in the vulnerable tension between risk and promise, between the agony of memory and the labor pains of hope, redemption is experienced as socio-transformative peacebuilding.

In his compelling reflections on the obligation to remember rightly in a violent world, Miroslav Volf emphasizes that learning "to remember well is the only key of redeeming the past" and that this redemption "is itself nestled in the broader story of God's restoring" the world to wholeness.[58] In light of this assertion, Volf proposes the following steps toward the redemption of memories: remembering truthfully (being essential to constructing justice and refusing to contribute to the deepening of a conflict); remembering therapeutically (a cornerstone in the healing of interhuman relationships as foundational for one's personal healing); learning from the past (solidi-

54. While borrowing the expression from Miroslav Volf and receiving the gift of his insights on "remembering rightly" (*Exclusion and Embrace: A Theological Exploration of Identity, Otherness, and Reconciliation* [Nashville: Abington, 1996], 132), I respectfully differ with his assertion of the need to forget and let go of our memory "in order to be fully redeemed." While I appreciate Volf's (Augustinian) argument, my theological imagination sees the culmination of the redemption of memory not in forgetting but in Christoformation, expressed as a sanctified vision of and relationship to the other (a relationship transfigured by love, imaging the divine communal life and including the other in one's future flourishing). In light of this, perhaps the promise that God will wipe away all tears (Rev 21:4) can be understood also as the redemptive eschatological renewal of memories, or as remembering (with memory illumined by this Christified perspective) without the agony of pain.

55. Lederach, *Moral Imagination*, 148.

56. Lederach, *Moral Imagination*, 148. Lederach's thoughts reassert the insights of Hannah Arendt's *The Human Condition*, reflecting on the search for societal healing after the traumatizing realities of World War II. He encapsulates Arendt's point in the following way: "We live in a certain paradox as human beings precisely because we are beings that live by the meaning things have for us. Our God-given place is this. We have the capacity to remember the past, but we have no capacity to change it. Not even God can change the past. We have the capacity to imagine a different future, but we have no capacity to fully predict much less control it."

57. Lederach, *Moral Imagination*, 149.

58. Volf, *End of Memory*, 42.

fying the redemption of memory through recapturing one's experience as a vehicle for compassion, solidarity with victims and socio-transformative action toward bringing justice and healing to others); and placing remembering into a larger moral framework[59]—that of God's mending the broken cosmos—a story stewarded by the Christian church as the "community of memory,"[60] dedicated to remember rightly for the life of the world.

The church is the transgenerational custodian of the firsthand witness of God's coming within the human story, redeeming and making all things new—the memory that *restorys* the world according to its creational intent and meaning and transfigures its ways of remembering. This redemptive transfiguration of memory is accomplished via incorporation into the incarnate, communal body of the redeemer through the agency of the Spirit, who births Christ in us and us in Christ, making us partakers of the divine nature, enabling us to see and know otherwise. In the generosity of the Spirit, we find ourselves engulfed in the one who alone knows and remembers all things rightly, and we discover that the hospitality of his grace is larger than all our memories. By reflecting back on the vastness of God's unconditional hospitality, inviting him to indwell us, we are enlarged by the Spirit to circumscribe and host the memories of others, carving within ourselves a consecrated time and space for their redemptive healing. Christ in us becomes the sacred space of memory redemption not only for us but for the entire cosmos. We become an in-Spirit-ed sanctuary for the memory of the other.

The sacramental life of the church depicts the proleptic enactment of this redemptive transfiguration within the creative tension of anamnesis and promise, magnetized with eschatological anticipation. In the words of John de Gruchy, "the sacraments link remembering the past with hope for the future in such a way that they enable the embodiment and practice of reconciliation now . . . they become means of grace for healing and renewal."[61] Grasping the teleology of sacred time as an "ancient future," in its peculiar way of remembering rightly, the sacrament becomes enactment of the future as "remembering" the world to come.[62] Thus, the prolepsis of

59. Volf, *End of Memory*, 93.

60. Volf, *End of Memory*, 17.

61. De Gruchy, *Reconciliation*, 100.

62. In his assertion of the need to place one's memory/story in the story of God, Volf lifts up particularly the exodus and the passion narratives and articulates the ways in which our memories undergo healing and redemption as we remember through the lenses of these narratives, which position the community of faith between the memory of these events and their eschatological promise. The author engages the thought of Johann Baptist Metz, highlighting

baptism as incorporation within the body of the redeemer "remembers" the day in which all creation will be brought by the Spirit in Christ's corporeality and he will be all in all. The enmity of the curse will be overturned, and the tangibility of God's shalom will permeate all relationships and spaces between his creatures vibrating from the inside out—from the very fibers of their beings to the extremities of the cosmos—consecrating them all as sanctuary of the divine presence. Similarly, the sacrament of chrismation (practiced in the Orthodox tradition immediately after baptism and prior to communion), as a symbolic depiction of the mystery of Spirit baptism (an evocation of a personal Pentecost, conceiving Christ in the believer), "remembers" the new creation as the redemption of difference. In the Pentecost's inbreaking of the eschaton, humanity recovers its ability to speak and understand the language of the other as a celebration of diversity in unity. In the sacrament's enacted vision of the world's Spirit-saturated future, the human community embodies the sociocultural polyphony and communion of difference that marks a reconciled world where the Spirit has transfigured the other into kin, while sustaining his or her otherness. In the Eastern Orthodox liturgical practice of chrismation, the newly incorporated believer in Christ is anointed toward Christoformation under the pronouncement of the anticipated memory of Pentecost—"Receive the Holy Spirit." The anointing oil (symbol of the Spirit's outpouring) is placed in the sign of the cross upon the believer's forehead, eyes, ears, lips, hands, and feet. He or she is to think, remember, see, hear, speak, act, and walk in the world as Christ does, so that the world may be touched, reconciled, healed, and gathered in him. In this new (marked-by-the-cross) creation, the Spirit transfigures one's memory and vision of the other into Christ's memory and vision, for the believer's life in the power of the Spirit is not a mere imitation of Christ, it is Christ's life reverberating in redeemed humanity.

The notion of sacrament as anticipatory memory culminates in the eucharistic celebration as the enactment of the very source and purpose of the church's sacramental life—union with God and neighbor in a wholesome, ontologically renewed creation. In the communal anamnesis of Christ's passion illuminated by the resurrection and the anticipation of his imminent

---

his statement, "We remember the future of our freedom in the memory of his suffering" (see Johan Baptist Metz, *Faith in History and Society: Toward a Practical Fundamental Theology* [New York: Seabury, 1980], 111). For Metz, the "Christian memory of suffering" is "an anticipatory memory" that "brings a new moral imagination into political life, a new vision of others' suffering which should mature into a generous, uncalculated partisanship on behalf of the weak and underrepresented" (117–18).

return, in the words of Alexander Schmemann, "we *create the memory of each other*,"[63] reconciled and joined to him, and in him to one another. Echoing Schmemann, Miroslav Volf states, "By remembering Christ's Passion, we remember ourselves as what we *shall be*—members of one communion of love, comprised of wrongdoers and the wronged."[64] Therefore, the Eucharist anticipates "*the formation of a reconciled community even out of deadly enemies.*"[65] It transitions humanity from the stage of forgiveness (as the divinely ordained remedy for redeeming the irreversibility of the past) to that of reconciliation in communion with the other, sustained by a covenantal promise (as the "remedy for the unpredictability of the future"[66] and an antidote for the anxiety of scarcity and competition for limited material resources). This sacramental enactment of the movement from forgiveness to covenant is the Christian answer to the seemingly insurmountable challenge to pursue the common good when it includes one's former oppressor, abuser, and victimizer—one's enemy. The Eucharist summons us into the community of the forgiven, where the Spirit has made us members of one another (Rom 12:5; Eph 4:25), opening our eyes to see Christ even in his most unexpected form—the visible image of the invisible God, manifested in those who have once upon a time trespassed against us.

It is not accidental that the entire sacramental life of the church, as the movement from proclamation of the Word to his communal embodiment, is possible only in the epiclesis of the Spirit as the agent of the incarnation. The church as the reconciled eschatological community of the world's redeemed memory is a theophany of the Spirit, saturating the communal body of the Son as it enacts the will of the Father—a body "enlarged" by the deifying Spirit with the divine "spaciousness" and enabled to extend unconditional,

63. Alexander Schmemann, *The Eucharist: Sacrament of the Kingdom* (Crestwood, NY: St. Vladimir's Seminary Press, 1988), 130. Reflecting on the commemoration (which he describes as "sort of verbal expression of the Great Entrance"), Schmemann states in his rapturous prose: "Through this commemoration we include the ones being remembered in the life-creating memory of Christ: God's memory of man, man's memory of God, that diune memory which is eternal life. We return each other in Christ, to God, and in this giving back we affirm that the one remembered and given back is *alive*, for he abides in God's memory. . . . The remembrance of Christ is the entry into his love, making us brothers and neighbors, 'brethren' in his ministry. His life and presence in us and 'among' us is certified *only* by our love for each other and for all whom God has sent into, has included in our life, and this means above all in the *remembrance* of each other and in the commemoration of each other in Christ."

64. Volf, *End of Memory*, 119.

65. Volf, *End of Memory*, 119.

66. Arendt, *Human Condition*, 237.

loving hospitality to all humanity and the rest of creation. Indeed, if redemption of memory requires truthful recollection, learning from the past and positioning of one's story/experience within the broader story of God's work in healing the world, then there is no redemption of memory (and enactment of authentic forgiveness) apart from the Holy Spirit. The Spirit of truth guides us into all truth (John 16:13), teaches us all things (John 14:26), incorporates us in Christ (Eph 1:13), transfigures us in the divine likeness (2 Cor 3:17), and builds the unity of Christ's communal body—the unity of the Spirit in the bond of peace (Eph 4:3). As Rowan Williams states,

> Truthfulness given to human beings and "sustained" in them, as a constant self-critical, alert, prayerful and receptive turning back to Jesus, is the gift of the indwelling Spirit. . . . If we search for the bridge connecting our forgiven-ness with the commission to forgive, it is found in the presence with the believers of the Spirit, given for recollection of Jesus and witness to Jesus. . . . The believer who lives in the furnace of this truth is being made a witness to the rest of humanity of the possibility of living in the truth—burning, but not being consumed; and thus he or she becomes part of God's act of giving back the world its memory.[67]

The Challenge of Forgiving the Unforgivable

The overarching Christian emphasis on forgiveness and its eschatological promise of reconciled cosmos is met on occasion, however, with the challenge of encountering crimes and atrocities that the broader society perceives as transcending the very limits of forgiveness—as being "unforgivable." Such accounts interface closely with the duty of memory to archive inerasably their occurrences within the chronicles of "universal conscience."[68] For if we are negligent and inattentive to this duty and allow ourselves to forget, we can be dehumanized by our own amnesia.[69] Reflecting on the prolifer-

67. Rowan Williams, *Resurrection: Interpreting the Easter Gospel* (London: Darton Longman & Todd, 2014), 42–43.

68. Derrida, "On Forgiveness," 33.

69. Elie Wiesel reflects on the duty of communal memory as a guardian not only of the humanity of its community of origin but of all people, serving as "shield against evil" (*From the Kingdom of Memory: Reminiscences* [New York: Summit, 1990], 239). Volf states that when "not born out of resentment, the memory of inhumanity is a shield against inhumanity."

ation of public (personal and national) repentance and forgiveness within domestic and international affairs in recent history, Derrida points out that this trend in geopolitics undoubtedly proceeds from "a universal urgency of memory,"[70] which binds all humanity in a common net of responsibility for "crimes against humanity," crimes "against itself." In light of this all-encompassing transgenerational summoning to accountability before the collective/shared face of humanness (and in response to the theatrical cheapening of repentance and forgiveness within global geopolitics as means to selfish political ends), Derrida reminds the reader that among humanity, there is no one who remains acquitted of bloodshed, of crimes against the fellow human. Therefore,

> if we were to begin to accuse ourselves in asking forgiveness, of all the crimes of the past against humanity, there would no longer be an innocent person on earth—and therefore no one in the position to judge or arbitrate. We are all heirs, at least, to persons or events marked, in an essential, interior, ineffaceable fashion, by crimes against humanity.[71]

Indeed, in our multifaceted, corporate identities (tribal and national, religious and ideological, political and economic), we are all guilty of refusing to be our brothers' keepers, of exterminating otherness (through annihilation or assimilation[72] via means ranging from persuasion and manipulation to repression and violent coercion). We are all in need of forgiveness and faced with its limits in light of what remains unforgivable.

As G. F. W. Hegel reminds us, all is forgivable except the crime against the Spirit—against the power of forgiveness itself, against what he calls

---

However, in anticipating the eschatological redemption of remembering suffering, he asserts that "where there are no swords, no shields will be necessary" (*Exclusion and Embrace*, 138).

70. Derrida, "On Forgiveness," 28. Derrida correctly notes that this new horizon within the "geopolitics of forgiveness" (30) has adopted the language and figures of speech belonging to the religious heritage of the Abrahamic religions (Judaism, Christianity, and Islam) and especially that of Christianity. Reflecting on the all-pervasive Christianization of the political language of reconciliation communities, between people groups and nation-states, Derrida states that this "'globalization' of forgiveness resembles an immense scene of confession in progress, thus a virtually Christian convulsion-conversion-confession, a process of Christianization which has no need for the Christian church" (31).

71. Derrida, "On Forgiveness," 29.

72. Regarding various manifestations/forms of exclusion, see Volf, *Exclusion and Embrace*, 75-77.

"the Spirit of Christianity."[73] However, according to Vladimir Jankélévitch, crimes against humanity (and no doubt, he writes with the Holocaust in mind), crimes against humanness itself, remain beyond the limits of forgiving because they are "inexpiable." For him, a crime is inexpiable when there is no punishment proportionate to it, and what is inexpiable is irreparable and therefore, he concludes, unforgivable. Jankélévitch asserts that forgiving crimes against humanity is not and cannot be a personal affair—for it "would not be to renounce one's rights but to betray *the* right."[74] This is why, he states, "Forgiveness died in the death camps."[75] Here Jankélévitch's view echoes Hannah Arendt's reflections on the correlation between punishment and forgiveness. She states:

> The alternative to forgiveness, but by no means its opposite, is punishment, and both have in common that they attempt to put an end to something that without interference could go on endlessly. It is therefore quite significant, a structural element in the realm of human affairs, that men are unable to forgive what they cannot punish and that they are unable to punish what has turned out to be unforgivable.[76]

Thus, according to the logic of Arendt's and Jankélévitch's arguments, crimes that are impossible to punish are eternally inexpiable and unforgivable. In Arendt's interpretation of the gospel narrative, the "reason for the

73. Hegel discusses blasphemy against the Holy Spirit in a number of writings. See, for example, "The Divine in a Particular Shape" and "Lectures in Philosophy of Religion," in *G. W. F. Hegel: Theologian of the Spirit*, ed. Peter C. Hodgson (Edinburgh: T&T Clark, 1997), 68, 251. No doubt, the association with the gospel statement regarding "a word" or "blasphemy" against the Holy Spirit (Matt 12:32; Mark 3:29; Luke 12:10) is intentional. While the common interpretations of the passage point to the essentiality of the Holy Spirit's convicting power (John 16:8), Hegel's statement asserts the essentiality of the Holy Spirit for the embodiment and enactment of forgiveness. In his work, L. Gregory Jones also emphasizes the work of the Holy Spirit as agent of forgiveness and reconciliation. In the process, he highlights John 20:22–23 as an evidence for "an inextricable relation between receiving the Holy Spirit and engaging in the practice of forgiveness" (*Embodying Forgiveness: A Theological Analysis* [Grand Rapids: Eerdmans, 1995], 129).

74. Vladimir Jankélévitch, *Forgiveness*, trans. Andrew Kelly (Chicago: University of Chicago Press, 2005), 48–50. See also his work *L'Imprescriptible* (France: Seuil, 1996).

75. Vladimir Jankélévitch, "Should We Pardon Them?" trans. Ann Hobart, *Critical Inquiry* 22 (1996): 567.

76. Arendt, *Human Condition*, 241.

insistence on the duty to forgive is clearly 'for they know not what they do' and it does not apply to the extremity of crime and willed evil."[77] For her, Jesus's instruction to practice repetitively the spiritual (and civic) duty of forgiveness for the same offence (Luke 17:3–4) supports such an interpretation. Differentiating between the use of *skandala* and *hamartanein* in Luke 17:1–4, Arendt concludes that Jesus points to the existence of offences that remain unforgivable, "at least on earth," which "will be taken care by God in the Last Judgment." For her, such cases of despicable crimes and premeditated acts of inconceivable evil are rather exceptional occurrences (what Kant terms "radical evil"), and we remain ignorant about their nature even after having been "exposed to one of their rare outbursts on the public scene."[78] We can "neither punish nor forgive" them. Therefore, they "transcend the realm of human affairs and the potentialities of human power, both of which they destroy wherever they make their appearance."[79] Indeed, humanity stands bewildered and speechless before that kind of radical evil that strips human beings from all that is recognizably human, as if intentionally testing the very boundaries of forgiveness. While Arendt's exegesis could be dismissed as decontextualized, inadequate, or outright erroneous, her reach to the gospel in search of answers to one of the most difficult questions—"interrogating" the limits of forgiveness and redemption—is, undoubtedly, noteworthy. Yet Arendt's reflections, moved by the post-Holocaust struggle to make sense of incomprehensible crimes against humanity and the seemingly unlimited capacity to distort and efface the image of God in the other, seem troubling to a tradition that places its hope for the world in a Creator whose redemptive grace circumscribes the cosmos and whose forgiveness cannot be limited by the nature of any human transgression.

No doubt, any Christian discussion on the limits of forgiveness would recollect Christ's crucifixion as *the* crime against humanity (and in view of his essence as being *the* human telos), as *the* crime against what constitutes humanness itself. Yet within the mystery of redemption, this cruel execution of the one and only completely innocent human being becomes the crime against humanity without which the humanization of the perpetrators is impossible; the unforgivable act that makes them forgiven; the emblematic event that displays forgiveness par excellence—forgiveness embodied in a dying human body, hanging on a cross and breathing its last

77. Arendt, *Human Condition*, 239.
78. Arendt, *Human Condition*, 241.
79. Arendt, *Human Condition*, 241.

breaths in intercession for the sins of the crucifiers—an intercession for all humanity. Indeed, forgiveness is the reality that transforms this crime into an act of redemption. Without it, humanity stands accused but unforgiven for the death of the innocent Son of Man. In this dying plea to the Father, the last Adam faces his killer—the first Adam (and his offspring)—forgiving the unforgivable and, thus, redeeming the inexpiable. Yet this act points to another important aspect of forgiveness—namely, that the victim is the only one who can forgive, no one else (neither a person nor an authority/institution/court/state) can do it on one's behalf or in one's name.[80] In the reconciling drama of the crucifixion, God the Son intercedes before God the Father on behalf of his executioners through the power of the Spirit. This is both a haunting and rapturous vision of forgiveness, residing at the heart of redemption as a Trinitarian act of justice and healing renewal of the world. Forgiveness becomes the point from which all things are liberated into newness—the possibility and beginning of the new (renewed) creation. Forgiving the unforgivable, putting an end to violent retribution, and thus reconciling the world to himself—this is how Christ, the incarnate God, begins to make all things new. Therefore, the cross marks forgiveness as an unconditional, unrepayable gift of grace that does not demand or depend on the repentance (remorse or asking for forgiveness) of the perpetrator. In a way, the undeserved generosity of forgiveness precedes repentance—it is a true gift of life to the other.

According to Derrida, in reality the unforgivable is the only thing to forgive (a notion that resonates with the incalculability of justice and "the gift"). He summarizes the paradox of this assertion by stating:

> If one is only prepared to forgive what appears forgivable, what the church calls 'venial sin', then the very idea of forgiveness would disappear. If there is something to forgive, it would be what in religious language is called mortal sin, the worst, the unforgivable crime or harm. From which comes the aporia, which can be described in its dry and implacable formality, without mercy: forgiveness forgives only the unforgivable . . . there is only forgiveness, if there is any,

80. Derrida, "On Forgiveness," 43–44. Here Derrida engages the experience of the Truth and Reconciliation Commission (TRC) in South Africa in order to assert his conclusions. In the process, he addresses another important question: What would happen if the victim is not ready to forgive? A more in-depth exploration of this issue in the context of the TRC is offered by Martha Minow, *Forgiveness, Law and Justice*, Annual Reconciliation Lecture, 2014 (14–20): http://traumareconcil.ufs.ac.za/dl/Userfiles/Documents/00000/78_eng.pdf.

> where there is the unforgivable. That is to say that forgiveness must announce itself as impossibility itself. It can only be possible in doing the impossible.[81]

For Derrida, forgiveness should be stripped of all conditionality; it should not come only in response to repentance and, thus, be reduced to a mere transaction/exchange of benefits. Since the process of repentance is a transformational experience, the person who asks for forgiveness in recognition of his or her sins is already a different human being—"already another, and better than the guilty one."[82] The *metanoia* has transformed the former perpetrator and his or her outlook toward oneself and the other; it has illuminated and transfigured one's sociality and the surrounding world, revealing it as a place for atonement and redemption and, therefore, as a place for worship in sacramental living—it has unveiled the sacramental essence of the cosmos as a sanctuary. Therefore, forgiving the repentant person is not forgiving the perpetrator—"it is no longer *the guilty as such* who is forgiven."[83] In light of this assertion, true forgiveness is understood as possible only when unconditionally granted to the unrepentant, unremorseful perpetrator who has not yet come to terms with his or her guilt, with the irreparable dehumanizing effect of his or her actions. Thus, Christ's intercession from the cross epitomizes the creative act of forgiveness par excellence—making all things new in the face of the irreversibility of the past.

No doubt, however, the question remains—how may one practice the sacrament of reconciliation through unconditional forgiveness without contributing to perpetuating social pathologies of injustice and oppression that commodify and objectify some while deforming others into monstrous abusers and victimizers? This question is further magnified by the demand to cultivate the practice of forgiveness as a global civic sacrament bringing it out of "religious captivity" and allowing it "to enter the ranks of ordinary political virtues."[84] While the ever-growing anxiety for sustaining (national, regional, and planetary) peace within an age marked by weapons of mass destruction and malignant proliferation of terrorism justifies the urge to cast forgiveness as a civic duty for the sake of the common good, one may wonder whether it can be formalized as a matter of public policy. Is it possible to

81. Derrida, "On Forgiveness," 32–33.
82. Derrida, "On Forgiveness," 35.
83. Derrida, "On Forgiveness," 35.
84. Shriver, *Ethic for Enemies*, 7.

legislate forgiveness without demeaning its authentic socio-transformative power and reducing it merely to a means to an end (for example, for avoiding retributive justice)?[85] Derrida insists that when "the language of forgiveness" is placed in "service of determinate finalities," it is "anything but pure and disinterested." He reasserts the irreducible nonconditionality of authentic forgiveness by stating:

> I shall risk this proposition: each time forgiveness is at the service of a finality, be it noble and spiritual (atonement or redemption, reconciliation, salvation), each time that it aims to re-establish a normality (social, national, political, psychological) by work of mourning, by some therapy or ecology of memory, then the 'forgiveness' is not pure. . . . Forgiveness is not, it should not be, normal, normative, normalizing. It should remain exceptional and extraordinary in the face of the impossible: as if it interrupted the ordinary course of historical temporality.[86]

Addressing the possibility of manipulating and abusing forgiveness for the sake of impure and oppressive ends, Donald W. Shriver asserts that "forgiveness thrives in the tension between justice-as-punishment and justice-as-restoration."[87] Creating precisely such a tension is the aim of domestic and international laws that construct and sustain mechanisms and institutions (such as human-rights courts and crime tribunals) for giving public voice to the suffering of victims (and empowering them to face their victimizers with courage and dignity) while holding the perpetrators accountable for their crimes against humanity. Yet, while providing the victims with the therapeutic opportunity to share their stories and outcries for justice, as well as to hear the perpetrators' public confessions of their crimes, these mechanisms (and legal platforms) do not guarantee the criminals' (human rights abusers') renewal and rehumanization through authentic repentance. If authentic social transformation within a given community amounts to the qualitative personal change of its members, then is it reasonable to expect the overturning of unjust, dehumanizing conditions without the moral transformation of their enacting agents and propagators? In the words of

85. These were precisely the types of questions surrounding the institution of South Africa's Truth and Reconciliation Commission in the aftermath of apartheid.

86. Derrida, "On Forgiveness," 31–32.

87. Shriver, *Ethic for Enemies*, 32.

John de Gruchy, "the sacrament of penance is the sacrament of restorative justice."[88] No doubt, one should not overlook "the significance and practice of penance" as "a sacrament of social accountability and reconciliation"[89] (nor the moral consequences of its absence in Protestantism).[90] Indeed, a true healing of intersocial relationships, a restored communion with the other, involves the transfiguring *metanoia* of both, the victim and the perpetrator, the forgiving and the forgiven.[91] Thus, repentance as a change of mind and perspective toward the other is essential to the experience of communal redemption manifested as just social transformation—as embracing of responsibility for the other's future, for securing their human flourishing. As such, repentance involves accepting the other's right to be as he or she is—to be different—with an alternative understanding, response to, and engagement of the same shared world. In a way, this is an act of reconciling with difference, opening space for it in one's reality—a first step toward the possibility of conscious community and communion with the other within the eucharistic essence of life and creation. Such a notion of reconciliation is not based on anticipating the other's conversion into our likeness; it is not predicated by sameness but sustains difference, carving an opening for the other in our world (in ourselves). Therefore, it seems to be counterintuitive, unnatural, impossible, or at least improbable. Indeed, it is not an act of the natural but of the supernatural (not according to the flesh but according to the Spirit—Rom 8:4)—or rather, of the ontologically renewed flesh infused by the Spirit—the eucharistic community-builder and perfector (*teleiōtēs*),

88. De Gruchy, *Reconciliation*, 101

89. De Gruchy, *Reconciliation*, 100, 107. The author offers a brief overview of the sacrament's historico-theological development and practice from the second century AD to its later Protestant reduction to a general confession of sins within the liturgy and personal confession in private devotions or during a time of pastoral counseling (100–112). He points to Carl Jung's reflections on "the serious negative consequences for human health and spiritual well-being" proceeding from the Protestant abandonment of the sacrament (105). In so doing, de Gruchy refers particularly to Jung's *Modern Man in Search of a Soul.*

90. See Dietrich Bonhoeffer, *Ethics* (New York: Macmillian, 1965), 292. Bonhoeffer emphasizes that the Protestant Church "ceased to possess a concrete ethic when the minister no longer found himself constantly confronted by the problems and responsibilities of the confessional" and suggests that it is "only by rediscovering the divine office of confession that the Protestant Church can find its way back to a concrete ethic such as it possessed at the time of the Reformation."

91.In his marvelous work, *Exclusion and Embrace*, Volf offers a compelling reflection on the need for repentance by both the victimizers and the victims as the path to authentic social transformation (113–19).

the eschatological gatherer/invocator of the new creation. As with unconditional forgiveness, so also with repentance, wherever encountered, it is the work of the Spirit self-pouring upon all flesh, groaning within the fibers of the cosmos in its labor pains, driving humanity from inside out (from the conviction of conscience to the commitment of self-giving in renewed covenantal community with the other) toward its transfigurational summoning into the one and only human telos—Christ, the beginning and completion of creation (Col 1:17).

One may ponder the question: to what extent does reconciliation as social transformation rely on understanding the other's vision of human flourishing? Does it need a translation of one's perspective into that of another's experience? According to Derrida, "a shared language" and conversational engagement are essential for the initiation of reconciliation as the beginning of authentic social change. Sharing a language involves more than utilization of a common vocabulary and syntax; it involves shared meaning of words (with their historically developed cultural contexts and experiences). For "when the victim and the guilty share no language, when nothing common and universal permits them to understand one another, forgiveness seems deprived of meaning." Then it becomes impossible.[92] While translation can facilitate a mechanical linguistic convergence, it cannot bridge the gap between the ethnographically, historically, culturally, or politically loaded meanings of words. A word is a shared communal experience, a common history of life together in world building, which can often get lost in translation. Therefore, according to Derrida, understanding the other (and *their* world/words) is essential to reconciliation. Yet, reflecting on the significance of mediation within this process of coming to terms with the other's viewpoint in light of the paradoxical, incomprehensible "madness" of absolute/unconditional forgiveness as plunging into "the night of the unintelligible," he states:

> As soon as the victim 'understands' the criminal, as soon as she exchanges, speaks, agrees with him, the scene of reconciliation has commenced, and with it this ordinary forgiveness that is anything but forgiveness. Even if I say 'I do not forgive you' to someone who asks my forgiveness, but whom I understand and who understands me, then a process of reconciliation has begun; the third has intervened. Yet this is the end of pure forgiveness.[93]

92. Derrida, "On Forgiveness," 48.
93. Derrida, "On Forgiveness," 49.

Thus, Derrida insists on sociopolitically differentiating between forgiveness and reconciliation. While the first is saturating the abyss between oneself and the other with unmerited grace as gift of life, the second is "reconstruction of 'normality', as necessary and desirable as it would appear through amnesties, the 'work of mourning', etc."[94] This thought compels us to ponder on the possibility (and impossibility) of legislated forgiveness.

Justice and Legislated Forgiveness as a Civic Virtue

While Derrida is right that within the scope of national and international affairs forgiveness "should never amount to a therapy of reconciliation," it still remains the key to the actualization of just peace—the key held only by the victims and not by any mediating (or policy-crafting) institutions.[95] Thus, the pressure to forgive and forget (as well as guilting individuals and communities to participate in legislated and formally organized civic rituals of reconciliation) is ever growing. Reflecting on this trend, Martha Minow insists that while the law "can promote or deter forgiveness whether by individuals or for groups as large as a nation," forced forgiveness "is not forgiveness." In light of this, she poses three significant questions:

> 1) Does looking to law to promote forgiveness invite too much public pressure on private emotions? 2) Does the analogy between interpersonal forgiveness and collective forgiveness work or does the analogy instead obscure how societies differ from individuals? 3) Does forgiveness amount to a "second-best" solution, turned to when true justice is not possible legally, politically, or psychologically?[96]

94. Derrida, "On Forgiveness," 50.

95. Derrida, "On Forgiveness," 41. As Martha Minow points out, despite all the mediating/reconciling efforts of the South African TRC, the statistics were rather discouraging. "The actual numbers of people involved in the TRC engaged in what they identified as forgiveness are small." One study indicates that of 429 participants in South Africa's process, only 72 discussed forgiveness; only 10 percent were willing to forgive if the wrongdoers took responsibility for their deeds, and only 7 were willing to forgive without conditions (*Forgiveness, Law and Justice*, 10–11). For information on the study mentioned by Minow, see Hugo van der Merwe and Audrey R. Chapman, eds., *Truth and Reconciliation in South Africa: Did the TRC Deliver?* (Philadelphia: University of Pennsylvania Press, 2008), 68.

96. Minow, *Forgiveness, Law and Justice*, 13.

Minow's answers highlight the rhetorical nature of these questions. She emphasizes the inherent dangers and limitations of legislated mediation toward forgiveness, pointing out that "the law cannot be neutral when it comes to the feelings and expressions of individuals who use it" and that "litigation can enlarge the distance between the disputing parties"; for if "the legal framework inevitably affects emotions, pushing toward forgiveness may be no worse than pushing toward revenge, adversariness, or bitterness."[97] Further, Minow magnifies the obvious differences between the functional realities of groups/nations and individuals and reasserts the shortcomings of attempts to translate the dynamics of personal forgiveness within the domains of international relations between states or ethnic groups. She points to the heart of the problem by stating:

> When a government makes steps in the direction of forgiveness, it seems to change forgiveness by making it no longer about reconciling primary relationships—relationships between the actual individuals directly involved in the wrong—but instead turns to secondary relationships—relationships between groups concerned ultimately with the legal consequences of obligations within primary relationships.[98]

If there is no healing of the interpersonal relation to the other, justice remains in the sphere of retribution but not in that of restoration and redemption. The magnitude of mass atrocities and crimes against humanity can easily obscure (in the sight of the international community) the reality that all crimes are ultimately committed against individuals and that the suffering (and consequent trauma) of the victim is never generic and impersonal. Indeed, states can judge each other (and their citizens) and negotiate conditions for ceasing conflicts or mutual isolation by restoring diplomatic relations, offering public apologies or paying reparations for past crimes (thus, attempting to put a manageable price tag to the other's suffering), but only people/individuals can forgive. Minow's answer to the final question naturally flows from this conclusion. She cautions against the temptation of "turning to forgiveness solely when more robust justice is unavailable" or is difficult to secure, especially "where very large numbers of wrongdoers are involved"[99] (as in the case of the Holocaust or the South African apartheid,

97. Minow, *Forgiveness, Law and Justice*, 15–16.
98. Minow, *Forgiveness, Law and Justice*, 17.
99. Minow, *Forgiveness, Law and Justice*, 18–19.

but also in postdictatorial, transitional democracies in Latin America or in African and Asian societies torn by past tribal and civil wars).

The communal/ethnic/tribal memories often pass down the trauma and resentment from generation to generation, which further complicates the healing of relationships between nations. The transmission of collective identity, marked by recollection of victimization by the other, demands to be addressed in each new generation within the context of redemptive (healing) restorying of the past and reenvisioning hope for a shared future with one's former enemy. In the painful, slow, seemingly impossible process of forgiveness and reconciliation between nations, the issues of the "duty of memory" as essential component of ethnic identity converge with the necessity for sociopolitical and economic survival, which demands functional relationships between former enemies. Ethnic identity's collective, narrative character diligently cherishes each wound (and torturous trauma) sustained in the process of its becoming—national tragedies and pains are faithfully remembered alongside victories and triumphs. Thus, Jewish identity is engraved with the survival of centuries of anti-Semitic persecution, culminating in the Holocaust of World War II. Bulgarians are marked by five hundred years of economic, political, and religious marginalization under Islamic, Ottoman rule and two national catastrophes during the World Wars. Armenians and Cyprians are imprinted by the experience of twentieth-century genocides and displacement as refugees. Serbs, Bosnians, and Croats bring flowers to mass graves, irreversibly stamped upon their recent history, and walk past shrapneled buildings, intentionally left unreconstructed—kept as memorials of the price paid for defending national identity and interests. In light of this, it is legitimate to pose the question: can reconciliation be accomplished without (repentance and) forgiveness? Can it take place as the building of a common future between victims and perpetrators when the act of forgiving is suspended indefinitely? If forgiving is considered a betrayal to the memory of the victims (and, thus, to national identity) and if no one is willing to forgive or to ask for forgiveness, could there be a sustainable peace as life together? It seems that this is precisely the peace attempted between the current Balkan countries (as well as in other contexts of protracted ethnic conflicts in Europe)[100] that are all looking toward a shared life and a new collective identity within the European Union. Only the future can show the extent of such a possibility.

100. For example, in the cases of the Basque separatists in Spain and of IRA in Northern Ireland.

Indeed, forced forgiveness is not forgiveness. Yet the Christian imperative to forgive is represented also by some significant gospel texts that seem to depict salvation as (more or less) a transactional reality in which one has no choice but to forgive in order to be forgiven by God. These disturbing passages could be perceived as abducting the possibility of choice and coercing victims of injustice to forgive under fear of inescapable divine retribution and eternal punishment. An example of such a text is the kingdom parable about the forgiving ruler and the unforgiving servant, punished for lack of mercy and compassion toward his debtor (Matt 18:23–34)—a passage recorded in the verses immediately following the instruction for unconditional forgiveness, in Matt 18:22. The passage ends with Jesus's warning: "So shall my heavenly Father also do to you, if each of you does not forgive your brother from your heart." A similar statement appears at the end of the landmark prayer of Christian discipleship (often referred to as "The Lord's Prayer"—Matt 6:9–13). There, the words of Jesus position the practice of forgiveness at the very heart of Christoformation, culminating in the verse "And forgive us our debts, as we also have forgiven our debtors" (Matt 6:12). The salvific dimension of embodied forgiveness for the other is further emphasized by Christ's statement recorded in the two verses following the prayer: "For if you forgive men for their transgressions, your heavenly Father will also forgive you. But if you do not forgive men, then your Father will not forgive your transgressions" (Matt 6:14–15).

In light of these passages, as well as their possible use to perpetuate abuse and injustice, one may wonder whether forgiving out of fear of punishment could be a truly transformative, Christoforming experience. Could such forgiveness be an act of the Spirit who transforms fear, exclusion, and prejudice into love that casts out all fear? Is it enough to ask forgiveness from God alone (in the anonymity of personal prayer or the confidentiality of confession), or should we face those against whom we have sinned? While the limits of the present work do not allow for an in-depth engagement of these questions, it is helpful to remember that all of Scripture should be read in light of its final purpose—making the Word flesh within the cosmos via the work of the Holy Spirit, incarnating it into a living communal body, for the life and mending of the world. Reading these passages, one should remember that their eschatologically nuanced teleology is not driven by thirst for vengeance and retributive justice at the great day of judgment but first and foremost by a longing for the healing of the cosmos and its gathering into union with the Creator. This eschatological unfolding demands the human agency of a redeemed, Christoformed humanity—humanity that has experienced ontological renewal in the likeness of God and has become living, enfleshed Word. In light of this assertion, mutual forgiveness could be perceived as a spiritual discipline that accomplishes both humanity's enactment of the divine likeness amidst the present and free-willed surrender to one's continual transfiguration toward that likeness. Through the liturgical asceticism of forgiveness, the believer commits him or herself to the Spirit's ongoing work of mending the world. This journey starts with the healing of relationships as a pathway to cosmic healing. Therefore, one is forgiven as they forgive, for this is the extent to which they have (or have not) attained to their creaturely telos, namely Christlikeness (as the likeness of God in flesh). Through these hermeneutical lenses, the story of the unforgiving servant sobers with its gravity—the servant's life becomes the location where God and his telos for the world are challenged by fallen humanity positing itself as the cosmic telos (humanity's self-centered introversion and self-proclamation as the end of existence)—the definition of sin (as idolatry), per se. Another obvious conclusion of such a reading would be that nonforgiveness imprisons us in the transgression to which we have been subjugated, robbing the soul of the healing for which it longs. It is a hellish, torturous experience; thus, the "wicked" servant is turned over to the "torturers" (*basanistais*) "and not merely 'jailers.'"[101] Reflecting on the narrative of the parable, John R. W. Stott states,

> Once our eyes have been open to see the enormity of our offence against God, the injuries which others have done to us appear by comparison extremely trifling. If, on the other hand, we have an exaggerated view of the offences of others, it proves that we have minimized our own.[102]

This interpretation could imply that the nonforgiving servant had not experienced salvation, for he did not bear evidence of having received the transformative, Christoforming grace of God in his life. For him, turning to "the king" in search of forgiveness was just a way to avoid well-deserved punishment. Therefore, the story portrays salvation in terms of faithful stewardship of the divine grace, purposed to transform its recipient into

101. D. A. Carson, *Matthew: Chapters 13 through 28*, The Expositor's Bible Commentary (Grand Rapids: Zondervan, 1995), 407.

102. John R. W. Stott, *Christian Counterculture: The Message of the Sermon on the Mount* (Downers Grove, IL: InterVarsity, 1978), 149–50.

the likeness of the giver. It implies that turning to God for forgiveness is not enough to inherit eternal life. Rather, one has to become like him, extending the same grace to their fellow humans. Acting in Godlikeness on this side of the eschaton means that the eschaton has arrived in the believers. They enter the kingdom, for the kingdom has first entered into them. The parable emphasizes the content of the gospel as being preoccupied with distributive (and restorative) justice—with enacting the divine grace of forgiveness and reconciliation as providing access to life for the needy (and the undeserving). In view of this, the story of the "wicked servant" stands in contrast with that of Zacchaeus (Luke 19:1–10). The tax collector welcomes the king and his kingdom not only in his home but also in himself, and this indwelling bears its fruit in the present in the form of distributive justice—the grace of God extended through its recipient to the needy, overflowing their lives with divine generosity. Thus, to Zacchaeus's public statement of faith and penance, "Behold, Lord, half of my possessions I will give to the poor, and if I have defrauded anyone of anything, I will give back four times as much," Jesus replies, "Today salvation has come to this house." The assertion that follows is "for he too is a son of Abraham." This is Christ's response to Zacchaeus's societal marginalization as tax collector, to his ceremonial "impurity" as collaborator with the gentile, Roman authorities—the enemies of Israel. His covenantal identity in God is reaffirmed by Jesus as a vocalization of reconciliation with God and the fellow humans. To be a son of Abraham means to keep the way of the Lord by doing righteousness and justice (Gen 18:19) and not a routinization of particular "liturgical rhetoric"[103] or the utilization of worship to justify injustice. Therefore, the story depicts distributive justice and restored communion as the visible, tangible mark of forgiveness and reconciliation.

The Challenge of "The Ways of Peace"

In facing the global struggle of peacebuilding as "*living with difference*" and pursuing the common good, Jonathan Sacks proposes that humanity should seize the wisdom of the sages and walk in what they have termed *darkhei shalom* or "the ways of peace"—an ancient rabbinical teaching that has become an ethical norm and way of life for the Jewish communities in the diaspora, living for thousands of years amidst religious (as well as cultural,

103. Meier, *Matthew*, 59.

ethnic, and racial) others. Sacks describes *darkhei shalom* as *hesed* (or "covenant love" between the members of the faith community) extended to or "applied to those who are not members of our faith."[104] Therefore, "the ways of peace" could be viewed as "universalized" covenant love.[105] No doubt, this is a radical and radically beautiful proposition. Indeed, it sounds remarkably similar to the Christian imperative for unconditional love toward the other—God and neighbor (despite their differences)—love extended even to the enemy.[106] We find one of the shortest formulations of "the ways of peace" in the Talmud, Gittin 61a: "Our Rabbis taught: We sustain the non-Jewish poor with the Jewish poor, visit the non-Jewish sick with the Jewish sick, and bury the non-Jewish dead with the Jewish dead, for the sake of peace."[107] According to Sacks, these statements constitute the rabbinical "*non*-utopian programme" for peace "in an *unredeemed world*."[108] The text is remarkable with its unconditional inclusion of the other into the communal access to life, with its understanding of well-being and shalom as rooted in the pursuit of the common good, and with its recognition of common humanity and, therefore, of common suffering. Here the shared experience of suffering becomes a bridge toward recognizing oneself in the other despite their difference and naming them as belonging to the same human community of life, death, and tears. *Darkhei shalom* are commitments for cosuffering with the fellow human in a recognition of the world's brokenness. They are gestures of companionate generosity and kindness to strangers that build peace as way of life with difference—life magnetized and held together by profound bonds of sameness, which run deep beneath the crust of otherness, through the core of indivisibly shared humanity.

Perhaps the third statement in the Gittin is the most striking and unexpected one, yet it is the most explicit evidence for embracing the humanity of others as one's own. "We . . . bury the non-Jewish dead with the Jewish dead, for the sake of peace." While the first two statements magnify charity

104. Sacks, *To Heal a Fractured World*, 98.

105. Sacks, *To Heal a Fractured World*, 98.

106. However, Sacks is careful to point out the particularly Jewish origin of the concept by asserting that in the period in which "these laws were formulated, there were no other monotheisms. Christianity, if it existed at the time (depending on the precise dating of the texts), was still a Jewish sect; Islam had not been born" (*To Heal a Fractured World*, 101).

107. Babylonian Talmud, Gittin 61a (http://www.on1foot.org/text/babyloniantalmud-gittin-61a). For accessing the full text of the Babylonian Talmud, see also https://www.jewishvirtuallibrary.org/jsource/Judaism/FullTalmud.pdf.

108. Sacks, *To Heal a Fractured World*, 100–101.

and compassion as imperative, the third one intensifies them to a new level of commitment to the other—to the recognition of him or her as family. Burials are marked by profound ethnographic and cultural particularities. They are intensified expressions of one's ethnic, familial and communal identity—events that link the living and the dead in one transgenerational community of common memory, shared story of beginnings, and joined hopes for the (eschatological) future. Therefore, burials gather the person together with his or her own in recognition of belonging that transcends the partitioning between life and death with bonds stronger than both time and eternity. Funeral ceremonies are also religious rites (even in the case of atheist convictions) and, as such, represent intense/compacted public proclamations of the community's faith confession. They affirm the faith identity of the departed with all the eschatological hopes that flow from it as an authentication of their rightful claim to a particular future of recompense for undeserved (or deserved) earthly travails—a future of justice and wholeness—a future of peace. Therefore, the instruction to bury the other as one's own is even more meaningful. It is a mandate to extend to the other one's own hope and future, to invite them into one's paradise/heaven, to share one's shalom and to profess an anticipation that, by the incomprehensible movement of grace, the other will enter into it. This is a gesture of radical hospitality—inviting the other to be family and treating him or her as such. The wisdom of *darkhei shalom* compels its practitioner to see through the otherness that polarizes, threatens, destabilizes, or shocks and to recognize the truth that we are all family and as such belong together, sharing a clear resemblance—the image of God. As Desmond Tutu's challenging words summon us to responsibility for the other's life and death in a shared world,

> Any death is one too many, and yet some were more important than others not only in life but also in death. This inequality in death results from our separating ourselves from one another in life. In war, for example, we keep score of our casualties and their casualties to see who is winning. God sees only His dead children. . . . Perhaps only when we care about each other's dead can we truly learn to live in the same world together without irrational prejudices and hatreds. Perhaps this will be possible when we eventually realize that God has no enemies, only family.[109]

109. Tutu, *No Future without Forgiveness*, 46–47.

Epilogue

Toward a Hagiography of a Community Committed to the Common Good

In her compelling book, *Saints and Postmodernism: Revisioning Moral Philosophy*, Edith Wyschogrod explores the concept of sainthood and the nature of hagiographic discourse in search of solutions to the apparent aporia between moral theory and practice (including ethical theories' inability to shape living moral communities or to account for the peculiar unfolding of saintly lives).[1] Analyzing the issue, Wyschogrod proposes that "by appealing directly to concrete moral lives" the nontheoretical framework of hagiography "can be brought to bear on questions of moral practice."[2] While recognizing the contextual particularity of hagiographical texts, the author outlines four distinct structural features of a saintly life, marking hagiography's discursive form—*narrativity*, *corporeality*, *textuality*, and *historicality*.[3] However, as Martin Hinterberger points out, despite the few common elements that can be traced throughout groups of texts, the wide variety of hagiographical works defy generalizations and categorizations. Due to this apparent challenge to systematization, the study of hagiography as a *genre* "remains perplexing"[4] and it seems more appropriate to speak instead

1. Edith Wyschogrod, *Saints and Postmodernism: Revisioning Moral Philosophy* (Chicago: University of Chicago Press, 1990), 3–4. According to Wyschogrod, this gap is the result "from the confusion of moral and scientific discourse." Alongside this assertion, the author reflects also on "the incommensurate presuppositions of theories from which follows the failure to produce moral dispositions" (4).

2. Wyschogrod, *Saints and Postmodernism*, 4.

3. Wyschogrod, *Saints and Postmodernism*, 5.

4. Martin Hinterberger, "Byzantine Hagiography and Its Literary Genres: Some Critical Observations," in *The Ashgate Research Companion to Byzantine Hagiography: Volume II: Genres and Contexts*, ed. Stephanos Efthymiadis (Burlington, VT: Ashgate, 2014), 25–60 (25). The author offers a brief overview of various hagiographical genres/groups and their specific features (e.g. *passio*, translation, narrations and collections of miracles, *apophthegmata*, ed-

of hagiographical *genres* and *subgenres*. Hinterberger notes that despite the shared features that nuance the texts in a given group, when examined not just as historical accounts but as literary works, each text exhibits distinct thematic and stylistic particularities and does not simply follow the expected topoi without introducing variations.[5]

Understanding the impossibility of finding a universal hagiographic blueprint could be both troubling and liberating for one who undertakes the task of articulating the flesh and blood of holiness in continuity with Christian tradition. The apparent space for variation in both forms and themes brings a degree of comfort alongside the weighty sense of inadequacy in facing the challenge.[6] Therefore, keeping in mind the perplexing complexity of hagiographical literature, this final chapter engages the characteristics of hagiographical discourse proposed by Wyschogrod (especially the first two—*narrativity* and *corporeality*) with caution and awareness of their limitations. It also brings the thematic unfolding of the volume full circle by returning to Sallie McFague's exploration of saintliness (highlighted in chapter 1) and offers a brief hagiographical account of the living community that has inspired this book by uplifting their *acts* of peacebuilding and reconciliation in pursuit of the common good.[7] The narrating voices in this hagiographic construct come not only from within the community's own self-reflective living memory but through the firsthand eyewitness accounts of the ethnic and religious others for whose life and well-being members of the community risked their own lives amidst the dehumanizing brutality of war and scarcity.

---

ifying stories, collective biographies, acts, etc.) while accounting for the variations between texts within each genre.

5. Hinterberger, "Byzantine Hagiography and Its Literary Genres," 25.

6. Wyschogrod begins her reflections on saintliness by posing on Dostoevsky's own literary struggle in depicting "a positive holy figure" and ultimately finding the inspiration for that in the life of Saint Tikhon of Zadonsk (*Saints and Postmodernism*, 3).

7. As Hinterberger points out, acts (*praxeis*) as hagiographical form were fashioned after the Acts of the Apostles and were used almost exclusively for narrating the hagiographies of the apostles or those named as "equal to the apostles"—for example, Saint Thecla. (Hinterberger, "Byzantine Hagiography and Its Literary Genres," 35.) While my retelling of the few selected stories in this chapter fits closer the hagiographic discourse of a different form discussed by Hinterberger—that of "edifying stories," I have chosen the term "Acts" in order to highlight a particular aspect that they have in common with that form—their historicity and significance as firsthand eyewitness accounts, as well as the pneumatological emphasis in the depiction of the post-Pentecost community's hallowed life, enlarged by the Spirit with the hospitality of God and empowered to enflesh the gospel, carrying its witness to the uttermost parts of the world (among the ethnic and religious others).

Pondering the Distinctives of Hagiographic Discourse and Saintly Lives

Reflecting on hagiography's specific *narrativity*, Edith Wyschogrod reaches to Jacques Derrida's distinct assertion of narrative as a form of "juridical discourse,"[8] seeking to "extort" something like a "secret-less secret" from the other, "something that they call the truth about what has taken place."[9] Indeed, for Derrida, the narrative begins with the demand for truth as "*demand for narrative*"[10] itself, going back to the origin of the story (to "the origin of origin," to the narrative of the narrative)—to the birth of what "sees the light of day" "when the present leads to presence."[11] This is the demand to see beyond the visible, to "see-beyond-sight" (or to "see-sight-beyond-sight"), to have a vision of the unseen.[12] This surprising language in Derrida's description of narrative resonates with iconographic theology. Keeping in mind the theological continuity between iconography (as the visualized narrative of the holy) and hagiography (as the narrated icon of the holy), such an assertion deserves further attention. Applied to hagiographical discourse, this understanding of narrative allows to receive the account of a saintly life as a vision of the life of God in flesh—a vision of Christ, the living Word. The saint's life becomes transparent to the readers so that they can behold God and commune with him in order that they may become like him. The life of the saint (a holy life) becomes a means of transfiguring/transformational communion with the one who is the destiny/telos of the hearer/viewer. They are to be caught by the Spirit's movement into the spaciousness of this life—the life of the pneumatized (united to God/the Spirit) other—until their life has become transparent for the divine presence in the world, making the invisible visible for others, giving sight to the spiritually blind so they can see what Adam beheld in Eden. Both hagiography and iconography are retelling (making visible) the *gospel* as the *narrative* of the narrative, the *origin* of the origin, the *story* of the story. Both are intended to facilitate proclamation and redemptive transformational encounter with the truth about oneself and the world (in light of its triadic theological understanding as *created* good by God, yet having become *fallen* and distorted by sin and finally *redeemed*,

8. Wyschogrod, *Saints and Postmodernism*, 5.

9. Jacques Derrida, "Living On: Border Lines," in *Deconstruction and Criticism*, ed. Harold Bloom (New York: Seabury, 1979), 87.

10. Derrida, "Living On: Border Lines," 72.

11. Derrida, "Living On: Border Lines," 72.

12. Derrida, "Living On: Border Lines," 75.

ontologically renewed in Christ).[13] Ultimately, as in iconography, so also in hagiography the beholder is to become, through the sanctifying agency of the Word and the Spirit, what they see, and the life of the saint is an elucidation of this pneumatic journey. Thus, the hagiographic (and iconographic) account of the saint's life is a theotic imperative—a demand for one's moral theoformation.

In light of Derrida's understanding of narrative as a truth-demanding, interrogating discourse, Wyschogrod defines hagiography not as one literary genre among others but as "a narrative linguistic practice that recounts the lives of saints so that the reader or hearer can experience their imperative power."[14] The saint's life is a narrative construct that is to serve as collective moral paradigm, transcending time and locality and maintaining an interactive open-endedness that allows the story's reshaping (and reapplication) within the sociopolitical dynamics of concrete living communities.[15] It is a textbook that invites the indigenization and incarnational contextualization of its lessons, upholding them not as a theoretical possibility but as living, enacted and eyewitnessed holiness in flesh and blood—the life of real human beings united to and moved by/in the Holy Spirit. Effectively, each saintly life (with all of its ethnic, racial, cultural, historical, geographical, sociopolitical particularities) is an authentication of the Incarnation with its scandalous radical particularity, and of the incarnational work of the Spirit, translating and indigenizing the life of Christ (as the content of the gospel) in diverse, living faith communities.

Indeed, the hagiographic narrative outlines the saint's upward progression toward Christification, usually propelled by an encounter with God/Christ and his holiness as summoning to responsibility for one's moral choices and relationship to the other (including the nonanthropic creation).[16] The saint's free-willed, cathartic response to this summoning by/in the Spirit results in his or her Christic transfiguring, which in turn confronts and challenges the world around them toward its Christifying

13. Alexander Schmemann, "The World in Orthodox Thought and Experience," in *Church, World, Mission: Reflections on Orthodoxy in the West* (Crestwood, NY: St. Vladimir's Seminary Press, 1979), 67–84 (74).

14. Wyschogrod, *Saints and Postmodernism*, 6.

15. Wyschogrod, *Saints and Postmodernism*, 7–8.

16. Healing of the relationship between sanctified humanity and the nonanthropic creation is an important theme, illustrating the Spirit's undoing of the consequences of the fall through the Christified human life. The hagiographies of Saint Francis of Assisi and Saint Ivan of Rila exemplify this theological theme within the hagiographic genres.

transformation.[17] In a way, both the saintly life and its hagiographic narrative become vehicles for the Spirit's socio-transformative work. Therefore, as Wyschogrod points out, "The story's success is not measured in aesthetic or cognitive terms but rather in regard to whether the addressees experience the saint's spiritual rebirth as an existential demand." Yet, as previously noted, the "tail is not intended to elicit replication but to inspire a new catena of moral events appropriate to the addressee's life."[18]

As the work of the Spirit who hallows the cosmos, holiness is never stereotypical, monotonous, or monochromatic. It surprises and even shocks by diverging from established norms and regulations. The saints' journey often appears as "breaking away from ecclesiastical authority" and their "antinomian acts provide an intratextual counterdiscourse to . . . institutional frameworks."[19] In the process, saintly lives display the creativity of holiness (reflecting the infinite creativity of the Spirit), carving unexpected openings for world-mending through the saint's Spirit-moved "moral imagination."[20] Thus, the hagiographic depiction of the holy articulates the saints' words and deeds not only as moral imperative and challenge toward sanctification for those around them, but also as interventions of grace, providing solutions to what seems to be unsolvable—for example, by mediating peace in the midst of violent conflicts[21] or by taking an uncompromised stand against injustice,

17. Wyschogrod, *Saints and Postmodernism*, 10. While Wyschogrod acknowledges that in Christian hagiographies *imitatio Christi* is the principle that "guides saintly conduct," she asserts that this is "an unrealizable imperative" since human nature "cannot conform itself to divine perfection" (13). Obviously, this understanding is antithetical to the vision of the present volume, uplifting the Spirit's agency toward humanity's Christification in perfect love toward God and neighbor.

18. Wyschogrod, *Saints and Postmodernism*, 10.

19. Wyschogrod, *Saints and Postmodernism*, 37. The author states: "The conflict between saintly desire and institutional norms that manifests itself in hagiographic plot constitutes a nodal point for the emergence of saintly achievement. Institutional structure and saintly will are rival sources of power."

20. See John Paul Lederach, *The Moral Imagination: The Art and Soul of Building Peace* (New York: Oxford University Press, 2005), ch. 2.

21. Hagiographies depict the saints' concern with the flourishing of all creation as inseparable from their commitment to pacifism/peacebuilding as a form of colaboring with the Spirit in mending creation and overturning the consequences of the curse. Two powerful examples of saintly peacebuilding come to us from the life of Saint Francis of Assisi. In 1219, Saint Francis and another monk called Illuminato traveled along with the armies of the Fifth Crusade to Damietta in Egypt. They preached pacifism to the Crusaders and shared the fundamentals of Christianity in their witness to Muslims. According to the account of Saint Bonaventure, Saint Francis was driven toward this apostolic mission by his deep desire to share

speaking truth to power and confronting both individuals and communities, summoning them to responsibility for the sociopolitical and economic disempowerment, marginalization, exploitation, and oppression of others.[22] Yet the Spirit presents the saint's life not only as an embodied prophetic critique of the dominant way of viewing the self, the other, and the world,[23] but also as the divinely inspired reimagining/reenvisioning, seeing, and knowing the other anew. This pneumatic epistemology is illuminated by

---

in the passion of Christ through embracing martyrdom (See Saint Bonaventure, *The Life of St. Francis of Assisi* [Charlotte, NC: TAN, 2010], 77–80). According to other accounts, Saint Francis attempted to stop the Crusaders from attacking the Muslims at the Battle of Damietta. Unfortunately, his attempts failed, and after the western armies suffered a heavy defeat, Saint Francis and Illuminato crossed the battle line in pursuit of their evangelistic mission. They were apprehended as spies by Arab soldiers, beaten, and consequently brought before sultan Malek al-Kamil, to whom and to whose court Saint Francis preached the gospel as a message of peace. After the encounter, according to Western accounts, sultan al-Kamil treated humanely and compassionately the defeated Crusaders, providing them with the needed sustenance for days, until they were strong enough to return home. For an overview of both the textual and visual accounts of the event, see John Tolan, "The Friar and the Sultan: Francis of Assisi's Mission to Egypt," *European Review* 16, no. 1 (2008): 115–26. The second example is articulated in the famous account of the encounter between Saint Francis and the fierce wolf of Gubbio. The saint tames the wolf that has terrorized the local community, transforming the conditions of long-lasting conflict between him and the citizens of Gubbio into a lifelong harmonious communion in sharing of resources and care for the well-being of the other ("How St. Francis Tamed the Very Fierce Wolf of Gubbio," in *From Christ to the World: Introductory Readings in Christian Ethics*, ed. Wayne G. Boulton, Thomas D. Kennedy, and Allen Verhey [Grand Rapids: Eerdmans, 1994], 496–98).

22. The hagiographical accounts of the holy "Fools for Christ," who spoke truth to power while taking "the mask" of foolishness or outright insanity, clearly exemplify this point. See Stavroula Constantinou, "Holy Actors and Actresses: Fools and Cross-Dressers as Protagonists of Saints' *Lives*," in *The Ashgate Research Companion to Byzantine Hagiography:* Volume II: *Genres and Contexts*, ed. Stephanos Efthymiadis (Burlington, VT: Ashgate, 2014), 343–57. The choice to embrace folly for the sake of Christ is based on Paul's statements in 1 Cor 1:25; 3:18; and 4:10. As Metropolitan Kallistos Ware points out, "folly for the sake of Christ" has its roots in the Byzantine tradition yet becomes especially prominent later in medieval Russia. He states: "the 'Fool' carries the idea of self-stripping and humiliation to its furthest extent, by renouncing all intellectual gifts, all forms of earthly wisdom, and by voluntarily taking upon himself the Cross of madness." The Fools confronted and criticized those in power with "frankness which no one else dared to employ," thus functioning, in a way, as their "living conscience." Saint Basil the Blessed, who openly critiqued Tzar Ivan the Terrible for his brutality and injustice, is perhaps the most famous among the Russian "Fools for Christ" (*The Orthodox Church*, 2nd ed. [New York: Penguin, 1993], 108).

23. Sallie McFague, *Blessed Are the Consumers: Climate Change and the Practice of Restraint* (Minneapolis: Fortress, 2013), 112–15.

the eschatological clarity of the world's theotic telos, where the hallowed human life is once again the home of the divine presence and the world is a Eucharist–Spirit-saturated means of communion with God and neighbor.

As in the Incarnation, so in the life of the saints, holiness's socio-transformative address to the world is never generic but always concrete in its contextual relationality, manifesting that "truth is in the service of the other's suffering,"[24] pointing to their need and striving for its alleviation. Therefore, hagiography functions as an *annunciation* to the hearers that if they will it, the Spirit will come and "overshadow" them, so that they may become *theophorous* and, like the saints, be Christ for the other in the cultural, ethnographic, linguistic, social particularity of their context. The hagiographical narrative is thus an assurance to the addressees (a testimonial authentication) of the Spirit's Christoforming agency, translating the life of Christ into ontologically renewed human beings until they recover their creaturely distinction as those made to live with and for the other. In the saint, the Word becomes flesh through the Holy Spirit, so that the saint's flesh (his or her being) may become a living word—heard, seen, tasted, and consumed as sustenance by others.

This Spirit-mediated enfleshment is reflected also in the second characteristic that marks hagiographic discourse—its *corporeality*. Edith Wyschogrod's articulation of this textual distinctive is informed by the hagiographies of Western medieval mystics as Saint Catherine of Siena and Saint Teresa of Ávila—particularly, by their accounts of bodily participation in ecstatic visions. Both saints "see" the visions not only with their spiritual eyes but also with their bodies, "entering" into the seen—witnessing Christ's passion (as in the account of Saint Catherine) by physically experiencing its torturous agony or feeling the painful, cathartic piercing of their hearts by the enflaming love of God (as described by Saint Teresa). Yet the physical agony of the vision engulfs the saintly body not only as an excruciating suffering but as a surprising "sweetness," for the participatory knowing of this pain is illuminated by the revelatory impartation of its redemptive, transfiguring, personal, and cosmic outcome.[25]

Engaging Sallie McFague's work, chapter 1 of the present book highlighted another depiction of saintly corporeality—that of living in compassionate ascetic and kenotic solidarity with the least of these—the ones with whom Christ has chosen to identify himself. This vision of askesis for the

24. Wyschogrod, *Saints and Postmodernism*, 37.

25. Wyschogrod, *Saints and Postmodernism*, 17–18.

sake of the other (both God and the anthropic as well as nonanthropic neighbor) is a mark of the saint's ontological renewal as a human being giving itself to and partaking in the Spirit's life and world-mending mission. As already noted, the saintly life presents a powerful deconstruction of materialism and self-indulging consumerism while affirming the goodness of creation's essential materiality. It unfolds not as a gnostic escape out of the world's material body but as an embodied commitment to the well-being of the other, perceiving their physical and spiritual flourishing as inseparable from one another. The hagiographical account challenges notions of disembodied holiness as being antithetical to the vision and witness of Christ. The saintly body is the body of the Spirit amidst the cosmos, not as an impersonal, temporary, borrowed vehicle but as the very home of God, made to be filled with and illumined by the divine presence. It points to the ontological purpose of all human bodies, of all matter, created to be permeated by the Spirit. The body is made for the Spirit who is to fall on all flesh—it is made for Pentecost.

Indeed, the body participates in theosis—in that Christoforming/Christifying union of the Creator with his creation. In light of this assertion, it is important to note Wyschogrod's conclusion that the corporeality of hagiographic discourse offers a critical distinction between saintliness and mysticism. While the saint may have an ecstatic/mystical experience, it is not a prerequisite (or requirement) of holiness. Saintly acts are marked instead by the centrality of altruism, by all-engulfing concern with the needs of others.[26] Therefore, hagiographies depict the *extrovertedness* of holy lives, following (and flowing from and with) the movement of the Spirit in the world, rushing toward the other in compassion and solidarity with their deprivation, pain, and brokenness. As a Christified, ontologically renewed Adam, the saints confront the condition of the world, yet not by passing the blame for it to others but by taking responsibility for its brokenness and affliction by systemic evils. The saints' *metanoic* ethos is not generic or anonymously collective but deeply personal—acutely aware of one's known and unknown (intentional and unintentional) contributions to the perpetuation of systemic injustice, accepting the blame for it, internalizing and not externalizing the responsibility for evil. Thus, in his or her new Christic identity, the saint does not seek to scapegoat the other (offering them as a substitutionary sacrifice)[27] but presents him or herself to God as a "living sacrifice"

26. Wyschogrod, *Saints and Postmodernism*, 38–39.

27. See chapter 2 of the present book.

(Rom 12:1), embodying the new life of all creation in its in-Spirit-ed eschatological fulness. For the saint's Christoformed sociopolitical imagination, in each given moment there is only one body (one life) to be offered—their own. They courageously refuse to succumb to the iconoclasm of violence and its skillful legitimation by civil religion (even when their commitment to nonviolence and pacifism condemns them as enemies or traitors of national interests and collective militaristic/expansionistic aspirations). The moral imperative of the saintly lives confronts violence with the face of Christ—the living icon of God.[28] The saintly life is, therefore, an undoing/overturning of the decreational force of the fall by taking responsibility for the postlapsarian fractures of creation. To God's "Adam, where are you?" the saint responds, "Here I am. I take responsibility for the condition of the world, for my fellow human, and the rest of creation. Let me suffer instead of them."

It is not surprising then that the saintly life entails nondefensive vulnerability in placing oneself with the entirety of his or her being—spiritual and physical (as well as all their material possessions) at the disposal of the other. It is a self-offering as a tangible gift of life to the other, in the name of the other's life. Therefore, Wyschogrod states that saints' lives "exhibit two types of negation: the negation of self and the lack of what is needful but absent in the life of the other."[29] The saint gives to the other often out of his or her lack (not out of abundance),[30] sharing sacramentally the little they have in solidarity with the lack of others. Thus, the saintly life tangibly embodies the eschatological vision of the new theotic creation, pneumatized and marked by its ontologically renewed ascetic ethos and eucharistic spirit. The saint's entire life becomes a Eucharist—sharing sacramentally

28. *The Russian Primary Chronicle* offer a famous example of saintly negation of violence through the story of Saint Boris and Saint Gleb, sons of Prince Vladimir (under whom Russia transitions to Christianity). After finding out that their father is dead and that their half-brother Svyatopolk is plotting to kill them in order to eliminate all competition for the throne, they refuse to retaliate or even hide from the coming assassins. Instead, they face death as imitators of Christ, worshiping God and interceding for his forgiveness upon Svyatopolk. For Boris and Gleb (as for the early martyrs), pacifism and nonretaliation authenticate their witness of Christ and the assurance that no longer they but he lives in them. See *The Russian Primary Chronicle: Laurentian Text*, trans. and ed. Samuel Hazzard Cross and Olgerd P. Scherbowits-Wetzor (Cambridge, MA: The Medieval Academy of America, 1956), 126–28.

29. Edith Wyschogrod, *Saints and Postmodernism*, xxiii.

30. Sallie McFague, *Blessed Are the Consumers*, 114. The author points out that the market-oriented vision of the self celebrates "the Bill Gates of the world" and their charity out of abundance as the hallmark of "saintliness." This is an ethic that devalues solidarity with the suffering and lack of others so often exhibited by Christian saints throughout the centuries.

oneself and the world in communion with God and neighbor. The saint is once again fully human—the Christified/restored *syndesmos* (living link) between heaven and earth, perfected in the divine love, in/through which the Spirit holds together the cosmos, revealing its divinely ordained relationality. The saintly life presents the true form of all life—Eucharist. It teaches that there is no true life but shared in communion, and no other holiness but social.[31] The saint's kenotic "incarnational inclusiveness"[32] of self-giving in communion with all others exhibits also the radicality of the eucharistic logic (already noted in chapter 3) that the one who eats the body and blood of Christ and becomes one with him (a member of his body) has to present him or herself as food for others.[33] This radical incarnationalism involves sharing in the suffering of all other beings—of all creation[34]—and striving for its alleviation while explicating the true meaning of creation as eucharistic inclusion and hospitality. Thus, enlarged by the Spirit with God's loving, unconditional hospitality, the saint's life partakes of the divine life in free-willed partnership with the Spirit's continual action of cosmic renewal, one life at a time.

31. While John Wesley's famous assertion of holiness's sociality is placed in the context of contrasting the content of the gospel with the isolation of the desert mystics (see John Wesley, *The Works of John Wesley*, vol. 14 [Peabody, MA: Hendrickson, 1991], 321), as one twentieth-century saint has argued—Mother Maria Skobtsova (Saint Maria of Paris)—the desert monastics continually showed care for those in need; their mysticism was not introverted and disconnected from the suffering of the fellow human. See Michael P. Plekon's biographical sketch of Saint Maria of Paris in his inspiring book, *The World as Sacrament: An Ecumenical Path toward a Worldly Spirituality* (Collegeville, MN: Liturgical, 2016), 35–49. Mother Maria is herself a striking example of saintly self-giving to and self-sacrifice for the fellow human. Daily feeding the poor and serving the needy, she believed in the continuity between "the table of the Lord" and "the table set for the hungry who lived in her hostel" (39). After being sent to a concentration camp for smuggling young Jewish children from Nazi-occupied Paris, on March 31, 1945 (just a few weeks before the camp's liberation by the allies), in a final act of love for God and neighbor, she laid down her own life for the life of the other, "volunteering to take the place of another woman being sent to the gas chambers" (43).

32. McFague, *Blessed Are the Consumers*, 119.

33. Sallie McFague illustrates this point by recounting Simon Weil's concept of "de-creation"—giving up the false sense of autonomous existence in recognition that not only does all life come from God but that he is "the 'food' of creation." Thus, in the midst of starvation-stricken Paris (during World War II), Weil prays that God may "devour" her, transform her into "Christ's substance," and give her "for food to afflicted men whose body and soul lack every kind of nourishment" (*Blessed Are the Consumers*, 118; this striking quotation comes from Simone Weil's *First and Last Notebooks*, trans. Richard Rees [London: Oxford University Press, 1970], 149).

34. McFague, *Blessed Are the Consumers*, 118.

Indeed, God's incarnate love for the other is the essence of sainthood (and, therefore, of authentic/complete/Christoformed humanness). Through the power of this all-circumscribing love, the saint is equipped with a new epistemology, making possible the true "knowing of the other," or as James Olthuis phrases it, "a knowing otherwise, a knowing of the heart with the eye of love."[35] For Olthuis, love is the source of all affirmation, a preliminary pledge to the other (and his or her context), which precedes any engagement in "language and action," as well as the sustaining principle of all existence—of all variations of life in their interrelated togetherness. Love is the divine gift and call that gracefully holds the world together, elucidating the meaning of life as being *with and for others*.[36] Therefore, as the embodiment of divine love, the saintly life is Christ's incarnation through the Spirit in redeemed humanity—the enfleshment of God's life as love for the other. As such, the saintly life becomes an authentication of the reality of Christ and of the Christifying agency of the Holy Spirit among the human community, enlarging humanity with the spaciousness of the divine love toward all creation, striving for its flourishing and correcting the distorted, dehumanizing perception of others as either "assets or obstacles" in the pursuit of one's self-interest.[37] In the language of Sallie McFague, the saints have acquired a "universal self"—recognizing oneself as standing in organic continuity and interconnectivity with all others, viewing them as an inseparable part of one's being. The world has become the saint's body as he or she becomes the world's living consciousness. Making this assertion, McFague offers a radical reinterpretation of the gospel imperative "love your neighbor as yourself" (Matt 22:39; Mark 12:31; Luke 10:27). She refuses to accept the unsettling, self-centered proposal that "self-love" must come first, before one is capable of loving others. Instead, the author proposes that the meaning of the phrase is: "you are the neighbor, the neighbors. The world is your body; you are a

35. James H. Olthuis, ed., "Introduction: Love/Knowledge Sojourning with Others, Meeting with Differences," in *Knowing Other-Wise: Philosophy at the Threshold of Spirituality* (New York: Fordham University Press, 1997), 1–15 (1). Olthuis states: "Knowing otherwise is meeting, not mastery. Knowing otherwise is mutuality, not competition. Knowing otherwise is of the body, not limited to mind. Knowing otherwise is ethics, intimacy with, not power over, the other. Knowing otherwise is love; opening, not closure; connection, not fusion; drawing nigh, not distancing. Knowing otherwise is celebrating with and suffering with the other. Knowing otherwise is spirit, shaping love even as we are shaped by Love. Knowing otherwise is spiritual process of mutual transformation in which everything arises. Knowing otherwise is to take the risk of loving the other, the risk of meeting in mutuality" (8).

36. Olthuis, "Introduction: Love/Knowledge," 12.

37. McFague, *Blessed Are the Consumers*, 113.

universal self, and hence to love others as yourself means the extension of the same feelings of empathy, attention to basic needs, and concern for recognition of intrinsic value [in other beings and things] that one 'naturally' has for oneself."[38] In light of this interpretation, McFague turns to the story of the Good Samaritan as the narrative that explicates the four landmark characteristics of the universal self: universal empathy (a refusal to limit one's concern to the "familiar or close neighbor"); both the anonymity and "impersonality"[39] of action on behalf of the other (without seeking gratitude, recognition, or expecting reward, and not based on a preexisting personal connection to the recipient of care); the material/physical goal of this action (meeting the recipient's physical needs—food, shelter, medical care); and, finally, demonstration through love toward neighbor "how one should love God" (not as an act of civic duty but of worship to God, driven by love).[40] As McFague points out, the story is "chilling"—its mandate is overwhelming—it does not leave space for "halfway measures," exceptions, or "qualifying circumstances."[41] Its weightiness is further intensified by the demand for "limitless" commitment to the other, continual active intervention on his or her behalf (Luke 10:35—"Take care of him; and whatsoever you spend more, when I come again, I will repay you"). Ultimately, both the story of the Good Samaritan and its perpetual replication in saintly lives elucidate the truth that, in the striking words of Dostoevsky's Father Zossima (mentioned repeatedly by McFague), "love in action is a harsh and dreadful thing compared to love in dreams."[42] For Dostoevsky, this juxtaposition between "love in action" and "love in dreams" is based on difference in goal and motivation. The first is patient, unglamorous, humble, often overlooked/unnoticed—it is "labor and fortitude" on behalf of alleviating the suffering of others; the second is impatient, "greedy for immediate action, rapidly performed in the sight of all."[43] A person committed to the Christic practice of active love may

38. McFague, *Blessed Are the Consumers*, 115.

39. Under "impersonal," McFague indicates the lack of prior personal knowledge of or relationship with the recipient of care/benevolence—the expression of Christic love toward absolute strangers.

40. McFague, *Blessed Are the Consumers*, 116.

41. McFague, *Blessed Are the Consumers*, 116.

42. Fyodor Dostoevsky, *The Brothers Karamazov*, trans. Constance Garnett (Louisville: CreateSpace, 2018), 21. Undoubtedly, Father Zossima's theological discourse on love throughout the book is a summary of Dostoevsky's own theology, elevating love toward the fellow human as the only cure for doubt and despair, as well as the one act that has the capacity to save the world.

43. Dostoevsky, *Brothers Karamazov*, 21.

see "in horror" how, despite all his or her efforts, the need remains unmet, the goal seems to be an unreachable, ever-drifting horizon. Yet grasping their own inadequacy in the face of the unbearable enormity of the other's deprivation, they discover the nearness of God and experience the adequacy of his presence in mending the world through the modesty and obscurity of their efforts. Thus, care for the suffering other becomes the means of communion with God, which re-creates anew the world through the power of love—the gift of the Spirit, empowering the human community with the life of the eschaton.[44]

While the first two characteristics of hagiographic discourse outlined by Wyschogrod, *narrativity* and *corporeality*, are of particular interest for the present project, it is important to mention briefly her thought on the remaining two—*textuality* and *historicality*. The author views hagiographic *textuality* as distinct precisely because (as noted earlier) the saints' lives "are not only communicated *in* texts but *as* texts,"[45] which need to be grasped and applied in practice. This understanding leads to the issue of factuality—or *historicality*—the last characteristic of hagiographic accounts. Indeed, the factuality of the text is an essential concern "because a sense of historical veracity is necessary to generate moral practices in the text's addressees."[46] The saint's life, while unique in its concreteness, must be relivable by the community of faith as a guide through the Christifying journey (with its challenges and struggles) as life with/in/through the Holy Spirit toward theosis. In light of this, what follows is a historical account of contemporary saintly acts amidst adverse circumstances.[47] The limitations of the present project allow for the narration of only a handful of stories; yet they illustrate the uncompromised corporeality of holiness and the moral demand of saintly lives to bridge the gap between faith and practice, leaving all of us without excuse for not doing likewise.

44. Dostoevsky, *Brothers Karamazov*, 21–22.

45. Wyschogrod, *Saints and Postmodernism*, 30.

46. Wyschogrod, *Saints and Postmodernism*, 30.

47. All accounts come from interviews with both those who performed the narrated saintly acts and from firsthand eyewitnesses. The interviews were compiled during my 2012 field research in Eastern Slavonia. I have done my best to protect the original words of the interviewees (and the attitude in which they were shared) from the potential imposition of my own theological agenda or distortion by sensationalism, keeping my own voice on the fringes of the narrative. The interviews were extraordinary in their straightforward simplicity and humility. Yet the power of the depicted saintly acts transcends the intentional austerity and minimalism of the prose.

Making Love Visible in the Midst of War

The following stories construct a brief semihagiographical account, narrating acts of Christian peacebuilding in the region of Eastern Slavonia during the 1990s war in former Yugoslavia.[48] Seizing on interviews and testimonies of firsthand witnesses, they articulate a vision of love toward the neighbor who has become the enemy in the midst of war. As communal creatures made of stories, we are compelled to commit them to shared memory for safekeeping and transgenerational transmission. We cannot afford to forget them, for they summon us to responsibility for our shared humanity, and if we forget them, we risk forgetting (and unmaking) ourselves.

Love Is Not Indifferent to the Suffering of the Other

By the autumn of 1991, the nightmares of raging war had engulfed the entire region of Eastern Slavonia. The front lines of combat had converged on the outskirts of Osijek, placing the city under a dreadful, suffocating siege. "Streams" of violent hatred were "cleansing" the city of Serbian Orthodox who were once considered neighbors but now labeled "the enemy"; their lifeless bodies were occasionally spotted floating in the nearby river. The perpetual, indiscriminate shelling and the chilling precision of sniper fire had forced life to flee into the cold, damp darkness of basements and meager, improvised shelters. Scarcity and starvation held all in their grip, further sharpening the fear of death and heightening the inescapable awareness of its ever-pressing nearness. The mounting desperation bent the city's resilience to a point of breaking, as (due to the lack of basic medical resources) the local hospital was forced to conduct emergency surgeries without anesthesia in the basement beneath the dilapidated, shrapnel-punctured skeleton of its bombarded edifice. This is when a distressed telephone call summoned Professor Peter Kuzmic away from the pages of his sabbatical project at Gordon-Conwell Theological Seminary. Tears mixed with ink on the pages of his manuscript as he heard the heart-piercing words coming from the other end of the line. God's unescapable demand for action on behalf of the suffering other summoned him in the words of the city's mayor, Dr. Vladko

48. The subtitles preceding the various stories in this section are symbolic and not exclusive to the accounts grouped beneath each of them. They, as the stories themselves, are overlapping thematically. Thus, most of the stories can be listed under each one of the subtitles.

Kramarić: "Peter, . . . as a Christian you cannot be indifferent." The call compelled Professor Kuzmic to enact what he was teaching others: If you are a Christian, "you cannot be indifferent, wherever there is pain, wherever the innocent suffers, wherever there is injustice—a true Christian who carries the love of Christ in his or her heart cannot be indifferent,"[49] for love always seeks its incarnation. Love refuses empty sentimentality; it does not shed tears while just watching the agony of others from safe distance. Love brings human beings in solidarity with the suffering of their fellow humans. Love took Peter on the next flight across the ocean to the convulsing, besieged city of Osijek. While all were trying to leave, love could not do otherwise but speed to the crisis.

Upon Peter's arrival, Mayor Kramarić took him to the basement of the hospital. There his hands touched "a small boy who had lost his limbs due to indiscriminate artillery shelling."[50] Peter wept at the haunting sight of his deformed body; yet the tears that he could not hold back only bolstered his determination to act. As presiding bishop of the Evangelical (Pentecostal) Church in Croatia (and its church plants in Bosnia-Herzegovina),[51] Profes-

49. Interview with Peter Kuzmic, Evangelical Theological Seminary, Osijek, Croatia, May 31, 2012. Professor Kuzmic is the Paul E. and Eva B. Toms Distinguished Professor of World Missions and European Studies at Gordon-Conwell Theological Seminary. He cofounded and directed the Evangelical Theological Seminary in Osijek, Croatia, the first evangelical theological school in Eastern Europe and the Balkans. He also founded Timisoara Theological Institute, a Romanian school affiliated with ETS. Professor Kuzmic was influential in bringing about the Dayton Peace Accord and served as an advisor on reconciliation for national leaders in the Balkans, the United Nations, and the US State Department.

50. Interview with Peter Kuzmic, Evangelical Theological Seminary, Osijek, Croatia, May 31, 2012.

51. Peter Kuzmic served as the last president of the Assemblies of God in former Yugoslavia before its fragmentation into seven independent countries. Reflecting on this turbulent time of transition (during our interview), he stated: "I had a very difficult role in this process, having to see to it that all church movements parted, peacefully, so that none of our national churches (though they weren't 'national' yet) would be left unorganized or fall prey to ethnocentric propaganda, nationalism, and so on. Through this process, we emerged as one of the very few church communities that were able to build some bridges across ethnic divisions and bring down the walls of animosity, although it was not easy. As things slowly normalized, it was wonderful to see how the Lord has kept us in spiritual fellowship even as we were politically and militarily kept apart. . . . What we have experienced is that those who are in Christ, 'under the cross,' or to use an old saying, 'those who have been washed by the Blood,' and filled with the Spirit have a fellowship and bond that is much stronger than any secular or political borders or animosities that would tear them apart. This fellowship continues." Interview with Peter Kuzmic, Evangelical Theological Seminary, Osijek, Croatia, May 31, 2012.

sor Kuzmic called a meeting of the church's leaders and persuaded them to start a humanitarian aid outreach—the Agape Humanitarian Relief and Development Agency. "We have to start the ministry to meet human needs, and we will give them daily bread because they are physically hungry, and then we'll give them eternal bread because they're also spiritually hungry," he solemnly told them.[52] After the war, Peter summarized one of the hard lessons learned by the Christian community during these days of torment: "You cannot evangelize by verbal proclamation alone when people are starving and religion is being abused. Proclamation alone could become counterproductive in such a context. People need to *see* love."[53]

During the war, Agape became one of the main relief organizations in the entire region (alongside the Red Cross and the Catholic humanitarian agency Caritas).[54] It delivered daily food and medicine to tens of thousands of people throughout the territories devastated by destruction and outbreaks of starvation across Croatia and Bosnia/Herzegovina (BiH).[55] The workers (all of whom were volunteers) often risked their lives, dodging bullets and shrapnel while driving through the frontlines and besieged towns, determined to reach all in need, regardless of their religion and ethnicity. Agape made God's love visible to Orthodox Serbians, Catholic Croats, and Bosnian Muslims, calling them to see beyond (the fueled-by-religion) nationalist extremism, remember their shared humanity, and recognize that they all speak the same language of tears.

Agape's Christic solidarity with the suffering other won the trust of many Muslim communities in the region.[56] Because two of the agency's

52. Interview with Peter Kuzmic, Evangelical Theological Seminary, Osijek, Croatia, May 31, 2012.

53. Interview with Peter Kuzmic, Evangelical Theological Seminary, Osijek, Croatia, May 31, 2012.

54. In order to assure access to the aid for all in need and prevent unequitable distribution, the three agencies partnered and coordinated their efforts. Interview with Antal Balog, Evangelical Theological Seminary, Osijek, May 29, 2012. At the time, Dr. Balog served as assistant professor at the Evangelical Theological Seminary in Osijek and at the College of Business and Management "Baltazar Adam Krčelić" in Zaprešić. He holds doctoral degrees in Applied Theology (Gordon-Conwell Theological Seminary, USA) and Economics (Faculty for Economics J. J. Strossmayer University in Osijek).

55. Antal Balog, *Agape International: The 1994 Annual Report on the Humanitarian Relief and Development Agency of the Evangelical Church in the Republic of Croatia and the Republic of Bosnia & Herzegovina* (Osijek, Croatia: Izvori, 1995).

56. During my research in Osijek, I was privileged to interview Effendi Enes Poljic, Chief-Imam for Osijek-Baranja and Virovitica-Podravina counties (Osječko-baranjska i Virovitičko-

young workers risked their lives to bring medicine to the Bosnian city of Bihać (where the artillery fire, which did not cease for three years, dissuaded all others from going),[57] Agape was able to establish a warehouse in the town's center, becoming the first relief organization in the area. After the city's liberation in August 1995, the mayor invited Peter Kuzmic and Antal Balog (one of Agape's main coordinators) to a special meeting, honoring the organization for its lifesaving humanitarian outreach in the region. During their fellowship around a shared meal, Peter asked the mayor: "Mr. Mayor, you are a Muslim and I am a Christian; how is it that we get along so well?" The mayor responded: "That is because I am not the kind of Muslim your

---

Podravska županija). Reflecting on his experiences with Agape's work in the region, he recollected the moving story about one of Agape's leaders, Antal Balog, traveling to BiH to visit Effendi Polijc's mother in the village of Lukavac near Tuzla and to deliver to her humanitarian aid. "Antal provided for my mother, whose life during the years of the war was very difficult (when a sack of flour was 1,000 Deutsch Marks). He brought to her a package of essentials [staples]. *One cannot forget that.* Later, whenever Agape received a donation, Antal or someone else (from Agape) would call me, asking if they could help us. I remember at least two to three occasions when we were given different donations . . . they were always cautious with the food, paying attention to the kind of food Muslims cannot take. . . ." Interview with Effendi Enes Poljic, Office of the Chief-Imam for Osijek-Baranja and Virovitica-Podravina, Osijek, May 29, 2012. Recollecting (in a separate interview) this trip to Lukavac, Antal Balog mentioned that upon his return to Osijek, he brought to Effendi Poljic a photograph of himself with the Imam's mother, accompanied by a letter from her. In response, overwhelmed with gratitude by this act of kindness, the Chief-Imam exclaimed: "I cannot believe it! You are my brother!" (Interview with Antal Balog, Evangelical Theological Seminary, Osijek, May 29, 2012). Effendi Polijic spoke with the same warmth about his relationship with Peter Kuzmic and the community of the Evangelical Theological Seminary. He stated: "Peter would often send me regards and share his impressions from his meetings with the religious leader of the Muslims in Bosnia and Herzegovina. Personal note: whenever I would meet Peter in the city, we would always share a brotherly hug! He is such a warm person. I would always come encouraged and supported from these meetings with him. Peter is like a brother to me. . . ."

57. The history of the city's siege, the devastation of its infrastructure (including the local medical facilities), the influx of tens of thousands of refugees and displaced populations, the resulting desperate humanitarian crisis, and the helplessness of the UN Security Council and the UN Peacekeeping Forces to intervene and alleviate the desperate starvation and suffering were well documented in the press, in UN reports, and in many consequent monographs reflecting on the war's sociopolitical dynamics. For example, see Tom Hedley, "Croatia, Serbia Face Off at Bihac," *Chicago Tribune*, July 30, 1995, http://articles.chicagotribune.com/1995-07-30/news/9507300180_1_bihac-bosnian-serb-bosnian-government; Tony Barber, "Defenseless Muslims Face the Final Agony: Tony Barber Witnesses the Relentless Demolition of Bihac by Serbian Guns," *The Independent*, August 12, 1992, https://www.independent.co.uk/news/defenceless-muslims-face-the-final-agony-tony-barber-witnesses-the-relentless-demolition-of-bihac-by-1540468.html.

friends in the West think about when they hear the word 'Muslim,' and you are not the kind of Christian that Muslims think about when they hear the name 'Christian.'"[58] The mayor continued, "I am a nominal [cultural] Muslim; I don't have a deep faith commitment. . . . But I am increasingly interested in *your* Jesus because you are different Christians than the ones we know. . . . You did not come with the sword in the one hand and a cross in the other, in medieval fashion. You came with no political aims nor territorial claims. Your young men did not rape our women and girls. You came lovingly feeding." Then he said, "Since I am the mayor, I can go anywhere [in the city], so I went to the back rooms [of your warehouse] and saw some boxes which contained little books titled *Novi Zavjet* (New Testament). There were other boxes that said 'Billy Graham: *Mir s Bogom* (Peace with God).' You obviously have some literature there. Feel free to distribute it!"

Peter was amazed. "A Muslim mayor was telling a Pentecostal minister to distribute Christian literature in his town!" Then the mayor added, "If you want to start a church here, go ahead and do it!" After the initial shock, Peter finally responded, "I don't know what to say! You're encouraging us to do something that we were reluctant to articulate even as a vision!" The mayor replied, "No, you can do it; we trust you." Peter asked, "What made you trust us?" The mayor responded, "You are credible to us, because *you became vulnerable with us*."[59]

Love Makes Space and Carves a Sanctuary for the Other

On July 23, 1991, the war reached the city of Vinkovci. The reverberating thunder of the shelling was occasionally interrupted by sudden silence, cutting through the thick, heavy air filled with smoke of crumbled mortar

58. There are a few accounts of this story, different in length and detail, besides the interview with Peter Kuzmic that I conducted in 2012. Some of them appear in various publications, for example, in Peter Kuzmic, "Historical Context: How Did We Get Here?" in *Bridges of Reconciliation: Reader on the Conflict in Bosnia*, ed. Craig Arban and Jo Marie Dooly (World Vision).

59. Interview with Peter Kuzmic, Evangelical Theological Seminary, Osijek, Croatia, May 31, 2012. A testament to the transformation of the Muslim population's attitude toward the Pentecostal Christians due to their humanitarian outreach during the war is also the fact that, while for the entire period between 1948 and 1992 there were only three Pentecostal churches in the territory of Bosnia-Herzegovina, statistics from the reports for 2003 are quite different. According to them, the Evangelical (Pentecostal) Church in BiH had 55 ministers and workers, 22 churches and preaching points, 723 members and adherents, and one Bible school with 10 students (see http://europemissions.org/about/countries/bosnia-herzegovina/).

and glare of shattered glass. Perplexed amidst war's surreality and unaccustomed to its lethal proximity, the local residents occasionally ventured out, trying to survey the damage and clear yards and streets from quickly accumulating debris. On one such instance, Milica—wife of the local Pentecostal (Church of God) pastor, Josip Jendričko[60]—was critically wounded by an artillery shell. Barely escaping death after an emergency surgery and weeks of treatment in the local hospital, she was transported to stay with relatives in Germany for further recovery.[61] During her absence, the Croat army and paramilitary units had moved into the city and settled in some of the houses vacated by Serbian Orthodox residents who had fled, fearing a potential massacre—a fear fueled by the vivid memories of atrocities committed against the region's Serbs during World War II.[62] The house of Josip and Milica's Serbian neighbors was among them. When the elderly couple returned to their home after a cease-fire agreement between the warring sides, they found themselves threatened at gunpoint by the soldiers who had settled in their house. Witnessing the scene, Josip walked into the street, stood between the soldiers and his neighbors, and brought the couple into his own home, where his family sheltered, cared for, and protected them for the next four and a half years. They were beloved as adopted members of the Jendričko family. Josip, Milica, and their children received continual death threats from Croat nationalists for the unconditional hospitality they had extended to their neighbors. Yet amidst the escalating harassment, God gave them peace and assurance of his protection. In the midst of the surrounding war, their home had become a sanctuary of peace.[63] The overwhelming

60. Josip Jendričko served as presiding bishop (national overseer) of Church of God in Croatia from the end of the war until the autumn of 2012.

61. A written (unpublished) testimony by Milica about her experience in the hospital and afterward during her recovery. Reflecting on the supernatural peace and love she felt for all humanity, including her enemy, Milica wrote: "In those long winter nights, deep down inside, I felt better than ever before. God was so real and near that my heart was melting. I was able to prayerfully talk with Him; pray for my husband who was still in Vinkovci, and those who were with him; for our children; for our parents; for brothers and sisters; for people suffering around me; for Christ's church; for enemies; and for the one who fired the grenade which wounded me."

62. For information about one of the notorious concentration camps (organized by the pro-Nazi Croat regime during World War II) where many Serbs, Jews, and Roma citizens lost their lives, see "Jasenovac," *Holocaust Encyclopedia* (https://www.ushmm.org/wlc/en/article.php?ModuleId=10005449).

63. With tears in her eyes, Milica recalled the extraordinary atmosphere of harmonious consensus and peace that filled their home for these four and a half years. There was no conflict, no argument, not even the slightest tension. Indeed, the Spirit had built for them a

sense of gratitude for the gift of the other and the cathartic experience of all-engulfing love for God and neighbor had transformed each shared daily meal at the war-induced scarcity of their dining table into a eucharistic feast filled with the abundant joy of life in the kingdom.

This Spirit-saturated life of radical hospitality quickly transcended the confines of the Jendričkos' household and transfigured the church they pastored into a home and sanctuary for the ethnic and religious other. On September 15, 1991, during one of the city's regular bombardments, the church building caught on fire and completely burned down. Refusing to despair, Josip contacted a friend—the pastor of the local Reformed church—who (as many others) had left town together with his family, closing the church for the duration of the war.[64] Their sanctuary, however, had survived the bombings, and Josip asked for the permission to use it—a request that was readily granted. In the weeks that followed, he tried to spread the news about the Pentecostal congregation's relocation into the Reformed sanctuary and to invite the Reformed Christians from the region to join them in worship. The first shared service of the two congregations took place in February 1992, opening the doors of the sanctuary for all others seeking spiritual comfort and hope. Soon the building was packed and overflowing with people standing outside in the courtyard, who numbered more than those sitting in the pews. A unique body of faith gathered there for weekly prayer and worship: Pentecostals, Reformed, Baptists, Orthodox, and Muslims, among whom were ethnic Croats, Serbians, and Bosnians—an extraordinary congregation of ethnic and religious others, defying the war with the peacebuilding of the Spirit. There the Spirit had demolished the walls of animosity and hatred, driven by the radical politics of ethnoreligious tribalism, transforming former enemies into one human family. The Spirit's subversive act of gathering together in one spiritual community the warring religious and ethnic others was also, in effect, redeeming religion itself by changing its role in the conflict—from an apologist of violent nationalism and accomplice in the craft of ethnic cleansing to becoming an essential part of peacebuilding and communal transformation in pursuit of the common good.

---

sanctuary—a place of safety and rest from the raging hatred and death around them. Interview with Josip and Milica Jendričko, Evangelical Theological Seminary, Osijek, June 9, 2012.

64. Many of the town's residents left either immediately prior to or during the beginning of the war. From approximately thirty-five thousand people, the population was reduced to about three thousand. Interview with Josip and Milica Jendričko, Evangelical Theological Seminary, Osijek, June 9, 2012.

The congregation in Vinkovci, however, was not an exceptional case. Solidarity with the suffering other had transformed many Pentecostal churches throughout Eastern Slavonia into ecumenical and interreligious community centers. They were involved daily in feeding the hungry, sheltering the homeless, and distributing humanitarian aid as local Orthodox Serbian residents, displaced Catholic Croats and Muslim refugees streamed through their doors in search of safety and means for survival.[65] In September of 1992, Lidia Stoiković, wife of the pastor of Orahovice's Pentecostal church, repeatedly heard God's voice prompting her to quit her job at the local school in order to serve the quickly growing numbers of refugees and displaced persons in the region. A German humanitarian-aid agency started sending regular shipments of food and clothing to the church, and the congregation decided to include also the impoverished local residents registered with the city's social services in the daily distribution of aid. Love's radical commitment to the well-being of the other had woven them into a community of solidarity and justice in shared access to life for all.

The church's sanctuary also became a place of healing broken relationships, bodies, and minds. It was a safe space to wrestle with distorted, politically expedient visions of the other while facing the challenging task of forgiveness and reconciliation. Sitting beside one another on the pews were Croat soldiers returning from the battlefield, Muslim families who had left the lifeless bodies of loved ones in bombarded villages, concentration camps, and mass graves in Bosnia, and Serbian women whose sons and grandsons may have slain them or been killed by them.[66] It was not easy to press through anger and apprehension of the other's immediate proximity, to pray and worship with them. Yet the shared pain and tears, mixed with the confessions of regrets and lament over the loss of life, dreams, and innocence by both victims and perpetrators,[67] transformed the sanctuary into a

65. Such was the case, for example, with the churches in Osijek, Tordinci, and Orahovice.

66. As Peter Kuzmic states, "No side in the Bosnian war is innocent. Bosnian Muslims and Croats have all committed atrocities and practiced ethnic cleansing. 'All are sinful' and there is no party to this war without guilt. But not all are equally guilty. This is why it is so important to review the genesis of the war, the role of Belgrade and the goals for which the war was fought. The international community also shares a considerable degree of responsibility for not stopping the carnage when it was still relatively easy to do so" ("On the Way to Peace in the Balkans," *The Christian Century* 6 [February 21, 1996]: 199–202 [201]).

67. Interview with Lidia Stoiković, Orahovice, June 1, 2012. Lidia recalls the challenge of the congregation's demographic dynamics: "We also had a contact with the families whose husbands were soldiers, some of whom were killed or injured in the war, and we made efforts to help them, as well. . . . Later, one of them came to our house, and he said he had been a

hospital for souls and minds traumatized by the dehumanizing brutality of war.[68] There the Spirit was mending creation from inside out—starting from the inner brokenness of those communing with the Lord, having seen him in the face of the ethnic and religious other and confronting the sacramental challenge of daily commensality at the shared dining table—so that this healing may reach the outer frontiers of their broken communities.

The Spirit's radical/unconditional hospitality became visible through this Pentecostal *darkhei shalom*[69] not only in feeding, sheltering, and caring for the physical and psychological wounds of the other, but in burying the other's dead as one's own. Many Pentecostal pastors were being asked during the war to conduct funerals for Reformed and Catholic Croats, Orthodox Serbians, and Bosnian Muslims. Often there were simply no other ministers/priests left in the region where performing a funeral for "the enemy" was considered a subversive and "unpatriotic" act. Therefore, the pastors had to be willing to lay down their own lives in order to bury the

---

defender in Vukovar, having gone there to avenge his grandfather who had been killed in the Second World War. He said, 'I have done a lot of awful things, and now I cannot sleep. I cannot do anything; all I do is drink.' We prayed with him and he started coming to the church. Even his wife was in danger, at the time, because he would become violent and crazy. She had to lock him in the toilet room [in Europe, it is customary for the toilet and the shower or bathtub to be separate]. He passed away, because his body was very badly affected by his heavy drinking, but before this happened, he received Christ. . . . When you think about it, we had contacts with people who had killed other people; we also had contacts with people who had escaped from certain terrible places."

68. During an interview, Lidia Stoiković shared some stories of healing of people with PTSD as a result of their war experiences. She recalled: "Once, through the association of Vukovarians, we met a [Catholic] family, and when they came to our house, the mother told me that her health situation was deteriorating and [that she] was going crazy, having to go to psychiatric screening in Osijek. When she realized how they were treating her, she no longer wanted to be admitted there, because all they were doing was prescribing her pills, which, of course, does not help [is not enough]. She then said, 'I heard your church can help me.' We replied, 'We cannot help you, but we do know who can. We can pray for you.' She said she could not sleep and needed six or seven pills before going to bed. This was because she could not forget everything she had been through in a Serbian prison camp; she said she did not trust the Serbian or the Croatian government, because she didn't trust anyone. She said 'I can only trust your church,' to which we replied, 'Just trust God.'. . . That night, she fell asleep just before the news ended, right before 8:00 p.m. The family observed her and said, 'She was crazy before, but now she is even more crazy,' because she had started to go to 'some sect.'. . . After some time, they realized she is not crazy, but rather that something good is happening to her." Eventually, they all started attending the church.

69. The Jewish notion of *darkhei shalom* is discussed in the concluding section of chapter 4 in the present book.

other's dead.[70] One of them, Matej Lazar Kovačević,[71] conducted over two hundred funerals of Catholics, Orthodox, and Muslims. He assumed the role of pastor of all in the town of Tordinci, but his pastoral care included also the Croat soldiers in the region, whose trauma often remained overlooked, repressed, and dismissed as a side effect of fulfilling one's duty. His chaplaincy without borders, extending "covenant love" and care to the ethnic and religious other, was consequently recognized and honored by both the local community and the Croat state, who named him "Defender of the Country" and decorated him with the Medal of the Order of Patriotic Memorial. Paradoxically, his journey in "the ways of peace" (once condemned as unpatriotic betrayal) had been vindicated and affirmed as courageous, self-sacrificial labor for the common good.

Love Summons the Other to Responsibility for the Brokenness of the World

On August 5, 1991, four coworkers were traveling from Vinkovci to Tordinci. They were riding in two separate cars, following from a distance a column of military vehicles. Suddenly, three heavily armed Serbian paramilitary soldiers (known as *chetnici*) jumped in front of the cars from the tall corn fields lining both sides of the road, pointing their guns at the startled passengers. The four men were ordered to get out of the vehicles and lie face down in the ditch with arms and legs spread, their heads propped up on the pavement. Among them were Pastor Matej Lazar Kovačević and

70. Reflecting on her husband's pastoral work during the war and on the community's transformation of attitude toward Pentecostals, Lidia Stoiković stated: "During the war, the Orthodox priests left, and if Orthodox people died, there was no one to bury them. So people came to my husband and asked if he could conduct the burial services, and he said yes. He conducted mostly Orthodox funerals. . . . Sometimes it was not easy because of the paramilitary soldiers . . . the only visible people [in the Serbian villages] were those that had their faces covered with balaclava masks. So every time my husband went to the villages to conduct a funeral, I would pray fervently, and I still remember several times that I felt he was in critical danger. However, nobody ever called him and threatened him, ever! The [Croat] paramilitary soldiers with the balaclavas were quietly standing, watching during the whole funeral. They listened to the gospel, and nobody asked us, "Why are you doing all this," because they knew that we were helping everybody who was in need."

71. During the war, Pastor Kovačević served as minister at the Church of God congregation in Tordinci. In the autumn of 2012, he became the presiding bishop of the Church of God denomination in Croatia.

Marko Šavanka, a local electrical engineer. One of the *chetnici*, evidently their commander, sat on Marko's back, pulled out a knife, placed it on his throat, and looked up to the other two, asking, "Should I cut his throat?"[72] One of them barked without any hesitation, "Do it!" but the other nervously objected. Then the first *chetnik* put away the knife, walked to the last of the men lying on the ground and started kicking his head with despicable brutality until the face of the other became an unrecognizable, deformed mass, covered with blood, dust, and grass. Seeing what awaited all of them, Marko cried out, "Lazar, pray!" Lazar Kovačević responded with anxious determination, shouting back, "I am praying." The response redirected the attention of the torturer, who rushed toward Lazar to resume the ceremonial effacing of the other in this iconoclasm of tribal violence. At that moment, deep inside his being, Lazar heard the voice of God—"Don't be afraid!"—and turned his face toward the approaching *chetnik* right when his foot lifted forcefully in the air, about to strike Lazar's head. As their eyes met, an invisible force swept the *chetnik* off his feet, throwing him in the air. His gun dropped on the ground, and he followed, landing in the dust. A higher power had suddenly disarmed him, disrupting the premeditated act of fratricide—the act of his self-dehumanization. The other two *chetnici* sprinted toward Lazar pointing their guns at his head. The panic in their voice crescendoed into curses and threats as they prepared to pull the trigger. Pale and confused, their commander got up from the ground and ordered them to put away their weapons. Then he turned toward Lazar and said, with a voice full of fearful anger, "Get up! Who are you? Who is responsible for all the evil in this land?" Lazar stood up and responded, "I am a preacher at the Church of God in Tordinci." Then, realizing that God had miraculously intervened on his behalf not just out of love for him but also for his enemy, "emboldened by the Spirit," Lazar proclaimed as loud as he could, "For the evil in the world are guilty all those who don't follow the way of Jesus Christ, the Son of God." He was determined to face the death raging in the tormented souls of his persecutors with the truth that could set them free—the truth that alone could summon them back to their humanity, challenging them to grasp and confess their own responsibility for the condition of the world. Visibly shaken, the commander changed the topic and, after a few more random sentences, told his captives to get in the cars and leave. Perhaps he had caught a glimpse of the face of God on the face of the ethnic other.

72. The story was narrated by Marko Šavanka during an interview in Tordinci, June 2012.

Love Stands in the Way of Death for the Other's Life in Mutual Safekeeping

During July of 1991, Vojislav Šešelj, leader of Serbia's Radical Party, had come to the village of Gaboš to promote his extremist nationalist program for ethnic cleansing throughout the territories of former Yugoslavia called "Greater Serbia."[73] He was inciting violence against the local non-Serbian population while actively recruiting for the party's paramilitary units—*chetnici* (known also as "Šešelj's Men"). During his speech, a local Serbian Orthodox farmer, Milorad (Mile) Kosanović, challenged Šešelj's hate-inciting political rhetoric by stating, "You have come here to promote war with my neighbor. . . . I cannot raise a weapon against my neighbor just because he is Catholic." Šešelj responded by turning toward the rest of the audience with the words, "If you have other[s] like him here, give them all to the Ustaša[74] [Croat paramilitary units]."[75] After this incident, Mile was isolated and harassed by his community. Eventually, the Serbian Militia requisitioned one of his tractors to transport supplies from a nearby village; yet after an unexpected encounter with Croat forces, they abandoned the tractor on the road. When Mile later approached the Croat soldiers at the barricade, requesting permission to retrieve his tractor, he was referred to

73. Šešelj was tried in The Hague by the International Criminal Tribunal for the Former Yugoslavia (ICTY) and charged with "three counts of crimes against humanity and six of war crimes in the ethnic cleansing for his role in mobilizing and motivating his followers. The charges included participating in a 'joint criminal enterprise' to create a so-called Greater Serbia that led to the forcible transfer of tens of thousands of civilians; torture, sexual assaults, beatings and other physical abuse of detained non-Serbs; the destruction of homes, religious sites and cultural institutions; and hate speech" ("Vojislav Seselj, Serbian Nationalist, Is Acquitted of War Crimes by Hague Tribunal," *The New York Times*, March 31, 2016, https://www.nytimes.com/2016/04/01/world/europe/vojislav-seselj-war-crimes.html). He was first acquitted of the charges in a first-instance verdict on all counts. The acquittal was consequently appealed by prosecutors from the MICT, a United Nations Security Council agency, which functions as successor to the ICTY. On April 11, 2018, the Appeals Chamber sentenced him to ten years in prison ("Appeal Chamber Reverses Šešelj's Aquittal, in Part, and Convicts Him of Crimes against Humanity," *United Nations Mechanism for International Criminal Tribunals*, April 11, 2018, http://www.unmict.org/en/news/appeals-chamber-reverses-šešelj's-acquittal-part-and-convicts-him-crimes-against-humanity).

74. The Ustaša (or Ustaše) was a Croatian fascist ultranationalist organization that was active in the territory of former Yugoslavia between 1929 and 1945. Reportedly, its members murdered hundreds of thousands of Serbs, Jews, and Roma during World War II.

75. The story was narrated during an interview with Milorad Kosanović, Gabos, Croatia, June 2012.

Tordinci's Municipal Office. An acquaintance advised him to contact Pastor Kovačević and ask for his support before the Croat city authorities. Shortly after Mile entered the municipal office of Tordinci, two policemen (one of whom was the director of the local police force) burst into the waiting room, grabbed Mile, and led him to a deserted nearby café. Ready to kill him, they pulled out their guns, saying, "Here your life ends." At this very moment, Lazar Kovačević (informed of Mile's detention) rushed into the café, interrupting the execution, and addressed the executioners with unshakable determination: "I will not permit you to kill him. I am a preacher of the gospel and will not let you kill him. He has come to take only what belongs to him. What you want to do is unjust and ungodly." The director of the police turned his rage toward Pastor Kovačević but, after a moment of hesitation, stormed out of the room. Still shaken by this near-death experience and fearing for his life, Mile turned to Lazar, pleading, "If you are a minister of the gospel, please come with me to the barricades and intercede for my safe passage; otherwise, they will kill me." Lazar readily agreed and requested, in turn, for Mile to escort him to the Serbian headquarters in the nearby town of Markušića in order to negotiate a prisoner exchange, to put an end to other pending executions and save lives. Grateful, Mile agreed to accompany Lazar, saying adamantly, "Don't worry! I will protect you, and if they want to kill you, they would have to kill me first." Until that point, no one had considered negotiating a prisoners' exchange, fearing the potentially deadly consequences of approaching the enemy. Yet love's creative force had opened the way to friendship and shared life in the midst of enmity and death.

Love Stands in Solidarity with the Suffering Other

The audacity of love's continual striving for the life of the ethnic and religious other was made visible amidst the war-torn, wounded region by the emergence of a small yet impactful Christian ecumenical peacebuilding movement. It involved a number of contributors, networking and collaborating in confronting the social pathology of violence and presenting a viable alternative vision of living in consensus with difference in commitment to the common good. Among them was the Center for Peace, Nonviolence and Human Rights in Osijek. The center was conceived as an idea, in the beginning of the conflict, as two Croat friends started discussing (after a weekly Catholic prayer meeting) what it means to love one's enemy in the days of war.[76] The war challenged their faith and Christian identity—it confronted and tested the authenticity of their Christlikeness, prompting them to examine their hearts and allow the Spirit to bring to the surface deeply seeded nationalist sentiments, chronic mistrust, and distorted attitudes toward the other. The center attracted Christians from different denominations (as well as some non-Christian members), becoming an impactful peacebuilding force in the city and the surrounding region. Its work was driven by a vision of a different future—an indigenous form of participatory democracy, marked by inclusion and empowerment of all voices toward a socio-transformative communal agency that unites into seamless wholeness the private and public domain in a commitment to shared flourishing.[77] The center's community realized that the only way to populate this reenvisioned future was to start living it here and now. This realization fueled their determination to "create a culture of resistance against atrocities and human-rights abuses."[78] Having understood that love for the enemy in the days of war is not a generic sentimentalism but a painfully concrete and unpopular choice, they embraced the loneliness of pacifism and committed to stand in solidarity with the Serbian community in Osijek, whose members were threatened and victimized from the very beginning of the war. Between the summer and winter of 1991, many civilian Serbs lost their lives at the hands of Croat paramilitary nationalist groups. The Serbians were also being forcibly evicted from their homes in order to make room for displaced Croats who were flooding the region from the contested territories. For the members of the center, this was a form of ethnic cleansing, which demanded immediate intervention. After publishing an article in the local newspaper, publicly taking a stand for peace, articulating their vision, and condemning human-rights abuses, they started receiving calls from threatened Serbian residents pleading for help. While committed to working for the cultural

76. Interview with Katarina Kruhonja, cofounder of the Center for Peace, Nonviolence and Human Rights and of the Croatian Branch of the Helsinki Committee, Osijek, June 4, 2012.

77. During the interview, Dr. Kruhonja outlined the NGO's vision, alongside the lessons of peacebuilding learned by its members. Their reenvisioning of the world started by asserting the foundational concern of building a nonviolent society. Reflecting on this key motive of their communal daydreaming with the Spirit, Dr. Kruhonja stated: "We said that we wanted a political society/state, in which problems and conflicts will not be resolved by violence, but rather that there would be an ongoing, nonviolent struggle for the improvement of society. This society will be reluctant and immune to participating in violence." Interview with Katarina Kruhonja, Osijek, June 4, 2012.

78. Interview with Katarina Kruhonja, Osijek, June 4, 2012.

transformation of the community, the members of the center realized that they had to do something more in the present, protecting the victims and protesting their mistreatment. Determined to live the future here and now, making it present and visible for all, they began "a program of nonviolent protection of people in their flats."[79] Many Serbian residents phoned the center sharing their experiences of harassment. Usually, a paramilitary unit or a group of armed nationalist neighbors "visited" the victims, giving them a day's notice to evacuate or face forceful eviction and, possibly, death. A number of the center's members would go to the apartment of the threatened Serbians and "sit" with them, "waiting for the armed group to come," willingly placing their lives in danger's way in order to protect the other's life. They also initiated active advocacy on behalf of the victims "by calling the police, the mayor's office, even the President [of Croatia], about each case. It was a [form of] nonviolent protection and struggle against injustice."[80] Their commitment to just peace drew growing threats, and the perpetual pressure of the persecution induced a crisis among the center's activists. Despite the moral, spiritual, and logistical support received from other, more experienced Christian peacebuilding organizations throughout Europe and the United States, some of the group's members, while supporting the campaign, did not feel ready for involvement in direct confrontation with the abusers through the "sittings for the others' lives." Yet they were also subject to persecution, losing their jobs and social standing "by publicly identifying with the anti-war movement."[81] It was the price they all had to pay for choosing to love their neighbor against the hate-fueled madness of war.

In the period between 1996 and 1998, the center's work proved crucial for the region's peaceful postwar reintegration. Realizing that the deeply traumatized local communities would not accept peace legislated and enforced from above, the center's members started traveling and mediating between all sides in the conflict. They cultivated a broad grassroot movement committed to facilitating just, sustainable peace and reconciliation. The movement networked individuals, communities, and nongovernmental organizations, contributing to shaping the foundations of the region's emerging civil society. From ecumenical prayers to common action toward communal healing, in all its efforts the movement's multiethnic, multireligious body enfleshed its bold Spirit-inspired vision for the future—a society

79. Interview with Katarina Kruhonja, Osijek, June 4, 2012.
80. Interview with Katarina Kruhonja, Osijek, June 4, 2012.
81. Interview with Katarina Kruhonja, Osijek, June 4, 2012.

of inclusion and consensus, where one is at home with the other and the different in shared access to life for all. Through them, the Spirit's *sobornost* was radiating its "freedom, concord and common life in secular society."[82]

Concluding Thoughts

Undoubtedly, hagiography presents an alternative to the monological character of moral theory by uplifting saintly life as a form of embodied, communicative ethical practice. The contextuality of hagiographic narrative incorporates the addressees, shaping their moral imagination while paradigmatically bridging the gap between theory and practice by offering a concrete, applied model of Christian ethics. Upholding the other's life as the location of ethical action (the location where practice corrects theory) concretizes hagiography's moral imperative. The concreteness of the saint's solidarity with the suffering other refuses mythologizing or cautious subjection to spiritual quarantine (pronouncing it as an admirable yet nonreplicable heroic [or wild] exception). Instead, as the ontologically renewed and eschatologically fulfilled image of God, the saint represents humanity's theotic destiny, affirming that sainthood is the creaturely vocation of each human being.

The acts of the saint's kenotic self-giving for the flourishing of others restate the gospel's summoning toward Christoformation ("Come, follow me!") as "labor in the form of dedication to the other."[83] This labor of in-Spirit-ed world mending is often lonely, misunderstood, and negated. It involves suffering ridicule, rejection, and abuse at the hands of the saint's own community (and at the hands of those whom he or she strives to help). The saintly response to this suffering is love, challenging and rehumanizing the other (even the enemy). The encounter with the saint unveils the patient, longsuffering creativity of love, making the unseen visible—the life of God as the eschatological destiny of the beholder—and carving him or her into its likeness.

Through the saintly life, the Spirit makes God's love tangible in surprising, unexpected ways, in which the hallowed human being itself becomes

82. Todor Subev, "The Nature and Mission of Councils in the Light of the Theology of Sobornost," *The Ecumenical Review* 45, no. 3 (July 1993): 261–70 (265–66). See the segment on *sobornost* in chapter 1 of the present book.

83. Wyschogrod, *Saints and Postmodernism*, 85.

the solution to impossible/insurmountable challenges. The Spirit uplifts the Christified human life as the visible means of invisible grace toward peacebuilding and reconciliation, economic justice, sociopolitical inclusion, and ecological renewal. Indeed, the healing of the entire cosmos starts from within hallowed, Spirit-saturated humanity. In the sanctified/saintly human community, the Spirit's world-mending artistry shapes communal consensus in pursuit of the common good while sustaining the challenging beauty of difference. There the Spirit calls forth the breathtaking *sobornost* of creation united to the Creator and enlarged with the spaciousness of the divine love. There the Word becomes flesh for the life of the world until the world becomes his flesh—the all-circumscribing, communal body of its Creator.

Bibliography

Alexander, T. Desmond. *From Paradise to the Promised Land*. Grand Rapids: Baker Academic, 2012.

Aquinas, Thomas. *Summa Theologiae*. Translated by Cornelius Ernst. London: Black Friars, 1972.

Arendt, Hannah. *The Human Condition*. Chicago: University of Chicago Press, 1998.

———. *On Violence*. New York: Harcourt, 1970.

———. *Viva Activa oder vom tätigen Leben*. Stuttgart: Kohlhammer, 1977.

Athanasius. *On the Incarnation*. Crestwood, NY: St. Vladimir's Seminary Press, 1996.

Augustine. *Tractates on the Gospel of John* 80.3. http://www.newadvent.org/fathers/1701.htm.

———. *The Trinity*. The Fathers of the Church 45. Translated by Stephen McKenna. Washington, DC: The Catholic University of America Press, 1963.

Augustine, Daniela C. "Creation as Perichoretic Trinitarian Conversation: Reflections on World-Making with Robert W. Jenson." Pages 99–113 in *The Promise of Robert Jenson's Theology*. Edited by Stephen Wright and Christopher W. Green. Minneapolis: Fortress, 2017.

———. "Image, Spirit and *Theosis*: Imaging God in an Image-Distorting World." Pages 172–88 in *The Image of God in an Image Driven Age*. Edited by Beth Felker Jones and Jeffrey W. Barbeau. Downers Grove, IL: InterVarsity, 2016.

———. "The Liturgical Teleology of Human Creativity and the City of God as *Theosis* of Culture." *Cultural Encounters: A Journal for the Theology of Culture* 10, no. 2 (April 2015): 3–26.

———. *Pentecost, Hospitality, and Transfiguration: Toward a Spirit-Inspired Vision of Social Transformation*. Cleveland, TN: CPT, 2012.

———. "Pentecost and Prosperity in Eastern Europe: Between Sharing of Possessions and Accumulating Personal Wealth." Pages 189–212 in *Pentecostalism and Prosperity: The Socio-Economics of Global Renewal*. Edited by Amos Yong and Katherine Attanasi. New York: Palgrave Macmillan, 2012.

Babylonian Talmud. https://www.jewishvirtuallibrary.org/babylonian-talmud-full-text.

Bakhtin, Mikhail. "Discourse in the Novel." Pages 259–422 in *The Dialogic Imagination*. Edited by Michael Holquist. Austin: University of Texas Press, 1981.

———. "Response to a Question from Novy Mir Editorial Staff." Pages 1–9 in *Speech Genres and Other Late Essays*. Translated by Vern W. McGee. Edited by Caryl Emerson and Michael Holquist. Austin: University of Texas Press, 1986.

Balog, Antal. *Agape International: The 1994 Annual Report on the Humanitarian Relief and Development Agency of the Evangelical Church in the Republic of Croatia and the Republic of Bosnia & Herzegovina*. Osijek, Croatia: Izvori, 1995.

Balthasar, Hans Urs von. *The Word Made Flesh*. Vol. 1 of *Explorations in Theology*. Translated by A. V. Littledale and Alexander Dru. San Francisco: Ignatius, 1989.

Barber, Tony. "Defenseless Muslims Face the Final Agony: Tony Barber Witnesses the Relentless Demolition of Bihac by Serbian Guns." *The Independent*, August 12, 1992. https://www.independent.co.uk/news/defenceless-muslims-face-the-final-agony-tony-barber-witnesses-the-relentless-demolition-of-bihac-by-1540468.html.

Barker, Margaret. "Beyond the Veil of the Temple: The High Priestly Origin of the Apocalypses." Presidential Address to the Society for Old Testament Study, Cambridge, January 1998. First published in the *Scottish Journal of Theology* 51, no. 1 (1998). http://www.marquette.edu/maqom/veil.html.

Barth, Karl. *Church Dogmatics: The Doctrine of Reconciliation*. Church Dogmatics 4.1. Edinburgh: T&T Clark, 1961.

———. *Dogmatics in Outline*. New York: Harper & Row, 1959.

———. *Preaching through the Christian Year: A Selection of Exegetical Passages from the Church Dogmatics*. Grand Rapids: Eerdmans, 1981.

Bartholomew I, H. A. H. Archbishop of Constantinople and Ecumenical Patriarch. *Encountering the Mystery*. New York: Doubleday, 2008.

Bauckham, Richard. "Jesus and the Wild Animals (Mark 1:13): A Christological Image for an Ecological Age." Pages 3–21 in *Jesus of Nazareth: Lord and Christ—Essays on the Historical Jesus and New Testament Christology*. Edited by Joel B. Green and Max Turner. Grand Rapids: Eerdmans/Carlisle: Paternoster, 1994.

Behr, John. *The Mystery of Christ: Life and Death*. Crestwood, NY: St. Vladimir's Seminary Press, 2006.

Berdyaev, Nicolas. *The Meaning of History*. Pages 299–514 in vol. 2 of *Collected Works*. Sofia: Zachari Stoyanov, 2003.

———. *The New Middle Ages*. Pages 515–607 in vol. 2 of *Collected Works*. Sofia: Zachari Stoyanov, 2003.

———. *Philosophy of Inequality*. Sofia: Prozoretc, 1995.

———. *Slavery and Freedom*. Paris: YMCA, 1939.

Bergson, Henri. *Creative Evolution*. New York: Cosimo Classics, 2005.

Blanchard, Kathryn D. *The Protestant Ethic or the Spirit of Capitalism: Christians, Freedom, and Free Markets*. Eugene, OR: Cascade, 2010.

Blount, Brian K. "The Apocalypse of Worship: A House of Prayer for All Nations." Pages 16–29 in *Making Room at the Table: An Invitation to Multicultural Worship*. Edited by Brian K. Blount and Leonora Tubbs Tisdale. Louisville: Westminster John Knox, 2001.

Boeve, Lieven. "Resurrection: Saving Particularity: Theological-Epistemological Considerations of Incarnation and Truth." *Theological Studies* 67 (2006): 795–808.

Bonaventure. *The Life of St. Francis of Assisi*. Charlotte, NC: TAN, 2010.

Bonhoeffer, Dietrich. *Ethics*. New York: Macmillan, 1965.

Brown, Raymond. *The Gospel According to John I–XII: A New Translation with Introduction and Commentary*. The Anchor Bible 29. Garden City, NY: Doubleday, 1966.

Bruce, F. F. *The Gospel of John: Introduction, Exposition and Notes*. Glasgow: Pickering and Ingles, 1983.

Brueggemann, Walter. *Genesis*. Interpretation: A Bible Commentary for Teaching and Preaching. Atlanta: John Knox, 1982.

———. *Journey to the Common Good*. Louisville: Westminster John Knox, 2010.

———. *The Practice of Prophetic Imagination*. Minneapolis: Fortress, 2012.

———. *Sabbath as Resistance: Saying No to the Culture of Now*. Louisville: Westminster John Knox, 2014.

Bulgakov, Sergius. "The Virgin and the Saints in Orthodoxy." Pages 65–75 in *Eastern Orthodox Theology: A Contemporary Reader*. Edited by Daniel B. Clendenin. Grand Rapids: Baker, 1995.

Bultmann, Rudolf Karl. *The Gospel of John: A Commentary*. Louisville: Westminster John Knox, 1971.

Byron, John. *Cain and Abel in Text and Tradition: Jewish and Christian Interpretations of the First Sibling Rivalry*. Leiden: Brill, 2011.

———. "Slaughter, Fratricide and Sacrifice: Cain and Abel Traditions in 1 John 3." *Biblica* 88, no. 4 (2007): 526–35.

Calder, Nigel. *Unless Peace Comes*. New York: Viking, 1968.

Caneday, A. B. "Mark's Provocative Use of Scripture in Narration: 'He Was with the Wild Animals and Angels Ministered to Him.'" *Bulletin for Biblical Research* 9 (1999): 19–36.

Cantalamessa, Raniero. *The Mystery of Pentecost*. Translated by Glen S. Davis. Collegeville, MN: Liturgical, 2001.

Carson, D. A. *The Gospel according to John*. Leicester: Inter-Varsity/Grand Rapids: Eerdmans, 1991.

———. *Matthew: Chapters 1 through 12*. The Expositor's Bible Commentary. Grand Rapids: Zondervan, 1995.

———. *Matthew: Chapters 13 through 28*. The Expositor's Bible Commentary. Grand Rapids: Zondervan, 1995.

Castro, Emilio. "Reconciliation." Pages 65–70 in *The Ecumenical Movement: An Anthology of Key Texts and Voices*. Edited by Michael Kinnamon and Brian E. Cope. Geneva: World Council of Churches, 1997.

Cavanaugh, William T. *Being Consumed: Economics and Christian Desire*. Grand Rapids: Eerdmans, 2008.

———. *The Myth of Religious Violence: Secular Ideology and the Roots of Modern Conflict*. New York: Oxford University Press, 2009.

Chardin, Teilhard de. *The Divine Milieu*. New York: HarperCollins, 2001.

Clausewitz, Carl von. *On War*. Princeton: Princeton University Press, 1984.

Coakley, Sarah. *God, Sexuality, and the Self: An Essay 'On the Trinity.'* New York: Cambridge University Press, 2013.

Connolly, William E. "Capitalism, Christianity, America: Rethinking the Issues." *Political Theology* 12, no. 2 (2011): 226–36.

Constantinou, Stavroula. "Holy Actors and Actresses: Fools and Cross-Dressers as Protagonists of Saints' *Lives*." Pages 343–57 in *Ashgate Research Companion to Byzantine Hagiography:* Volume II: *Genres and Contexts*. Edited by Stephanos Efthymiadis. Burlington, VT: Ashgate, 2014.

Cox, Harvey. *The Future of Faith*. New York: HarperOne, 2010.

Cross, Samuel Hazzard, and Olgerd P. Scherbowits, trans. and ed. *The Russian Primary Chronicle: Laurentian Text*. Cambridge, MA: The Medieval Academy of America, 1956.

Crossan, John Dominic. *God and Empire: Jesus Against Rome, Then and Now.* New York: HarperOne, 2007.

Crouch, Andy. *Culture Making: Recovering Our Creative Calling.* Downers Grove, IL: InterVarsity, 2008.

Cunningham, Laurence S. *The Meaning of Saints.* New York: Harper and Row, 1980.

Damascene, John. *An Exact Exposition of the Orthodox Faith.* http://www.orthodox.net/fathers/exacti.html.

De La Torre, Miguel A. *Genesis.* Louisville: Westminster John Knox, 2011.

Derrida, Jacques. "Living On: Border Lines." Pages 62–142 in *Deconstruction and Criticism.* Edited by Harold Bloom. New York: Seabury, 1979.

———. *Of Grammatology.* Translated by Gayatri Spivak. Baltimore: Johns Hopkins University Press, 1998.

———. *On Cosmopolitanism and Forgiveness.* Thinking in Action. New York: Routledge, 2007.

———. "The Villanova Roundtable: A Conversation with Jacques Derrida." Pages 3–28 in *Deconstruction in a Nutshell: A Conversation with Jacques Derrida.* Edited by John Caputo. New York: Fordham University Press, 1996.

Dionysius Aeropagite. *The Divine Names.* Patrologia Graeca 3:700A–B. Edited by J.-P. Migne.

Dostoevsky, Fyodor. *The Brothers Karamazov.* Mineola, NY: Dover, 2005.

Ecumenical Press Service. "Churches Urged to Play Their Part in Ex-Yugoslavia." *Ecumenical Press Service.* February 22, 1993.

Engels, Friedrich. *Herr Eugen Dühring's Revolution in Science.* https://www.marxists.org/archive/marx/works/download/pdf/anti_duhring.pdf.

Fagerberg, David. "A Century on Liturgical Asceticism." *Diakonia* 31, no. 1 (1998): 41.

Finger, Reta Halteman. *Of Widows and of Meals: Communal Meals in the Book of Acts.* Grand Rapids: Eerdmans, 2007.

Flam, Nancy. "'Pass Not Away': Yearning for a Seamless Life of Connection." Pages 3–14 in *Jewish Mysticism and the Spiritual Life: Classical Texts, Contemporary Reflections.* Edited by Lawrence Fine, Eitan Fishbane, and Or N. Rose. Woodstock, VT: Jewish Light, 2010.

Flesher, Andrew Michael. *Heroes, Saints, and Ordinary Morality.* Washington, DC: Georgetown University Press, 2003.

Foucault, Michel. *Society Must Be Defended.* Translated by David Macey. Edited by Mauro Bertani and Alessandro Fontana. New York: Picador, 2003.

Francis of Assisi. "How St. Francis Tamed the Very Fierce Wolf of Gubbio."

Pages 496–498 in *From Christ to the World: Introductory Readings in Christian Ethics*. Edited by Wayne G. Boulton, Thomas D. Kennedy, and Allen Verhey. Grand Rapids: Eerdmans, 1994.

Francis, Pope. *Homily for the Canonization of Mother Teresa*. Holy Mass and Canonization of Blessed Mother Terese of Calcutta. St. Peter's Square, September 4, 2016. http://en.radiovaticana.va/news/2016/09/04/homily_for_the_canonization_of_mother_teresa_full_text/1255727.

Fresko, J. V. "Preaching as a Means of Grace and the Doctrine of Sanctification: A Reformed Perspective." *American Theological Inquiry* 3, no. 1 (January 15, 2010): 35–54.

Freud, Sigmund. *Beyond the Pleasure Principle*. London: Hogarth, 1920.

Fromm, Erich. *The Fear of Freedom*. London: Routledge, 2001.

Gaventa, Beverly. *The Acts of the Apostles*. Abingdon New Testament Commentaries. Nashville: Abingdon, 2003.

George, Henry. "Moses: A Lecture." http://www.cooperativeindividualism.org/george-henry_moses-a-lecture-1878.html.

Gieschen, Charles A. "Why Was Jesus with the Wild Beasts (Mark 1:13)?" *Concordia Theological Quarterly* 73, no. 1 (January 2009): 77–80.

Gilligan, James. *Violence: Reflections on a National Epidemic*. New York: Vintage, 1996.

Girard, René. *Le Bouc emissaire*. Paris: Grasset, 1982.

———. *Je vois Satan tomber comme l'éclair*. Paris: Grasset, 1999.

———. *Violence and the Sacred*. Translated by Patrick Gregory. Baltimore: Johns Hopkins University Press, 1979.

Glenny, Misha. *The Fall of Yugoslavia: The Third Balkan War*. London: Penguin, 1996.

Godzieba, Anthony. "'Stay with us. . .' (Lk. 24.29)–'Come, Lord Jesus' (Rev. 22.20): Incarnation, Eschatology, and Theology's Sweet Predicament." *Theological Studies* 67 (2006): 783–95.

Greenberg, Irvin. "Religion as a Force for Reconciliation and Peace: A Jewish Analysis." Pages 88–112 in *Beyond Violence: Religious Sources of Social Transformation in Judaism, Christianity, and Islam*. Edited by James L. Heft, S.M. New York: Fordham University Press, 2004.

Gregory of Nyssa. *The Life of Moses*. Patrologia Graeca 44:374. Edited by J.-P. Migne.

Groody, Daniel G. "Globalizing Solidarity: Christian Anthropology and the Challenge of Human Liberation." *Theological Studies* 69 (2008): 250–68.

Gruchy, John W. de. *Reconciliation: Restoring Justice*. Minneapolis: Fortress, 2002.

Habermas, Jürgen. "The Crisis of the Welfare State and the Exhaustion of Utopian Energies." Pages 285–99 in *Jürgen Habermas on Society and Politics: A Reader*. Edited by Steven Seidman. Boston: Beacon, 1989.

Hardt, Michael, and Antonio Negri. *Declaration*. Argo Navis, 2012.

Hauerwas, Stanley. *Approaching the End: Eschatological Reflections on Church, Politics, and Life*. Grand Rapids: Eerdmans, 2013.

Havel, Vaclav. "Politics, Morality, and Civility." Pages 391–402 in *The Essential Civil Society Reader: Classic Essays in the American Civil Society Debate*. Edited by Don E. Eberly. New York: Rowman & Littlefield, 2000.

Hayes, Zachary. "Christology-Cosmology." *Spirit and Life* 7 (1997): 41–58.

Hedley, Tom. "Croatia, Serbia Face Off at Bihac." *Chicago Tribune*. July 30, 1995. http://articles.chicagotribune.com/1995-07-30/news/9507300180_1_bihac-bosnian-serb-bosnian-government.

Hegel, G. W. F. *G. W. F. Hegel: Theologian of the Spirit*. Edited by Peter C. Hodgson. Edinburgh: T&T Clark, 1997.

Heinrich, Mark. "Eastern Slavonia Agrees to Join Croatia." *Independent*. November 13, 1995. https://www.independent.co.uk/news/world/eastern-slavonia-agrees-to-rejoin-croatia-1581721.html.

Hengel, Martin. *Property and Riches in the Early Church*. Philadelphia: Fortress, 1974.

Hill, David. *The Gospel of Matthew*. New Century Bible Commentary. Grand Rapids: Eerdmans, 1981.

Hill, Lisa. "The Hidden Theodicy of Adam Smith." *European Journal of the History of Economic Thought* 8, no. 1 (2001): 1–29.

Himes, Michael J., and Kenneth R. Himes. "The Sacrament of Creation: Toward an Environmental Theology." *Commonweal* 117 (1990): 45–46.

Hinterberger, Martin. "Byzantine Hagiography and Its Literary Genres: Some Critical Observations." Pages 25–60 in *The Ashgate Research Companion to Byzantine Hagiography:* Volume II: *Genres and Contexts*. Edited by Stephanos Efthymiadis. Burlington, VT: Ashgate, 2014.

Hobbes, Thomas. *Leviathan (Or the Matter, Form and Power of a Commonwealth Ecclesiastical and Civil)*. New York: Simon and Schuster, 1962.

Howard, Michael. *The Invention of Peace*. London: Yale University Press, 2000.

Ignatius. *Letter to the Romans*. http://www.newadvent.org/fathers/0107.htm.

Irenaeus. *Against Heresies*. The Apostolic Fathers with Justin Martyr and Irenaeus, Christian Classics Ethereal Library. http://www.ccel.org/ccel/schaff/anf01.ix.vii.xv.html.

Jacques, Peter. "Ecology, Distribution, and Identity in the World Politics of

Environmental Skepticism." *Capitalism Nature Socialism Journal* 19, no. 3 (2008): 8–28. http://www.cnsjournal.org/wp-content/uploads/2014/09/Jacques.19.3.Sep_.08.pdf.

Jankélévitch, Vladimir. *Forgiveness*. Translated by Andrew Kelly. Chicago: University of Chicago Press, 2005.

———. *L'Imprescriptible*. France: Seuil, 1996.

———. "Should We Pardon Them?" Translated by Ann Hobart. *Critical Inquiry* 22 (1996): 552–72.

Jenson, Robert W. *The Triune God*. Vol. 1 of *Systematic Theology*. New York: Oxford University Press, 1997.

———. *Visible Words: The Interpretation and Practice of Christian Sacraments*. Minneapolis: Fortress, 2010.

———. *The Works of God*. Vol. 2 of *Systematic Theology*. New York: Oxford University Press, 1999.

John of Damascus. *An Exposition of the Orthodox Faith*. http://www.newadvent.org/fathers/33042.htm.

Johnson, Luke Timothy. *Sharing Possessions: Mandate and Symbols of Faith*. Philadelphia: Fortress, 1981.

Jones, L. Gregory. *Embodying Forgiveness: A Theological Analysis*. Grand Rapids: Eerdmans, 1995.

Kant, Immanuel. *Perpetual Peace: A Philosophical Essay*. Translated by M. Campbell. New York: Grand, 1972.

Keegan, John. *A History of Warfare*. London: Hutchinson, 1993.

Kim, Angela Y. "Cain and Abel in the Light of Envy: A Study in the History of Interpretation of Envy in Genesis 4.1–16." *Journal for the Study of Pseudepigrapha* 12, no. 1 (2001): 65–84.

Kuzmic, Peter. "Historical Context: How Did We Get Here?" Pages 6–12 in *Bridges of Reconciliation: Reader on the Conflict in Bosnia*. Edited by Craig Arban and Jo Marie Dooly. Washington, DC: World Vision, 1997.

———. "On the Way to Peace in the Balkans." *The Christian Century*, no. 6 (February 21, 1996): 199–202.

———. "Reconciliation in Eastern Europe." Pages 47–55 in *Reconciliation in Difficult Places: Dealing with Our Deepest Differences, The Washington Forum: Perspectives on Our Common Future*. Monrovia, CA: World Vision, 1994.

Levinas, Emmanuel. *Beyond the Verse: Talmudic Readings and Lectures*. London: Continuum, 2007.

———. "The Ego and Totality." Pages 25–46 in *Collected Philosophical Papers*. Translated by Alphonso Lingis. Dordrecht: Martinus Nijhoff, 1987.

———. *In the Time of the Nations*. Translated by Michael B. Smith. London: Athlone, 1994.

———. *Totality and Infinity: An Essay on Exteriority*. Dordrecht: Kluwer, 1991.

Lederach, John Paul. *The Moral Imagination: The Art and Soul of Building Peace*. New York: Oxford University Press, 2005.

Lossky, Vladimir. *The Mystical Theology of the Eastern Church*. Crestwood, NY: St. Vladimir's Seminary Press, 1976.

———. *Orthodox Theology: An Introduction*. Crestwood, NY: St. Vladimir's Seminary Press, 1978.

Loth, Andrew. "From Doctrine of Christ to Icon of Christ: St. Maximus the Confessor on the Transfiguration of Christ." Pages 260–75 in *In the Shadow of the Incarnation: Essays on Jesus Christ in the Early Church in Honor of Brian E. Daley, S.J.* Edited by Peter W. Martens. Notre Dame: University of Notre Dame Press, 2008.

Luther, Martin. *Lectures on Romans*. Vol. 25 of *Luther's Works*. Saint Louis: Concordia, 1972.

Luxemburg, Rosa. "Socialism and the Churches." *Marxist Classics*. http://www.newyouth.com/archives/classics/luxemburg/socialismandthechurches.html.

Marx, Karl. "Introduction." *A Contribution to the Critique of Hegel's Philosophy of Right*. http://www.marxists.org/archive/marx/works/1843/critique-hpr/intro.htm.

Marx, Karl, and Frederick Engels. *Communist Manifesto*. https://www.marxists.org/archive/marx/works/1848/communist-manifesto/ch04.htm.

Mass, Peter. *Love Thy Neighbor: A Story of War*. New York: Alfred A. Knopf, 1997.

Maximus the Confessor. *Ambigua*. Patrologia Graeca 91:1072B–C. Edited by J.-P. Migne.

———. *Gnostic Chapters* 1.67. Patrologia Graeca 90:1108B. Edited by J.-P. Migne.

———. *Mystagogy*. Patrologia Graeca 91:684C–685A. Edited by J.-P. Migne.

———. *On the Cosmic Mystery of Jesus Christ*. Crestwood, NY: St. Vladimir's Seminary Press, 2003.

McChesney, Robert W. Introduction to *Profit over People: Neoliberalism and Global Order*, by Noam Chomsky. New York: Seven Stories, 1999.

McFague, Sallie. *Blessed Are the Consumers: Climate Change and the Practice of Restraint*. Minneapolis: Fortress, 2013.

———. "An Ecological Christology: Does Christianity Have It?" Pages 29–46 in *Christianity and Ecology: Seeking the Well-Being of Earth and Humans*.

Edited by Dieter T. Hessel and Rosemary Radford Ruether. Cambridge, MA: Harvard University Press, 2000.

———. "Epilogue: Human Dignity and the Integrity of Creation." Pages 199–212 in *Theology That Matters: Ecology, Economy, and God*. Edited by Darby Kathleen Ray. Minneapolis: Fortress, 2006.

———. *Life Abundant: Rethinking Theology and Economy for a Planet in Peril*. Minneapolis: Fortress, 2001.

———. *A New Climate for Theology*. Minneapolis: Fortress, 2008.

McGill, Arthur. *Sermons of Arthur C. McGill: Theological Fascinations*. Edited by Daniel Cain. Eugene, OR: Cascade, 2007.

Meeks, M. Douglas. "The Church and the Poor in Supply-Side Economics." *Cities*, no. 1 (Fall 1983): 6–9.

———. *God the Economist: The Doctrine of God and Political Economy*. Minneapolis: Fortress, 1989.

Meier, John P. *Matthew*. New Testament Message 3. Wilmington, DE: Michael Glazier, 1980.

———. "The Present State of the 'Third Quest' for the Historical Jesus: Loss and Gain." *Biblica* 80 (1999): 459–87.

Merwe, Hugo van der, and Audrey R. Chapman, eds. *Truth and Reconciliation in South Africa: Did the TRC Deliver?* Philadelphia: University of Pennsylvania Press, 2008.

Metz, Johann Baptist. *Faith on History and Society: Toward a Practical Fundamental Theology*. New York: Seabury, 1980.

Meyendorff, John. "Doing Theology in an Eastern Orthodox Perspective." Pages 79–96 in *Eastern Orthodox Theology: A Contemporary Reader*. Edited by Daniel B. Clendenin. Grand Rapids: Baker, 1995.

Midlarsky, Manus I. *Origins of Political Extremism: Mass Violence in the Twentieth Century and Beyond*. New York: Cambridge University Press, 2011.

Minow, Martha. *Forgiveness, Law and Justice*. Annual Reconciliation Lecture, 2014. https://www.ufs.ac.za/docs/librariesprovider47/trauma-forgiveness-and-reconciliation-studies-documents/programme-and-actvities-documents/annual-reconciliation-lecture-2014-78-eng.pdf?sfvrsn=0

Moberly, R. W. L. "Did the Interpreters Get It Right? Genesis 2–3 Reconsidered." *Journal of Theological Studies* 59, no. 1 (April 2008): 22–40.

Moloney, Francis J., and Daniel J. Harrington. *The Gospel of John*. Sacra Pagina. Collegeville, MN: Liturgical, 1998.

Moltmann, Jürgen. *Creating a Just Future: The Politics of Peace and the Ethics of Creation in a Threatened World*. London: SCM, 1989.

———. *Ethics of Hope*. Minneapolis: Fortress, 2012.

———. *The Living God and the Fullness of Life*. Translated by Margaret Kohl. Louisville: Westminster John Knox, 2015.

———. *The Trinity and the Kingdom*. Minneapolis: Fortress, 1993.

Morgan, Maria Teresa. "Tongues as of Fire: The Spirit as Paradigm for Ministry in a Multicultural Setting." Pages 106–25 in *The Spirit in the Church and the World*. Edited by Bradford E. Hinze. New York: Orbis, 2004.

Murove, Munyaradzi Felix. "Perceptions of Greed in Western Economic and Religious Traditions: An African Communitarian Response." *Black Theology* 5, no. 2 (2007): 220–43.

Nation, R. Craig. *War in the Balkans, 1991–2002: Comprehensive History of Wars Provoked by Yugoslav Collapse; Balkan Region in World Politics, Slovenia and Croatia, Bosnia-Herzegovina, Kosovo, Greece, Turkey, Cyprus*. Progressive Management, 2014.

Nauta, Rein. "Cain and Abel: Violence, Shame and Jealousy." *Pastoral Psychology* 58, no. 1 (March 2009): 65–71.

Nazianzus, Gregory. *Epistle CI. To Cledonius the Priest against Apollinarius*. Christian Classics Ethereal Library. http://www.ccel.org/ccel/schaff/npnf207.iv.ii.iii.html

———. *The Fifth Theological Oration: On the Holy Spirit*, XXVI, in *Cyril of Jerusalem and Gregory of Nazianzen*. Christian Classics Ethereal Library. http://www.ccel.org/ccel/schaff/npnf207.iii.xvii.html.

———. *Oration* 38. http://www.newadvent.org/fathers/310238.htm.

Neshev, Kiril. *The Philosophical Postmodernism*. Sofia: Filvest, 1997.

Niebuhr, H. Richard. *Christ and Culture*. New York: Harper & Row, 1975.

Nussbaum, Martha C. *Political Emotions: Why Love Matters for Justice*. Cambridge, MA: Harvard University Press, 2015.

Olthuis, James. "Introduction: Love/Knowledge Sojourning with Others, Meeting with Differences." Pages 1–15 in *Knowing Other-Wise: Philosophy at the Threshold of Spirituality*. Edited by James Olthuis. New York: Fordham University Press, 1997.

Ouspensky, Leonid. "The Meaning and Content of the Icon." Pages 33–63 in *Eastern Orthodox Theology: A Contemporary Reader*. Edited by Daniel B. Clendenin. Grand Rapids: Baker, 1995.

Peters, Rebecca Todd. "Examining the Economic Crisis of Values." *Interpretation* (April 2011): 154–66.

Pfeil, Margaret R. "Liturgy and Ethics: The Liturgical Asceticism of Energy Conservation." *Journal of the Society of Christian Ethics* 27, no. 2 (Fall/Winter 2007): 127–49.

Philo. *Questions and Answers on Genesis* 1.4. The Works of Philo, Early Jewish Writings. http://www.earlychristianwritings.com/yonge/book41.html.

———. *The Special Laws*. The Works of Philo. http://www.earlychristianwritings.com/yonge/book30.html.

Plekon, Michael. *The World as Sacrament: An Ecumenical Path toward a Worldly Spirituality*. Collegeville, MN: Liturgical, 2016.

Rad, Gerhard von. *Genesis*. Translated by John Marks. Philadelphia: Westminster, 1961.

Renan, Ernest. "What Is a Nation?" Pages 143–55 in *The Nationalism Reader*. Edited by Omar Dahbour and Micheline R. Ishay. Atlantic Highlands, NJ: Humanities, 1995.

Rieff, David. *Slaughterhouse: Bosnia and the Failure of the West*. New York: Touchstone, 1995.

Riggs, Marcia Y. "The Globalization of Nothing and Creation Ex Nihilo." Pages 141–53 in *Theology That Matters: Ecology, Economy, and God*. Edited by Darby Kathleen Ray. Minneapolis: Fortress, 2006.

Ringe, Sharon H. *Jesus, Liberation, and the Biblical Jubilee: Images of Ethics and Christology*. Philadelphia: Fortress, 1985.

Rosenblatt, Naomi H., and Joshua Horwitz. *Wrestling with Angels: What the First Family of Genesis Teaches Us about Our Spiritual Identity, Sexuality, and Personal Relationships*. New York: Delacorte, 1995.

Sacks, Jonathan. *The Politics of Hope*. London: Vintage, 2000.

———. *To Heal a Fractured World: The Ethics of Responsibility*. New York: Schocken, 2007.

Schaab, Gloria L. "Incarnation as Emergence: A Transformative Vision of God and the Cosmos." *Heythrop Journal* 54, no. 4 (July 2013): 631–44.

Scheler, Max. "Repentance and Rebirth." Pages 38–63 in *On the Eternal in Man*. Translated by Bernard Noble. Hamden, CT: Archon, 1972.

Schmemann, Alexander. *The Eucharist: Sacrament of the Kingdom*. Crestwood, NY: St. Vladimir's Seminary Press, 2003.

———. "Fast and Liturgy." *St. Vladimir's Seminary Quarterly* 3, no. 1 (Winter 1959): 2–9. https://oca.org/reflections/fr-alexander-schmemann/fast-and-liturgy.

———. *For the Life of the World: Sacraments and Orthodoxy*. Crestwood, NY: St. Vladimir's Seminary Press, 1963.

———. "Liturgy and Theology." Pages 49–69 in *Liturgy and Tradition: Theological Reflections of Alexander Schmemann*. Edited by Thomas Frisch. Crestwood, NY: St. Vladimir's Seminary Press, 1990.

———. "The Missionary Imperative in the Orthodox Tradition." Pages 195–

210 in *Eastern Orthodox Theology: A Contemporary Reader*. Edited by Daniel B. Clendenin. Grand Rapids: Baker, 1995.

———. *Of Water and Spirit: A Liturgical Study of Baptism*. Crestwood, NY: St. Vladimir's Seminary Press, 1974.

———. "The World in Orthodox Thought and Experience." Pages 67–84 in *Church, World, Mission: Reflections on Orthodoxy in the West*. Crestwood, NY: St. Vladimir's Seminary Press, 1979.

Shepherd of Hermas. http://www.earlychristianwritings.com/text/shepherd.html.

Shriver, Donald W. *An Ethic for Enemies: Forgiveness in Politics*. Oxford: Oxford University Press, 1998.

The Sibylline Oracles. Translated by Milton S. Terry. New York: Eaton and Mains, 1899.

Simmons, Marlise. "Vojislav Seselj, Serbian Nationalist, Is Acquitted of War Crimes by Hague Tribunal." *The New York Times*. March 31, 2016. https://www.nytimes.com/2016/04/01/world/europe/vojislav-seselj-war-crimes.html.

Smith, Adam. *An Inquiry into the Nature and Causes of the Wealth of Nations*. London: William Benton, 1955.

———. *The Theory of Moral Sentiments*. New York: Augustus M. Kelley, 1966.

Smith, James K. A. *Desiring the Kingdom: Worship, Worldview, and Culture Formation*. Vol. 1 of *Cultural Liturgies*. Grand Rapids: Baker Academic, 2009.

Smith, Roger M. "Citizenship and the Politics of People Building." *Citizenship Studies* 5, no. 1 (2001): 73–96.

Sneed, Mark. "Israelite Concern for the Alien, Orphan, and Widow: Altruism or Ideology?" *Zeitschrift für die alttestamentliche Wissenschaft* 111, no. 4 (1999): 498–507.

Staniloae, Dumitru. *Revelation and Knowledge of the Triune God*. Vol. 1 of *The Experience of God: Orthodox Dogmatic Theology*. Brookline, MA: Holy Cross Orthodox Press, 1994.

———. *The Sanctifying Mysteries*. Vol. 5 of *The Experience of God: Orthodox Dogmatic Theology*. Brookline, MA: Holy Cross Orthodox Press, 2012.

———. *The World: Creation and Deification*. Vol. 2 of *The Experience of God: Orthodox Dogmatic Theology*. Brookline, MA: Holy Cross Orthodox Press, 2005.

Stavropoulos, Christoforos. "Partakers of Divine Nature." Pages 183–92 in *Eastern Orthodox Theology: A Contemporary Reader*. Edited by Daniel B. Clendenin. Grand Rapids: Baker, 1995.

Stott, John R. W. *Christian Counterculture: The Message of the Sermon on the Mount*. Downers Grove, IL: InterVarsity, 1978.

Straus, Scott. *Making and Unmaking Nations: War, Leadership, and Genocide in Modern Africa*. Ithaca, NY: Cornell University Press, 2015.

Stronstad, Roger. *The Prophethood of All Believers*. Journal of Pentecostal Theology Supplements Series 16. Sheffield: Sheffield Academic, 1999.

Subev, Todor. "The Nature and Mission of Councils in the Light of the Theology of Sobornost." *The Ecumenical Review* 45, no. 3 (July 1993): 261–70.

Tanner, Kathryn. *Theories of Culture: A New Agenda for Theology*. Minneapolis: Fortress, 1997.

Taylor, Charles. "Notes on the Sources of Violence: Perennial and Modern." Pages 15–42 in *Beyond Violence: Religious Sources of Social Transformation in Judaism, Christianity, and Islam*. Edited by James L. Heft, S.M. New York: Fordham University Press, 2004.

Tertullian. *Apology*. http://www.newadvent.org/fathers/0301.htm.

Thatcher, Tom. "Cain and Abel in Early Christian Memory: A Case Study in 'The New Use of Old Testament in the New.'" *The Catholic Biblical Quarterly* 72, no. 4 (October 2010): 732–51.

Theokritoff, George. "The Cosmology of the Eucharist." Pages 131–35 in *Toward an Ecology of Transfiguration: Orthodox Christian Perspectives on Environment, Nature, and Creation*. Edited by John Chryssavgis and Bruce V. Foltz. New York: Fordham University Press, 2013.

Tillich, Paul. *Love, Power, and Justice*. New York: Oxford University Press, 1960.

Tilton, John E. "Depletion and the Long-Run Availability of Mineral Commodities." *Mining, Minerals and Sustainable Development* 14 (March 2001). http://www.iied.org.

———. *On Borrowed Time? Assessing the Threat of Mineral Depletion*. Washington, DC: Resources for the Future, 2003.

Tolan, John. "The Friar and the Sultan: Francis of Assisi's Mission to Egypt." *European Review* 16, no. 1 (2008): 115–26.

Tschuy, Theó. *Ethnic Conflict and Religion: Challenge to the Churches*. Geneva: World Council of Churches, 1997.

Tutu, Desmond. *God Has a Dream: A Vision of Hope for Our Times*. New York: Image/Doubleday, 2004.

———. *No Future without Forgiveness*. New York: Doubleday, 1999.

———. *The Rainbow People of God*. New York: Doubleday, 1994.

Vermulen, Karolien. "Mind the Gap: Ambiguity in the Story of Cain and Abel." *Journal of Biblical Literature* 133, no. 1 (Spring 2014): 29–42.

Vogels, Walter. "The Tree(s) in the Middle of the Garden (Gen. 2.9; 3.3)." *Science et Esprit* 59, nos. 2–3 (2007): 129–42.

Volf, Miroslav. *The End of Memory: Remembering Rightly in a Violent World.* Grand Rapids: Eerdmans, 2006.

———. *Exclusion and Embrace: A Theological Exploration of Identity, Otherness, and Reconciliation.* Nashville: Abingdon, 1996.

———. *Flourishing: Why We Need Religion in a Globalized Word.* New Haven: Yale University Press, 2015.

———. *Public Faith: How Followers of Christ Should Serve the Common Good.* Grand Rapids: Brazos, 2011.

Walton, John H. *Genesis.* The NIV Application Commentary. Grand Rapids: Zondervan, 2001.

Ware, Timothy (Bishop Kallistos). *The Inner Kingdom.* Vol. 1 of *Collected Works.* Crestwood, NY: St. Vladimir's Seminary Press, 2000.

———. *The Orthodox Church.* New York: Penguin, 1993.

———. "*Sobornost* and Eucharistic Ecclesiology: Alexei Khomiakov and His Successors." *International Journal for the Study of the Christian Church* 11, nos. 2–3 (May–August 2011): 216–35.

Weber, Max. "Ethnic Groups." Pages 52–66 in *Theories of Ethnicity: A Classical Reader.* Edited by Werner Sollors. New York: New York University Press, 1996.

Weil, Simone. *First and Last Notebooks.* Translated by Richard Rees. London: Oxford University Press, 1970.

Wenk, Matthias. *Community-Forming Power: The Socio-Ethical Role of the Spirit in Luke-Acts.* Journal of Pentecostal Theology Supplements Series 19. Sheffield: Sheffield Academic, 2000.

Wesley, John. *The Works of John Wesley.* Vol. 14. Peabody, MA: Hendrickson, 1991.

Wiesel, Elie. *From the Kingdom of Memory: Reminiscences.* New York: Summit, 1990.

Williams, Rowan. *On Christian Theology.* Oxford: Blackwell, 2000.

———. *Resurrection: Interpreting the Easter Gospel.* London: Darton Longman & Todd, 2014.

Wright, N. T. *The Challenge of Jesus: Recovering Who Jesus Was and Is.* Downers Grove, IL: InterVarsity, 1999.

———. "Jesus' Self-Understanding." Pages 47–61 in *The Incarnation.* Edited by Stephen T. Davis, Daniel Kendall, S.J., and Gerald O'Collins. New York: Oxford University Press, 2002.

Wyschogrod, Edith. *Saints and Postmodernity: Revisioning Moral Philosophy*. Chicago: University of Chicago Press, 1990.

Yong, Amos. *Hospitality and the Other: Pentecost, Christian Practices, and the Neighbor*. Maryknoll, NY: Orbis, 2008.

———. *In the Days of Caesar: Pentecostalism and Political Theology*. Grand Rapids: Eerdmans, 2010.

Zappen, James P. "Mikhail Bakhtin." Pages 7–20 in *Twentieth-Century Rhetoric and Rhetoricians: Critical Studies and Sources*. Edited by Michael G. Morgan and Michelle Ballif. Westport: Greenwood, 2000.

Zizioulas, John D. *Being as Communion: Studies in Personhood and the Church*. Crestwood, NY: St. Vladimir's Seminary Press, 1995.

———. *Communion and Otherness*. New York: T&T Clark, 2006.

Index of Subjects

Abel, 67–72
Abraham, 111
abuse, 103, 175, 194, 223n73
accountability, 103, 151, 183, 189
acts, 200n7
Adam, 16–18, 26, 27, 31, 39, 42, 55, 105, 135, 139, 140, 177
Agape Humanitarian Relief and Development Agency, 214–16
"already and not yet," 146–47
American dream, 74, 158
anger, 67–69, 158, 166, 219
annunciation, 39, 205
anthropology, 1, 7, 12, 15n8, 40, 139
anti-war, 226
Arendt, Hannah, 47, 63–64, 95n95, 163, 169, 170–71, 184
ark of the covenant, 33
Armenians, 193
art, 54–55
ascension, 37, 87, 150, 152, 177
asceticism, of Christoformation, 21, 22, 23, 205, 207; and dignity, 110; of fasting, 151, 152; of forgiveness, 167, 195; and hospitality, 44–45, 51; as liturgical, 130, 131–32n45, 147; and prayer, 53; and repentance, 103
askesis, 45, 48, 49, 52, 108, 131–32n45, 136, 137, 159, 205–6
Athanasius, 19, 36, 39, 79n51
atheism, 90
atrocities, 2, 100, 182, 192, 217, 219n66, 225
Augustine, 53, 86n64
authenticity, 14, 21, 41, 46, 118, 165, 188, 205, 209, 225

Babel, 46–47, 49–51
Bakhtin, Mikhail, 57
Balkan countries, 193
Balog, Antal, 215
Balthasar, Hans Urs von, 35n71
Baptists, 218
Barker, Margaret, 38
Barth, Karl, 86, 96n96
Bartholomew I, H. A. H., 53, 54, 94, 127, 135, 153
Basil the Blessed, 204n22
Basque separatists, 193n100
Bauckham, Richard, 73–74
Behr, John, 78n49, 78–79n51, 84, 87–89
belief, 54
Berdyaev, Nikolai, 65n18, 85n63, 125–26
Bergson, Henri, 82n56
bitterness, 192
body, 40
Boeve, Lieven, 41
Bonaventure, 203n21
Bonhoeffer, Dietrich, 189n90
Bosnia, 1–3
Bosnia/Herzegovina (BiH), 214
Bosnians, 193, 218

brokenness, 77, 97, 221-22
Brown, Raymond E., 36n76
Brueggemann, Walter, 92, 97n99, 115, 133, 134, 145, 149
brutality, 2, 89, 115, 118, 200, 204n22, 220, 222
Bulgakov, Sergius, 50
burials, 198
Byron, John, 69n21

Cain, 54, 67-72
Calder, Nigel, 63
Cantalamessa, Raniero, 86n64
capitalism, 76n45, 121-26
categorical violence, 98, 100n105
Catherine of Siena, 205
catholicity, 10n38, 23-25, 59
Cavanaugh, William, 90n80, 149, 156
Center for Peace, Nonviolence and Human Rights, 224
charity, 86n64, 110-11, 115, 197-98, 207n30
chrismation, 180
Christian ethics, 118-19, 168, 227
Christianity, 183n70, 197n106
Christification, 202, 206
Christlikeness, 17, 28, 46, 195, 225
Christoformation, 20, 48, 87, 137, 172, 178n54, 180, 194, 206, 227
Christology, 11, 35, 88
church, as "community of memory," 179, 181; as crown of creation, 18; as icon of Trinity, 58-60; and justice, 173; theosis of, 34
"cities of refuge," 158
civic virtue, 92n85, 174, 191-96
civil covenant, 103
civilization, 54, 112n135, 167n19, 175
civil religion, 76n44, 92n85, 207
classism, 144
Clausewitz, Carl von, 62
Coakley, Sarah, 45n105, 46
cocelebrant, 80, 149, 161
coequality, 108
Cold War, 63
common good, and capitalism, 122, 126; commitment to, 64n14, 66, 92n85, 221, 224; and eschatology, 162-64; and the Eucharist, 145, 149; and forgiveness, 187; and guilt, 68n20; language as, 56; practice of, 15-25; pursuit of, 4, 84, 181, 196-97, 200, 228; responsibility for, 72, 96
communicative freedom, 94-95
communion, 11, 26, 28, 31, 45-51, 57, 115, 127, 131, 139, 161, 181-82, 189
Communism, 63n6, 91, 99n102
community, 22-23, 94, 166
compassion, 21, 153
competition, 1, 13, 47, 62, 71, 80, 84, 90, 95, 127, 144, 181
conciliarity, 10, 23, 24
conditionality, 187, 188
confession, 189n90
conflict, 1-5, 42n101, 77, 102, 203, 225n77
Connolly, William E., 123
conscience, 56, 89, 90, 104, 165, 182
consecration, 35, 66, 117, 145, 147, 180
consensus, 10, 24, 49, 65, 217n63, 224, 227, 228
consubstantiality, 49, 59, 108
consumerism, 14, 103, 145-55, 158, 206
consumption, 11, 21, 80, 122-24, 135, 149, 157, 158
conversion, 162-63
corporeality, 199, 200, 205, 211
cosmology, 32n62, 35n71
cosmos, as a book, 30; consecration of, 145, 147, 180; healing of, 195, 228; renewal of, 10, 171
cosuffer, 22, 197
Council of Churches for Britain and Ireland, 5
covenant, 93, 103, 112
creation, divine presence in, 11, 14; eschatology of, 8; icon of, 26-27; ontology of, 115; seven days of, 129; and world-mending, 29-44
creativity, 47, 49, 54, 203
creator Spirit, 96n96, 160, 172

crimes against humanity, 182–91, 192, 223n73
Croatia, 5, 193, 214, 218
Crossan, John Dominic, 89n77, 115, 133
crucifixion, 185–86
culture, 8, 54–55, 94, 128
Cunningham, Lawrence S., 6
curse, 42
Cyprians, 193

darkhei shalom, 196–98, 220
David, 105
Day, Dorothy, 19
Dayton Peace Accord, 213n49
death, 43, 78, 84, 87–88, 222
debt, 121n2
Decalogue, 93, 101, 173
"decreation," 207, 208n33
dehumanization, 101
De La Torre, Miguel A., 70, 71n31
democracy, 124, 174, 225
Derrida, Jacques, 101n109, 168, 169, 173–74, 175n47, 183, 186–87, 188, 190–91, 201
desensitization, 89–90
desires, 145–55
dignity, 109
dining table, 145
Dionysius Aeropagite, 42
discernment, 48
discipline, 151
distributive justice, 111, 115, 117, 157, 172, 173, 196
divine face, 25–29
divine self-revelation, 36
divine will, 18
dominion, 75, 133
Dostoevsky, Fyodor, 22, 91, 97n99, 210–11
Dühring, Eugen, 63n5

Eastern European Pentecostals, 150, 154
Eastern Orthodox, 15, 16, 23, 26–27, 28, 44, 58, 136, 145, 150, 154, 177, 180, 218
Eastern Slavonia, 4–5, 6, 211n47
ecclesiology, 23, 58
"ecological catholicity," 24–25
ecological disasters, 106–7
ecological justice, 114
economic justice, 114, 118, 125
economics, 12, 121–24, 157
ecotheological, 81–83
Eden, 31, 134, 161
edifying stories, 200n7
embodiment, 16, 40
empathy, 21, 210
enemy, 165, 175, 181, 225
energy, 82n56
enflesh, 9, 26, 31, 106, 137, 142, 205
Engels, Friedrich, 62, 92n86
enōsis, 19
environmental research, 12
envy, 68n20
epiclesis, 145, 181
epicletic, 146, 148, 151
epistemology, 14, 209
equality, 108–20
eschatology, 8, 152, 162
eschaton, 30, 33–34, 59, 170, 172, 180, 196, 211
eternal life, 43, 44
eternity, 129
ethics, 11n44, 227
ethnicity, 2n11
ethnocentrism, 9
Eucharist, 147–55, 180–81, 207–8
eucharistic priesthood, 128, 143
Eve, 27, 105, 177
evil, 98, 185
execution, 224
ex nihilo, 47
exploitation, 104
externalization, 102

"facial mutilation," 3
fall, 78–79n51, 80, 97
family, 141
fasting, 150–53, 167
fear, 3, 14, 85n63
Feast of the Holy Face, 29
female, 27
Finger, Reta Halterman, 144–45n78

finiteness, 81, 84
foolishness, 204n22
forgiveness, as cosmic, 119; as forced, 194; and memory, 175–82; in past and present, 163; and Pentecost, 10; and punishment, 184–85; versus reconciliation, 190–91; and repentance, 103; as unconditional, 164–74; of unforgivable, 182–91
Forgiveness Sunday, 154
Foucault, Michel, 62n4
Francis (pope), 21–22
Francis of Assisi, 202n16, 203–4n21
fratricide, 66–76
freedom, 32, 47, 50, 53, 85n63, 93–95, 126–27
free-willed, 16, 17, 85, 139, 171, 195, 202, 208
Friedman, Milton, 124
friendship, 170n36, 224
Fromm, Erich, 96–97n98
funeral ceremonies, 198

Garden of Eden, 31, 134, 161
Gaventa, Beverly, 142n72
genocide, 100n105
George, Henry, 112
gift, 130, 173–74, 186
Gilligan, James, 61n1
Girard, René, 61n1, 99n103
Glenny, Misha, 2–3
globalization, 75, 121, 183n70
gnosticism, 42
God, communion with, 11; face of, 66; hospitality of, 43; omnipresence of, 32n62, 166; omniscience of, 32n61; "self-limitation" of, 136; visions of, 70n24
Godlikeness, 107, 130, 196
Godzieba, Anthony, 40, 118n149
Gomorrah, 53n132, 111
Good Samaritan, 210
Gordon-Conwell Theological Seminary, 212
gospel, 168, 196, 201
grace, 186
Graham, Billy, 216
gratitude, 96n96, 143, 149, 174
greatness, 136n56
greed, 81–83, 104, 122n5
Greenberg, Irvin, 104n117, 106n121
Gregory of Nazianzus, 41, 52n124, 140
Gregory of Nyssa, 4
Groody, Daniel G., 125
Gruchy, John W. de, 175n47, 176, 179
guilt, 68n20, 187, 219n66

Habermas, Jürgen, 83
hagiography, 6n24, 19, 155, 199–227
hamartanein, 185
Hardt, Michael, 121n2
harvest, 161
hatred, 67
Havel, Vaclav, 103
healing, 83, 219, 228
Hegel, G. F. W., 183–84
hell, 173, 176–77
helplessness, 97
hesed, 116, 197
heteroglossia, 57
Hill, David, 76
Hinterberger, Martin, 199, 200
historicality, 199, 211
history, 90
Hobbes, Thomas, 1, 62
holiness, 155–59, 203, 206
Holocaust, 185, 192, 193
holy misfits, 8
holy of holies, 31
Holy Spirit, agency of, 26; *charisms* of, 139; empowerment of, 22; and freedom, 53; image of, 58–60; intercession of, 54; love of, 45–46; new life in, 96n96; outpouring of, 51, 157, 180; presence of, 7–8; sanctifying of, 19, 84–85; socio-transformative work of, 203; transfiguration of, 16–17, 28; work of, 165
holy war, 163n6
homecrafting, 173
homesickness, 172
homo adorans, 52, 137, 138, 140

hospitality, 43, 45–51, 133, 218
household, 140–41
human civilization, 54
human flourishing, 4, 13–14, 21, 47–48, 65, 80, 107, 141–42, 149, 189, 225, 227
humanity, creativity of, 47, 54; crimes against, 182–91, 192, 223n73; dignity of, 157; as free moral agent, 93–94; ontology of, 26; will of, 18, 32n63
human-rights abuses, 175
hunger, 149

iconography, 201
idolatry, 28, 75, 134, 137, 195
Ignatius, 88n75
image of God, 16, 50, 143, 167
imitatio Christi, 203n17
Incarnation, authentication of, 202; and catholicity, 25; and Eucharist, 132, 208; and Holy Spirit, 16, 22, 202; and Pentecost, 19, 142n72, 155; and possessions, 142–43; and resurrection, 87; and world-mending, 29–44
inclusivity, 172, 227
indifference, 212–16
individualism, 103, 126, 159
injustice, 90, 91n83, 92, 194
insanity, 204n22
in-Spirit-ed, 12, 14, 21, 45, 49, 95, 127, 139, 160, 172, 179, 207, 227
intercession, 52
interdisciplinary dialogue, 12
internalization, 102
Irenaeus, 83n75, 117, 159
Islam, 183n70, 197n106
Ivan of Rila, 202n16
Ivan the Terrible, 204n22

Jankélévitch, Vladimir, 184
jealousy, 68n20
Jendričko, Josip, 217–18
Jendričko, Milica, 217–18
Jenson, Robert W., 35, 47n112, 51, 52, 53
Jesus Christ, as antipode of Cain, 72; crucifixion of, 185–86; face of, 26; as last Adam, 31, 34–44; passion of, 118–20; as perfect Eucharistic Being, 50, 139
John of Damascus, 87, 135–36n56
Jones, L. Gregory, 184n73
Jubilee, 112, 115, 133, 157
Judaism, 91n83, 98n100, 106, 166n15, 171, 183n70
judgment, 151
Jung, Carl, 189n89
juridical discourse, 201
justice, as civic virtue, 191–96; as divine, 166; versus law, 168; and memory, 175–76; and peace, 108–20, 162

Kant, Immanuel, 138, 163, 185
Keegan, John, 99n103
kenosis, 6, 15n8, 19, 47–50, 136, 156, 165
Kim, Angela Y., 67–68n20, 77
King of kings, 75, 136n56
kinship, 3
koinōnia, 145n78, 146
Kosanović, Mile, 223–24
Kovačević, Matej Lazar, 221–22, 224
Kramaric, Vladko, 212–16
Kruhonja, Katarina, 225
Kuzmic, Peter, 1n2, 212–16, 219n66

land degradation, 82–83n57
language, 55, 190
last Adam, 34–44
law, 112, 114, 168, 191–96
Lederach, John Paul, 8n32, 178
legislated forgiveness, 191–96
Levinas, Emmanuel, 4, 55–56, 109, 158, 168
liberation theology, 167n19
life, 66, 80, 81, 130, 177
likeness, 17
limited goods, 77–89
liturgical asceticism, 131–32n45, 147, 195
"liturgical askesis," 131
liturgies, 92n85
logocentric binaries, 101
logoi, 30
Logos, 30, 55
Lossky, Vladimir, 18–19, 47n109, 54

love, 45, 47, 49, 85–86, 95, 153, 209, 212–27
lust, 104
Luther, Martin, 69n22
Lyotard, Jean-François, 55n140

macroanthropos, 17, 18n18
male, 27
Mammonism, 126
manna, 149
Maria of Paris, 208n31
Martin, Lee Roy, 97n99
martyrdom, 88, 163
Marx, Karl, 62, 92n86
Marxism, 144, 157
Mary (mother of Jesus), 50
materialism, 126, 206
matter, 82n56, 137
Maximus the Confessor, 18n18, 30, 37, 79n51
McChesney, Robert W., 124
McFague, Sallie, 7, 14, 15n8, 19–21, 22, 23, 24, 117, 125, 155, 159, 200, 205, 208n33, 209–10
McGill, Arthur, 15
Meeks, M. Douglas, 122, 125, 147
Meier, John P., 40n93, 74, 75
memory, 25–29, 175–82
metanoia, 187
metanoic, 206
metaphysics, 41
Metz, Johann Baptist, 179–80n62
Meyendorff, John, 44
minority, 7
Minow, Martha, 191–92
mishpat, 110, 111, 116
mistrust, 3
Moloney, Francis J., 36
Moltmann, Jürgen, 5n19, 9, 13–14, 15–16, 23, 94–96, 108, 114
moral imagination, 8n32
murder, 67
Muslims, 214–16, 218
mystery, 87
mysticism, 206

narrativity, 199, 200, 201, 211
national identity, 193
nationalism, 1, 5, 9, 214
nationality, 2n11
natural resources, 13, 80n53, 82n56
natural theology, 16
Nauta, Rein, 68n20, 71n31
negation, 207
Negri, Antonio, 121n2
neighbor, 6, 115, 133, 149, 209–10, 212, 217, 223, 226
neoliberalism, 121–24, 156
Neshev, Kiril, 83
new creation, 33, 186
Niebuhr, H. Richard, 128n34
Nietzsche, Friedrich, 95
nonanthropic, 20, 25, 27, 34, 45, 48, 77, 84, 102, 115, 147, 202, 206
noncovenantal, 115, 165
nonretaliation, 207n28
nonviolence, 65, 226
Northern Ireland, 193n100
nostalgia, 172

obedience, 51
oikonomia, 124–25, 140, 144
oikos, 124–25
old covenant, 37
Olthuis, James, 209
ontology, 17, 26, 31, 32, 39, 54, 72, 78, 115, 139
oppression, 90, 92, 167n19
optimism, 106–7
original sin, 136
Orthodox ecclesiology, 58
orthodoxy, 137
orthopraxy, 137
other, communion of, 45–51; face of, 138; fear of, 13, 14; and reconciliation, 190; responsibility for, 11, 89–108; sacrament of, 9–10; suffering of, 212–16, 224–27; as "wild space," 7
Ouspensky, Leonid, 29

pacifism, 203n21, 207n28
pantheism, 32n62

paradise, 31, 161, 177
parousia, 151–52
passion, of Christ, 118–20
peace, 80, 108–20, 160–64, 217, 226
peacebuilding, 5–6, 156, 173, 203n21, 226
pedagogy, 130, 173
penance, 103, 189
Pentecost, versus Babel, 49–51; and chrismation, 180; community of, 127, 139–42; as icon of Trinity, 58–60; and Incarnation, 19, 142n72, 155; Spirit of, 9–10
Pentecostals, 5, 218
perichoresis, 11, 26, 43, 49, 51, 59, 79, 95, 108, 137, 142, 143, 144, 173
persecution, 226
personhood, 95, 169
Peters, Rebecca Todd, 123
Pfeil, Margaret, 131n45
philanthrōpia, 137
Philo of Alexandria, 39, 113
philoxenia, 48
Plekon, Michael P., 9n37
pneumatological anthropology, 12, 16, 139
pneumatology, 9, 15n8
poiēsis, 172
political philosophy, 12, 61
Poljic, Effendi Enes, 214–15n56
possessions, 142, 155
poverty, 20, 74, 104, 125, 149
power, 64, 75
praktikē, 47
prayer, 51–57, 150
preeucharistic, 150–51, 152
priests, 39, 75, 135–45
privilege, 72n31
promise, 163
prophet, 74
prosōpon, 27, 137
prosperity gospel, 76
pros ton theon, 49
Protestantism, 189
protocommunity, 34, 35, 45, 47, 60, 66, 165, 173
proto-holy of holies, 31
protosanctuary, 161
prototemple, 68
punishment, 184–85, 194

racism, 9
Rad, Gerhard von, 69, 70, 71
radical evil, 185
rape, 3
rebellion, 69
reconciliation, as authentic, 165; and the Eucharist, 154; versus forgiveness, 190–91; and Pentecost, 10; and redemption, 164; and repentance, 187, 189
redeemer, 32n61, 171, 179–80
redemption, as communal affair, 101, 173; of desires, 76; forgiveness as heart of, 186; and justice, 93, 192; of memory, 175–82; and reconciliation, 164; and world-mending, 29–44, 79
reenvision, 7, 8, 170, 172, 177, 193, 204, 225n77
Reformed, 218
refugees, 23, 158, 193, 215n57, 219
relationality, 14
religion, 70n24, 89–90
remembering, 175–82
Renan, Ernest, 2–3n11
renewal, 105, 171
repentance, 102–5, 183, 187, 189
resentment, 193
respect, 170n36
responsibility, for brokenness of world, 221–22; and fasting, 151; and holiness, 155–59; for the other, 22, 85, 89–108; refusal of, 70, 97; theology of, 32n61
restoration, 192
restorative justice, 188–89, 196
restorying, 178, 179, 193
resurrection, 43, 85, 86–87, 95, 132, 177
retribution, 116, 186, 192, 194
retributive justice, 110, 111, 188
revenge, 169, 192
Riggs, Marcia, 157
Roma, 99n102

Sabbath, 83, 113n136, 115, 133–34
Sacks, Jonathan, 32–33, 47n111, 59, 91, 93, 98, 102, 110–11, 112, 119n152, 160, 166, 196–97
sacrament, and memory, 179–81; as mystery, 87; of the other, 9–10; world as, 128–35
sacrifice, 130, 132
saintliness, 6–7
saints, 20, 28, 201–27
salvation, 32, 79
sanctification, 76, 127, 132
Satan, 73–74, 75, 152
Šavanka, Marko, 222
scapegoating, 98–100
scarcity, 14, 77–89, 149, 162
Schaab, Gloria L., 41n98
Schmemann, Alexander, 29, 40, 50n116, 81, 139, 146, 147–48, 150, 151, 152, 154, 181
Scripture, on forgiveness, 168, 194; foundational values of, 124; on humanity, 136, 139, 143; on justice, 92–94; on redemption, 79, 104–5, 165; on responsibility, 171; on resurrection, 87; on violence, 67, 77–89
second law of thermodynamics, 82n56
secularization, 144
self-criticism, 104n117
self-dehumanization, 222
self-denial, 155
self-destruction, 32
self-interest, 126
self-revelation, 36
self-sacrifice, 49
self-sharing, 136, 140n70, 141
sentimentality, 213, 225
Serbia, 5, 193, 218, 223, 225
Šešelj, Vojislav, 223
seventh day, 133
sexism, 9
shalom, 25, 80, 83, 156, 160–64, 196–98
shame, 68n20
shared language, 190
sharing, 142, 155
shekinah, 38, 112n133
Shepherd of Hermas, 18
Shriver, Donald W., 163n8, 167n20, 188
Sibylline Oracles, 113–14
Silouan of Mount Athos, 176n50
sin, 9, 28, 69, 79, 88
skandala, 185
Skobtsova, Maria, 9n37
slavery, 85n63
Smith, Adam, 122
Smith, James K. A., 158
Sneed, Mark, 109n128
sobornost, 10, 23–24, 65, 126–27, 228
socialism, 125–26
social justice, 113
social responsibility, 22
social sciences, 61n1
social Trinity, 44
socioeconomic, 13, 70n24, 75, 100n105, 112, 126, 133, 138, 141, 157
sociology of religion, 12
socium, 127, 142, 158
Sodom, 53n132, 111
solidarity, 219
Solovyov, Vladimir, 24
soteriology, 15n8
South African apartheid, 192
speech, 55
spirituality, 103
spontaneity, 142
Staniloae, Dimitru, 30, 57, 129, 130, 131, 132
starvation, 74
Stavropoulos, Christoforos, 19
stewardship, 49, 133, 135–45
Stoiković, Lidia, 219
Stott, John R. W., 195
Straus, Scott, 100n105
Subev, Todor, 24
suffering, 7, 21, 197, 205, 208
syndesmos, 30, 208

tabernacle, 33
Talmud, 106
Taylor, Charles, 98–101
Teilhard de Chardin, Pierre, 25, 119–20
telos, 17, 31, 146, 190, 195

temple, 37, 38, 39, 117
temporality, 84
temptation, 76, 97, 153
Teresa of Ávila, 205
Tertullian, 88n73
textuality, 199, 211
theoformation, 7, 48, 54, 55, 202
Theokritoff, George, 148
theology, of the face, 15, 28, 66; of iconography, 177, 201; of martyrdom, 88n72, 88n75; as natural, 16; of reconciliation, 164; of responsibility, 32n61
theophany, 58, 181
theophorus, 205
theosis, 16, 17, 23, 26, 46, 137, 139, 206
Theotokion, 50
theoumenon, 52
thermodynamics, 82n56
"Third Balkan War," 1-3
Thomas Aquinas, 41n98, 86n64
Torah, 32, 44, 105-6, 109, 171
tower of Babel, 46-47, 49-51
transfiguration, 37-38, 58, 136
transformation, 106-7, 202-3
trauma, 163, 176, 192, 193, 221
tribalism, 9, 218
tridirectional, 25, 27, 60, 66, 177
Trinity, 26, 34, 44
Troeltsch, Ernst, 86
truth, 92, 102, 162, 182
tsedaqah, 110, 111, 116
Tutu, Desmond, 103, 165n12, 167n19, 172n41, 198

unconditional forgiveness, 164-74, 175
unconditional hospitality, 45-51
uncurve, 79
unforgivable, 182-91
United States, 158
unity, 46, 49, 157, 182
"universal self," 20-21, 209-10
unrepentant, 187
utopically, 83-84, 100n105, 160, 197

veil, 38
vengeance, 169, 171
violence, brutality of, 2; as categorical, 98, 100n105; iconoclasm of, 66-76; and limited goods, 77-89
vocation, 17, 39, 72, 128, 136
Vogels, Walter, 77n48
Volf, Miroslav, 70n24, 71, 75, 90n80, 178, 179n62, 181, 189n91
voluntary poverty, 20
vulnerable, 216

Ware, Timothy (Bishop Kallistos), 23, 24n40, 204n22
warfare, 63, 212-27
"ways of peace," 196-98, 221
"ways of the Lord," 93, 105, 110, 161
wealth, 63, 113, 122, 141
Weber, Max, 3n11
weekly life, 129
Weil, Simone, 19, 25, 308n33
well-being, 13-14, 21, 101, 103, 115, 117, 141-42, 149
Wesley, John, 208n31
Wiesel, Elie, 182n69
wild animals, 73-74, 88-89n75, 106
wilderness, 76, 149, 151, 152, 153
"wild space," 7-9
Williams, Rowan, 175, 182
Woolman, John, 19
work, 130
world, changing of, 106-7; dependence on, 81; as Eucharistic sacrament, 128-35; as gift, 130; making of, 51-57, 128; mending of, 29-44, 54
World War II, 1, 3n12, 178n56, 193, 208n33, 217, 220n67, 223n74
worship, 21, 51, 115-17, 129, 134-35
Wright, N. T., 37, 118
Wyschogrod, Edith, 155, 199-207

xenophobia, 100-101

Yong, Amos, 10

Zacchaeus, 196
Zizioulas, John D., 46

Index of Scripture Citations

Old Testament

Genesis
1 16
1:26-27 89
1:26-28 134
1:27 39
1:28 31
2-3 78n50
2:7 139
2:9 77n48
2:16-17 97
2:17 78, 78n50
3 71, 98n100
3:2-3 48
3:3 77n48
3:3-4 78n50
3:5 81n54
3:8-12 97
3:9 70
3:14-19 42n101, 77
3:22-24 77
4:1-16 67
4:6 68
4:7 68, 78n49
4:9 70
4:11 71
4:14 71
4:16 71
4:22 54
6:5 79n51
6:11 79n51
11:7-8 46
18:1-15 56
18:17-19 110
18:17-33 53n132, 111
18:19 93, 196

Exodus
2:23-24 92
3:7-8 92
20:1-17 93
20:3-5 93
20:3-17 173
24:15 37
25:20 33
34:21 134
40:34 38

Leviticus
19:18 138
25:23-55 110

Numbers
35 158

Deuteronomy
5:14 133
6:6 137
6:16 75
8:3 74
10:17-18 109
11:26 114
15:7-11 112
16:19-20 109
24:17-22 109, 110, 112
30:15-20 134
33:27 78

Joshua
24:14-15 134

1 Kings
8:10-11 38
18:21 134

Job
24:14-15 14
32:18 14
38:4-7 51

Psalms
1 134
2:6-8 75
2:7 73
2:8 75
17:15 110, 111
19 24
24:1 153
33:5 111

37:28 111
51 105
51:1-2 105
51:3 105
51:4 105
51:5 105
51:6 105
51:7-12 105
51:13 105
69:32 69n21
89:14 111
91 76n42
91:11-12 75
97:2 111
119:133 106

Isaiah
1:11 71n31
1:13 71n31
1:14-17 116, 117
1:16-17 71n31
1:27 111
2:4 161
5:7 111
11:1-9 107
11:2 73, 107
11:4-5 107
11:6-9 107, 160
29:13 117

Jeremiah
6:20 116
7:3-7 116
7:14 118
9:24 116
22:13 111
31:33 112

Ezekiel
22:29 111
22:29-30 111

Hosea
2:19 112
4:1 106
4:2 106
4:3 106
6:6 115

Amos
5:21-24 117
6:12 111

Micah
4:1-3 161
4:2 161
4:3 161
4:4 162

New Testament

Matthew
2:1-2 42
2:9-11 42
4:1 151
4:1-11 72
5:17 37
5:21-22 67
5:21-48 67
5:38-45 118
6:9-13 194
6:11 145
6:12 194
6:14-15 194
6:24 117
9:14 152
12:32 184n73
15:5-9 117
17 37
17:2 38
17:3 38, 57
17:5 38
17:21 152
18:22 168, 194
18:23-32 194
18:35 171
19:19 138
21:12-16 117
21:14 118
22:37 137
22:37-40 79
22:39 209
24:42 152
25 110
25:14-30 132
25:31-40 80
25:31-46 22, 66, 132, 138, 154
25:34 154

Mark
1:9-11 73
1:10-11 72
1:12 72
1:12-13 72
1:13 73, 73n34, 74n35
2:18 152
3:29 184n73
7:10-13 117
8:1-10 143
9 37
11:15-17 117
11:17 117
11:25 171
12:30 137
12:31 209
14:36 39

Luke
1:38 50
2:8-20 42
3:21-22 140
4:1-2 151
4:1-14 72
4:14 72, 73
5:33 152
8:21 106
10:27 137, 209
10:35 210
11:3 145
12:10 184n73
12:23 75
16:13 117
17:1-4 185
17:3-4 185
19:1-10 44, 196
19:45-46 117
22:42 19

24:29 40n89, 118n149

John
1:1 26, 33, 49
1:1–2 36n76
1:1–3 35
1:9 76
1:14 26, 35, 36n76, 50
1:18 35, 36, 57
2:19–22 37
4:34 74, 74n37
6:51 130
6:68 44
8:12 29
8:32 92, 165
8:51 106
11:25 177
14:2 158
14:6 76, 86, 173
14:26 182
15:26 58
16:8 184n73
16:13 182
19:5 89
19:30 89
20:22–23 184n73

Acts
1:1 142n72
1:8 50
2 105
2:5 51
2:6 51
2:42 145n78
2:43–47 144
2:44 144
2:46 144
3:1–16 142n72
4:30 142n72
4:32–33 157
4:34 144
4:34–35 157
7:55–56 142n72
9:5 142n72
9:10 142n72
13:39 142n72
17:6 105
17:7 142n72
17:28 47
18:10 142n72
19:15 142n72
22:4 105
25:19 142n72

Romans
2:12–16 165
5:5 79, 85, 86n64
5:12 88
6:3–4 85
6:4 85
6:5 88
6:6 85
6:19 143
7:5–25 104
8 177
8:4 189
8:5–8 104
8:11 84
8:18–22 8
8:19–22 42
8:20–21 78
8:21 83
8:26 54, 167
12:1 207
12:5 181

1 Corinthians
10:17 150
11:20–22 149
11:21 149
11:24–25 146
11:26–28 153
11:27–34 147, 149
11:33 149
13 47
13:8 86n64
13:8–13 86
13:10–11 86
15:26 43
15:28 34, 60
15:45 26

2 Corinthians
3:3 35
3:17 95, 182
3:18 17, 96
5:18 156
5:18–19 164
6:16 60

Galatians
2:20 19, 86
5:22 86

Ephesians
1:13 182
1:18 86n64
1:23 135
2:14 76, 80
2:19–22 60
3:17–19 36
4:3 182
4:25 181
6:12 103
6:18 53

Philippians
2:7 19

Colossians
1:15 17, 29, 36, 50, 89, 139
1:15–16 33
1:17 30, 190
2:9 26, 32

1 Thessalonians
4:3–8 143
5:17 53
5:23 143

Hebrews
1:1–2 34, 36
4:15 43, 73
8:8–13 37
9:13–14 143
11:4 72n33
12:1 28
12:14 154

James
4:7 151

1 Peter
1:2 79

2 Peter
1:4 39, 52, 139, 144

1 John
3:12 69n21, 72n33
3:15 67
4:7-8 85
4:8 86n64
4:16 66, 170
4:17 66
4:18 47, 85, 177
4:19 85, 170
4:20 66, 138

Jude
11 72n33

Revelation
1:8 33
21-22 51
21:1 95
21:4 178n54
21:5 86
21:6 37, 138
21:24-27 162
22:20 40n89, 118n149